Baedeker
Provence/Côte d'Azur

# Baedeker's

# PROVENCE/ COTE D'AZUR

## Imprint

158 illustrations, 12 ground plans, 6 general maps, 3 drawings, 1 large map at end of book

Original German text: Dr Bernhard Abend, Peter M. Nahm, Dr Fritz Nohr

Editorial work: Baedeker (Dr Bernhard Abend)
English language edition: Alec Court

General direction: Dr Peter Baumgarten, Baedeker Stuttgart

English Translation: Julie Bullock, David Cocking, Alec Court, Crispin Warren

Cartography: Christoph Gallus, Hohberg-Niederschopfheim; Gert Oberländer, Munich, Mairs Geographischer Verlag GmbH & Co., Ostfildern-Kemnat (large map)

Source of Illustrations: Abend (60), Anthony/Jogschies (2), Grosskopf (1), Artemis Verlag, Zurich (1), Baedeker-Archiv (2), The Baltimore Museum of Art, The Coene Collection (1), Bucher/Thomas (1), Berne (3), Photographie Giraudon (2), Historia (2), Hohenacker (1), IFA/COMNET (1), Ortel (1), Selma (1), Staatsmuseum Kröller-Müller, Otterlo (1), Lade (1), Direction du Tourisme Monaco (1), Müller (6), Nahm (12), Pfaffinger (2), Reinhard (1), Toni Schneiders (2), Schuster/Barnes (1), Bull (1), Jogschies (1), Kasch (1), Löhr (1), Strüber (6), Thomas (16), Ullstein Bilderdienst (3), ZEFA/Eugen (1), Barnes (1)

Following the tradition established by Karl Baedeker in 1844, sights of particular interest and hotels and restaurants of particular quality are distinguished by either one or two asterisks. To make it easier to locate the various places listed in the "A to Z" section of the Guide, their co-ordinates on the large map are shown at the head of each entry.
Only a selection of hotels, restaurants and shops can be given; no reflection is implied therefore on establishments not included.
In a time of rapid change it is difficult to ensure that all the information given is entirely accurate and up-to-date, and the possibility of error can never be entirely eliminated. Although the publishers can accept no responsibility for inaccuracies and omissions, they are always grateful for corrections and suggestions for improvement.

2nd English edition 1992



US and Canadian edition
Prentice Hall Press

Distributed in the United Kingdom by the Publishing Division of the Automobile Association, Fanum House, Basingstoke, Hampshire RG21 2EA



Licensed user:
Mairs Geographischer Verlag GmbH & Co., Ostfildern-Kemnat bei Stuttgart

The name *Baedeker* is a registered trade mark
A CIP catalogue record of this book is available from the British Library

Printed in Italy by G. Canale & C.S.p.A – Borgaro T.se –Turin

ISBN UK 0 7495 0560 5
US and Canada 0–13–059502–0

## Contents

# The Principal Sights at a Glance





*(Continued on page 296)*

## Preface

This guide to Provence/Côte d'Azur is one of the new generation of Baedeker guides.

These guides, illustrated throughout in colour, are designed to meet the needs of the modern traveller. They are quick and easy to consult, with the principal places of interest described in alphabetical order, and the information is presented in a format that is both attractive and easy to follow.

The subject of this guide is the French region of Provence–Alpes–Côte d'Azur, but is also concerned with places which are generally considered to be within the Provençal area.

The guide is in three parts. The first part gives a general account of Provence and the Côte d'Azur – its geographical divisions and landscape, its climate, flora and fauna, population, economy, history, famous people, art and culture. A selection of quotations and a number of suggested itineraries provide a transition to the second part, in which the country's places and features of tourist interest – towns, provinces, regions, rivers – are described. The third part contains a variety of practical information. Both the sights and the practical information are listed in alphabetical order.

The new Baedeker guides are noted for their concentration on essentials and their convenience of use. They contain numerous specially drawn plans and colour illustrations; and at the end of the book is a large map making it easy to locate the various places described in the "A to Z" section of the guide with the help of the co-ordinates given at the head of each entry.

2 CAROMB
St-PIERRE 1

# Facts and Figures

## General

### Definition of Region

The expressions "Provence" and "Côte d'Azur," however familiar they may be, are geographically, historically and politically not easy to define.

Provence

The regional name "Provence" comes from the Roman Provincia Gallia Narbonensis which was founded from 125 B.C. onwards, after the conquest of what is present-day France. Subsequently the political borders and affiliations of the Provence area altered frequently and today it comprises the political region Provence-Alpes-Côte d'Azur, one of the 22 Régions of France, the Départements of Alpes-de-Haute-Provence, Hautes-Alpes, Alpes-Maritimes, Bouches-du-Rhône, Var and Vaucluse. Surrounded by this territory on the Mediterranean coast is the independent Principality of Monaco.

Côte d'Azur

Even the expression "Côte d'Azur" is difficult to define. It indicates the "azure blue coast" between St Raphaël and the French-Italian frontier but it is generally applied to the whole French Riviera as far west as Marseilles.

The area described in this guidebook does not completely coincide with Provence-Alpes-Côte d'Azur as a political region. On the one hand it takes in the chief places of interest (Georges de l'Ardèche, Nîmes, Montpelier, etc.) on the edge of the area, on the other hand it only briefly refers to the purely winter sports areas far to the north-east.

### Regional Structure

Provence, which comprises the south-east of the French mainland, is richly blessed with beauties and cultural monuments. It is divided into three regional areas each with its own character and wealth of scenic forms – the lower Rhône Valley, the coast and the mountainous hinterland.

Rhône Valley

The Rhône is France's second longest and most abundant river. It rises in Switzerland near the Furka Pass, flows through the Valais and Lake Geneva and divides in the Défilé de l'Ecluse in the Jura Mountains. Its lower valley begins near Lyons, where the more abundant Saône joins it. Below Lyons the Rhône flows southwards through the Rhône rift valley (part of the Mediterranean-Mjosen-Zone), between the foothills of the French Alps and the Massif Central (Cevennes) to its mouth. In this area the wide valley is terraced and used for intensive cultivation of grapes, fruit and vegetables. South of Avignon the river has many tributaries. It finally reaches Arles, where heavy sediment has extended its mouth towards the sea by between 10m/33ft and 55m/181ft a year. The Rhône forms a delta here, bordered by the Grand Rhône (with its mouth in the east at Port St-Louis in the Gulf of Fos) and the Petit Rhône (with its mouth in the west at St-Marles). The Rhône delta encloses the Camargue, an unspoilt area of particular charm.

Long before Greek and Roman times – and certainly no later than the Bronze Age – the Rhône Valley was a much-used transport route and an important cultural link between the Mediterranean on the one hand and Britain and Gaul on the other.

◀ *The "Barbarotte", the town-gate of Modena (Modène)*

## General

Coastal region

Provence's coastal region extends between Cap Couronne in the west and Capo Mortola in the east and is divided into four sections; the Côte à Calanques (Blue Coast), the Côte des Maures (Crimson Coast), the Côte de l'Esterel and the Côte d'Azur in its narrowest sense.

The **Côte à Calanques** forms the first section. With the Rade de Marseille (Roadsteads of Marseilles) and some offshore islands it is characterised by the Calanques, torturous coastal indentations which are difficult to reach – the name comes from the Provençal *calenco* (falling steeply) – and forms part of the ancient karstic limestone massifs of the Provençal coast. The imposing coastal formation arose as a consequence of the combination of considerable sinking of the level of the sea during the Pleistocene age and a simultaneous rise in the limestone heights, in which karstic development played an important role.

The **Côte des Maures** or Côte Vermeille (purple coast) begins at Sanary-sur-Mer and is bounded in the east by the estuary of the River Argens. With the offshore Hyères Islands this coastal area has to be included with the mountains of the Département of Var, as is illustrated by the nature of the Massif des Maures, consisting of granite, gneiss, mica-schist and phyllite, some 60km/37 miles long, 30km/17 miles broad and rising to a height of 779m/2557ft. Extensive bays with, in places, excellent beaches form the line of the coast and sometimes, for example near Toulon and St-Tropez, penetrate deeply inland.

The **Massif de l'Esterel**, extending between St-Raphael and Cannes, is geologically of the same nature as the Massif des Maures. This mountainous gneiss area is 20km/12 miles long, about 12km/7 miles broad and up to 618m/2028ft in height which in many places, particularly on the coast is broken by volcanic outcrops. The reddish porphyry of the coast with its numerous bays and offshore islets contrasts charmingly with the blue of the sea.

*Côte d'Azur: view from the Esterel Massif over Nice and the Alps*

**Provence and the Côte d'Azur are among the most visited holiday areas of France.**

To the east of the estuary of the Siagne this coastline is characterised by the dipping of the sub-Alpine chain and the western Alps to the south into the Ligurian Sea. To the east beyond Cannes the coast rises in terraces; the Cap d'Antibes stands out impressively, and then there follows the estuarial area of the Var, the course of the river reveals clear tectonically-limited boundaries. Bays and promontories, with the backdrop of mountain slopes like an amphitheatre, give the landscape its particular attraction which, however, is more and more becoming spoiled by development as big business has transformed the whole area into a unique centre of tourism.

Between Nice and Menton (where the Italian border begins) the chalk foothills of the **Maritime Alps** fall away steeply into the sea. This leaves little room for human habitation, only the Principality of Monaco (covering an area of about 2sq.km/¾sq.miles and able to increase its size through deposits building up in the sea) and Eze, lying at an altitude of 427m/1401ft above sea-level.

The coastal hinterland, comprising Haute-Provence and Basse-Provence, is bordered in the extreme west by the **Crau**, once the delta of the Durance, whose smooth pebbles had been washed down from the Alps during the Ice Age. Originally dry, about 60% of the area is now irrigated and used as pasture and for market-gardening. The territory around the Etang de Berre,

*Provençal landscape*

a lake of about 160sq.km/62sq.miles in area but only up to 10m/33ft deep, serves as an industrial relief zone for Marseilles.
To the east lies a stratified region, consisting primarily of chalk, clay and conglomerates, the highest terrace of which forms part of the basin of Aix-en-Provence. To the east and south-east of Aix the mountain chains of Provence become more prominent. Examples are the steep slopes of the Montagne Ste-Victoire, the Montagne du Cengle, the Chaîne de l'Etoille and the Chaîne de la Ste-Baume. But even ranges such as the Chaîne de l'Estaque between the Etang de Berre and the Golfe du Lion or the Montagne du Lubéron to the east of Avignon, consisting predominently of Jurassic and cretaceous limestone, belong to the mountain system of the Pyrenees and Provence. The depression zone around Toulon – Cuers – Le Muy, with its extensive vineyards, separates these chains from the uplands of the coast.

The deposits of bauxite in the vicinity of Brignoles bear witness to the emergence of an upland zone from the inlet of the sea which once covered an extensive area of Provence. The products of a considerable weathering of laterite became accumulated in karstic hollows forming storage places for this basic material of aluminium production.

The river systems of the Durance and the Verdon characterise the north of the hinterland. The Lower Valley of the Durance, between Avignon and Mirabeau, is broad and follows the Pyrenees–Provence axis. It has only a few tributaries and a relatively small gradient. North of Mirabeau there is an increase in gradient and in the number of tributaries, and the Durance turns towards the north-east.

The central reaches of the Verdon which is controlled by important flood-barriers is an exception. It has cut its bed into great Jurassic limestone banks, in part like the Dolomites.

*Surfers on the Rhône (near Marcoule)*

This stretch, called the "Grand Canyon of the Verdon", with the deepest gorges in Europe, is an example of an ancient breach valley. Even the tributaries of the Verdon reveal an astonishing independence from the present structure of the land. North of the Lower Verdon stretches the Plain of Valensole, a hollow filled with huge mounds of gravel. South of the Grand Canyon of Verdon extend the undulating old karstic reliefs of the Grand Plan de Canjuers and the Plain of Comps.

The east of the hinterland is mainly formed by heavily fissured fold mountains of the Alpine foothills of Grasse, to which the Montagne de Thorenc, the Montagne de Cheiron and the Montagne de l'Audiberque also belong. The rivers, however, sometimes follow the north–south direction of the Maritime Alps to the east of the Var, as is shown by the example of the Loup. The highest point of the Maritime Alps, the Cime dell'Argentera (3297m/10821ft) is actually in Italy.

Mediterranean

The waters around the Mediterranean coast (Golfe du Lion, Ligurian Sea) are relatively warm; because of latitude, evaporation and salt content are relatively high. Even at quite great depths the temperature is rarely below 13°C (55°F). The surface temperature in winter ranges between 10 and 13°C (50 and 55°F) and in summer can reach 25°C (77°F).

High and low tides have a difference of only 25cm/10in, but the waves are frequently subject to fluctuation; quite often strong air currents cause short-lived but violent waves which can be dangerous to swimmers.

Unfortunately the quality of the sea water in several places leaves much to be desired. Sewage from coastal settlements, pollution of the rivers and rubbish from ships have recently necessitated regular monitoring of rivers, bacteriological control and the setting up of a warning service when excessive pollution is threatened.

This warning service proved of little use against the oil pollution which occurred when the tanker "Haven" exploded and sank off Genoa in April 1991. In just two weeks the escaped oil reached the beaches of the Côte d'Azur and threatened the Hyères beaches and the National Park Port-Cros. Special ships which were meant to vacuum up the oil could not be used as the waves were too high and the carpet of oil had broken up. Fortunately the tanker did not break up and so the spillage was only relatively light;

even in the bay of St-Tropez, which faces east, only a few patches of oil were washed ashore.

Beaches

The beaches vary in nature, depending on the one hand on the sea currents, and on the other hand on the morphology of the coasts. Long-standing tourist centres such as Monaco and Nice have partly rocky coasts and very coarse sand, while more modern resorts, such as St-Tropez and Hyères, can offer spacious beaches with fine sand. Artificial beaches have been and continue to be laid down.

The submarine terrain has naturally the same geological conditions as the coast. Steep shelving, shallows and precipitous rock formations require constant vigilance from those in boats. There are excellent opportunities for experienced sub-aqua sportsmen and sportswomen.

## Climate

Coastal Area

Most of the built-up areas near the coast – and above all the Côte d'Azur – are extraordinarily well favoured from the point of view of climate. Although the annual precipitation is between 550mm/22in and 820mm/32in and is, therefore, not very different from that in northern regions, the annual sunshine total amounts to about 3000 hours. In the east especially, where the mountains rise like an amphitheatre and the slopes are exposed to the sun for the whole of the day, cool north winds are kept at bay. In the west the Mistral occasionally makes its unpleasant presence felt.

For the coastal area favourable pressure distribution provides clear sunny days with fresh winds and predominently dry air in winter. In this season average day temperatures of between 6°C (42°F) and 12°C (57°F) are reached; maximum temperatures are between 2°C (36°F) and 4°C (39°F) higher, corresponding approximately to conditions to the south of Rome. Frost and snow are rare on the coast. The windiest month is March which is also rainy; April and May are the most suitable months for a visitors seeking a healthful holiday. Summer is not too hot (July average 24°C (75°F)). Sultry weather and storms are rare in the vicinity of the coast, but there is a considerable drop in temperature at night and at times heavy dew. Moderate rainfall occurs mainly in autumn and it is almost possible to talk of a rainy season in October (maximum 97mm/3¾in) and November. Precipitation and the frequency of frost increase in relation to altitude and topography.

Upland Region

Climatic conditions in the more northerly upland mountain areas are quite different, as a continental type of climate competes more strongly with the moderating influence of the sea. In this region precipitation occurs throughout the year, without noticeable maxima in spring or autumn. In the higher parts the snow lies for quite a long time; in the high Alpine regions generally excellent conditions for winter sports prevail. Even in the summer months cool "climatic" islands occur here.

Mistral

The Mistral, a notorious wind, which hurls itself down the Rhône Valley and roars over Provence, occurs when there is low pressure over the Golfe du Lion and simultaneous high pressure over the Massif Central. The constriction of the air currents between the latter and the Alps causes, by means of a kind of jet effect, high wind speeds. At the same time low-pressure areas which are caused by solar heat rising from the North African shotts – saline depressions – and the flat expanses of sandy desert, contribute in causing localised Mistrals.
The Mistral generally blows in periods of from three to ten days, normally beginning about 10am and lasting until sunset. When such a period comes to an end, several pleasant days without any wind follow.

Sirocco

Sometimes in summer the Sirocco reaches Provence. This is a hot dry wind from North Africa (the Sahara).

Holm oaks in bloom in the Lubéron

Thyme in the Tricastin

## Flora and Fauna

Flora

As a consequence of the favourable Mediterranean climate the flora is exceptionally varied. Silver-grey olive trees, which are found everywhere on the slopes up to 500m/1640ft and more above sea-level, orange and lemon plantations, vines, pines, palms, cypresses, aloes, agaves, cacti and many more are now taken for granted as typical plants of the Côte d'Azur, but were in some cases brought here from various other countries in Roman times.

Of the original vegetation which has suffered from human intrusion as well as catastrophic fires in forest and plain, pines take a leading place (Aleppo, maritime, stone and northern pines), in addition there are holm, kermes and cork-oaks, hornbeam and sweet chestnut. The principal plant of the Garrigue (in Provençal *Garoulia*), a special form of the maquis (undergrowth of hard-leafed evergreens, bushes, shrubs, etc.), is the holm oak. The outer surface of its leaves are thickened and covered with a wax layer, and the underside is protected with a felty coating. This prevents evaporation occuring too quickly.

The large number of sweetly scented bushes and herbs (lavender, rosemary, thyme, cistus, etc.) is striking. Edible fungi often occur in the forests, particularly truffles in Vaucluse which are tracked down with the help of trained dogs. The flowers of the Riviera have become a legend, the intensive cultivation of cut flowers such as mimosa for export (in winter) or of sweet-smelling blossoms (violets, roses, lavender, oranges, etc.) for perfume production plays an important role in the economy.

Fauna

There is a wide variety of fauna, particularly reptiles (tortoises, lizards, geckos, snakes, vipers, etc.) and insects, which find perfect living conditions in areas which are difficult of access. Fairly few animals suitable for hunting survive in the hinterland as the sport is traditionally very popular.

Thrushes and other songbirds, quails, pheasants, partridges, hares, roe deer and deer as well as trout, whitefish and river crabs are all sought-after outside the few protected areas. The sea is being equally intensively exploited so that (just as with hunting) stocks are being increasingly exhausted. Sea creatures under particular protection include mussels, prawns and octopuses as well as sea-eels, perch, bream, tuna and sardines together with fur seals and ray.

## Economy

General

The natural potential of Provence has led to land development which is characterised on the one hand by agriculture, forestry and fishery (the last named partly in decline), and on the other hand, by reason of a rapid development of industry, mining, energy production and tourism, a heavy concentration of population and the urbanisation of entire stretches of the coast.

Population

The Provence–Alpes–Côte d'Azur region is one of the most densely populated areas of France, with the coastal region being one of the most densely populated anywhere. The intensity of settlement here continues as shown by the increase in population (doubled since the Second World War) and the density of settlement; from about 100 inhabitants per square kilometre at the end of the 1970s to 136 per square kilometre today. The numbers appear even more drastic when compared to the corresponding numbers (1989) in various other départements: Alpes-de-Haute-Provence 19, Hautes-Alpes 20, Var and Vaucluse 128, Alpes-Maritime 226, Bouches-du-Rhône 346 inhabitants per square kilometre. In total the region has about 4¼ million inhabitants of which 1½ million form the working population employed in the following fields – 4.2% in primary industry, 22.4% in the secondary sector and 73.4% in the service industry.

### Industry

Marseilles/Toulon

The favourable geographical situation of the coastal area is of extreme economic importance. Marseilles, at the "Gateway to Africa and the East" has become a first-class industrial and commercial centre, and the zone of the Etang de Berre is a major petro-chemical "Europort". An annual turnover of about 100 million tonnes (about 90% of the imports consists of oil) makes the port of Marseilles one of the largest in Europe. With an annual refining capacity of 30 million tonnes, this industrial zone holds second place in France (a pipeline from Fos to Karlsruhe in Germany is 782km/486 miles long.

As well as large complexes of the chemical and petro-chemical industries, there are also aluminium works which produce about 85% of the total French output. In addition there are large iron and steel plants, aircraft and engineering works and shipyards. Another important branch of the economy is the food industry (sugar, bread, cakes and pastries, jams, milling and abattoirs).

In addition to Marseilles, Toulon is also notable as a regional economic centre, owing to its natural advantages as a military and commercial port (1138ha/2812 acres; the largest naval port in France).

Côte d'Azur

The Côte d'Azur has also developed over the last 20 years into an important industrial centre, concentrating mainly on new "chimneyless" technology. The turnover of the tourist trade is being surpassed in the meanwhile by the development of service, electronic and computer companies (e.g. Texas Instruments, IBM, Digital Equipment, Thomson) and of chemical and biotechnological research and business centres. Nice airport is France's

*Cruas power-station*

second largest and deals with five million passengers a year; about 20 flights a week arrive here from Paris. Direct flights connect Nice with the rest of the world. The long-term goal is to establish Nice as a second centre of industry after Paris and the location of the technology park (Sophia Antipolis at Antibes with 2300ha/5683 acres, Toulon) is intended to be a step in this direction. Jacques Médecin, mayor of Nice from 1966 to 1990 and initiator of the "Côte d'Azur Developpement" company founded in 1983 to provide support for the economy, believed that the region could become the centre of an economically successful southern Europe. Médecin considered it to be an exaggeration to suppose that the limit of the ecological maximum capacity of the area could be reached.

Further industries

A not unimportant role is played by bauxite-mining in the vicinity of Brignoles (about 70% of the total French supply); this supply is important for the industrial area of Marseilles.

Of regional importance is the limestone and cement industry between Marseilles and Cassis. Productive salt-pans are located in the area of the Etang de Berre as well as near Hyères and Giens.
The fresh and preserved food industry, which processes agricultural produce plays an important role.

Perfume industry

The centre of the highly developed and traditional perfume industry is the little town of Grasse and the countryside around it. Here more than 30 large concerns annually process several million kilograms of flower blossoms (orange, rose, jasmine, thyme, rosemary, mignonette, violet, etc.). There are also undertakings producing synthetic perfume and these are gaining in importance. The distillation of lavender is primarily confined to the catchment area of the Verdon, where almost 80% of the world's lavender oil is produced.

*Lavender harvest near Valensole*

## Energy

Water exploitation

A decisive factor in the provision of water is the landform with its deeply incised valleys, especially in the catchment area of the Durance. The numerous dams and canals leading to the south are not only used to generate electricity, but also to control the water supply by holding back floodwater, thus creating a reserve for periods of drought, irrigation (for example in the Crau) and providing a supply of drinking-water. The waters of the larger rivers, especially the Rhône, are used for cooling the reactors in nuclear fuel plants (Cruas, Marcoule, Tricastin). Cruas and Tricastin combined have more than eight reactor blocks which produce almost 50 billion kilowatt hours a year, supplying about 14% of France's electricity requirements. Tricastin and Marcoule are also important for their enriched areas of fissile uranium. Cadarache, the centre for atomic development, is located south of Manosque at Verdon.

Nuclear Power

## Agriculture and Fishing

Irrigation

Agriculture and forestry have great importance as suppliers of basic materials. Once poorly supplied with water, Provence developed into the fertile region it is today through the building of a network of tightly-knit canals. The initiator of this project was Adam de Craponne (1527–76). Born in Salon-de-Provence, he built the canal between the Durance and the Crau (opened in 1554) which carries his name.

Cultivable areas and products

Extensive areas devoted to vegetable and fruit-growing as well as numerous vineyards are to be found principally in the fertile valleys of the hinterland but also on the artificially irrigated fields of the Crau. The produce is not only valuable for the local food and canning industry but is also exported.

The less fertile land (the gravelly areas of the Durance karst and the high terrain of the Alpine foothills) serves either as pasture or for growing fodder for cattle or for sheep. Increasing demands for beef and veal in the tourist centres has led to a considerable increase in the rearing of cattle.

In the mountainous regions near the coast supplies of timber (olive, oak, beech and erica arborea – briar roots, especially for pipes) are much in demand. The production of olive oil and cork plays an important agricultural role.

Between Toulon and Menton some 8000 specialist firms are engaged in the growing of flowers (principally under glass). The blossoms are used for the production of perfume and ethereal oils. The Alpes-Maritimes département alone produces about 50% of France's cut flower exports.

The main source of income for the farmers on the plateau between the Durance and the coast is the harvesting of lavender, together with a small amount of cereals and hay.

Transhumance

Flocks of sheep graze everywhere between Crau and the Maritime Alps. The ancient custom of transhumance – the seasonal moving of livestock to new pastures – is adhered to strongly here. For centuries in early summer, when the grass on the plains had already withered, flocks of sheep were driven along paths (known as *drailles* or *carraires*) up into the heights of the Cevennes, the Massif Central and the Alps. They often covered distances of 100km/62 miles or more. Nowadays the flocks total in all some 500,000 animals, a fraction of former numbers, and are mostly transported by freight train or lorry. The sight of the brightly marked and decorated animals, bleating noisely and with their bells jingling as they are moved across the fields and through the villages, presents a unique picture (see Practical Information, Walking).

Fishing

Fishing both in the sea and in inland waters only plays a subordinate commercial role today, increasing water pollution and the decline in fish stocks through over-fishing being largely responsible. On the other hand inshore fishing and fishing on the high seas is of increasing popularity among tourists.

## Tourism

Beginnings

Already in the first half of the 18th c. the great beauty and mild climate of this coastal region was talked about in circles where people could indulge in journeys for pleasure and recuperation. At first it was the wealthy English who spent winters here, first in Nice and later in Cannes. Nice, the climate of which was found to be very healthy, became fashionable as a health resort.

War and revolution caused a considerable reduction in the the already burgeoning tourism, but the Côte d'Azur experienced a considerable rise in prosperity in the 19th c., not least through the building of railway lines and roads. The pattern of settlement was considerably altered when promenades along the shore, splendid gardens, luxury villas and well-appointed inns were built, and there arose here an attractive winter health resort area of international status. Cannes, Nice, Monaco and Menton were the resorts preferred by the European aristocracy.

Côte d'Azur

In 1887 the dandy and author Stephen Liégeard published a book about the life of the upper crust on this as yet nameless coast, entitled "Côte d'Azur". The book's success caused its title to be included in "Larousse", France's famous dictionary, in 1888. The world's playground had acquired its name.

Development of mass tourism

The First World War brought another crisis. However, through skilful advertising wealthy people from all over the world were attracted to Provence

*Cannes around 1920 . . .*

*. . . and today*

for holidays for their health. After 1930 new coastal and beach settlements came into being, dependencies of villages situated further inland, and this relieved pressure on the older seaside resorts, while their beaches attracted more summer visitors. From the original health resorts, which were visited only in winter, there arose a holiday area with visitors the whole year round, and with summer as the high season.

Economic and ecological importance

The favourable climatic conditions, the beauty of the coasts with their bays and sandy shores, convenient sites for building and the relative proximity of the winter sports area resulted after the Second World War in the development of a tourist region which has few equals and which fulfils the requirements of today's visitors. In the wake of modern mass tourism there succeeded hectic building of hotels, holiday colonies, second homes, marinas, camp sites and leisure complexes. Warnings given by biologists and town planners about the destruction of flora and fauna and about the enormous intrusion into the delicate ecology of the coastal region have, until now, been ignored. With the increase in local holiday traffic, difficulties have arisen, including bottlenecks on roads, pollution and shortage of accommodation. There has also been a considerable increase in criminal activity (theft, stealing from vehicles, mugging). Recently, in addition to local and holiday tourism, business meetings and congresses have contributed to the growth of the tourism industry. Cannes, Nice and Monte Carlo in particular have made great efforts to stage various events – fairs, festivals and congresses – and the international airport Nice-Côte d'Azur has been of great service in this respect.

# Famous People

The following list is composed of famous historical personalities, all linked to Provence either through birth, residence, work or death and famous throughout the world. The list is arranged alphabetically.

André-Marie Ampère
1775–1836

The mathematician and physicist André-Marie Ampére, born in Lyons on January 22nd 1775, did fundamental work in the field of natural science. He developed a theory of electro-magnetism, built an electro-telegraph and discovered the direction of circulation of a magnetic field surrounded by a conductor through which the current was flowing. Even today the measure of the strength of a current is named after him. Ampère died on June 10th 1836 at the age of 61 in Marseilles.

Louis Bréa
*circa* 1450–1522/23

Louis Bréa, born in Nice, was the most important artist living between the end of the 15th c. and the beginning of the 16th c. in the Nice–Liguria region, a region remote from contemporary trends. Little is known about the models he chose or his influences. He worked mainly in Genoa, Taggia, Ventimiglia, Monaco and Nice. For a long time he remained closely attached to the antiquated taste of his patrons, mainly orders of penitent monks; his altarpieces consist of several fields mounted in wooden frames, each depicting only a few figures portraying deep contemplation and peace. The simplicity and naïvity of his figures cause him to be known as the "provincial Fra Angelico". From 1500 onwards he painted in the Renaissance style and after 1510 the influence of the Lombardy School became noticeably stronger. Bréa died between March 1522 and March 1523 in Nice. His paintings can be found in churches in Monaco, Nice, Biot, Antibes, Gréolières, Lucéram and Fréjus.

Paul Cézanne
1839–1906

Born the son of a prosperous banker on January 19th 1839 in Aix-en-Provence, Paul Cézanne came to painting after studying law for a short time. At first he modelled himself on classical masters; he admired and copied Michelangelo, Delacroix and Tintoretto. His schoolfriend Zola introduced him to the Impressionists, of whom Camille Pissarro influenced him most strongly. In 1873 Cézanne accompanied Pissarro to Auvers-sur-Oise and worked with him there in the open air outside the studio – a novelty of the Impressionists' form of art. He began to use strong colours to reproduce distinctive moods of light, air and nature. After taking part in the first group exhibition mounted by the Impressionists in 1874 and reaping only scorn, he moved back to Aix and spent the next 27 years there in strict seclusion.

Only after 1899 did he gradually become known to a wider public. He is regarded as the master of post-Impressionism; and from his words *"La réflection modifie la vision"* ("Contemplation alters what one sees") he is counted as one of the forerunners of modern art. By returning to classical aesthetics and to form he gave considerable impulse to modern representational art (Fauvism, Cubism). Cézanne died on November 22nd 1906 in Aix.

Marc Chagall
1887–1985

Marc Chagall, born in Vitebsk (White Russia) on July 7th 1887, studied at the Petersburg Academy of Art and then lived from 1910 to 1914 in Paris, where he became friends with Cendrars and Apollinaire; at that time his tendency to fantasy was already becoming apparent. He made the acquaintance of the Cubists, whose influence can only be sensed, however, in his composition. His first solo exhibition was arranged by Herwarth Walden in 1914 in his Berlin gallery "The Storm". Chagall returned to the Soviet Union until 1923, when he finally turned his back on his homeland. After another period in France he went to live in America from 1941–47 (in 1945

*André Maria Ampère*

*Jean-Henri Fabre*

*Vincent van Gogh*

he designed the staging and costumes for Stravinsky's ballet "The Firebird") and then returned to France to live in St-Paul-de-Vence from 1949. Chagall's work has its roots in the Jewish tradition of the East and in Russian popular art. From Jewish-mystic and rural elements he created mysterious, melancholy or effusive compositions in a uniquely fantastic style; his works contain mainly lyrical characters. Chagall is also important as an illustrator of books (Gogol, La Fontaine, the Bible) and he also worked with ceramics and stained glass, including the windows of the Frauenmunster in Zürich in 1970 and Rheims Cathedral in 1974. The most important museum in Provence featuring Chagall is the Musée National Message Biblique in Nice. Chagall died on March 28th 1985 in St-Paul.

Alphonse Daudet
1840–97

Alphonse Daudet first saw the light of day in Nîmes, but spent his youth in Lyons. In 1860 he obtained the post of Private Secretary to the Duke of Morny, through whose patronage he gained entry to interesting literary circles and thus acquired the basis of a commercially successful career in writing. Daudet's mainly cheerfully ironic stories make him the most important humorist of his time. Under the influence of the Naturalists he also turned his hand to themes critical of society, although he did not adopt their general ideological claims. Through Frédéric Mistral, Provence plays a large part in his works. He used the windmill near Arles as the fictitious place of origin of his "Lettres de Mon Moulin" (the stories were written in Paris). The museum now houses a Daudet museum and has become a leading French tourist attraction. Georges Bizet wrote the music to accompany a dramatisation of one of the letters, "l'Arlesienne." Daudet also created the well-known figure of Tartarin of Tarascon, an ironically-drawn Frenchman of the south on whom the ever present discrepancy between fantasy and reality plays many tricks. Daudet died on December 16th 1897 in Paris.

Auguste Escoffier
1846–1935

Escoffier, the "creator of the modern culinary art", was born on November 28th 1846 in Villeneuve-Loubet and died on February 12th 1935 in Monte Carlo. He served his apprenticeship with his uncle in Nice and then went on to work in Paris, Lucerne and Monte Carlo before making a great career for himself in London, becoming "the king of chefs and the chef of kings". In 1898 he became chef de cuisine at the London Carlton and remained in this position until he retired in 1921 at the age of 75. He was decorated with the Order of the Legion of Honour.

Escoffier's extensive works still form the basis of professional cookery, especially "Le Guide Culinaire" (1903), "Livres des Menus" (1912) and "Ma Cuisine" (1934). He not only created many classic recipes (Peach Melba is merely his best known) but also reorganised and rationalised the working kitchen and its employees and introduced a code of behaviour (cooks were to practise cleanliness and precision in the kitchen and they were not to smoke, drink or shout there). Escoffier modernised some methods of preparation such as making heavy Spanish and German sauces more subtle. A cookery museum was set up in 1966 in the house in which he was born at Villeneuve-Loubet.

Jean-Henri Fabre
1823–1915

Fabre was a brilliant scientist and is regarded as the father of modern behavioural research – a fact little known outside France. Born the son of a poor farmer in 1823 in St-Léons (Aveyron), the intelligent boy discovered his love of nature at an early age but satisfied his thirst for knowledge with a variety of interests. At the age of sixteen he gained a scholarship to a teacher training college in Avignon, eventually teaching in Carpentras, Ajaccio and Avignon. He gained his doctorate although, in order to support his large family, he had to supplement his meagre income by giving private lessons. Fabre's first and greatest discovery, the behaviour of digger wasps, brought him to the attention of Darwin, with whom he exchanged letters over many decades.

Fabre was already over 60 years old when, with the help of a loan from the famous English philosopher John Stuart Mill, he was able to buy an estate at Sérignan-du-Comtat called Harmas (Provençal for fallow land). Here he could continue with his experiments. The publication of his ten-volume major work "Souvenirs Entomologiques" between 1879 and 1907 introduced him to a wider audience. Fabre died on November 11th 1915 in Sérignan; Harmas has been turned into a museum.

Vincent van Gogh
1853–90

Vincent van Gogh was born on March 30th 1853, the son of a pastor in Zunden near Breda in the Netherlands. To begin with he was an assistant to an art dealer in Den Haag, then a lay preacher in the southern Belgian workers' settlements of the Borinage. After failing at theological studies, he began to paint in 1880 without any artistic training, portraying the farmers and workers of his native land in heavy, dark colours. In 1886 he went to Paris to live with his brother Theo, a successful art dealer, and came into contact with many other artists, including Paul Gauguin. Van Gogh began to paint in the Impressionist style, brightening the colours of his still life subjects and his portraits, and even verged on Pointillism.

On moving to Arles in 1888 van Gogh was completely overcome by the intensity of light and colour, and developed a completely new and unique style. He painted landscapes and town scenes, still life (such as "Sunflowers"), and portraits in loud, expressive colours with his characteristically rough strokes. After several attacks of mental derangement (after a fight with Gauguin in December 1888 he cut off one of his ears) van Gogh first entered a psychiatric home at St-Rémy-de-Provence in 1889, then one at Auvers-sur-Oise, all the time working with vehement energy until his suicide on July 29th 1890 at the age of 37.

During his lifetime van Gogh remained almost unknown and depended on the financial help of his brother. It was some decades after his death that he was discovered as the successor to Impressionism; his work inspired the Expressionists. Today such pictures as "Sunflowers" and "The Bridge at Arles" fetch astronomical prices.

Henri Matisse
1869–1954

Henri Matisse, born on December 31st 1869 at le Cateau-Cambresis, belonged in his early days as an artist to the school of Impressionism. Under the influence of Gauguin, Cézanne and Monet he became in about 1900 one of the most important artists to overcome the direction into which this style was leading; his paintings became more two-dimensional and more intensive in colour. Matisse and the painters of his circle were first disparagingly called "Les Fauves" ("The Wild Ones"). Fauvism preferred to compose pictures with large expanses of colour, abstaining from the delicate shades of Impressionism, and the effect was only obtained by colour and contrast. Matisse's book illustrations and drawings are also important; his last great fresco is the painting of the rosary chapel in Vence (1947–51). Matisse died on November 3rd 1954 in Nice-Cimiez.

Darius Milhaud
1892–1974

The composer Darius Milhaud who was born in Aix-en-Provence and was a pupil of the famous Conservatoire de Paris, belongs to the Groupe des Six, which included Arthur Honegger; the group had been formed in 1918 and its aim was to give new life to contemporary music. Milhaud was an extraordinarily prolific composer; his works include operas ("Christophe Colombe," "Medée", etc.), ballet music, opera, symphonies and chamber music. From 1947 until 1962 he gave lessons in composition at the Paris Conservatoire.

Hippolyte
Mège-Mouriès
1817–80

In 1869 this food chemist, born in Draguinan, developed a butter substitute based on beef suet as an entry for a competition run by Napoleon III, who was looking for a cheap and long-lasting fat for sailors. It was called margarine on account of its mother-of-pearl appearance (from the Greek *margaron* meaning pearl). Only after 1900, with the discovery of fat hardening, was plant oil substituted.

Prosper Mérimée
1803–70

After studying art and architecture, this son of an affluent merchant family (born on September 29th 1803 in Paris) became an inspector of historical statues and in this capacity travelled around France and the Mediterranean countries, in particular Spain. Many important historical monuments, which make up an essential part of Provence's cultural landscape owe their preservation to him. His literary works are characterised by a preference for romantic, spine-chilling, exotic and unusual themes; nevertheless, he wrote in a deliberately factual, anti-romantic style. He achieved true mastery of the novella and through the operatic production of his novella "Carmen" in 1845 by Georges Bizet he remains famous until this day. In 1848 he became a member of the Académie Française and in 1853 a senator; nevertheless he maintained friendship with Stendhal and other opponents of the Restoration. He died on September 23rd 1870 in Cannes.

Frédéric Mistral
1830–1914

Frédéric Mistral was born in Maillane, not far north of St-Rémy, the son of a farmer. The impetus for his literary work and his enthusiasm for the sonorous Provençal dialect came from his earlier acquaintance with Joseph Roumanille who was twelve years his senior. In 1859 appeared the first of the major works of Mistral, the novel "Mirèio" (in French "Mireille").
Mistral (the name is not a pseudonym!) is the most important innovator of the Provençal language and its poetry. With Théodore Aubanel and Joseph Roumanille he founded in 1854 the group of the Félibres, the members of which devoted themselves totally to this revival. Their work and aims are still highly regarded in Provence. In 1904 Mistral received the Nobel Prize for Literature.

Nostradamus
1503–66

Michel de Nostre-Dame was born in St-Rémy-de-Provence, the son of a family converted to Judaism. After studying liberal arts in Avignon and medicine at Montpellier University (founded in 1289 and the most famous medical faculty in the western world) he became the personal physician of Catherine de Medici and Charles IX of France. Like many Humanists he Latinised his name and henceforth called himself Nostradamus.

Considerable success in treating patients in several epidemics, mainly by the use of disinfected implements and by insisting on rules of hygiene, earned him the mistrust of his colleagues and forced him into hiding. During this time his intensive preoccupation with astrological and cosmic subjects began. From his observations of the constellations he drew conclusions which he set down in his sombre esoteric prophecies. His work, composed in gloomy four-lined verse, was published in 1555 in Lyons under the title "The Centuries". It caused a great furore (the Vatican blacklisted it as it foresaw the decline of the papacy) and has continued to exert influence in later centuries.

*Nostradamus*

*Francesco Petrarca*

*Pablo Picasso*

Less well-known is his book which appeared in the same year in which he foresaw the production of make-up and perfumes and of jams. Nostradamus died on July 2nd 1566 at Salon-de-Provence where he had lived since 1547.

Francesco Petrarca 1304–74

The Italian poet, philosopher and Humanist, born in Arezzo, moved with his family to Avignon in 1311 and studied law from 1317 in Montpellier and then from 1323 in Bologna. Having moved back to France he met in 1327 the lady whom he immortalised in his poetry as "Laura". It was a meeting that held importance for the whole of the rest of his life and for his artistic development. Between 1330 and 1347 he was the servant of Cardinal Giacomo Colonna. After extensive journeys through France, the Netherlands and Germany, where he searched for old manuscripts in libraries, he moved back to Fontaine-de-Vaucluse near Avignon in 1337 to fulfil his poetic inclinations there. In 1353 he left Provence and worked for eight years for the Milanese Visconti as an envoy (including some time in Prague), from 1362 he lived entirely in Venice. Petrarca was a pioneer of Humanism and of the Italian Renaissance. His writings in Latin gave new life to what was old and the content of his Italian poems, which are characterised by the formation of the suffering and reflective soul and by an inner-worldly ideal of the beautiful woman, became formal models for European love poetry (Petrarchism). He has become known as the "First Modern Man", proof of which is his famed ascent of Mount Ventoux on April 24th 1336, a climb made not for gain but with the sole purpose of experiencing the landscape.

Gérard Philipe 1922–59

The actor Gérard Philipe, born in Cannes, lived only for 37 years. Better known than his stage appearances were the films in which he appeared abroad ("Fanfan la Tulipe", "Le Diable au Corps", etc.). He is buried in the upland village of Ramatuelle near St-Tropez.

Pablo Picasso 1881–1973

Pablo Ruiz Picasso, the Spanish painter, sculptor, illustrator and potter, was born on November 25th 1881 in Malaga. He is held to be the greatest artist of modern time, having determined this century's art for eight decades.

After having been apprenticed to his father, Picasso studied at the academies of Barcelona and Madrid (from 1896) and, following several extended stays in Paris, moved to his chosen homeland of France in 1904. He finally settled on the Côte d'Azur in 1936 – "Then I realised that this landscape was my landscape" – after repeated trips to Provence and the coast. He worked chiefly in Mougins, Golfe-Juan, Antibes, Vallauris, Cannes and Vauvenargues. His early works, which are divided into the Blue and the Pink Periods according to the most-used colour, are characterised by melan-

choly, yet graceful figures. With his epoch-making key work, the "Demoiselles d'Avignon" of 1907, Picasso (together with Georges Braques, and later also Juan Gris and Férnand Léger) created the requirements necessary for the development of Cubism. After the First World War Picasso returned to figurative representation and came close to Surrealism; his use of forms now became blurred, his pictures were filled with motifs of movement and extremely vivid people. At the end of the 1920s he devoted himself increasingly to sculpture. Book illustrations, works portraying the Spanish Civil War and the greyness of war in general ("Guernica", created after the bombardment of the Basque town by the German Condor Legion, was a further highpoint), depictions of bull fights, portraits and variations on the theme of "artist and model" were now his main subjects.
After the Second World War Picasso became very involved with ceramics and also produced many graphics (drawings, etchings and lithographs). This resulted in a life's work which shows a unique mastery of using the history of art, of his own history and of the most varied artistic methods and techniques. Picasso died on April 8th 1973 in Mougins; his grave is at Vauvenargues where he worked for three months in 1958.

# History

| | |
|---|---|
| 900,000 B.C. | First signs of human life (cave finds at Vallonet near Roquebrune-Cap-Martin); objects made of bone and pebbles. |
| 700,000 B.C. | Oldest burnt spots in the cave at L'Escale, near Saint-Estéve-Janson (Bouches-du-Rhône). |
| 380,000 B.C. | Terra Amata finds at Nice: coastal settlement of large huts, burnt spots. |
| 300,000 B.C. | Cave finds at Baoussé-Roussé near Menton. |
| 4000–3000 B.C. | Stone Age culture, decorated and painted pottery; cave-dwellings, burial-grounds (finds at Roquepertuse, near Velaux). |
| about 800 B.C. | Ligurians take the coastal area and set up strongpoints; development of modest trade along the Riviera. |
| about 600 B.C. | Greeks from Phocaea in Asia Minor found the port of Massalia, later Marseilles. They introduce the vine and the olive tree as well as their important ceramic industry. Greek culture spreads through Gaul from here. |
| 600–100 B.C. | Further Greek settlements on the coast, increasing clashes with the Celto-Ligurian population. |
| 181/154 B.C. | The Greeks from Massalia summon their Roman allies to help against the Celto-Ligurians. |
| 150–50 B.C. | Roman incursions into the present-day area of Provence: Provincia Gallia Narbonensis. |
| 125–121 B.C. | The amalgamation of the Celts leads the Romans to occupy the land (destruction of the Oppidum d'Entremont, an important stronghold of the Saluvier). |
| 124 B.C. | Founding of Aix to protect the land route to Spain; construction of the Via Domitia. Founding of the first Roman province on the other side of the Alps: Gallia Transalpina or Gallia Narbonensis (founding of Narbonne 118 B.C.). |
| 58–52 B.C. | Caesar's conquest of Gaul. |
| 50/49 B.C. | Julius Caesar conquers Massalia (Latin Massilia), which had taken the side of Pompeii against him. Roman veterans are settled in Arles and Fréjus, etc. Further colonies in Avignon and Orange. |
| until A.D. 14 | Augustus conquers the Alpine tribes. Construction of the Trophée des Alpes, the victory monument near La Turbie. Various magnificent buildings of the Imperial Age such as the triumphal arch in Cavaillon. |
| 2nd c. A.D. | Heyday of the Pax Romana, which lasted until the 3rd c. A.D.<br>Extension of the Gallo-Roman towns and the first beginnings of Christianity. |
| 3rd c. A.D. | Arrival of nomadic peoples |
| 4th/5th c. A.D. | Christianity gains in importance; coffins are produced in Marseilles and the church of St-Victor is built. |

| | |
|---|---|
| Legend of the landing of the three Maries (Stes-Maries-de-la-Mer). | |
| The West Goths conquer Arles and occupy the area south of the Durance; Burgundians settle north of the Durance. | 419–478 |
| After their victory at Vouillé the East Goths take control of the Riviera. | 507 |
| The Franks gain the ascendancy. | 536 |
| Plague in Marseilles | 591 |
| Saracens invade southern France; emergence of many refuge settlements (*villages perchés*). Construction of *baptisteries* (baptismal churches). | 736–739 |
| Charles Martel defeats the Saracens and invades Provence. | 714–741 |
| Charlemagne brings "peace" to the region. | 768–814 |
| As a result of the Verdun treaty, in which the Carolingian empire was divided, Provence gains Lothar. | 843 |
| Provence first becomes a kingdom. | 855–863 |
| Charles the Bald, King of France, annexes Provence. | 869 |
| Under Boso, brother-in-law of Charles the Bald, Provence becomes part of the kingdom of Lower Burgundy. | 879 |
| Spasmodic incursions by the Saracens who settle in the Massif des Maures. | 9th c. |
| Lower and Upper Burgundy combine into one kingdom with Arles as the main city. | 933 |
| Kingdom of Provence-Burgundy under Conrad, founding of the new earldoms of Arles, Apt, Avignon. | 947 |
| Saracens are expelled from Fraxinetum (La Garde-Freinet?). | 973 |
| Affiliation of the kingdom of Burgundy with the Salic empire (Emperor Conrad II). | 1033 |
| First Romanesque church building. The family of the counts of Provence break into three factions, the counts of Barcelona, Toulouse and Forcalquier, who feud against one another. | 11th c. |
| Raimond Bérenger III, Count of Barcelona, receives the land between the Rhône, the Durance, the Alps and the sea, the Count of Toulouse, Alphonse Jourdaine, the land north of the Durance. | 1125 |
| Battles between the Catalan counts and the Dukes of Les Baux (1142–62). Participation in the Crusades. | |
| Flourishing of the ports following the Crusades (trade with the Levant). | 12th c. |
| Founding of Silvacane Abbey. | 1175 |
| Charles I of Anjou, brother of Ludwig the Holy, becomes Duke of Provence by marriage and, through the conquest of the kingdom of Naples in 1266, King of Provence. | 1246 |
| Flourishing of courtly poetry (troubadours). | 12–14th c. |

| | |
|---|---|
| 1308 | The Grimaldi family from Genoa purchases the estates of Monaco. |
| 1309–76 | Avignon is the residence of seven Popes during the time of the "Babalonian Exiles" and of the schism in the church. |
| 1348 | Countess Jeanne (also Queen of Naples) sells Avignon to the Pope. |
| 1388 | After the death of Ludwig I of Anjou his widow sells Nice and the Dukedom of Barcelona to the Dukedom of Savoy, with whom it remains (interrupted by Napoleon) until 1860. |
| 1434–80 | Flowering of the province under René of Anjou (Good King René). |
| 1442 | King René, driven from Naples, settles in Aix-en-Provence. |

Provence is united with the French kingdom; Ludwig XI, Count of Provence. 1482

Building of the Château d'If on the island of Marseilles. 1524

Royal troops (from 1536 under Charles V) penetrate into Provence and are repelled by a popular uprising. From 1524

More than 2000 Huguenots and other Protestants are put to death in the Lubéron Mountains; 800 are sold as galley slaves. 1545

Marseilles develops into an important trading centre. 1580–95

Great epidemic of plague. 1629

## History

| | |
|---|---|
| 1635 | Louis XIV makes Toulon a naval port. |
| 1641–60 | After uprisings Marseilles is subjected to the central power of Louis XIV. |
| 1691 | The French take over Nice. |
| 1710 | Prince Eugene advances to the Riviera. |
| 1720–22 | Years of severe plague. |
| 1715–50 | Flowering of the art of faience in Moustiers-Ste-Marie and Marseilles. |
| 1792 | The "Song of the Rhine Army" is made known in Paris by a voluntary corps from Marseilles. As "The Marseillaise" it becomes the national anthem. |
| 1793 | Siege of Toulon by the young Bonaparte; Nice annexed by French. |
| 1814 | After his abdication Napoleon leaves St-Raphaël for Elba. |
| 1815 | On March 1st Napoleon, returning from exile, lands in the Golfe-Juan. He proceeds in the direction of Paris via the route which was later called the "Route Napoléon" and arrives there on March 20th. One hundred day rule. |
| 1839 | The painter Paul Cézanne is born in Aix-en-Provence. |
| 1859–69 | Construction of the Suez Canal, which is of great importance for the port of Marseilles. |
| 1860 | After a popular vote King Victor Emanuel II of Piedmont-Sardinia cedes Nice and the Maritime Alps to France (alteration of the French eastern border).<br>The Côte d'Azur becomes a winter holiday resort. |
| 1861 | Menton and Roquebrune are sold to France by the Prince of Monaco. |
| 1866 | Founding of Monte-Carlo. |
| 1870/71 | Franco-Prussian War. |
| 1878 | Opening of casinos in Monte-Carlo. |
| 1914–19 | The First World War does not affect Provence. |
| 1939–45 | The Second World War. Menton is occupied by the Italians in 1940. At the end of 1942 German troops occupy the Riviera in retaliation for the Allied landing on November 8th in North Africa. The French war fleet is scuttled on November 27th at Toulon.<br>Within the framework of the invasion strategy which has been proceeding since the beginning of June in Normandy, on August 15th enormously strong Allied forces land on the Côte des Maures. With the support of the Resistance they take Toulon (August 26th), Marseilles (August 28th) and Nice (August 30th). German units remain in the mountainous hinterland until April 1945. |
| 1947 | Italy cedes the territory of Col de Tende to France. |
| 1956 | Inauguration of the first French ceramic works, Marcoule on the Rhône. |
| 1959 | On December 2nd the town of Fréjus is stricken by a catastrophic flood caused by a breach in the Malpasset Dam. This kills 421 people. |
| 1962 | The airport Nice-Côte d'Azur is opened and quickly becomes of more than regional importance. |

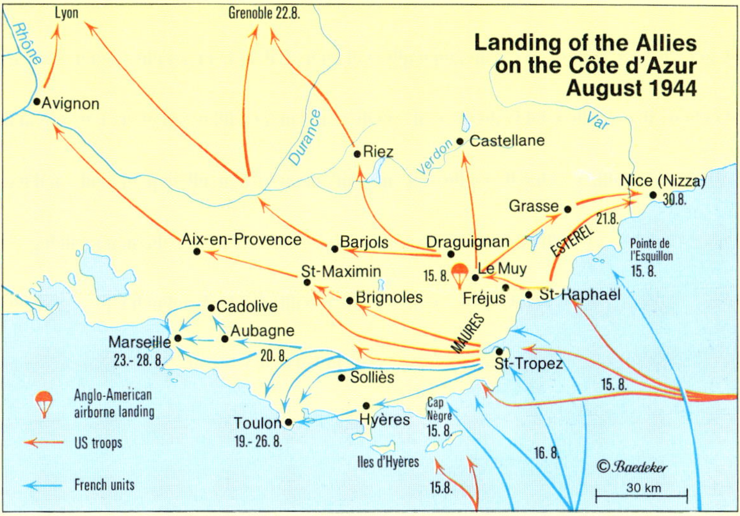


Construction of the industrial harbour of Fos at the Etang de Berre after Marseilles harbour becomes too small. From 1965

During the course of regionalisation the départments of Bouches-du-Rhône, Vaucluse, Hautes-Alpes, Alpes-Maritimes and Alpes-de-Haute-Provence are combined into the Provence-Alpes-Côte d'Azur region. 1972

The painter Pablo Picasso is buried in Vauvenargues. 1973

Motorway A 8 "La Provençal" links Provence to the French and the Italian motorway networks. 1980

A new policy of decentralisation begins under the newly-elected President François Mitterrand; the aim is to bring more political independence to the regions. 1981

Huge forest fires destroy almost the entire stock of trees, especially in the Esterel Mountains. 1982

# History of Art

Pre- and Early History

The first monuments of significance date from the time of pre- and early history; these include the finds from the Sanctuary of Roquepertuse near Velaux, from the Oppidum of Entremont near Aix-en-Provence and from Cavaillon near Avignon.

About 600 B.C. Greeks from Phocaea bring the first breath of free Classical Mediterranean culture to the Riviera with the founding of Massalia (Marseilles). There are also traces of settlement in Nice, Antibes and Greek Antipolis.

Roman Times

There are many remains of the Roman era including the arena and baths of Cimiez (part of Nice), fine granite pillars in Riez, the Greek-Roman town of Glanum near St-Rémy, the arena and theatre in Arles, the arena and theatre in Fréjus, the fine victory statue in La Turbie, the triumphal arches in Orange and Cavaillon as well as the temple site at Vernègues near Salon.

A large amount of stonework is kept and displayed in the museums in the relevant towns.

Ancient Christendom

From the early Christian period and the Carolingian era date remarkable round buildings (baptisteries), which can still be admired today in Fréjus, Aix-en-Provence and Riez. The crypt of St-Maximin contains the sarcophagi of, amongst others, Saints Maria-Magdalena, Sidonius and Maximin; there are more sarcophagi in the Musée d'Art Chrétien in Arles. One of the most important monuments of this age is the Church of St-Victor in Marseilles.

*Arles: the Roman arena*

*Cloister of Le Thoronet*

Romanesque

In the 12th c. architecture in this region experiences a considerable uplift, which manifests itself particularly in secular building of the Romanesque-Provençal style. Under the influence of the Cistercians there arise churches of uncomplicated design, with simple façades and plain interiors, generally with a single aisle; the square bell-towers reveal the influence of Lombardy. The best-known buildings of this period are the cathedrals at Aix-en-Provence and Avignon and the abbeys of Sénanque, Thoronet and Silvacane.

Gothic

French Gothic which is influenced by mysticism reaches its zenith in Avignon with the church of St-Pierre and the famous Papal Palace. Other leading buildings of this time are the Basilica of St-Maximin and the cathedrals of Fréjus.

Renaissance

Few architectural monuments remain from the Renaissance but, on the other hand, it left a legacy of very many paintings. Of note is the Avignon School which developed further to the work of Simone Martine who came from Tuscany and which united artists from different countries at the court of the popes. The most important examples are "Coronation of the Virgin Mary" by Enguerrand Quarton (1453) in the museum at Villeneuve-lèz-Avignon (see A to Z) and Nicolas Froment's triptych "Maria in the Burning Bush" (1485) in the Cathedral of Aix-en-Provence (see A to Z).
Inspired by the Italian Renaissance, a remarkable school of painting flourished in Nice, the head of which, Louis Bréa (about 1440 to 1523) is considered the "Fra Angelico of Provence". Works of the school of Bréa, which are characterised by a naïve purity and simplicity, are to be found in numerous rural churches of south-eastern Provence.

Baroque/ Classicism

During the time when Baroque art was gaining momentum, above all in Italy and Germany, Classicism was developing in France. This movement consciously and intentionally dissociates itself from the Baroque, and in

*Avignon: the Papal palace*

*Aix-en-Provence: Pavillon de Vendôme*

essence also preserves a greater formal strictness and discipline. Yet in south-eastern France the influence of the Italian view of art cannot be ignored and here one can confidently speak of Baroque art.

The most prominent examples of this form of art are to be found in the old town of Aix-en-Provence; as a single work the Pavilion de Vendôme, a little outside the town, is outstanding. Also belonging to this period is the good ceramic work of Moustiers-Ste-Marie. Definitely influenced by Baroque was the Marseilles painter and architect Pierre Puget (1620–94), who was at the same time probably the most important French sculptor of the 17th c.; as well as many other striking sculptures he created the caryatides on the portal of the Old Town Hall in Toulon.

Classicism

Eighteenth century Classicism is reflected in the works of Parrocel, Van Loo and Fragonard. Fragonard, born in 1742 in Grasse, was as it were the court painter of the Parisian aristocracy and is famous today for his stately boudoir and pastoral scenes.

Neo-Romanesque

In the 19th c. an architectural style based on neo-Romanesque-Byzantine historical models was widespread. Shining examples are the Church of Notre-Dame-de-la-Victoire in St-Raphaël, the Church of Notre-Dame-de-la-Garde and the Cathedral of La Major in Marseilles.

19th and 20th c.

Increasing numbers of artists of more modern and contemporary painting have been attracted to the Riviera since the end of the 19th c.. Impressionists, the master of whom is Cézanne, born in Aix-en-Provence, include Berthe Morisot who painted in Nice, Monet in Antibes and Renoir in Cagnes. In 1892 Signac, an exponent of Pointillism, chose St-Tropez as his home and brought others, including Bonnard and Matisse, with him. The reaction in the form of Fauvism was principally represented by Dufy and Matisse who were later resident in Nice. Picasso, one of the initiators of

*The new theatre in Nice (by Yves Bayard and Henri Vidal)*

Cubism, spent his time principally in Vallauris, Cannes and Mougins. The Cubist Léger was active in Biot, the Surrealist Chagall found in Vence themes for his colourful dream pictures. Other famous artists who lived and worked on the Riviera include Braque in St-Paul-de-Vence, Kandinsky in La Napoule, Cocteau in Menton and Van Dongen in Cannes. Their works can be seen in many local museums.

The "Unité d'Habitation", built in Marseilles by Corbusier between 1947 and 1952, together with modern marinas and leisure and residential layouts, such as Port-Grimaud, Port Camargue or Marina Baie des Anges, are impressive (if not of great merit in all respects) examples of contemporary architecture. The important art centre, Fondation Maeght in St-Paul-de-Vence, is a work of art in itself. In earlier times Nîmes and Nice distinguished themselves as centres of modern architecture.

Villages Perchés

Amid the long line of scarcely indistinguishable picturesque coastal villages and small and large towns with their inimitable atmospheres the many *"villages perchés"* are of particular interest. These hill settlements, also known as *"Nids d'Aigle"* (literally eagle's nests), situated on the hilltops, slopes, outcrops, ridges or terraces, were once used as refuges against foreign invaders or would-be conquerors, especially those threatening attack from the sea. They are situated relatively close to the coast but in places which are difficult to reach. Lack of space compelled the inhabitants to build their houses on the smallest possible piece of ground (*maisons en hauteur, maisons tour*), as close together as possible and frequently intermingled. Typical examples are Castellar, Eze, Gorbio, Gourdon, Peillon, Roquebrune, Tourette-sur-Loup and Vence.

Some years ago these hill villages were being abandoned by their inhabitants as a result of the unfavourable economic situation and problems of access and supply (for example, drinking water). Today, when money and technology make a more comfortable life possible, they are inhabited once more and restored as second and holiday homes, protected from total decay but robbed of their originality.

# Language of Provence

Provençal, which is widely spoken in south-eastern France, has considerable differences from classical French. It is known as *la langue d'oc* in southern France ("oc" being the word originally used to mean "yes"), whereas in the rest of the country the word was "oil" and French spoken elsewhere was called *la langue d'oil.*

History

Like all living Romance languages, Provençal was derived from vulgar Latin, which had penetrated into the country with Roman colonisation. In Provence about the year 1000 this dialect was the basis of the language of the troubadours and of Courtly poetry, a trend which was to be parelleled in German-speaking countries with the Minnesänger. This old Provençal was basically an artificial language. From the 13th c. the concept of "Proencal" gained currency at the expense of the former idiom known as "Lenga Romana". In subsequent centuries although Provençal was still being used as a spoken language, it was surpassed by written French, and more particularly in the field of literature by "classical" French which had developed from the northern French tongue, the so-called "langue d'oil.

Provençal Renaissance

It is certainly no accident that at the time when nation-states were beginning to come into being, that is in the first half of the 18th c., there arose in Provence a new awareness of its own history and a new assessment of its own language. In 1854 the Association of Félibres was founded, a group of poets of whom Fréderic Mistral was the most important. One of the principal contributions of the Provençal renaissance of that year was the comprehensive stock-taking of the linguistic heritage of the south of France. The

*Fréderic Mistral*

*A symbol of self-confidence – a signpost in two languages*

conscious nurture of the "Langue d'Oc" and the pride of the people of southern France in belonging to the area where it is spoken, are now increasingly apparent. In spite of this the "Langue d'Oc" is rarely their first language; indeed, a survey of 1987 could not find as many as 1% of speakers who named French *and* the "Langue d'Oc" as their mother tongue.

Linguistic Characteristics

Basically Provençal differs from standard French through the richness of its vowels. Whereas in classical French unstressed vowels tend to become reduced to a voiceless "e" or in some cases to disappear altogether, Provençal still makes use of the whole range of vowels. The chief characteristics are the maintaining of "a" in an open syllable (Provençal "pra" = French "pré", the mutation of the "a" to "ié" (Provençal "marchié" – from the Latin "mercatus"), the distinction of four final vowels (a, e, i, o; Provençal a, e; French e), the "o" ending of the first person of the verb, the regional distinction between Nominative and Accusative and the shaping of certain sounds. There are, of course, unusual features in the vocabulary, both in the stock of words and in the meaning.

# Provence in Quotations

Henry Swinburne (18th century)

"The Provençal is all alive, and feels his nerves agitated in a supreme degree by accidents and objects that would scarce move a muscle or a feature in the phlegmatic natives of more northern climes; his spirits are flurried by the slightest sensations of pleasure or of pain, and seem always on the watch to sieze the transient impressions of either; but to balance this destructive propensity, nature has wisely rendered it difficult for those impressions to sink into their souls; thus daily offering a surface smoothered afresh for new pains and pleasures to trace their light affections upon. But this by no means excludes warm attachments and solid friendships; when time and habit afford leisure for the impression to penetrate deep enough, it will, no doubt, acquire and retain as firm a hold in their breast as in any other, and perhaps be stamped with still greater warmth and energy."
*A Journey from Bayonne to Marseilles*, 1775 and 1776

Charles Lewis Meryon (1821–68)

"The Provençal language . . . is a most disagreeable jargon, as unintelligible even to those who understand French, as to those who do not, and delighting in intonations of the voice, which always reminded me of a crying child."
*Travels with Lady Hester Stanhope*, 1846

**Aigues Mortes**

Henry James (1843–1916)

"Aigues Mortes presents quite the appearance of the walled town that a school-boy draws upon his slate, or that we see in the background of early Flemish pictures – a simple parallelogram, of a contour almost absurdly bare, broken at intervals by angular towers and square holes. . . . It is extraordinarily pictorial, and if it is a very small sister of Carcassonne, it has at least the essential features of the family. Indeed, it is even more like an image and less like a reality than Carcassonne."
*A Little Tour in France*, 1882

**Aix-en-Provence**

Charles Dickens (1812–70)

"The town was very clean; but so hot, and so intensely light, that when I walked out at noon it was like coming suddenly from the darkened room into crisp blue fire. The air was so very clean, that distant hills and rocky points appeared within an hour's walk; while the town immediately at hand – with a kind of blue wind between me and it – seemed to be white hot, and to be throwing off a firey air from the surface."
*Pictures from Italy*, 1846

**Avignon**

Philip Thicknesse (1720–92)

"Avignon is remarkable for the number seven; having seven ports, seven parishes, seven colleges, seven hospitals, and seven monasteries; and I may add, I think, seven hundred bells, which are always making a horrid jingle; for they have no idea of ringing bells harmoniously in any part of France."
*A Year's Journey through France and Spain*, 1789

J. C. Hare (1795–1855)

"At Avignon I saw some large baths in the garden by the temple of Diana, built on the foundations of the old Roman ones. 'Does anybody bathe here now?' we askt; for we could see no materials for the purpose.
'No'; the guide answered. 'Before the Revolution, the rich used to bathe here; but they wanted to keep the baths to themselves; and the poor wanted to come too; and now nobody comes'.
What an epitome of a revolution!"
*Guesses at Truth* (with A. Hare), 1847

**Cannes**

"'Decent men don't go to Cannes with the – well with the kind of ladies you mean.' 'Don't they?' Strether asked with an interest in decent men that amused her. 'No; elsewhere, but not to Cannes. Cannes is different.'"
*The Ambassadors*, 1903

Henry James

**Menton**

"Of all the beasts of countries I ever see, I reckon this about caps them. I also strongly notion that there ain't a hole in St. Giles's which isn't a paradise to this. How any professing Christian as has been in France and England can look at it, passes me. It is more like the landscape in Browning's 'Childe Roland' than anything I ever heard tell on. A calcined, scalped, rasped, scraped, flayed, broiled, powdered, leprous, blotched, mangy, grimy, parboiled, country, without trees, water, grass, fields – with blank, beastly, senseless olives and orange-trees like a mad cabbage gone indigestible; it is infinitely liker hell than earth, and one looks for tails among the people. And such females, with hunched bodies and crooked necks carrying tons on their heads, and looking like Death taken seasick. Ar-r-r-r-r! Gr-r-r-rn!"
*Letter to Pauline Trevelyan*, January 19th 1861

Algernon Charles Swinburne (1837–1909)

**Montpellier**

"I have been dangerously ill, and cannot think that the sharp air of Montpellier has been of service to me – and so my physicians told me when they had me under their hands for above a month – if you stay any longer here, Sir, it will fatal to you – And why good people were you not kind enough to tell me this sooner?"
*Letter to Mrs. Fenton*, February 1st 1764

Laurance Sterne (1713–68)

"There are places that please, without your being able to say wherefore, and Montpellier is one of the number. . . . The place has neither the gaiety of a modern nor the solemnity of an ancient town, and it is agreeable as certain women are agreeable who are neither beautiful nor clever."
*A Little Tour in France*, 1882

Henry James

**Nice**

"When I stand upon the rampart and look round me, I can scarce help thinking myself enchanted. The small extent of country which I see, is all cultivated like a graden. Indeed the plain presents nothing but gardens full of green trees, loaded with oranges, lemons, citrons, and bergamots, which make a delightful appearance. If you examine them more nearly, you will find plantations of green pease ready to gather; all sorts of sallading, and pot herbs, in perfections; and plats of roses, carnations, ranunculas, anemonies, and daffodils, blowing in full glory, with such beauty, vigour, and perfume, as no flower in England ever exhibited."
*Travels through France and Italy*, 1766

Tobias Smollett (1721–71)

"This place is so wonderfully dry that nothing can be kept moist. I never was in so dry a place in all my life. When the little children cry, they cry dust and not tears. There is some water in the sea, but not much: – all the wet-nurses cease to be so immediately on arriving: – Dryden is the only book read: – the neighbourhood abounds with Dryads and Hammer-dryads; and weterinary surgeons are quite unknown. It is a queer place, – Brighton and Belgravia and Baden by the Mediterranean: odious to me in all respects but its magnificent winter climate. . . ."
*Letter to Chichester Fortescue*, February 24th 1865

Edward Lear (1812–88)

**Nîmes**

"I took Wordsworth to see the exterior of both the Maison Carrée and the Arena. He acknowledged their beauty, but expressed no great pleasure. He says: 'I am unable from ignorance to enjoy these sights. I receive an impression, but that is all. I have no science, and can refer nothing to

Henry Crabb Robinson (1775–1867)

principle.' He was on the other hand delighted by two beautiful little girls near the Arena, and said: 'I wish I could take them to Rydal Mount.'"
*Diary*, April 3rd 1837

Philip Thicknesse

The Maison Carrée
"It is said, and I have felt the truth of it, in part, that there does not exist, at this day, any building, ancient or modern, which conveys so secret a pleasure, not only to the connoisseur, but to the clown also, whenever, or how often soever they approach it. The proportions and beauties of the whole building are so intimately united, that they may be compared to good breeding in men – it is what every body perceived, and is captivated with, but what few can define."
*A Year's Journey through France and Spain*, 1789

**Toulon**

Tobias Smollett

"Toulon is a considerable place, even exclusive of the basin, docks, and arsenal, which indeed are such are justify the remark made by a stranger, when he viewed them, 'The king of France (said he) is greater at Toulon than at Versailles.'"
*Travels through France and Italy*, 1766

# Recommended Routes

Foreword

These recommended routes are intended to offer plenty of ideas to those travelling by car or by motorcycle without denying them the freedom of individual planning and choice. The triangular area enclosed by Avignon, Aix/Marseilles and Agues-Mortes, in particular, contains so much of interest that it is almost an impossible task to select one outstanding itinerary in this region.

The routes have been devised to include the main places of interest in the area. Nevertheless, many of the places described in this guide can only be reached by making detours. The suggested routes can be followed by using the map that accompanies this travel guide, which should help to simplify the detailed plans.

Places which are included in the "A to Z" section under a main heading appear in the recommended routes in **bold type**. Descriptions of other places included can be found by referring to the index.

Timetable

Those who follow the complete routes described here (including all detours they cover a total of approximately 4500km/2796 miles) and who want to have sufficient time to visit the principal points of interest, must allow about four weeks for the itinerary (including, thanks to convenient and fast motorways, getting to the area). Even when the detours are omitted, the whole tour will still take three weeks.

Provence

In its most general sense the Provence of scenic beauty and of important cultural monuments encompasses the area of land between the lower Rhône (approximately between Montélimar and Aigues-Mortes) and the Var at Nice as well as the French Alps rising in the hinterland. In contrast the historical province of Provence stretches across the area of the present-day départements of Bouches-du-Rhône and Vaucluse as well as the Languedoc-Rousillon region in the Département du Gard (Nîmes).
The first section of these recommended routes deals with this triangular area usually considered by tourists to be Provence.

Côte d'Azur

The second section covers the French holiday resorts par excellence, the Mediterranean coast between Marseilles and the Italian border at Menton as well as its immediate hinterland.

Haute Provence/ Alps

By following these recommended routes it is possible to return to northern France via Gap – Grenoble, or Geneva and Lyon. One possibility is to follow the Route Napoléon (described in the third section of the recommended routes); however, not from the south to north but from the north to the south as an interesting alternative to the "normal" way of getting to Provence by car.

Splendid views of the French Alps can be enjoyed by following the Route des Grandes Alpes (also known as the Route d'Eté des Alpes) which is another alternative for the return journey. From Nice it passes through Briançon and Chamonix and on to Geneva. The third section of the recommended routes details the stretch as far as Barcelonette, from where Serre-Ponçon Lake and Gap can be reached.

## 1a: Loriol–Orange (150km/93 miles)

Itinerary

Provence begins – so it is generally said – at Loriol: landscape, vegetation and light soon take on a Mediterranean flavour. Leave the motorway here and cross to the right bank of the Rhône. Enter Cruas with its noteworthy Roman church, its medieval ruins and its nuclear power station. From Rochemaure Castle enjoy a wonderful view across the Rhône Valley to **Montélimar**. This old Provençal town, famous for its white nougat, is dominated by a 12th–14th c. castle.

Heading towards Orange it is worth making a detour through the Tricastin, a hilly triangular area enclosed by Montélimar, Nyons and Orange. The hillsides are mainly planted with olive trees, holm oaks and pines, while fruit and vegetables are grown wherever possible in the valleys. Discerning gourmets associate truffles in particular with this area. Leaving Montélimar on the D4 drive through **Grignan** with its splendid 16th c. castle where Madame de Sévigné, famed for her letters, lived. Continue to Suze either in an easterly direction through Valréas, centre of the "Enclave des Papes" (Enclave of the Popes), and Nyons or proceed westwards past the ruins of the chapel of Val des Nymphes to the small medieval town of **La Garde-Adhémar**, located on a mountain spur across the Rhône and offering, as well as an impressive Romanesque church, a good general view of the whole Tricaston region. The principal town, St-Paul-Trois-Châteaux (the wrong translation of the Celtic word Tricastin), contains remains of a former fortress and a 11th/12th c. cathedral built in the Provençal-Romanesque style. The imposing castle in Suze-la-Rousse bears witness to the town's great importance during the Middle Ages. Looking up from the Var Valley, Boliène, becomes visible, with the remains of its 14th c. fortress built on a hill blessed with fine views across the Rhône Valley.

It is possible here to make a round trip to view the Gorge of the **Ardèche** and the famous stalactite caves; to do this cross the Rhône at Pont-St-Esprit.

An excursion to the north can be undertaken from Boliène. Where the Rhône is diverted by the Rhône dam at Donzère pass the enormous Blondel power station and ascend to Barry, a small hamlet built on a rocky outcrop. Here experience a fantastic panoramic view across the complex of the **Donzère-Mondragon** dam and KKW Tricastin.

Leaving Mondragon, Orange can soon be reached via the N7 (A7) from Montélimar. It is more interesting, however, to follow the route along the D12 through Rochegude (detour along the D206), Uchaux and across to Sérignan where the scientist Fabre lived and worked. At last we come to Orange, located in a fertile plain exposed to the Mistral. Its ancient Roman theatre is one of the largest and best-preserved.

## 1b: Orange–Mont Ventoux–Apt–Aix–Marseilles (310km/193 miles)

General Information

This varied journey demonstrates Provence's differing landscapes; first Orange's fertile plain with its olive and mulberry trees, then Mont Ventoux with its wooded slopes but bare limestone crest offering a view right across Provence as far as the Alps, then the Vaucluse plateau with its picturesque gorges and Fontaine-de-Vaucluse made famous by Petrarch (where the Sorgue has its source). After crossing the Lubéron Mountain in the densely forested Combe de Lourmarin the visitor finally reaches the plain of Aix-en-Provence, surrounded by bare mountain chains and intensively farmed. The route from here to Marseilles passes through Vauvenargues, St-Maximin, Nans-les-Pins and the Col d'Espigoulier and reveals the many unique characteristics of Provence.

Itinerary

Begin the journey from **Orange** to **Mont Ventoux** by driving east along the D950 and D55 to Beaumes-de-Venise, a village famous mostly for its Muscat wine. Then proceed northwards along the foot of the Dentelles-de-Montmirail a mountain chain resembling the edge of lace. On the way pass the Romanesque chapel Notre-Dame-d'Aubune, with its elegant belltower visible from some distance, the famed wine villages of Vacqueyras, Gigondas and Séguret, finally reaching Vaison-la-Romaine. Countless excavations verify the importance of the town as a trading centre in Roman times. Continue to Malaucène at the western foot of Mont Ventoux (Provencal *Ventour* = windy mountain, after the many heavy storms). The impressively towering chalk ridge is an isolated continuation of the Pyrenees.

From the summit, it is worth continuing via Sault through large fields of lavender (destined for the perfume industry) along "Lavender Road" (this tourist route, not described here, leads from Avignon via Carpentras and Malaucène to Sault and on through the little old town of Forcalquier and Gréoux-le-Bains, a little spa town located in the lower Verdon Valley, to the Gallo-Roman township of Riez, from there via Moustiers-Ste-Marie, Castellane and Grasse to Nice).

From Sault, drive through the Gorges de la Nesque, a wooded rocky valley cut into the Vaucluse plateau, a high chalky plain adjoining the south face of Mont Ventoux. Pass through Villes-sur-Auzon, noted for its ochre production, to **Carpentras**, an industrial town rich in tradition, located on the Auzon with France's oldest maintained synagogue. Not far away to the south east, the village of Venasque contains a noteworthy church and a baptistry (6th and 12th c.). From Carpentras the journey continues through Pernes-les-Fontaines with its several pretty fountains, its remains of an old fortress and its 12th c. church, to **Fontaine-de-Vaucluse**, picturesquely situated in a rocky amphitheatre (vallis clausa) and dominated by the ruins of a castle once belonging to the bishops of Cavaillon. Allow time here for a stroll to the source of the Sorgue which begins as a spring at the end of a hollow surrounded by high chalk rocks and which was mentioned by Petrarch who lived in Avignon and Fountaine-de-Vaucluse for many years.

A detour through the pretty little town of **Gordes**, located on a rocky slope of the Vaucluse plateau (its castle accommodates a Vasarély museum) and past medieval cottages called "bories" and constructed from stone slabs and without mortar, leads to **Senanque**, a Roman Cistercian monastery. Continue to Rousillon, France's main ochre-producing centre built on a plateau of ochre. Apt, with its fruit and preserves industries, lies in the Coulon Valley; of note is the Cathedral of St Anne in the town centre.

Further south, drive through fine fertile countryside reminiscent of Tuscany to the **Montagne du Lubéron**, a mountain chain between the valleys of the Coulon and the Durance. Continue to Bonnieux, a pretty hillside town, either directly along the D943 or by travelling further east through Fort-de-Buoux. Bonnieux affords a fine view northwards to Mont Ventoux. The road winds its way southwards among forests of holm oaks and chalk rockfaces through the Combe de Lourmarin; the village of Lourmarin possesses a Renaissance castle as well a cemetery where the author Albert Camus is buried. He spent the later years of his life in this town. From here, either follow a direct route to Cadenet in the Durance Valley or arrive there via the former Waldenses (see A to Z; Lubéron) villages of Cucuron and Ansouis, with its impressive castle. Cadanet's church contains an ancient font.

After visiting the former Cistercian abbey at **Silvacane** (cross the Durance and then turn right towards La Roque-d'Anthéron), continue to Aix-en-Provence; drive along the D543 past Bassin-de-St-Christophe, a reservoir supplying water to Marseilles, and the small town of Rognes to the D10. Head west again to Ventabren and the Roquefavour aqueduct and then on via Les Milles (D65) to **Aix-en-Provence**, Provence's historical centre. Allow plenty of time to visit its many places of interest.

Beyond Marseilles, use the motorway A51, which cuts through a hilly landscape, offering a very impressive panoramic view of surrounding bare mountain chains. The visitor is recommended to drive east and follow the eroded and twisty road around the Montagne-Ste-Victoire to the Massif de la Ste-Baume and on down into Marseilles. The D10 passes Bimont reservoir and on to Vauvenargues, famous for its castle where Picasso lived for some years. Walkers would find the climb to the Croix de Provence a unique experience. Passing through Puits-de-Rians and Pourrières, the tour then reaches **St-Maximin-la-Ste-Baume**. This attractive little town nestles in the basin of a former lake and possesses Provence's only important Gothic church.

Leaving Tourves and Nans-les-Pins, Plan d'Aups is reached at the foot of the Massif de la Ste-Baume, which like St-Maximin and Stes-Maries-de-la-Mer is bound up with the legend surrounding St Mary Magdalene. Another real feast for walkers is the ascent of St-Pilon; also of interest here is the wood, whose plant life is not typical of the area. The double bends of the Col d'Espigoulier lead down to Gemenos, a holiday resort, and to Aubagne, birthplace of Marcel Pagnol (his stories are mainly based in this area) and headquarters of the Foreign Legion. The Etoile mountain chain rises in the north west with the characteristic rocky peak of the Garlaban. Follow the D2 to Marseilles, France's second largest and oldest town, on the Golfe du Lyons; the entrance to Marseilles is dominated by the view of high densely-built tower blocks in front of the towering rocks.

## 1c: Marseilles–Arles–Nîmes–Avignon (310km/193 miles)

Itinerary

Leave Marseilles in a north-westerly direction and arrive first at L'Estaque, a seaside resort frequented by local people; it has a small fishing harbour and some industry. The N568 leads via the picturesque bare Chaîne de l'Estaque which separates the Etang de Berre from the Mediterranean and through the Val de l'Aigle up to the coast at Carry-le-Rouet, a small seaside town. Then follow the coastline to Sausset (and to Cap Couronne), finally head inland to **Martigues**, once the centre of a principality on the **Etang de Berre** which is linked to the Mediterranean by the Canal de Caronte. Traversed by several channels, the old town is known as "the Venice of Provence".

The harbour areas of Lavéra, Port-de-Boux and the enormous Port de Fos (industrial zone) form Marseilles' new giant harbour. Cross the Rhône canal and also a side-canal by a small "Pontet" (bridge) and drive along the west bank of the Etang de Berre whose white chalk rocks and park-like landscape offer a charming alternative to the industrialised east bank around Marignane (airport, saltworks, natural gas refineries, chemical industries, etc.). The route continues via St-Mitre-les-Remparts, with its medieval fortifications, eventually by means of a detour via the Chapelle St-Blaise across the Etang de Lavalduc, near to which the remains of a Greek castle (4th c. B.C.) and a basilica have been excavated, to Istres (Latin for "oyster pond") on the bank of the small Etang d'Olivier where remains of an ancient Greek town have been found. Allow time to visit the hill town of Miramas-le-Vieux, which still has its walls, before travelling along rural roads lined with plane trees via St-Chamas and the well-known small wine village of Cornillon-Confoux finally reaching **Salon**, centre of olive processing and the home town of Nostradamus.

The straight N113 leads immediately from here through the Crau, called "Campus Lapideus" or "Cravus" by the Romans, a bare plain formed by Pleistocene gravels of the Durance where sheep graze and where market gardening is carried on to **Arles**, Provence's unofficial capital, with its unique atmosphere and impressive historical monuments from Roman and medieval times.

From here, choose either the direct route to Stes-Maries-de-la-Mer or a round journey via Les Baux: to the north-east outside Arles the ruins of the former 10th c. Benedictine abbey of **Montamjour** and the unusual chapel Ste-Croix-en-Jérusalem (12th/13th c.) lie on a mountain ridge. Then comes the small town of Fontvieille with its impressive limestone quarries and the windmill made famous by Alfonse Daudet in his "Lettres de Mon Moulin". Continue into the white mountain chain of the Alpilles to the ruined town of **Les Baux**, picturesquely located on a rocky plateau and once the chief town of a medieval barony and centre of troubadors. In 1632 Les Baux was destroyed and today is only a small place, living exclusively by tourism; it has restored 14th/15th c. houses, a former Waldenses (Protestant) church, the grandiose fortress ruins and a fantastic view.

Continuing in the direction of St-Rémy-de-Provence, cross the **Alpilles** chain whose richly-fossilised white Miocene rocks proved an excellent building material (partly quarried underground). To the south of **St-Rémy-de-Provence** with its classical domed church, worthy of a visit, lies the Greek-Roman settlement of Glanum, destroyed by the West Goths in A.D. 480, of which extensive excavations bear witness; still preserved are a triumphal arch and the 18m/59ft high "Julier's Monument". To the north-west of St-Rémy is the village of Maillane, birthplace and resting place of the Provençal poet Frédéric Mistral, a champion of the maintenance of Provençal traditions.

Next head for the town of **Tarascon** on the left bank of the Rhône, known through Alphonse Daudet's Roman character "Tartarin de Tarascon". Next to the bridge leading to neighbouring Beaucaire stands the imposing 12/15th c. castle of King René. Beaucaire, on the right bank of the Rhône, once famous throughout the western world for its market dating from 1217 but today of lesser importance, is crowned by the ruins of a fortress (there is a fine panoramic view from the tower); also to be recommended is an excursion to the Abbaye de St-Roman across the Grand Rhône.

From Beaucaire either follow the D999 directly to **Nîmes** or travel along the Canal du Rhône to Sète which forms a connection to the Mediterranean at Aigues-Mortes to **St-Gilles**. This small town, which grew up around one of the abbeys founded by St Egidius, possesses a Roman church famous for its extraordinarily richly-decorated façade. From St-Gilles, on the northern edge of the **Camargue**, a trip can be undertaken through the Rhône delta with its flat lagoons and reed marshes, extensive salt-works and sand dunes; either follow the D37 southwards and along the east bank of the Etang de Vaccares to Salin-de-Giraud and to Plage du Piémanson or follow the D570 (from Albaron) to **Les Stes-Maries-de-la-Mer**, the Camargue's largest town. The route continues along the Petit Rhône to **Aigues-Mortes** about 6km/4 miles from the sea, located between marshes and ponds which give the town its name "Dead Waters" (acquae mortuae). The medieval harbour and crusader town still possesses its mighty fortified walls. To the south-west of Aigues-Mortes lie the "artificial" seaside resorts of Le Grau-du-Roi and **La Grande-Motte**, loved by French holidaymakers.

After driving through St-Laurent and Aimargues (east of Codognan is the bottling plant for Perrier mineral water), reach **Nîmes** (the French town most blessed with historic buildings) and continue via **Uzès** with its castle and the elegant round Tour Fenestrelle to **Pont du Gard** (in summer only via Remoulins, one way street). The 49m/161ft high and 275m/903m long aqueduct, probably built around 19 B.C., spans with its three rows of arches the deep valley of the Gard and is one of the most spectacular and best-maintained Roman constructions in existence. From here continue along the N100 through hilly country (to the north the vineyards from which comes Tavel, the best known rosé wine of Provence) to the old papal residence of **Avignon**, the centre of tourism in Provence.

## 2a: Marseilles–Toulon–Cannes–Nice (250km/155 miles)

Itinerary

Leaving **Marseilles**, the route leads first to the little port of Cassis, located on a small semi-circular bay and famous for its excellent white wine. A detour exists to the west of Cassis to the Calanques, narrow deep inlets between steep white chalk cliffs. Well worth experiencing is the drive from Cassis to La Ciotat on the Corniche des Crêtes, which encircles Cap Canaille, at 363m/1191ft France's highest cliffs. The red cliffs of the Bec de L'Aigle tower boldly above the port of La Ciotat. The journey continues via the seaside towns of La Ciotat-Plage, Les Lecques and **Bandol** to Sanary-sur-Mer from where there is a fine view of the coast and also from where an excursion to Ollioules and to Gros Cerveau can be made. At this point the D559 divides the Cap Sicle peninsula and passes Fort de Six-Fours, with its many excellent views, before reaching **Toulon**, France's largest military port.

The N98 provides a direct link to Hyères. However, it proves more interesting to follow the coast road to the Glens peninsula, an island first linked to the mainland during Roman times. Trips to the Hyères islands, with their impressive cliffs and rich plant life, depart from La Tour-Fondeau. The most important island in this group is the Île de Porquerolles with its port of the same name. About 10km/6 miles to the east lies the island of Port-Cros, a nature reserve with wonderful walks. **Hyères**, built not far from the sea on a steep hillside, is the oldest health resort in the Mediterranean. The old town is bordered to the south by Hyères-les-Palmiers, a new town named after its many date palms. The hill to the north, where a castle once stood, offers an extensive panoramic view although this remains surpassed by the view from the Fenouillet, the highest peak of the Maurettes.

Now follow the N98 as it returns inland, past extensive salt fields, through Monts des Maures covered with woods (cork extraction), moorland and maquis. Behind Mauvanne the D559 turns off to the small old town of Bornies, arriving at the coast again at **Le Lavandio**. The splendid Corniche des Maures runs along this part of the coast, rich in bays and cliffs and with a number of seaside resorts, continuing via the charming hillside health resort of Le Rayol to the sheltered bay of Cavalaire. Cross magnificent forests (partly planted with cork trees) to the Cap Camarat peninsula and continue via Moulins de Paillas and a detour to Cap Camarat (a far-reaching view of the Plage de Pampelonne, the Côte d'Azur's largest and finest beach) to **St-Tropez**, the famous little port lying on the south bank of the gulf of the same name. This small town still thrives as a meeting place for artists and the international "in crowd", even though its prominent inhabitants have long since retired into quieter areas and well-protected villas.

The N98 continues through the Giscle estuary and along the Gulf of St-Tropez to **Port Grimaud**, a harbour and holiday town built in the mid 1960s in a Venetian style by the architect François Spoerry, and to the resort of Ste-Maxime. The coast road continues around the Cap des Sardinaux, Les Issambers and encircles further foothills, all with fine views. Behind St-Aygulf (good sandy beach) cross the estuary of the Argens to reach **Fréjus**, a small town located between the Monts des Maures and the Esterel mountains, which in Roman times as *Forum Iulii* was an important port. The old and medieval buildings, especially the cathedral with its font and cloisters, are well worth visiting.

Beyond Cannes the N7 from Fréjus leads in a north-easterly direction through the **Esterel** mountains. It is worth climbing Mont Vinaigre, the highest peak of the Massif. The coast road, meanwhile, follows the Gulf of Fréjus via the seaside resort of **St-Raphaël** (whose old town contains an impressive Templar church) to the red porphyry rocks Lion de Mer and Lion de Terre. The Corniche de L'Esterel (Corniche d'Or) continues on to Agay. Behind Agay the coast road passes through the seaside resort of Anthéor on the Calanque of the same name, with its many cliffs, and then follows a picturesque route via the Pointe du Petit-Caneiret, with its view of the fire-red porphyry cliffs of Cap Roux and the less impressive Rocher de St-Barthélemy. An excursion should be planned here to the Grand Pic du Cap Roux, the Esterel's best vantage point with a fine view of the coast of St-Tropez as far as Bordighera, the Maritime Alps and sometimes Corsica.

Drive through St-Barthélemy, nestling in a valley, across the Cap Roux peninsula and around the Baie de la Figueirette until Miramar appears. Behind the Point de L'Esquillon ascend many twisty mountain roads admiring the view of Napoule Bay, Cannes, the Lérins islands and the Maritime Alps. Above the popular seaside resort of La Napoule, a 14th/18th c. castle stands in solitary splendour on a ridge.

Crossing the wide estuary of the Siagne, we reach fashionable **Cannes**, regarded as the most distinguished health resort on the Côte d'Azur thanks to its mild climate, varied sub-tropical vegetation, splendid beaches and international film festival. Boats sail several times a day to the Lérins islands of Ste-Marguerite and St-Honorat. The trip crosses the fine Juan Bay to the port of Golfe-Juan where Napoleon I landed in 1815 on his return from Elba. The somewhat inland little town of Vallauris is known for its pottery, Picasso having worked here. On the western side of Cap d'Antibes lies the famous resort of Juan-les-Pins. Its yearly summer jazz festival enjoys international acclaim.

From here to Antibes the route passes around Cap d'Antibes with its villas and gardens of which the Jardin Thuret, laid out in the 19th c., invites a stroll. **Antibes**, in an impressive location on the north-east side of the like-named cape between the small bays of Anse St-Roch in the north and Anse de la Salis in the south, is a centre of flower cultivation and export. Visit Fort Carré, a remainder of the fortifications, and the medieval town wall with the Front de Mer promenade, which borders the heart of the old town on the seaward side, as well as the former Grimaldi Castle, which houses a Picasso museum.

For the journey from Antibes to Nice, choose either the N7, a little away from the sea, or drive directly (N98) along the wide Baie des Anges (Bay of Angels) – with a detour to Biot – past the enormous pyramid-shaped apartment buildings, Marina Baie des Anges and, on the other side of the Var past the Nice-Côte d'Azur airport, to the "main town of the Riviera" – **Nice**. Stroll through the narrow alleys of this lovely, lively old town and along the palm-lined Promenade des Anglais.

An alternative recommended route from Cannes to Nice is via Mougins to **Grasse**, the centre of the perfume industry, then on to Gourdon and to the Gorges du Loup and across to Tourrette-sur-Loup. The appealing little towns of **Vence** and St-Paul-de-Vence hold particular interest for art-lovers (Fondation Maeght). Rejoin the coast either at Villeneuve-Loubet or Cros-de-Cagnes.

## 2b: Nice–Monaco–Menton (30km/19 miles)

Summary

From Nice, three different roads called "Corniches" (road along edge of cliff, coastal road with extensive views), of which the Moyenne Corniche and the Grande Corniche count among Europe's finest roads, follow the slopes or the feet of the Maritime Alps to Menton.

The distance between Nice and Menton on all three routes measures about 30km/19 miles and 35km/22 miles. Those wishing to make the journey twice, perhaps as a round trip from Nice, should choose for the outward journey the Moyenne Corniche, as it reveals the full beauty of the landscape, while the return journey on the Grande Corniche offers a grandiose panoramic view.

## Recommended Routes

*Corniche du Littoral

The Corniche due Littoral (N98), also called the Corniche Inférieure or Petite Corniche, follows the edge of the sea and offers fine views but takes second place to the two higher routes. Traffic is heavy here and this leads above all to congestion through the many towns.

After leaving Nice, the Corniche du Littoral leads first around the foothills (many fine views) of Mont Boron, past the excellent roadstead of Villefranche harbour and to the like-named holiday resort with its romantic old town. Behind here a road branches to the south to the elegant villa town of St-Jean-Cap-Ferrat on the eastern side of the peninsula. Here a round trip to a vantage point (*belvédère*) and up on to the headland can be made.

The road continues to the pleasant little town and holiday resort of **Beaulieu-sur-Mer**, located very close to Villefranche on a broad waterway, dominated by steep rocky cliffs. After Menton, Beaulieu counts as France's warmest town, this having earned the town the name of "Little Africa". Now drive through the magnificent chalk cliffs of Cap Roux to reach the elegant seaside town of Eze-Bord-de-Mer. The journey continues via Cap d'Ail, whose wonderful cliff-hidden bays are excellent for swimming, and St-Antoine, with its impressive Château de l'Ermitage, to the principality of Monaco, whose people are so closely linked to their neighbours in France. Crossing Pont St-Roman leave the principality again and follow the N7 to **Menton**, at the foot of the Maritime Alps right on the Italian border. In contrast to many other seaside resorts Menton, despite some new building, has managed to preserve the character of a developed Mediterreanean town.

**Moyenne Corniche

Completed in 1939 and ending in Monaco, the Moyenne Corniche passes half way up the cliffs across several bridges, from where there are fine views, and through galleries. It is certainly the finest of the three routes, as it lies closer to the sea than the Grande Corniche, and offers the chance to sample the beauty of the coast in a more detailed way.

Continue along the N7 via the Col de Villefranche (view of Nice, the coast and the Maritime Alps, south of the pass across the Vallon de la Murta) to the Col de Caire, to drive beyond here via a picturesque route over cliffs and through a long tunnel to the St-Michel valley, with its olive groves and across a 57m/187ft high viaduct to the old mountain settlement of Eze-Village. The village was built in a bold, scenic position high above the sea on a cliff crowned with a Ligurian refuge. After leaving Eze-Village the road soon curves through the Vallon de St-Laurent and around the Tête de Chien, where a fork leads past the Jardin Exotique (worth visiting) to **Monaco** and from there to **Menton**.

**Grande Corniche

The highest route is the Grande Corniche, climbing to 530m/1740ft. Built during the time of Napoleon I, it offers a splendid extensive view.

The Grande Corniche (D2564) follows a wide curve from Nice past the observatory around Mont Gros, with its magnificent view across the Paillon valley and the Maritime Alps to Nice and the western coastline. Following the Col des Quatre Chemins are the Belvédère (view across the coast) and the Col d'Eze, from where the peaks of the Maritime Alps are visible. Drive along the southern slope of Mont Camps de l'Allé to La Turbie, a small old Provençal coastal town on the saddle between the Tête de Chien (fantastic view down across Monaco) and Mont de la Bataille, dominated by the "Trophée d'Auguste" or "Trophée des Alpes". The road continues along the slopes of Mont Agel, past the village of **Roquebrune**, picturesquely built on a group of cliffs with narrow, vaulted, stepped alleys and the fine ruins of a castle, to climb finally to the start of the Corniche du Littoral, leading to the health resort of **Menton**.

# 3a: Gap–Digne–Nice/Cannes (220km/137 miles)

General information

The Route Napoléon, a tourist route inaugurated in 1932 and generally open to traffic throughout the year, stretches from Grenoble via Gap and Grasse to Cannes. It encompasses the extremely charming and varied landscape of the high Alpine peaks around Gap, the mountainous scenery of Haute Provence to the Mediterranean coastal region. The route follows in reverse that which Napoleon took after he landed in Golfe-Jun on March 1st 1815 on his return from Elba and is marked by small eagles. Using a legacy from Napoleon, six shelters (named *Réfuges Napoléon* after him) were built on the particularly exposed mountain passes, of which only three still remain. From Barrème the most southerly section of the Route d'Hiver des Alpes forms the connection to Nice.

The descriptions in this guide do not cover the whole appromimately 350km/217 mile Route Napoléon but only the stretch between Gap and Cannes/Nice. As a result some information about the route between Grenoble and Gap is included in the following suggestion.

Itinerary

Behind Grenoble pass first Vizille with its imposing 17th c. castle built by Connétable Lesdiguières. The "Monument du Centenaire" stands outside it, dedicated to the group of representatives who, on July 21st/22nd 1788, decided to refuse to pay their taxes thus sparking the French Revolution. After La Mure it is worth making a detour along the Corniche du Drac, past the old monastery of Notre-Dame-de-Commiers and the Château de la Motte, while the N85 (which the Route Napoléon follows) ascends to the lakeland district of Laffrey, a small area much visited for its delightful situation, where Napoleon encountered the regular troops opposing him on his return from Elba. Continue either via the Col de la Morte or past Laffrey's pretty lakes to La Mure, a small mining town, then onward and upward through Beaumont, in the foothills of the Alps, to Obiou at the summit. Next head for Corps, departure point for visits to the Sautet reservoir and La Salette, the famous place of pilgrimage with its imposing church on the slopes of Mont Gargas.

Beyond Gap there is a worthwhile alternative route to the Route Napoléon exists. Drive around Lac de Sautet on the D537, then through the narrow pass Défilé de la Soulolse and Les Etrolts and continue via St-Etienne-en-Dévoluy to Col du Noyer, with its fine views. The Route Napoléon can be rejoined at St-Bonnet as it climbs from Corps to Col Bayard, where a fine view of the Dauphiné Alps exists.

With a look back at the Massif des Ecrins, enter the ever-widening Gap valley. **Gap**, called *Vapincum* in Roman times, is the principal town of the Hautes-Alpes Département, with a 19th c. cathedral and a noteworthy departemental museum. Continuing on the N85, the Route Napoléon reaches the Durance valley and follows its left flank through the little town of Tallard up to Lac de Serre-Ponçon while, just before **Sisteron**, the Route d'Hiver des Alpes descends the valley and joins it.

The Route d'Hiver des Alpes, identical to the Route Napoléon from Sisteron to Barrême, now follows the course of the mainly dried-up Durance downstream to the elongated town of Château-Arnoux, crosses the Durance and continues alongside a canal to Malijai and then into the Bléone valley to **Digne**, the Roman *Dinia*. Its old town is a maze of streets and has a noteworthy church. Finally the traveller reaches Barrême where the Route Napoléon turns off to Castellane (Grand Canyon du Verdon), while the Route d'Hiver des Alpes leads into the Asse de Moriez valley and via the Col des Robines into the Verdon valley, wide at this point, to St-André-les-Alpes. From there it passes Verdon's fine reservoir the Lac de Castillon, via Annot and **Entrevaux** to **Nice**.

From the little town of **Castellane** in the Verdon valley, dominated by an impressive chalk cliff with the Notre-Dame-du-Roc Chapel, an excursion around the **Grand Canyon du Verdon** can be undertaken. At this point, take the road through the Verdon valley with the two narrow passes Porte de St-Jean and Clue de Chasteuil, then continue via Trigance to the Balcons de la Mescla with a breathtaking view down into the deep Verdon gorge and beyond on to the Corniche Sublime high above the Falaises des Cavaliers. Drive around Vaumale, encircled by rocks, across the Col d'Illoire and via the Verdon, dammed here, to reach the small old town Moustiers-Ste-Marie, famous for its faience, with a notable Roman-Gothic church as well as the Chapel of Notre-Dame-de-Beauvoir. Return to Castellane via La Palud and Point Sublime.

Leave the Verdon valley behind Castellane and drive through a partly-wooded mountain landscape via the Col de Luens, Escragnolles, the Pas de La Faye and St-Vallier-de-Thiey, from where an excursion via the Col de la Leque and past the tumulus to the medieval village St-Cézaire and the dripstone cave Grotto Dozol can be made, down to **Grasse**, in a sheltered location on the slopes of Roquevignon. Now only a further 17km/11 miles remain to the luxurious seaside resort of **Cannes** on the Golfe de la Napoule.

Alternative route

A very interesting alternative to one side of these "well-trodden paths" is the "Sprint Final" route, the final stage of the 1960 Monte-Carlo rally. In contrast to those drivers, two or three days should be allowed to enjoy the landscape and Provençal hospitality. From Gap follow the D942 or the A/D900B to Lac de Serre-Ponçon; at Ort L'Hotel change on to the D900C across the Durance to Selonnet. The D900 leads via the Col de Maure Pass and the Col de Labouret Pass as well as La Javie Pass to Digne. Follow the Route Napoléon (N85) as far as Séranon, then the D81/D79 to Gréolières and Coursegoules and finally the D8 to Bouyon and the D1 to Le Broc and Carros in the Var valley. Head north on the N202 and after 2km/1 mile turn off to the right after Castagniers at Les Moulins on the D614. From here follow the D719 to Tourrette-Levens and the D19 to St-André, pass twice under the motorway, and reach La Turbie and Monaco on the D2204A.

## 3b: Nice–Barcelonnette (160km/99 miles)

General information

The following route is part of the Route des Grandes Alpes (Route D'Eté des Alpes), the most splendid journey through the French Alps. The very varied route leads from the sub-tropical Mediterranean coastal landscape through narrow valleys and gorges and the Maritime Alps, partly forming part of Provence, to the southern French High Alps belonging to the Dauphiné.

Itinerary

From **Nice** ascend the at first wide Var valley upstream between the rocky slopes of the Maritime Alps via Plan-du-Var, behind which the D2565 turns off into the Gorges de la Vésubie to the health and winter sports resort of St-Martin-Vésubie and through the narrow Défilé du Chaudan to the Tinée estuary.

Here the driver can take the uphill Route de la Bonette through Tinée valley via Isola and St-Etienne-de-Tinée to Col de la Bonette, the highest Alpine pass, eventually climbing to the Cime de la Bonette with its breathtaking panoramic view. Crossing the smaller Col de Reste Fond the Route des Grandes Alpes is rejoined in the Ubaye valley at Jausiers.

The Route des Grandes Alpes meanwhile leads from the Tinée estuary via the picturesque little hillside town of Touët-sur-Var in the direction of Puget-Théniers and **Entrevaux** with its impressive citadel. Immediately beyond Pont de Cians at Touët make time for a worthwhile detour through the wild and romantic Gorges du Cians, first through the 450m/1477ft high chalk sides of the towering Gorges Inférieures and then into the even wilder

*Panorama on the Col de Turini*

and deeper Gorges Supérieures which are carved into the dark red porphyry rock. Via Beuil and Col de Valberg in the centre of a small winter sports region, climb to Guillaumes where those drivers who have continued on the N202 from Entrevaux and later turned off right on the D902/D2202 through the Gorges de Daluis rejoin the route.

From Guillaumes the D2202 continues mostly along the slopes of the upper Var valley via the prettily-located village St-Martin-d'Entraunes and past the source of the Var to the bare Col de la Cayolle where a fantastic view can be enjoyed. **Barcelonnotto**, in the Ubaye valley, soon appears. From here, by following the Route des Alpes across passes or through the Ubaye and Durance valleys, Briançon can be reached – alternatively, change to the Route Napoléon after Gap.

Col de Turini

To conclude these recommended routes, the final stage of the Monte Carlo Rally route can be referred to again – in particular the journey along the Col de Turini ("Night of the Long Knives"). From Monaco take the D2204A to St-André and then ascend to L'Escarène on the D2204. Follow the D2566 up through Lucéram (whose church contains the most important collection of work by the Nice School of painting) and Peira-Cava to the top of the pass (1607m/5274ft) from where the outstanding view is ample reward for the strenuous journey.

# Provence from A to Z

Note

In the following description of places (including their surroundings) the individual headings are so arranged that they follow a circular walk or circular drive.

The name of the "Région" is given if the town or place concerned does not lie within the Provence–Alpes–Côte d'Azur region.

## Aigues-Mortes D2

Région: Languedoc-Rousillon
Département: Gard
Altitude: sea-level
Population: 4500

Location

Famous for its medieval fortifications, the little town of Aigues-Mortes lies some 30km/20 miles east of Montpelier on the western edge of the Camargue, the delta of the Rhône, which is here dotted with numerous lagoons. Two navigable canals, the Chenal Maritime and the Canal du Rhône à Sète, link the town with the sea, 6km/4 miles distant.

History

The town owes its name of the "town of the dead waters" (aquae mortuae) to the bogs and shallow lagoons of the surroundings. St Louis (King Louis IX) possessed no lands bordering on the Mediterranean, so in 1240 he purchased the region from the monks of Psalmody (the remains of their abbey some 4km/2½ miles to the north are currently being excavated). He then bestowed a number of privileges on the town, which rapidly developed and prospered in the field of commerce and trade as well as in the traditional spheres of fishing and salt-mining. The seventh Crusade in 1248 and the eighth in 1270 sailed from here. The building of the town walls, financed by means of taxes, was expensive and lasted – with some interruptions – from 1266 to the end of the century. At that time Aigues-Mortes had 15,000 inhabitants. It started to decline in the middle of the next century as the waterways gradually silted up, but nevertheless remained an important trading port until the end of the 15th c., when Marseilles was elevated to the status of "royal town".

In the Hundred Years' War, the great controversy about the succession to the French throne, the Burgundians, supported by England, conquered the town in 1418 and settled here. Afterwards the Gascons laid siege to Aigues-Mortes, penetrated the town one night and defeated the Burgundians. Their corpses were thrown into the south-west tower (now known as the Burgundian Tower) of the town walls and covered with salt in order to prevent decay.

In the Wars of Religion Aigues-Mortes became a refuge for the Huguenots, but following the Edict of Nantes in 1685 its towers served as their prison.

### Sights

**Town Walls

The massive walls took over 30 years to build; they form a rectangle which is still complete and which surrounds the town. The ring of walls has fifteen towers and is penetrated by ten gates, some protected by towers; it comprises an area with sides measuring 567m/620yds, 497m/544yds, 301m/329yds and 269m/292yds.

◀ *Orange: a symbol of Roman power – the Triumphal Arch*

Because of the narrow streets in the Old Town a visit on foot is recommended. There are car parks on the northern edge of the Old Town, near the Tour de Constance (fee-paying) and outside the south-west town wall.
The tour of the ring of walls starts at the Porte de la Gardette, a few yards east of the Tour de Constance. A broad path inside the wall enabled the defenders of the town to get quickly from one place to another to repulse invaders.
It is also worthwhile following the ring of walls on the outside. There is a fine view of the Tour de Constance to be had from the bridge which spans the canal, the Chenal Maritime. The south-west front – of cyclopean proportions, measuring nearly 500m/550yds in length – is particularly impressive. At one time the quays were situated here, which is why it has the most defensive towers.

Tour de Constance

The mightiest tower in the town walls is known as the "Tour de Constance"; its name is said to come from that of a daughter of King Louis VI. It is also sometimes called the "Tower of Steadfastness". Forming the northern corner of the ring of walls, it is separated from them by a moat filled with water and spanned by a bridge. 54m/177ft in height and with walls 6m/20ft thick and measuring 22m/72ft in diameter, it is the epitome of a medieval defensive construction. From the earliest times it served as a State prison, for it was considered impregnable. Among those imprisoned here were, at the beginning of the 14th c., members of the Order of Templars, who had been taken prisoner by Philipp IV on the pretext of heresy and immorality, from the 17th c. many Huguenots, and finally a group of Protestant women who were released in 1768 by clemency of the Governor; among these prisoners was the well-known Marie Durand, who spent 38 years in this dungeon and was renowned in France for her steadfastness. It was last used to imprison Napoleon's officers when the Royalists took Aigues-Mortes.

*Aigues-Mortes: town walls and the Tour de Constance*

*Tour Carbonnière, outpost of Aigues-Mortes*

*Flamingoes in the Camargue*

It is interesting to climb up to the little turret which is crowned by an iron cage and served as a lighthouse for centuries when the town was still a port. From here there is a charming panoramic view of the town and the surrounding countryside, as far as the Cevennes in the north and the concrete pyramids of La Grand-Motte in the west, salt-mines and the Camargue in the east.

Tour Carbonnière

The 14th c. Tour Carbonnière, about 3km/2 miles to the north-east along the D58 road, guards the only entrance to the town from the land side. The road passes through the tower, the gates of which used to be secured by means of a portcullis and mantraps inside. The little round tower, which protrudes from the top of the square edifice, probably dates from the 16th c., when the tower was in Protestant hands.

## Aix-en-Provence

D3

Département: Bouches-du-Rhône
Altitude: 177m/581ft
Population: 155,000

Location and importance

Aix (Provençal Ais), the former capital of Provence, lies barely 30km/19 miles north of Marseilles in a fertile plain surrounded by mountains. Four old palaces, dating mainly from the 17th and 18th c., and many fine churches and museums bear witness to the town's glittering past. As the home of a famous university and the seat of an archbishop it remains the spiritual centre of Provence to this day.

As well as being a spa town and deriving considerable income from tourism, an important part of its economy lies in the preparation of almond-nuts for the confectionery trade; its "Calissons d'Aix", a tangy almond sweet, are famous.

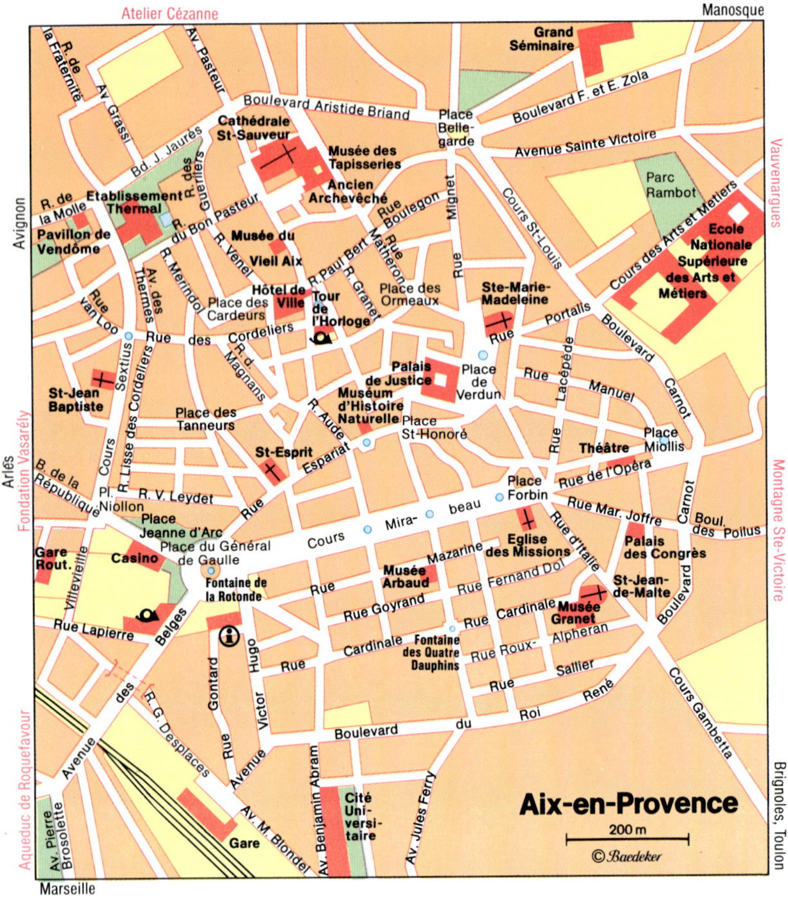


The lightly radio-active hot springs, rich in minerals, were already known in Roman times. Their chief constituents are bicarbonates, calcium, sulphates, silicates, chlorine and magnesium.

Music Festival

The International Music Festival which is held annually in July/August attracts large audiences. Further information can be obtained and tickets booked (by post or by telephone) from Service Location Festival d'Aix, F-13100 Aix-en-Provence; tel. 42 17 34 34, fax. 42 96 12 61.

History

Soon after the destruction of the Celtic settlement (121 B.C.) to the north near Entremont, Aix-en-Provence was founded by Caius Sextus as the first Roman settlement in Gaul and called "Aquae Sextiae Saluviorum". Twenty years later the Roman commander Marius defeated the Teutons near here as they advanced into Italy. Its medicinal springs, which had been known for a long time, and its favourable position from the point of view of communications on the Via Aurelia, led to a rapid development of the new settlement.

After serious setbacks, caused by migrations and attacks by the Saracens, Aix became the capital of the county of Provence and also, especially in the time of the art-lover René of Anjou (1409–80), a cultural centre of Provençal poetry. In 1409 the university was founded, and in 1481 the town passed to France. It was badly affected in the Wars of Religion. From 1630 there were violent clashes with Richelieu and Mazarin which could be settled only by the good offices of Michel, the brother of Mazarin and Archbishop of Aix. An extensive building programme in the 17th and 18th c. determined the town's architectural image. Count Mirabeau, a lawyer and revolutionary leader (1749–91) and the painter Paul Cézanne (1839–1906) were born in Aix. In 1958 Picasso lived in the palace at Vauvenargues (see Surroundings), where he is also buried.

## Sights

*Cours Mirabeau

The broad Cours Mirabeau, laid out in 1651, borders the Old Town in the south, separating it from the newer parts. This idyllic shady promenade is planted with old plane trees (which, however, are regularly and heavily pruned); in the middle of the roadway stand three beautiful fountains, the centre one of which, the "Fontaine Chaude", is fed with warm spring water, and in the Place du Général de Gaulle, which forms the western boundary of the line of streets, stands the great Fontaine de la Rotonde. There are several impressive buildings in the street, among them the Hôtel des Villiers (No. 2; 1710), the Hôtel d'Isouard de Vauvenargues (No. 10; 1710), the Hôtel d'Arbod Jouques (No. 19; early 18th c.), the Hôtel de Forbin (No. 20; 1656) and the Hôtel de Maurel de Pontèves (No. 38; 1647–50; now the offices of the Principal of the University). At the east end of the Cours Mirabeau stands the Fontaine du Roi René, the work of David d'Angers (19th c.) and the Chapelle des Oblats, part of the Carmelite Monastery designed by a pupil of Puget and restored about 1700. The "Deux Garçons" café dates from the 18th c.

Hôtels

*Hôtel de Ville and Tour de l'Horloge*

*The Hôtel Fourbin on the Cours Mirabeau*

North of the Cours Mirabeau the Old Town extends as far as the Hôtel de Ville (Town Hall) and is largely a pedestrian precinct.

Museum of Natural History

Near the central one of the three fountains on the Cours Mirabeau, Rue Clemenceau leads into the heart of the Old Town. At the end of the little Place St.-Honoré Rue Espariat branches off to the left, and near it stands the Muséum d'Histoire Naturel (Museum of Natural History). Its collections, particularly the dinosaur eggs which were found in Provence, are well known in specialist circles. The museum is housed in the Hôtel Boyer d'Eguilles, a town mansion built in the 17th c. Open: Mon.–Sat. 10am–noon, 2pm–6pm, Sun. 2pm–6pm.

Place d'Albertas

The Place d'Albertas lies a short way west of the Museum of Natural History. On its south side stands a town house of three wings grouped around a fountain. Here the visitor should turn right and follow the Rue Aude in a northerly direction, noting on the left the 16th c. Hôtel Peyroneti, built in 1562 and one of the oldest in Aix, with an interesting façade of double rectangular columns and a frieze of bulls' heads. Continue along Rue du Maréchal Foch, with the 17th c. Hôtel d'Arbaud on the left, until the Place de l'Hôtel de Ville is reached.

## Place de l'Hôtel de Ville

The Place de l'Hôtel de Ville, the central point of the Old Town, is adorned with a fountain (1755) around which the busy flower market is held every day. On the south side of the square stands the former Halle aux Grains (grain market), with a magnificent gable, built in 1759–61 and embellished with sculptures by Jean Pancrace Chastel. It now houses the post-office.

Hôtel de Ville

On the west side of the square stands the Hôtel de Ville (Town Hall), built between 1652 and 1668 and modelled on Italian Baroque; it encloses the courtyard and was badly damaged during the French Revolution. Its wrought-iron balcony rail and the beautiful gateway are also 17th c.

Tour de l'Horloge

On the right side of the façade of the Hôtel de Ville rises the Tour de l'Horloge (Clock-tower of 1510), which was erected on the Roman foundations of a former town gate. In 1661 the astronomical clock below the balustrade was installed.

Palace of Justice

On the Place de Verdun to the south-east stand the palace of Justice, completed in 1831, and the Church of Ste-Marie-Madeleine, which contains an Annunciation *c.* 1440. The Renaissance-style façade of the church dates from 1860, while the church itself was re-built in 1905.

Musée du Vieil Aix

Passing through the clock-tower and continuing north along Rue Gaston de Saporta, with its fine town-houses, we come to the Musée du Vieil Aix (museum of civic history), which is located in the 17th c. Hôtel Estienne de St-Jean (No. 17). Open: Tues.–Sun. 10am–noon, 2.30pm–6pm, in winter 2pm–5pm.
Also in Rue Gaston de Saporta are the Hôtel de Châteaurenard, with its richly decorated staircase, and the Hôtel de Maynier d'Oppède, once the seat of the Faculty of Letters.

*Cathédrale St-Sauveur

In Rue J. De la Roque, in the north of the Old Town, stands the Cathédrale St-Sauveur (St Saviour's Cathedral). It was built in various stages from the 12th to 17th c., and dedicated in 1534.

Doorway

In the 15th–16th c. Gothic doorway, where the stone figures were severely damaged during the French Revolution, hang beautiful walnut doors carved mainly between 1508 and 1510 by Jean Guiramand; these are normally concealed behind protective shutters, which the sacristan will

◄ *"Mary in the burning thorn-bush" (1475/76) by Nicolas Froment* open on request. The lower part of the doors already reveals elements of the Early Renaissance.

Interior

The cathedral is entered through a Romanesque doorway, to the right of the Gothic part of the façade. On the right is an Early Christian Baptistry, dating from the 6th c. and renovated in 1577, with a 4th c. font. On the right of the main nave can be seen the triptych "Mary in the Burning Thorn Bush", by Nicolas Froment (1435–84); in the left wing will be found a portrayal of "Good King René" (1434–80). In the central nave and south aisle hang Flemish tapestries from 1511 representing the Passion and the story of the Virgin, with likenesses of English courtesans.
Behind the High Altar lies the Chapelle de St-Mitre, dedicated to the patron of the town, whose tomb can be found in the first chapel on the right. There is a small Romanesque cloister adjoining the church on the south wall.

*Musée des Tapisseries

The Musée des Tapisseries (Gobelin Museum) is housed in the Ancien Evéché (former episcopal palace; 1648), adjoining the cathedral on the west in the Place des Martyrs de la Résistance. On show are tapestries from Beauvais in Picardy which date from the 17th and 18th c. and include scenes from "Don Quixote de la Mancha" by Cervantes. Open: Wed.–Mon. 10am–noon, 2pm–5pm.
Musical events are held in the inner courtyard during the summer.

Établissement Thermal (Thermes Sextius)

The Établissement Thermal (thermal baths), which is reached from the cathedral by following Rue du Bon Pasteur in a south-westerly direction, was built in the 18th c. on the foundations of the Roman Baths of Sextius (2nd c. B.C.). The water issues at a temperature of 36°C/97°F and is used both for drinking and bathing, especially for metabolic disturbances, circulatory disorders, nervous diseases and post-operative complaints.

Pavillon de Vendôme

In Rue Celony, not far west of the Établissement Thermal and outside the town walls as they were at that time, stands the pavilion built in 1664–67 for the Duc de Vendôme and reconstructed in the 18th c. It is surrounded by a small park. The sculptural decoration is noteworthy, and inside can be seen some 17th and 18th c. furniture and paintings. Open: 10am–noon, 2pm–6pm, in winter 2pm–5pm.

Atelier Paul Cézanne

The studio of the famous Impressionist painter Paul Cézanne, born in Aix, is situated to the north outside the Old Town at Avenue Paul Cézanne 9, and is reached along Avenue Pasteur. In addition to mementoes of the master painter there is an audio-visual information exhibition. Open: Wed.–Mon. 10am–noon, 2.30pm–6pm, in winter 2pm–5pm.

Quartier Mazarin

In the years 1646–53, at the suggestion of Michel Mazarin, archbishop of Aix and brother of the famous cardinal and politician, the Quarter named after him and the broad street known as Cours Mirabeau were laid out, necessitating the demolition of part of the town walls. The rectangular area is characteristic of 17th c. town planning; it is bounded on the south by the Boulevard du Roi René and the Boulevard Carnot, part of which follows the line of the Old Town Walls. The centre of the area is formed by the Place des Quatre Dauphins, with the 1667 fountain of the same name which is adorned with sculptures of four dolphins.

Musée Paul Arbaud

Standing to the north of the Fontaine des Quatre Dauphins on Rue du Quatre Septembre, the Hôtel d'Arbaud is one of the finest town mansions in the quarter. Built in the 18th c. it now houses the Académie d'Aix and the Musée Paul Arbaud. This collection contains important examples of faience and pictures and also possesses a large library. Open: Mon.–Sat. 2pm–5pm.

*Musée Granet

The Musée Granet (Museum of Fine Arts and Archaeology) in the Place St-Jean-de-Malte, east of the Fontaine des Quatre Dauphins, is one of the most comprehensive museums in Provence. It is housed in the former palace of the Commandant of the Order of Malta (Palais de Malte), dating from 1671. Most of the exhibits were formerly the property of the collector and painter François Marius Granet (1775–1849); they include Celto-Ligurian sculptures from the Oppidum d'Entremont (see below), Greek reliefs, Roman fragments, an Early Christian sarcophagus, medieval sculpture and works by European painters (including Jost van Cleve, Hans Holbein the Younger, Rubens, Rembrandt, Cézanne and Pissarro). Open: Wed.–Mon. 10am–noon, 2pm–6pm.

St-Jean-de-Malte

The Church of St-Jean-de-Malte, which adjoins the palace on the east, was once part of the property of the Commandant of the Order of Malta. Erected late in the 13th c., it is the earliest Gothic building in the town. In 1682–93 it was extended by having chapels added to it. The 14th c. bell-tower is 67m/220ft high. Inside, note the graves and paintings.

Cité Universitaire

The Cité Universitaire is located in the Quartier des Fernouillères, south of the Boulevard du Roi René. The foundation of the University with its Faculty of Philosophy (1409) dates from the reign of Louis II. University institutions are still housed in the old buildings in the Place de l'Université, but in 1950 it became necessary to remove a considerable part of the University out of the Old Town. There are now about 20,000 students in Aix.

Bibliothèque Méjanes

The valuable collection of the Mejanes Library – 350,000 18th c. volumes, manuscripts, incunabula – was once housed in the Hôtel de Ville (Town Hall), but now forms part of the Espace Culturel Méjanes, an old match factory converted into the municipal library at 8–10 Rue des Allumettes in the west of the town. The nucleus of the collection was provided by the Marquis de Méjanes (1726–86), a teacher born in Arles, who donated 80,000 volumes to the native town.
The St John Perse Foundation, a research centre for poets, diplomats and 1960 Nobel Prize Winners, has also been transferred here. Temporary exhibitions are held twice a year.

*Fondation Vasarély

The Vasarély Foundation lies in Avenue Marcel Pagnol, in the Jas de Bouffan district in the west of the town. In this modern and unconventionally styled building, some 87m/286ft in length, visitors can see 42 huge wall-paintings – "integrations murales" – as well as some 800 studies by the Hungaro-French artist Victor Vasarély (b. 1908), the main advocate of the Abstract Constructivist school of painting and of Op Art (see Gordes). Open: Wed.–Mon. 9.30am–12.30pm, 2pm–5.30pm. Open Tues. in summer.

*Oppidum d'Entremont

The archaeological site of the Celto-Ligurian settlement of Oppidum d'Entremont lies some 3km/2 miles north of Aix, off the D14 road. This settlement, which comprised an Upper and a Lower Town, was strategically placed on high ground. About 4ha/10 acres have been uncovered, and pieces of broken pillars enable one to discern the outlines of some individual buildings and parts of the settlement. A mosaic floor and remains of what were apparently charnel-houses are all that is left of a sanctuary on the hill, destroyed in 123 B.C. Open: Wed.–Mon. 9am–noon, 2pm–6pm.

## Surroundings of Aix-en-Provence

Vauvenargues

The D10 road leaves Aix and leads northward through the charming countryside on the north bank of the Bimont reservoir. The latter is in fact not visible from the road, and it is worth making a detour to the wall of the reservoir in order to enjoy the impressive view of the bold triangular mountain peak, the Montagne Ste-Victoire.
About 12km/7½ miles east of Aix, above the river which supplies into the reservoir, lies the village of Vauvenargues, known for the abundance of game and wild-life in the surrounding countryside. The pretty village

*The noble place d'Albertas in Aix*

*Vauvenargues Castle, near Aix*

church dates from the 12th and 16th c., and the Renaissance palace, where Luc de Clapiers, Marquis de Vauvenargues, wrote his famous 18th c. philosophical maxims, was purchased by Picasso in 1958. Picasso and Jacqueline Roque, his second wife, are buried in the park.
Today the palace is owned by the daughter of Jacqueline Roque and is not open to visitors. Jacqueline wanted to instal a Picasso Museum here, but the local authorities would not allow it, for fear that the little village and quiet valley would be spoiled by hordes of artists and other visitors.

**Croix de la Provence

To the south of Vauvenargues towers the Montagne Ste-Victoire ridge, made famous by Paul Cézanne. From the little hamlet of Les Cabassols to the west a road – part of the GR9 walking trail – leads to Croix de la Provence (945m/3100ft). The climb – about 5km/3 miles and taking about 1½ hours – is mainly over gravel and rocky ground; sure-footedness, stout shoes and a good standard of fitness are essential. The superb panoramic view – on a clear day – from the Camargue in the west across the Maures massif as far as the Alps in the south make the effort so worthwhile. The masses of flowers among the rocks are also most impressive.

*Ventabren

Ventabren is a picturesque "village perché", or hillside village, dominated by a ruined castle high above the Valley of the Arc, some 15km/9 miles west of Aix. Few other places can so clearly portray what is meant by the term "perché": "like a bird perched high up in a tree" is one description of it. The 11th–12th c. Parish Church of St-Denis is worth visiting; there is a magnificent 180° view from the castle ruins over the idyllic landscape to the north of the Etang de Berre and Martigues on the southern bank of the river.

*Roquefavour Aqueduct

4km/2½ miles to the south of Ventabren along, a charming lateral valley of the Arc, we come to Roquefavour Aqueduct, an imposing construction conveying the Durance Canal over the valley towards Marseilles. The aqueduct – three storeys, internal height 83m/272ft and length

*"A quarry and Montagne Ste-Victoire" (1898) by Paul Cézanne*

375m/410yds – was constructed between 1842 and 1847; although modelled on the Pont du Gard and in fact considerably larger, its modern construction is rather too perfect and thus it fails to achieve the same powerful effect.
The upper level of the aqueduct is accessible from the D64; coming from Ventabren, turn left towards Petit Rigoués just before reaching the D65, and then turn right to the watchman's house.

Roquepertuse

4km/2½ miles west of Ventabren in the Valley of the Arc lies the Celtic rock-sanctuary of Roquepertuse; an unsigned footpath leads southward from the junction of the D65 and D10. Most of the important finds made here can be seen in the Borély Museum in Marseilles (see entry).

Les Milles

During the Second World War, when France was occupied by the Germans, some 3000 German Jews who had fled from Nazi Germany were interned here in the local brick-works. Some escaped, but the remainder – together with a further 2000 Jews betrayed by the Vichy Government – were sent to German concentration camps. There is a plaque in memory of this sad tale to be seen near the loading bay at the railway station.
In a beautiful park south of Les Milles, by the D59, stands the 18th c. Lenfant Palace.

## Alpilles

D2

Département: Bouches-du-Rhône
Highest point: La Caume 387m/1270ft

Location

The chain of the Alpilles (Little Alps) extends east of the Rhône between St-Rémy-de-Provence (see entry) to the north and Les Baux (see entry) to the south. In spite of its relatively modest height the steep limestone massif has a thoroughly Alpine appearance. Geologicaly the Alpilles are a continuation of the Lubéron (see entry), the mountain range adjoining on the east which runs parallel to the northern bank of the Durance. The western (Alpilles de Baux) and the eastern (Alpilles d'Eygalières) parts are different in character. The first discoveries of bauxite were made in the Alpilles.

La Caume

The highest point of the Alpilles is the Caume (387m/1270ft). The summit, from which there are excellent views, can be reached on a road – sometimes closed – which branches off to the east on road D5 between St-Rémy and Les Baux. The panorama extends as far as the mouth of the Rhône and the Camargue in the west and to Mont Ventoux and the Valley of the Durance in the east.

## Antibes D5

Département: Alpes-Maritimes
Altitude: sea-level
Population: 63,000

Location and importance

The town of Antibes – to which the resorts of Cap d'Antibes and Juan-les-Pins belong – lies to the east of Cannes at the western end of the Baie des Anges (Bay of Angels), which reaches as far as Nice. Cap d'Antibes, which extends south into the Mediterranean, closes off the huge sweep of the bay. The actual area of the town occupies the Peninsula of Garoupe.
The well-known "Jazz à Juan" jazz festival is held here every July.

Economy

Flower-growing is of great importance to the economy; roses, carnations, etc. are grown under about 3sq.km/1·2sq.miles of glass.

Sophia Antipolis

8km/5 miles inland along the D35/103 the Sophia Antipolis Industrial and Technological Park has been developing since 1972. At the end of 1990 it covered an area of 580ha/1450acres, on which 834 firms with 14,000 employess had become established. Of those some 60 were foreign firms, and 700 companies and organisations were working in advanced fields of technology such as electronics and telecommunications, energy and environmental research, chemistry and biotechnology. More than a half of the work force are "white collar workers", and of them 40 per cent are foreigners from 50 different countries. A further 3200ha/8000 acres are expected to be developed by the year 2000. There should be advantages in the proximity of the Sophia Antipolis University, which is expected to take 25,000 students.

History

Antibes was founded in the 5th c. B.C. by Greeks from Phocaea and named "Antipolis", meaning the town lying opposite the settlement of Nikaia Polis (Nice). The settlement became a Roman municipium, later a bastion against the barbarians. From the 14th c. onwards it was a frontier town between Savoy and France. In 1481 the town together with the whole of Provence fell to the French throne. Later the old fortifications were remodelled by Vauban and Fort Carré, of which only a few remains still exist, was built. The castle in the Old Town was for many years the seat of a bishop and a holiday residence of the Grimaldi family.
Today Antibes, Cap d'Antibes and Juan-les-Pins (see below) form a three-part community.

*The Town

Antibes has a fine situation on the north-east side of the cape between the little bays of Anse St-Roche in the north and Anse de la Salis in the south. Above Anse St-Roche rises the picturesque 16th c. Fort Carré, a relic of the town defences. Nearby is a sports and youth centre.
South of the old fort lies the harbour (Port Vauban) which was laid out by Vauban himself.

Cathedral

South of the harbour – with a good general view from the Avenue de Verdun on its south side – on the coastal road (Avenue Amiral-de-Grasse) stands the Church of the Immaculate Conception which in the Middle Ages was an episcopal church. The nave dates from the 17th c., so that there is not much to see of the former 12th c. Romanesque building. The church houses a notable altar-painting from 1515 by Louis Bréa, "The Madonna with Rosary", as well as a figure of Christ dating from 1447.

Château

*Musée Picasso

The former castle of the Grimaldis stands to the south of the cathedral. When it was built in the 16th c. remains of the Roman fort were used in its construction. However, the defensive tower dates from the 13th/14th c. Today the castle contains the interesting Musée Picasso, a collection of modern and contemporary art, with works by Pablo Picasso, de Stael, Ernst, Mirò, Léger, Hartung, Atlan, Richier, Adami, Modigliani, Saura, Cesar, Arman and Alechinsky. There is also a wall tapestry "Judith and Holofernes", by Jean Cocteau.

The first floor is devoted to Picasso himself, with exhibits of pictures, ceramics and sculptures which he produced during a two-month stay in the castle in 1946. Open: Wed.–Mon. 10am–noon, 3pm–7pm, in winter 2pm–6pm; closed in Nov. and on public holidays.

*Antibes: the Old Town, with the Bastion St-André*

Musée Archaeologique

The coastal promenade continues south to the Bastion St-André, also a relic of the Vauban fortifications. Here is situated the Musée d'Histoire et d'Archaeologie (Museum of History and Archaeology). Among its exhibits are some portraying the history of the old Greek town, especially submarine archaeological finds. Open: Wed.–Mon. 9am–noon, 2pm–7pm, in winter to 6pm; closed in Nov. and on public holidays.

## *Cap d'Antibes

The spit of land about 4km/2½ miles long which leads to Cap d'Antibes is dotted with villas and gardens. Its highest point is the Plateau de la Garoupe (78m/256ft; lighthouse) on which stands an observation platform and an orientation table. The panorama takes in the town and the coast with the offshore islands of Lérins (see Cannes, Surroundings of) as well as the Esterel Mountains and the Maritime Alps rising behind them.

*Notre-Dame-de-la-Garoupe

Also on the plateau stands the old Pilgrimage Chapel of Notre-Dame-de-la-Garoupe; among its internal features are many votive tablets, frescoes, a 14th c. icon from Sebastopol and two gilded wooden statues.

Jardin Thuret

The Jardin Thuret is situated not far west of the Plateau de la Garoupe on the Boulevard du Cap. The garden commemorates the botanist Gustave Thuret, who laid it out about 1856. In the botanical garden, which boasts many exotic plants, the eucalyptus tree, originating in Australia, was first planted.

Musée Naval et Napoléonien

To the south-west not far from the end of the cape – where there is a rock-pool and luxury restaurant – we come to the Batterie du Grillon. This former defensive work now houses the Musée Naval et Napoléonien (Naval and Napoleonic Museum).

Antibes: drawings in the Picasso Museum

Façade of the Musée Léger

## Juan-les-Pins

Picturesque Juan-les-Pins lies on the Golfe Juan which extends between Antibes and Cannes (see entry). The name is derived from an old pine-grove. Juan-les-Pins is an international and very popular resort with many hotels and a casino.

## Surroundings of Antibes

Biot

Biot (pronounced "beeyot"), once a chief place of the Ligurians, is a village with steep little streets and bumpy paths climbing up a hill slope. It is noted for its arts and crafts, which include gold and silver work, ceramics, glass-blowing, carving in olive-wood, weaving and silk-screen printing. In the Church of Ste-Madeleine-St-Julien are two beautiful altar-pictures from the Nice school and a "Madonna with Rosary" by Louis Bréa.

*Musée Fernand Léger

Biot has become known especially for its Musée National Fernand Léger, which is reached by taking the Chemin du Val de Pome, a little way out of Biot in the direction of the sea, and then turning left. The museum, established by Léger's widow Nadja in the 1950s, displays all the periods of his works in a most comprehensive fashion. The enormous mosaic on its outside wall was originally intended for the sports stadium in Hanover, Germany, but was found to be too expensive. The portrait of the artist in wire on the staircase is by Alexander Calder. Open: Wed.–Mon., Apr. 1st–Sept. 30th, 10am–noon, 2pm–6pm: Oct. 1st–Mar. 31st until 5pm.

Marina Baie des Anges

See Cannes

Vallauris

See Cannes

## **Ardèche** (Gorges de l'Ardèche) C2

Régions: Languedoc-Rousillon, Rhône-Alpes
Départements: Gard, Ardèche

Location

The Ardèche is a tributary on the right bank of the Rhône, which it joins near Pont St-Esprit, about 100km/66 miles north of the Mediterranean coast.

Course of the river

The Ardèche, which has a total length of 120km/75 miles, rises at a height of 1467m/4815ft in the area of Vivarais on the eastern edge of the Massif Central. It drops steeply in its upper course.
The most impressive reach of the river from the point of view of scenery is between Vallon-Pont d'Arc and Pont St-Esprit, a stretch which is also designated as the "Gorges de l'Ardèche". The following description is confined to this part of the river, which is about 30km/17 miles long as the crow flies.

Boat trips

Boats can be hired at many places on the road which follows the river. Canoeing down the Ardèche is a popular sport, sometimes unfortunately leading to overcrowding. Occasionally there are rapids in the river; also when there is heavy rainfall the water-level can rise rapidly by several metres. For these two reasons boating is advised only for experienced canoeists. During the high season in May and June there are very many boats on the river, which tend to spoil it as a place of natural beauty.

**Warning**

The scrub and bushes – the "garrigue" – which cover a large part of the higher slopes are extremely dry in summer and, therefore, fire is always a danger. Because of the extensive nature of the area and its lack of paths these fires are practically impossible to fight. Visitors should be extremely

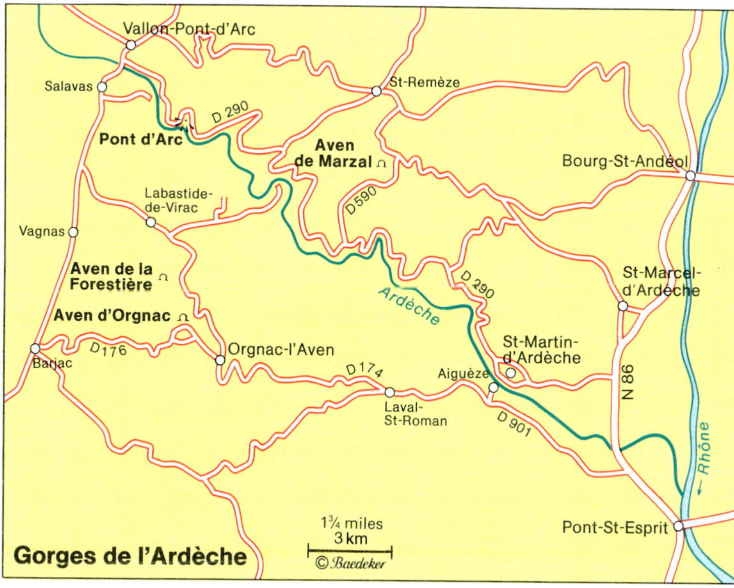


careful with naked flames and avoid discarding lighted matches, cigarettes, etc.

## **Circular tour through the Gorges de l'Ardèche

General

The circular tour described below is approximately 150km/93 miles long. In addition to the wildly romantic scenery this trip is also impressive for the karst caves, especially those of the Aven d'Orgnac, which are among the most important caves in France open to visitors. The vistas which open up on this drive are extremely impressive, particularly the many ever-changing views downwards to the rushing turquoise river.
The visitor who wants ample time to appreciate the scenery is recommended to devote a whole day to this tour.

Leaving Pont St-Esprit the road crosses the Rhône – not far north of its confluence with the Ardèche – on an old stone bridge nearly 1000m/1100yds long. There is an exceptionally charming view of the river frontage of the Old Town.
From Pont St-Esprit follow the N86 for a short distance and then bear left on to the D901, signposted "Gorges de l'Ardèche". This road, which is not within sight of the river, gradually climbs to the undulating higher slopes which are covered with scrub and bushes. Near Laval-St-Roman turn right off the D901 on to the D174 and, following the signs "Aven d'Orgnac", it is a further 9km/6 miles to the village of Orgnac l'Aven, near which lies the cave.

**Aven d'Orgnac

Aven d'Orgnac is one of the most splendid caves in the country which are open to the public. In this dripstone cave, which was discovered on August 19th 1935, there is an almost constant temperature of 13°C/55°F, so that in addition to stout footwear warm clothing is recommended. A vist, with a guide, lasts about an hour. Open: Mar., Oct. 1st–Nov. 14th 9am–noon, 2pm–5pm; Apr.–Sept. to 6pm.

In the hall of the building at the entrance a plan of the cave can be seen on the wall, and above it are displayed a number of objects which have been found there, including bones, pottery, etc. The cave is entered by an artificially constructed tunnel which leads to the "Great Hall" with its almost 25m/82ft high stalagmites. Visitors are photographed inside the cave and can take the photographs away with them when they leave.
Only those parts of the extensive system of caves which were opened up by 1939 are accessible to the public. Continuations have been discovered since 1965 and to a great extent have been explored. Near the entrance stands a memorial to Robert de Joly (1887–1968), the discoverer and first investigator of the caves.

Aven de la Forestière

Not far north-west of the Aven d'Orgnac we find the Aven de la Forestière, a dripstone cave with some interesting sinter formations; it was discovered in 1966 and since 1968 has been accessible to the public. It must be said, however, that it is not nearly so impressive as the Aven d'Orgnac. Open: Apr. 1st–Sept. 30th 10am–7pm.
Leaving Orgnac l'Aven, follow the D317 (which later becomes the D176) west. In a few kilometres there is a rewarding view on the right. In Barjac, turn north and cross the Ardèche this side of Vallon-Pont d'Arc. On the far side of the bridge turn right and follow the sign "Route Touristique des Gorges de l'Ardèche". The road (D290) now follows the course of the river for the most part. At first it winds through rock galleries; here there are some little grottoes including the Grotto of the Tunnel.

*Pont d'Arc

About 4km/2½ miles from Vallon-Pont d'Arc a large bridge-like rock arch can be seen on the right and through it flows the River Ardèche. The arch has headroom of 34m/112ft above the normal water-level and a breadth of 60m/197ft at water-level. The sandy stretches on the banks are popular as stopping-places for people in boats. The best view of the Pont d'Arc is from a short distance away after driving round a little bluff.

*Pont d'Arc*

The road continues at varying distances from the river, which in this reach has dug its bed many hundred metres deep into the chalk. At the viewpoints (belvédères) there are adequate parking places; falling rocks are often a danger on this stretch.

On this part of the route lie the viewpoints of Belvédère du Serre de Tourre, Belvédère de Gaud, Belvédère d'Autridge and Belvédère de Gournier. Beyond the last-named the D590 branches off, and after just over 5km/3 miles on this road we reach the Aven de Marzal.

*Aven de Marzal

The dripstone cave Aven de Marzal was systematically investigated in 1892 by the famous French speleologist Edouard Martel (1859–1938), then it was forgotten again. Not until 1949 was it rediscovered, and it is now open to the public. There are guided tours every day between April and October; these last about one hour, and warm clothing is recommended.
The cave is notable for its wealth of stalactites and stalagmites, sinter formations and crystals, the colours of which range from pure white through shades of ochre to brown. In the cave museum can be seen equipment – ladders, boats, diving apparatus, etc. – which was used in the various phases of the exploration of the Aven de Marzal.

Grotte de la Madeleine

On the right away from the tourist road and near the above-mentioned fork along a narrow road lies the Grotte de la Madeleine. It has beautiful dripstones – among them the completely irregular "excentriques" – and sinter formations. A guided tour lasts about an hour. Nearby is the viewpoint Belvédère de la Madeleine.

**Belvédères de la Corniche

The stretch of the D290 beyond the D590 turning follows the river; this section is known as the "Haute Corniche" and is especially charming. Here lie the best viewpoints – Belvédère de la Cathédrale (a view of the Cirque de la Madeleine), Balcon des Templiers and Belvédère de la Maladrerie (a

*The great bend of the River Ardèche, from the Belvédere de Maladrerie*

magnificent view of the huge bend of the Ardèche), Belvédère de la Rouvière, Belvédère de la Coutelle, Grand Belvédère at the end of the gorge, Belvédère du Colombier and Belvédère du Ranc-Pointu, above the last bend of the river, with a fine view into the Rhône valley.
The return route to St-Esprit, where the tour started, is via St-Martin d'Ardèche.

A shorter alternative

The visitor with little time at his or her disposal can curtail the tour by taking the last part, the Haute Corniche, in the opposite direction from Pont St-Esprit. In this case the views become more impressive as far as the Balcon des Templiers. The visit can end with the Aven de Marzal.

## Arles D2

Département: Bouches-du-Rhône
Altitude: 9m/30ft
Population: 51,000

Location and importance

The ancient town of Arles lies on the Rhône south of the point where the river divides into two arms – the Grand Rhône to the east and the Petit Rhône to the west – and flows through the Camargue, with its ponds and lakes, before entering the Mediterranean.
Impressive Roman and medieval historical monuments serve as a reminder of its great past.

History

Arlath (the "town in the marsh") was originally a Greek settlement, from 46 B.C. a Roman colony and competed with Massilia (Marseilles) as a port.

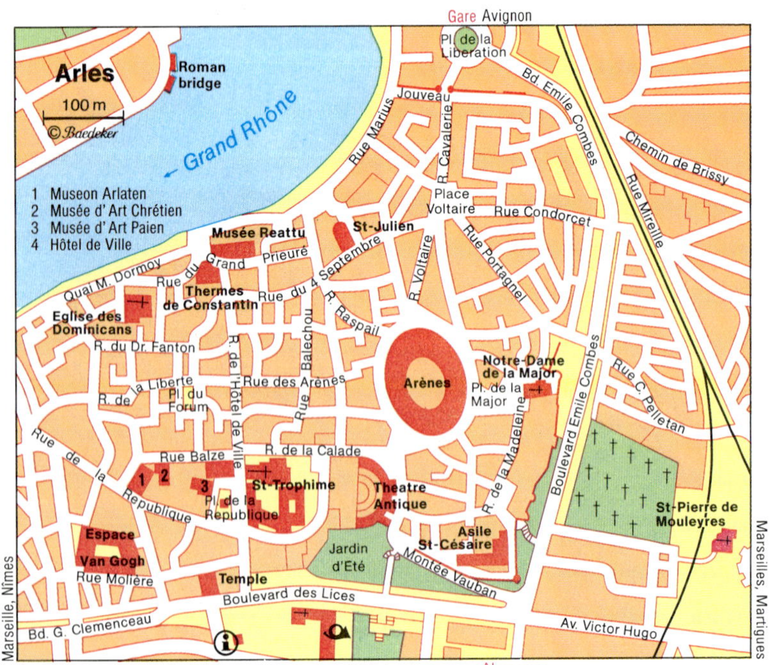

Quite early in its history it had a Christian community and was the venue in 314 for the first Council of the Roman Empire in the West. In 406 the city was the seat of the Roman Civil Government for the whole of Gaul. From the 10th c. it belonged to the Kingdom of Burgundy (Arelate) and later to the Holy Roman Empire. In 1481 it and Provence fell to France.
The painter van Gogh resided here in 1888–89; the famous "Bridge of Arles" in his picture no longer exists, and Arles possesses none of his works.
Today Arles extends over 750sq.km/290sq.miles and in area is the largest commune in France, Paris being only 105sq.km/41sq. miles.
The beauty of the maidens of Arles was immortalised by Georges Bizet in his two-part concert suite "L'Arlésienne", from the music written in 1872 for the drama of the same name by Alphonse Daudet (see Montmajour, Fontvieille).

Note

The streets of Arles are very narrow and there is a labyrinth of one-way streets, so motorists are recommended to leave their vehicle outside the Old Town which is partly surrounded by walls, and to visit the town on foot. Collective tickets at a reduced rate are obtainable from all ticket offices, and they provide admittance to all the sights in the town.

## Sights

***Arènes**
(amphitheatre)

**Opening times:**
June–Sept. 8.30am–7pm;
Oct. 9am–12.30pm, 2pm–6pm;
Nov., Dec. 9am–noon, 2pm–4.30pm;
Jan., Feb. 9am–noon, 2pm–4.30pm;
Mar. 9am–12.30pm, 2pm–6pm;
April 9am–12.30pm, 2pm–6.30pm;
May 9am–12.30pm, 2pm–7pm

The Roman amphitheatre is the largest and most complete ancient monument in the town, dating probably from early in the first century A.D. The great oval once had accommodation for 21,000 spectators. With a length of 136m/149yds and a width of 107m/117yds the arena was one of the largest in Gaul. The façade has a double row of arcades with 60 archways each 3·38m/11ft wide; the four arches used as main entrances are 4·80m/16ft wide.

Seating for the spectators was once on 34 rows of tiered steps; the arena itself was built into the bedrock of the site. In Roman times a wooden floor was provided over the rock; the holes in which the supporting joists were fixed can still be seen in the wall surrounding the arena.

In the Middle Ages the citizens converted the amphitheatre into a fortress by the addition of towers and the walling up of the arcades, of which there were originally three rows; the third no longer exists. When Prosper Mérimée cleared and restored the arena 150 years ago three of the towers were left standing. The one over the entrance can be climbed and from it there is a charming view over the roofs of the Old Town and of the nearby ancient theatre. Nowadays in summer bull-fights take place in the arena.

Van Gogh Foundation

The Fondation Vincent van Gogh was installed in 1984 in the nearby Palais de Luppé, at 26 Rond-Point des Arènes. Many famous artists, painters, photographers, writers and composers paid homage to van Gogh, and there are exhibits and documents covering his life on display. Thus his dream of a "House of the Artist" has been realised. Open: 10am–12.30pm, 2pm–7pm.

Théâtre Antique
(Roman theatre)

The Roman theatre is located in Rue de la Calade/Rue du Cloître; opening times are the same as those for the Arènes.
It was built in the time of Augustus and, with seating for 8000 on 33 tiers of steps, was as large as the theatre in Orange (see entry). In the early Middle Ages the theatre was used as a quarry, and with the material it provided the town wall was erected. Of the rear wall of the stage only a few stumps of pillars and two more or less complete columns remain. Since the theatre is now used again during the summer it is protected on the outside by screens and the interior is somewhat spoiled by the necessary technical apparatus.

Most of the relics brought to light during excavation can be seen in the Musée d'Art Païen (Museum of Pagan Art, see below) – the most important of these is the "Venus of Arles", a representation of the goddess Diana, which was discovered near a fountain in 1651 and is now in the Louvre in Paris.

Place de la République

Further west lies the Place de la République with an Egyptian obelisk 15m/50ft high. It was found in the amphitheatre and erected here in 1676. On the north side of the square stands the Hôtel de Ville (Town Hall) built in 1673–75. Its bell-tower dates from 1553 and came from the building which previously stood on the site.

***St-Trophime**

The Church of St-Trophime in the Place de la République, once the cathedral, was founded it is believed in the year 606. Its patron was a Greek disciple who brought Christianity to Provence. In its present form it is a Romanesque basilica, built 1152–80, the interior of which reveals Early Gothic forms.

**Doorway

The recently restored façade facing the square has a magnificent doorway with some most impressive figures – a masterpiece of Provençal sculpture. It was placed in front of the existing Carolingian building in the 12th c. and shows a certain similarity to the doorway of the Church of St-Gilles (see entry). On the pillars are figures of saints and Apostle: on the extreme inside of the front on the left is St Trophime being crowned with a mitre by two angels and on the right the Stoning of St Stephen. Above the door in the tympanum can be seen the Last Judgment with glory, surrounded by the symbols of the Evangelists and with the Twelve Apostles at his feet. This frieze is continued on the left and the right in the portrayal of the Last Judgment, with the "chosen" on the left and the "damned" on the right; below on the capitals on the left is the Annunciation and on the right the Birth of Jesus.

*Cathedral of St-Trophime, with the cloisters*

*Musée d'Art Chrétien*

Both side doorways are considerably smaller than the main doorway and were added in the 17th c. They give access to the rather dim interior. All three aisles are very narrow and high and show the transition from Romanesque to Gothic, the transept being 11th c. and the centre aisle 12th c. In the first bays on the right and the left hang large Gobelin tapestries. The choir and the choir ambulatory are 15th c. High Gothic.

**Cloisters

The Cloisters of St-Trophime adjoin the church on the south-east. They are accessible through the building to the right of the façade of the church and the courtyard behind it.

In the cloisters pillars alternate with columns in pairs, the capitals of which are decorated with fine sculptures of Biblical scenes; on the pillars will be found figures of Apostles and saints, and between them reliefs of stories of Christ and the saints. The 12th c. north and east wings are the oldest parts, while the south and west wings date from the 14th c.; thus the cloisters reveal both Romanesque and Gothic elements. The Chapter House adjoins the cloisters; in it hang two Gobelin tapestries and in the gallery is a small lapidarium. The other rooms adjacent to the cloisters are used for temporary exhibitions. The stairs leading to the galleries and the rooms above also provide access to the terrace-like roof gallery which encircles the cloisters and provides a charming view of the latter. Opening times: Jan. 10am–noon, 2pm–4.30pm; Feb. 10am–12.30pm, 2pm–7pm; Mar.–May 9.30am–12.30pm, 2pm–7pm; June–Sept. 9am–7pm; Oct. 9.30am–12.30pm, 2pm–6pm; Nov., Dec. 9.30am–noon, 2pm–4.30pm.

Musée d'Art Païen
Museee Lapidaire

The Musée d'Art Païen (Museum of Pagan Art) or Musée Lapidaire (lapidarium) is located opposite St-Trophime in the former Church of Ste-Anne (1630). It exhibits works of the Roman Age and especially of Hellenism. Most of the exhibits come from the Roman theatre, the former Forum and other ancient buildings in Arles.

Musée d'Art
Chrétien

The Musée d'Art Chrétien (Museum of Christian Art; open; May–Sept. 9am–12.30pm, 2pm–7pm; other months as for Arènes – see entry) lies a short distance north-west of the Musée Lapidaire on Rue Balze. Housed in the chapel of the former Jesuit college which was built in 1652, it possesses one of the most important collections of Early Christian sarcophagi from the 4th c.; many of them come from the Necropolis of the Alyscamps (see below) and from the Early Christian burial-place of St-Genest in the present-day suburb of Trinquetaille. The sarcophagi are decorated with reliefs showing scenes from the Old and New Testaments.

The "Cryptoporticus", a partly subterranean arcade of the ancient Forum (see below), can be reached from the museum.

*Museon Arlaten

The Museon Arlaten (Museum of Arles) was founded in 1899 by the famous Provençal poet Frédéric Mistral. The Palais de Laval-Castellane, in which it is housed, is built on the remains of an ancient basilica, and was first a nobleman's palace and then a Jesuit college. Mistral, a Nobel Prize-winner of 1904, donated the amount of his prize in order to create in his native region a permanent museum. It is now the most important collection of Provençal folk art, displaying furniture, costumes, ceramics, tools and farming implements. Open: July, Aug. daily 9am–noon, 2pm–7pm; other months Tues.–Sun. 9am–noon, 2pm–5pm.

Forum

The Forum, the market and meeting-place of the Roman town, was situated on the south side of the present-day Place du Forum, north of the above-mentioned museums. The best-preserved part is known as the "Cryptoporticus" (crypto doorway *c.* 40 B.C.), a horseshoe-shaped loggia 89m/97yds by 59m/65yds in extent, built probably to compensate for the slope of the site. Entrance is from the Musée d'Art Chrétien.

Place du Forum, with statue of F. Mistral

"Maid of Arles", Festival of Gardians

Thermes de Constantin

The Thermes de Constantin (Baths of Constantine), the Roman bathing complex, dates from the 4th c. A.D. and is situated on Rue D. Maisto in the north of the town near the arm of the river called the "Grand Rhône". Of the once-extensive series of buildings, which resembled a palace, only the Caldarium (warm bath) and parts of the Hypocaust (underfloor heating) and the Tepidarium (warm air room) remain. Open: Nov.–Feb., 9am–noon, 2pm–4.30pm; Mar.–Oct., 9am–12.30pm, 2pm–6pm; Apr., 2pm–6.30pm; May–Sept., 2pm–7pm.

Espace Van-Gogh

The Dutch painter Vincent van Gogh (1853–90) spent fifteen productive months in Arles in 1888–89. The artist – together with Cézanne and Gauguin one of the main pioneers of modern painting – lived in this former hospital for a time, and included it in several of his paintings. The 16th c. building is now a cultural centre and equipped as a "School of Books".

"Pont de Langlois"

The Pont de Langlois, which once stood at the end of the Avenue du Plan-du-Bourg and was made famous by van Gogh, no longer exists. The drawbridge in Rue G. Monge, which is often referred to as the Pont de Langlois, is some 2km/1¼ miles from the "genuine article" and is a copy.

*Musée Réattu

The Musée Réattu, housed in a 15th/16th c. building on Rue G. Monge once the Grand Priory of the Knights of Malta, stemmed from the collection of the painter Réattu (1760–1833) and exhibits drawings and paintings by Provençal artists of the 18th and 19th c., as well as a collection of contemporary art, largely owing to the generosity of Pablo Picasso. In addition to the gallery of photographs by Lucien Clergue and others, the drawings by Picasso himself make this friendly little museum particularly interesting; in the main they are portraits with the faces wreathed in loving or amused smiles, evidence of the humanity and sense of humour of the artist. Open: Nov.–Jan., 10am–12.30pm, 2pm–5pm; Feb.–Apr., 2pm–7pm; May, 9.30am–12.30pm, 2pm–7pm; June–Sept., 9am–12.30pm, Oct., 10am–12.30pm, 2pm–6pm.

*Vincent van Gogh: "Pont de Langlois" (1888)*

*Alyscamps

Opening times see Arènes (amphitheatre)

Along the Avenue des Alyscamps, on the south-eastern edge of the Old Town, stretch the Alyscamps (the "Elysian Fields"), an extensive Roman burial-place which, according to the legend of St Trophime, was dedicated as a Christian cemetery and, in the Middle Ages, was so famous that the dead were brought here for burial from considerable distances; Dante refers to it in his "Inferno". This led to the curious procedure of bringing the dead – in cleverly designed barrels together with a sum of money – along the Rhône to Arles, where they were fished out of the water by people employed for the purpose and duly interred. Their marble sarcophagi, which were later neglected, sold or destroyed, were not assembled again until the 18th c. Along the idyllic Allée des Tombeaux (Street of Graves), the only coffins now standing are the plain stone ones of the Middle Ages; the best ones are housed in the museums, especially in the Musée d'Art Chrétien, and in the Church of St Trophime.

At the end of the Allée stands the Church of St-Honorat (12th c.), the only remains of which are the choir and the adjoining 15th–18th c. chapels. In the side-chapel on the left will be found a beautiful sarcophagus dating from the 4th c. A.D.

## Surroundings of Arles

Camargue

See entry

Montmajour

See entry

Moulin de Daudet

See Montmajour

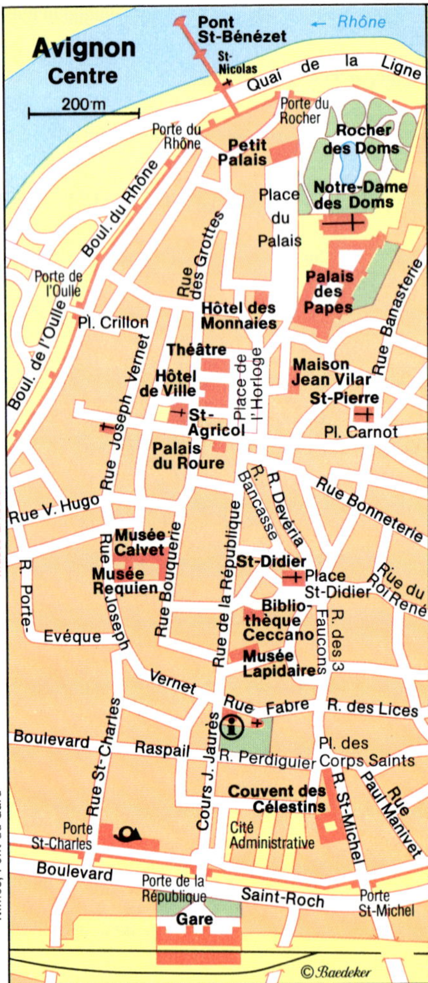


# Avignon
## Palais des Papes

Old Palace
New Palace

FIRST FLOOR

A Tour de Trouillas
B Tour de la Glacière
C Tour des Cuisines
D Tour St-Jean
E Tour de l'Etude
F Tour des Anges
G Tour de la Garde-Robe
H Tour St-Laurent
I Tour de la Gache
K Tour d'Angle
L Tour de la Campane

GROUND FLOOR

PAPSTPALAST

PAPAL PALACE
GROUND FLOOR
1 Conclave wing
2 Consistory Hall
3 Wine store, bakery
4 St John's Chapel
5 Treasury
6 Wardrobe, bathroom
7 Large Audience Chamber
8 Small Audience Chamber
9 Porte des Champeaux
10 Porte de Notre-Dame

FIRST FLOOR
11 Guest room
12 Confidants' wing
13 Chapel of St Benedict
14 Banqueting Hall
15 Ante-room
16 Study
17 Papal bedroom
18 Room of the Stag (above St Michael's Chapel)
19 Great Chapel
20 Window of Indulgence
21 Servants' quarters
22 Wing of the Dignitaries

# Avignon

D2

Département: Vaucluse
Altitude: 23m/75ft
Population: 93,000

Location and importance

The former Papal Residence of Avignon, today the capital of the Département of Vaucluse, lies on the left bank of the Rhône where the river is divided into two by the island of Barthelasse, and at the foot of a limestone cliff on which stand the Papal Palace and the Cathedral. South of Avignon its tributary the Durance flows into the Rhône. Avignon is much favoured by tourists for its art treasures and because it is an excellent setting-out point for excursions into Provence.

Festivals

More than twenty festivals are held annually in Avignon, the major and most attractive one being the great International Festival in July/August; including jazz and rock concerts which are held against the impressive backdrop of the Papal Palace.

Information is obtainable from Festival d'Avignon, 8 bis, Rue de Mons, F-84000 Avignon; tel. 90 82 67 08.

History

Avennio (or Avenio), the capital of the Gallic Cavares, later became a thriving Roman colony. In turn the town fell into the hands of the Burgundians and the Franks, and in the 13th c. it was acquired, together with Provence, by Charles of Anjou. In the Albigensian Wars it supported the Duke of Toulouse and the Albigens and was consequently conquered by Louis VIII in 1226.

Between 1309 and 1377 there resided here Popes Clement V (1305–14), John XXII (1314–34), Benedict XII (1334–42), Clement VI (1342–52), Innocent VI (1352–62), Urban V (1362–70) and Gregory XI (1370–78), a nephew of Clement VI. Only the return of Gregory XI to Rome ended the almost 70 years of "Babylonian Exile" of the Church. After his death when schism set in, the Popes Clement VII (1378–94) and Benedict XIII (1394–1424), resided in Avignon until 1403. The town with the surrounding county of Venaissin remained a possession of the Curia until the Revolution united the "Papal City" with France in 1791.

After the Popes had employed Italian masters, especially the Siennese Simone Martini who died here in 1344, an important school of painting flourished in Avignon right until the 18th c.

## **Palais des Papes (Papal Palace)

**Location**
Place du Palais

The immediate reason for the erection of the Papal Residence was the removal of the Curia from Rome to Avignon under Clement V. His successor, John XXII (Pope 1316–34), chose the palace of the Bishop of Avignon, his nephew Arnaud de Via, as his official seat and initiated the first extensions. The present aspect of the fortress-like block of buildings is due mainly to the erection of the east and north-east wings (Palais Vieux=Old Palace) by Benedict XII (Pope 1334–42) and the west wing (Palais Nouveau =New Palace) by Clement VI (Pope 1342–52). Later Popes who resided in Avignon were responsible only for small extensions and completions.

Opening times: Easter–June daily 9–12.15am, 2–6pm; July 1st–Sept. 30th, daily 9am–7pm; Oct.–Easter daily 9–12.15am, 2pm–5.15pm (Guided tours).

*Avignon: the Papal Palace*

**Exterior**

The east of the Place du Palais is dominated by the mighty façade of the Palais Nouveau, more a fortress than a centre of spiritual power. The irregular buildings of the façade are articulated in the lower part by great pointed arches over wall columns. To the wall above the entrance gateway cling two octagonal towers with pointed spires. On the right the façade is flanked by the Tour de la Gache and on the left by the Tour d'Angle, two somewhat insubstantial stump towers protruding from the surface of the wall. On the left, set back a little towards the façade, it is joined by the Palace Vieux (Old Palace), articulated completely by wall pillars and pointed arches. At the corner of the building rises the Tour de la Campane with its battlemented pinnacle making it a defensive tower. Near the Palais Vieux, above a mighty open stairway, stands the Cathedral of Notre-Dame des Doms (see entry).

**Interior**

Although the entire furnishings of the inside of the Papal Palace, except for some remains of sculptures and frescoes, have disappeared, the interior of this complex of buildings offers a compulsive impression of space. Passing through the Porte des Champeaux, the entrance from the open-air stairway, the Grande Cour comes into view; this great inner courtyard, around which the old and new parts of the palace are grouped, is from time to time the scene for open-air dramatic performances.

Consistory

In the left-hand corner of the courtyard will be found the entrance to the Consistoire (Consistory), and, opposite, the Cloister of Benedict XII (see below). In the Hall of the Consistory measuring 11m/36ft by 48m/158ft can be seen the remains of some frescoes by Simone Martini; adjoining the longer wall lies the Chapelle St-Jean (Chapel of St John), the lower part of the chapel tower. Here will be found some well-preserved frescoes created between 1346 and 1348 and attributed to the Italian Matteo Giovanetti. They depict the life-stories of St John the Baptist and St John the Evangelist.

Cloister

Opposite the entrance to the Consistory Hall lies the Cloister of Benedict XII, dating from 1339 and completely restored in 1940; this was the site of the earlier palace of John XXII. A staircase leads to the covered gallery above the cloister; note the alternation of double and considerably smaller simple windows up above.

Banqueting Hall

Adjoining this gallery is the former Banqueting Hall (Grand Tinel or Magnum Tinellum). It is situated immediately above the Consistory Hall and has the same measurements; the wooden vaulted ceiling is modern. Hanging here can be seen four huge 18th c. Gobelin tapestries; from the short linking corridor in the left-hand corner of the hall which gives access to the Kitchen Tower (Tour des Cuisines) there is a charming view to the south-west over the Old Town.

St-Martial

The Chapelle St-Martial, which occupies the upper storey of the chapel tower, is – like its counterpart on the ground floor – decorated with frescoes by Matteo Giovanetti which date from 1344–45. They portray the miracles of St Martial, the 3rd c. patron saint of Limousin.

Bedchamber

The end of the Banqueting Hall leads into the Robing Chamber, the ante-room to the Papal Bedchamber, in which two 18th c. Gobelins and a model of the Papal Palace are to be seen. The Papal Bedchamber lies immediately adjoining in the Tour des Anges. Of interest here are the (restored) polychromatic tiled floor, the painted beamed ceiling and the walls painted in tempera, predominantly arabesques on a blue ground; in the window niches are lodged painted birdcages. The Tour de la Garde-Robe, the tower adjacent to the Tour des Anges, houses the former study of Clement VI, known as the Chambre du Cerf (Room of the Stag), so called from the secular scenes, especially of hunting and fishing, painted on the walls. Also of interest is the painted coffered ceiling. The floor tiles are, like those in the bedchamber, of more recent date but copied from old designs.

Grande Chapelle

A staircase now leads into the North Sacristy where there are plaster replicas of numerous tombs of cardinals and other spiritual dignitaries. Then comes the Grand Chapelle (Great Chapel), also called the "Chapelle Clementine", a huge single-aisled church with a coffered roof. On the walls hang a considerable number of Baroque paintings; to the right of the altar stands the entrance to the South Sacristy in which will be found replicas of the tombs of Innocent VI, Clement V, Clement VI and Urban V. From the Great Chapel there is an entrance to the loggia where through the large traceried Fenêtre de l'Indulgence (Window of Indulgence) there is a view of the Great Courtyard. From this window the Pope used to give his blessing to the assembled faithful.

Grande Audience

Following the broad vaulted staircase down to the ground floor leads on the left to the door of the Grand Audience, the Great Audience Chamber, a twin-naved audience hall beneath the Chapelle Clementine. This, too, was embellished by Matteo Giovanetti in 1352 with wall-paintings of Prophets and Sybils. In the Small Audience Chamber (also called the "Audience des Contredites") ornamental grisaille paintings were introduced in the 17th c.

The way back to the entrance doorway is through the Corps du Garde (Guardroom).

## Other places of interest

Notre-Dame des Doms

Near the Papal Palace on the north towers the Cathedral of Notre-Dame des Doms; its present architecture is mainly of the 12th c., but it was altered several times in the 14th–16th c. On the arch and gable of the main doorway are remains of frescoes by Simone Martin. The gilded statue of the Virgin on the tower and the Crucifixion group in front of the cathedral date from the 19th c.

*Frescoes in the Chapelle St-Martial*

*Hôtel de Ville in the Place de l'Horloge*

In the interior, in the crossing to the left, can be seen a 12th c. bishop's chair of white marble; in the first side chapel on the north stands the former Romanesque main altar; in the fourth chapel on the south side the partly restored Late Gothic monument to John XXII. At the entrance to the Baptistry Chapel – the ante-room on the right – can be seen early 15th c. frescoes portraying the Baptism of Christ and also showing the donor's family, the Spiefami from Luca. A beautiful silver sculpture of the "Scourging of Christ" is to be found in the north aisle. The Chapel of the Resurrection, the third chapel on the south side, was a gift from Archbishop Cibelli and also contains his tomb.

Rocher des Doms

The Rocher des Doms is a rocky spur which rises to the north of the Papal Palace and then falls steeply down to the Rhône. There is a fine panoramic view from the beautiful park on its summit of the famous Pont St-Bénézet (see below) and the islands of Barthelasse and Piot in the river, as well as Villeneuve-lès-Avignon on the far bank.

*Pont St-Bénézet
Pont d'Avignon

**Opening times:**
Apr.–Sept. daily 9am–6.30pm; Oct.–Mar. Tues.–Sun. 9am–5pm. Closed on public holidays

Jutting out into the river at the foot of the Rocher des Doms lies what is probably the most famous bridge in the whole of France, immortalised in the children's song "Sur le pont d'Avignon, on y danse tous en rond . . .". Built in 1177–85, this fortified bridge over to Villeneuve-lès-Avignon originally had 22 arches and was 900m/985yds long. A large part of it was destroyed in 1668, and only four arches remain; in the centre of these stands the two-storey Chapelle St-Nicholas (St Nicholas' Chapel), the lower part of which is Romanesque and the upper Gothic and with a bell-gable. The chapel was restored in the 19th c.

The bridge to St-Bénézet (Provençal for Benedict) is also well-known because of the following legend attributed to it: it is said that in the year 1177 the shepherd Bénézet was instructed by the angels to build a bridge over the Rhône. The town fathers and citizens both mocked the idea, but he

*Villeneuve-lès-Avignon: Pont St-Bénézet and Tour Philippe-le-Bel*

was given the strength to raise a giant lump of rock, which they then recognised as being a sign from God, further evidenced by the fact that the bridge was built in only eight years.

Musée du Petit Palais

**Opening times:** Wed.–Mon. 9.30am–noon, 2pm–6pm. Closed on public holidays

On the north side of the Place du Palais stands the 14th c. Petit Palais, a Gothic fort which used to serve as episcopal offices and residence. It has a beautiful arcaded courtyard and the core of the building dates from the 13th c. At present it houses the Campana Collection of paintings by 13th–15th c. Italian masters, as well as a collection of works by the Avignon School of Painters, established by Simone Martini (c. 1280–1344) and Matteo Giovanetti. At one time Napoleon II had purchased the collection for the Louvre.

A little way to the north the town wall is pierced by the Porte du Rocher, a gateway leading to the Pont St-Bénézet.

Hôtel des Monnaies

Opposite the Papal Palace stands the Hôtel des Monnaies, the former mint. Built in the early 17th c., this baroque building still displays a strong Italian influence; the façade is decorated with large figures of animals and bears the coat-of-arms of Pope Paul V, who came from the House of Borghese and whose vice-legate resided here. Today the palace houses the Conservatoire.

*Town walls

The whole of the Old Town is surrounded by a complete ring of walls, constructed by Pope Innocent VI between 1355–68. At irregular intervals eight gates and 39 towers were incorporated into the wall, the total length of which is 4·8km/3 miles. Some detailed restoration work was carried out in the 19th c.

St-Symphorien

At some distance east of the Papal Palace, on the Place des Carmes. stands the Church of St-Symphorien, dating mainly from the 15th c. It belonged to the former Monastery of the Unshod Carmelites, and was therefore also named the Eglise des Carmes. Inside will be found some 16th c. statues as well as paintings by Pierre Parrocel, a lesser-known member of the Parrocel family of artists, and others. A flea-market is held on Sunday mornings on the Place des Carmes.

Place de l'Horloge

The idyllic Place de l'Horloge south-east of the Papal Palace, dominated by street-cafés beneath shady plane trees, is the very centre of Avignon life. On its west side stand the theatre and the Hôtel de Ville (Town Hall; 1845) incorporating a 14th c. clock-tower; life-sized figures on the top, known as "jacquemarts", strike the hours.

St-Pierre

A little to the east of the square stands the Church of St-Pierre; built in 1356 and extended in the late 15th c. and restored in the 19th c., it possesses a very beautiful Gothic façade and carved Renaissance wooden doors dating from 1550. Inside the church will be found some 16th c. statues of burial groups and a splendid Baroque choral scene from the mid-17th c.

St-Agricol

A short distance south-west of the Town Hall is the Gothic Church of St-Agricol, a very sombre triple-aisled basilica with no transept, built by Pope John XXII in 1321–26.

St-Didier

To the east of the Rue de la République, the main street of the Old Town leading south from the Place de l'Horloge, stands the single-aisled Church of St-Didier, dating from the mid-14th c. It provides a further example of the stern Provençal Romanesque style. It contains one of the earliest Renaissance works of art, a Way of the Cross created between 1478 and 1481 by the Italian painter Francesco da Laurana, who had been working in France since 1476. Also worthy of note is the Late Gothic pulpit with richly flamboyant-style decoration. More recently wall-paintings dating from the 14th c. depicting the Crucifixion and Interment, etc. have been uncovered in the church.

*Musée Calvet

The Musée Calvet is the town's major museum; it is, however, likely to remain closed until some time in 1992 for renovation work to be carried out. The museum has its origin in the private collection of the doctor, a native of Avignon, François Esprit Calvet (1729–1810) together with municipal collections. Since 1833 it has been housed in the Hôtel de Villeneuve-Martignan which dates from 1750 and is situated at 65 Rue Joseph Vernet, south-west of the Place de l'Horloge. The contents embrace antique sculptures, medieval paintings by Provençal masters, as well as an instructive cross-section of French painters from the 16th to the 19th c., together with collections of coins and ceramics.

Musée Requien

The Musée Requien is located close to the Musée Calvet. A well as a large scientific library it possesses geological and botanical collections, including a large herbarium. Open: Tues.–Sat. 9am–noon, 2pm–6pm; closed on public holidays.

*Musée Lapidaire

The Musée Lapidaire (lapidarium) can be found at Rue de la République 27, in the Baroque former Jesuit Church, joined by a bridge to the Jesuit college – now a secondary school – which was founded in 1564. The exhibits include Roman mosaics, fragments of the former triumphal arch, reliefs and ancient sculptures. Open: Wed.–Mon. 9am–noon, 2pm–6pm; closed on public holidays.

Couvent des Célestins

In the south of the Old Town, near the Porte St-Michel on the street of the same name, stands the former Célestine monastery, once the largest monastery in the town. The interesting church has a superb apse by Perrin Morel; in the cloister (*c.* 1400), which unfortunately is only partially preserved, is a 17th c. gateway.

Musée Louis Vouland

In the west of the Old Town, in the Rue Victor Hugo near the Porte St-Dominique, can be found the Musée Louis Vouland, with French furniture, especially from the 18th c., pictures, Gobelin tapestries and ceramics. Of interest here too is the collection of Chinese porcelain and ivory sculptures. Open: June–Sept. Tues.–Sat. 10am–noon, 2pm–6pm; afternoons only Oct.–May.

Other cultural institutions

The Bibliothèque Ceccano, the public lending library, is contained in a restored 15th c. building at 2 Rue Laboureur.

The Palais du Roure at 3 Rue Collège du Roure is the home of an institute specialising in archaeology and ethnology and the promotion of the Provençal language. There are guided tours on Tuesdays at 10am and 3pm.

In Maison Jean Vilar at 8 Rue de Mons (open: Tues.–Fri. 9am–noon, 2pm–6pm; Sat. 10am–5pm) exhibitions are held depicting the history of the theatrical festival and providing information on the work of the producer Jean Vilar (1912–71), who was the festival director from 1947.

St-Ruf

Some distance to the south, outside the Old Town on the other side of the station on Boulevard Gambetta, stands the artistic Church of St-Ruf, the remains of a monastic foundation – Abbatiola Sancti Rufi – which goes back to Carolingian times; it was formerly a place of honour where the relics of St Justus were revered.

## Surroundings of Avignon

### Villeneuve-lès-Avignon

Location and townscape

A bridge over the southern part of the island of Barthelasse leads from Avignon to the little town of Villeneuve-lès-Avignon, which was laid out by Philip the Fair as a bastion against the Papal residents.

*Villeneuve: the mighty Fort St-André*

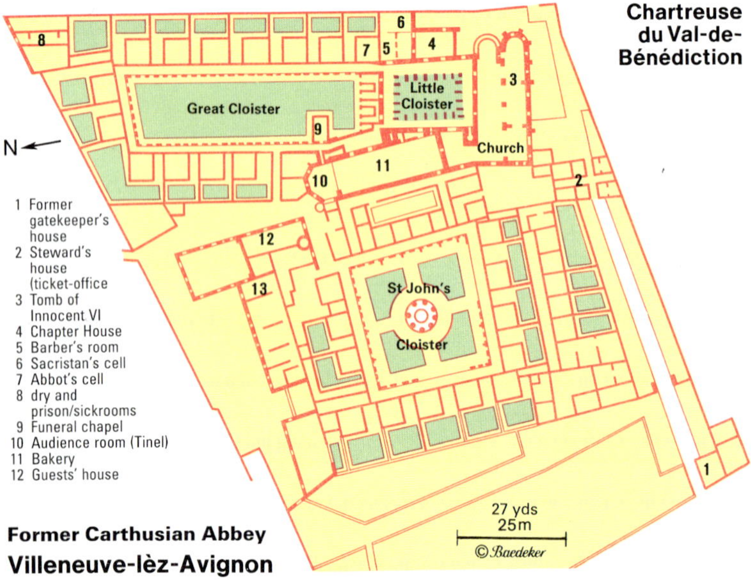


**Former Carthusian Abbey**

**Villeneuve-lèz-Avignon**

On the bank of the Rhône opposite the Pont St-Bénézet (see above) stands the Tour Philippe le-Bel, built in 1307. In the collegial Church of Notre-Dame, dedicated in 1333, are some good panels, a copy of the pietá and a noteworthy treasury.

**Museum

The "pièce de résistance" of the Musée Municipal Pierre de Luxembourg on the Rue de la République is the "Coronation of the Virgin Mary", painted by Enguerrand Quarton (or Charonton) in 1453, accompanied by works by Nicolas Mignard in the mid-17th c. and a 14th c. Madonna of painted ivory, carved from an elephant's tusk. Some pieces removed from the Carthusian monastery (see below) are also to be found here, including a 17th c. door and cupboard and some pewter-ware.

Fort St-André

From Fort St-André with its two mighty round towers, built in the second half of the 14th c. by John the Good and Charles V, there is a magnificent view of Villeneuve, Avignon, Mont Ventoux and the Lubéron and Alpilles mountain ranges. The massive walls enclose the little town of St-André, a Benedictine monastery and the Romanesque Church of Notre-Dame-de-Belvézet. Open: Apr.–June and Sept. 9.30am–12.30pm, 2pm–6.30pm; July, Aug. 9.30am–7pm; Oct.–Mar. 10am–noon, 2pm–5pm.

*Chartreuse du Val de Bénédiction

In the northern part of Rue de la République can be found the former Chartreuse du Val de Bénédiction (Carthusian monastery), which was founded in 1356 by Pope Innocent VI and soon became larger than its mother priory, the Grande Chartreuse at Isère. In the church – the choir of which is in ruins, thus giving a clear view of the fort – can be found the tomb of Innocent VI, in the first bay on the right; dating from 1362, it was preserved thanks to the efforts of Prosper Mérimée in 1834.
To the north of the monastic church lies the Petit Cloître (Little Cloister) and the elongated Cloître du Cimetière, measuring 20m/66ft by 80m/263ft, adjoining which were the monks' cells.

Open: Apr.–Sept. 9am–6.30pm, Oct.–Mar. 9.30am–5.30pm.

*Enguerrand Quarton: "Coronation of the Virgin" (Villeneuve Museum)*

## Cavaillon

Location

The little provincial town of Cavaillon – a centre of melon-growing and of the canning industry – lies on the right bank of the Durance and on the western edge of the Montagne du Lubéron (see entry).

St-Veran

In the centre of the town stands the notable former Cathedral of St-Véran, which was probably founded in the 12th c, as indicated by its Romanesque Provençal architecture. Its exterior is rather less attractive, but inside can be seen beautiful capitals in the apse and a fine cloister.

Open: Apr. 1st–Sept. 30th 10am–noon, 3pm–6pm; Oct. 1st–Mar. 31st 10am–noon, 2pm–4pm; closed Sun. and Mon. morning.

Synagogue

The beautiful synagogue on Place Castil-Blaze is easily recognised by its arcades. Built in the Rococo style in 1772 it was later altered on many occasions and today houses the little Musée Judéo-Contadin, or Jewish Museum, which is not open to the public.

Museum

In the chapel of the old hospital on the Cours Gambetta, with its Rococo façade, can be found the Archaeological Museum with exhibits mainly from the Gallo-Roman period, including an interesting Merovingian altar-table. One room contains some interesting items of equipment from the old hospital dating from the 17th and 18th c.

Triumphal Arch

South-west of St-Véran, in the Place F. Tourel on the edge of the town, can be found the only preserved building of the Roman era, the little triumphal arch of the former Roman Oppidum Cabellio. It was restored in 1880.

# Bandol D3

Département: Var
Altitude: sea-level
Population: 7000

Location and townscape

The port and holiday resort of Bandol lies on the pretty bay between Marseilles and Toulon. It possesses a casino and three beaches; Plage de Casino (500m/550yds long, fine sand), Plage de Rènecros (500m/550yds long, fine sand) and Plage Dorée (also 500m/550yds, coarse sand and pebbles). The promenades, Allées Alfred-Vivien and Allées Jean-Moulin, are charmingly planted with palms, pines and flowers.
In the church the Baroque woodwork is worth seeing. The surroundings of Bandol are among the best wine-producing areas of the French Mediterranean coast (see Wine).

## Surroundings of Bandol

St-Cyr-sur-Mer

St-Cyr-sur-Mer, a community of several parts situated 9km/6 miles north-west of Bandol, has highly developed agriculture – flowers, capers, olives, grapes – and a ceramic industry.
The principal tourist area is the stretch of coast between the yacht harbours of Les Lecques in the north-west and La Madrague in the south.
The Musée de Tauroentum – once the site of a Roman villa – has some well-preserved mosaics from the 1st c. A.D., remains of pillars and amphorae.

Île de Bendor

The Île de Bendor is a rocky island only 1km/½ mile south of Bandol, a trip of only seven minutes by boats which leave the mainland every 30 minutes. Its attractions include a reconstructed Provençal harbour, the Musée de la Mer (Marine Museum), the Fondation Paul Picard, with art exhibitions and courses and a huge painting by Salvador Dali, the Exposition Universelle des Vins et des Spiritueux, a wine and spirits exhibition, the diving centre known as the Centre International de Plongée, a little zoo and a sea-water swimming-pool.

Sanary-sur-Mer

Sanary-sur-Mer, 4km/2 miles south-east of Bandol, is a pretty former fishing village surrounded by wooded hills and with an extensive colony of villas. On a hill to the west of the village stands the Chapel of Notre-Dame-de-Pitié, built in 1560, which is well worth seeing and from which there is a splendid view. In the early part of the Second World War a number of well-known German intellectuals fleeing from the Nazis settled in Sanary.

Six-Fours-la-Plage

Six-Fours-la-Plage, 10km/6 miles south of Bandol, is a large community of several parts situated at the foot of a hill 210m/689ft high, with magnificent views of the Roads of Toulon (see Toulon) and the Fort de Six-Fours. At the foot of the hill stands the Church of Vieux-Six-Fours, part of which is a well-preserved Romanesque building, containing a fine 16th c. winged altar.
Along the beach stretches an extensive complex of holiday homes.

Cap Sicié

Cap Sicié, south of Six-Fours-la-Plage, is the imposing steep slope of a wooded promontory. To the east in the sea can be seen the two rocks known as Les Deux Frères (The Two Brothers). Not far west on the 358m/1175ft high summit of the cape stands the pilgrimage church of Notre-Dame-du-Mai, from which there is an excellent panoramic view.

Îles des Embiez

About 5km/3 miles south of Six-Fours-la-Plage, on the southern edge of the Bay of Sanary, lie the Îles des Embiez. The Île de la Tour-Fondue (95ha/235 acres) is the chief island in this diverse group and has been developed into a centre for water sports. The south of the island, which is 64m/210ft high and steeply sloping, is characterised by a salt-works, vineyards and bathing beaches. The Observatoire de la Mer, a marine observation station and museum, is worth a visit.

## Barcelonnette

C4

Département: Alpes-de-Haute-Provence
Altitude: 1135m/3725ft
Population: 3300

Location and importance

Barcelonnette, the headquarters of the Sous-Prefecture des Départements Alpes-de-Haute-Provence, is situated some 70km/44 miles east of Gap in the Ubaye valley. This little town, reminiscent of many in the southern hemisphere, lies in magnificent mountain country, surrounded by fruit-fields and meadows. The roads to the south lead over the well-known passes of Col d'Allos, Col de la Cayolle and Col de la Bonette; the latter, 2802m/9196ft above sea-level, is the highest pass anywhere in the Alps.

History

Raimond Bérenger, Count of Barcelona and Provence, built a fortress here in 1231; it was named Barcelone, from which developed the present name of Barcelonette. From 1388 Barcelonette, together with the whole of the Ubaye region, belonged to the House of Savoy until it was ceded to France under the Treaty of Utrecht in 1731.
Barcelonette was the birthplace of the politician Paul Reynaud (1878–1966), a staunch opponent of European unity after the Second World War. In 1940 he was made President of the Council, resigned and was replaced by Marshal Pétain. He was interned by the Vichy government and deported to Germany between 1942 and 1945. After the liberation he was elected to and made president of the European Economic Commission.

"Mexicains"

In 1821 the Arnaud brothers from neighbouring Jausier emigrated to Mexico and opened a textile and clothing shop in Mexico City. From 1830 onwards they encouraged more emigrants from the valley, and by the end of the century more than 100 such shops in Mexico were owned by "Barcelonnettes". Over a number of years more than a half of the men aged over twenty left the Ubaye valley to go to Mexico. Some of them became financially very successful; dealings in gold and silver began, and a group of them bought the Bank of London, Mexico and South America, which had the licence to issue banknotes for the whole of Mexico. In the 1880s the "Mexicans" started to build luxurious villas in their home town, and these give the townscape its unusual character.
This golden age came to an end with the Mexican Revolution between 1910 and 1920, and a wave of the "Mexicains" émigres returned to Barcelonnette to settle.
The Musée de la Vallée (Ville de Barcelonnette) in the "La Sapinière" villa on the Avenue de la Libération has a department devoted to the Mexican history of the Barcelonnettes; open: Wed., Thur. Sat. 3pm–6pm, to 7pm in summer; open every day during the school holidays in winter and summer.

Townscape

The Avenue de la Libération is lined with fine parks containing the villas built by the "Mexicains". One of the most lavish, known as "La Sapinière", houses a museum and also the offices of the Mercantour National Park (Maison du Parc National du Mercantour); another villa is now a hotel.
The Place Manuel lies outside the chessboard pattern of the old bastion. This broad square, with its colourful house-fronts and cafés, is now a favourite meeting place for tourists. The Tour Cardinalis, the old bell-tower of the Dominican priory, dates from the 15th c.

## Surroundings of Barcelonnette

St-Pons

This little village some 3km/2 miles to the north-west, has an interesting church, a relic of a Benedictine priory. The Romanesque parts – the west door and the choir and section immediately adjoining – date from the 12th c. The 15th c. south door has rich figure decoration, the theme of the simple scenes being that of Death.

Le Sauze

The well-known winter sports resort of Le Sauze, 4km/2½ miles south-east of Barcelonnette at a height of 1380m/4530ft, is one of the oldest anywhere in the Alps. Its sister resort of Super-Sauze lies at 1700m/5580ft.

Col de la Bonette

The direct road link with Nice, 149km/92 miles away, passes along the Route de la Bonette, built in 1832; the present road dates from 1963–64. Fortifications along the way are reminders of the strategical importance this route has always had, including the period of the Second World War. A winding road – with a fine view of the Ubaye valley along the way – leads up to the top of the pass at 2802m/9196ft. From here it is a half-hour climb there and back to the Cime de la Bonette (2862m/9393ft) from where there is a superb panoramic view, from Mont Pelvoux to Monte Viso in the north and from the foothills of the Alps in Digne to the Maritime Alps in the south.

Col d'Allos

This road over the Col d'Allos (2240m/7350ft) together with the Col de la Cayolle (2327m/7637ft) provides the link with the valley of the Upper Var (see Mercantour). While a wide road leads to the Pra-Loup winter sports region, the road through the pass – closed in winter – is in a dreadful condition and requires strong nerves to negotiate it. Any barriers along the edge afford little more than token protection; large stretches should be taken at a snail's pace and a lookout kept for vehicles coming from the opposite direction!

Foux d'Allos

The Alpine view around this popular winter sports resort (1425m/4677ft) is extremely impressive, but tends to be spoilt in summer when skiing takes over. Large areas of the grass turf on the gently rounded slopes have been badly damaged.

# Les Baux-de-Provence D2

Département: Bouches-du-Rhône
Altitude: 280m/920ft
Population: 450

Location

The ruined town of Les Baux is situated in the extreme west of Provence on the southern edge of the Alpilles (see entry), north-east of Arles. This unique ruined site occupies the plateau of a rock mass which rises above the Lower Town.

The entire place can be visited only on foot; parking is available outside the entrance to the Lower Town.

History

This elevated site was settled as long ago as the Early Stone Age. The first signs of overlords in Les Baux are found around the year 950. In the 12th and 13th c. Les Baux (Provençal Li Baus = The Rocks) was the chief town of a county which embraced a great part of Provence and numbered more than 3000 inhabitants. The Cour d'Amour, the rendezvous of the troubadours in the 13th c., was famous as the centre of courtly poetry which was later to find a parallel in German-speaking countries in the Minnesang. Being a stronghold of Huguenots – there still exists a window from the former Protestant church of 1571 with the watchword "post tenebras lux", or "after the dark comes light" – and a refuge for rebels from Aix, in 1631

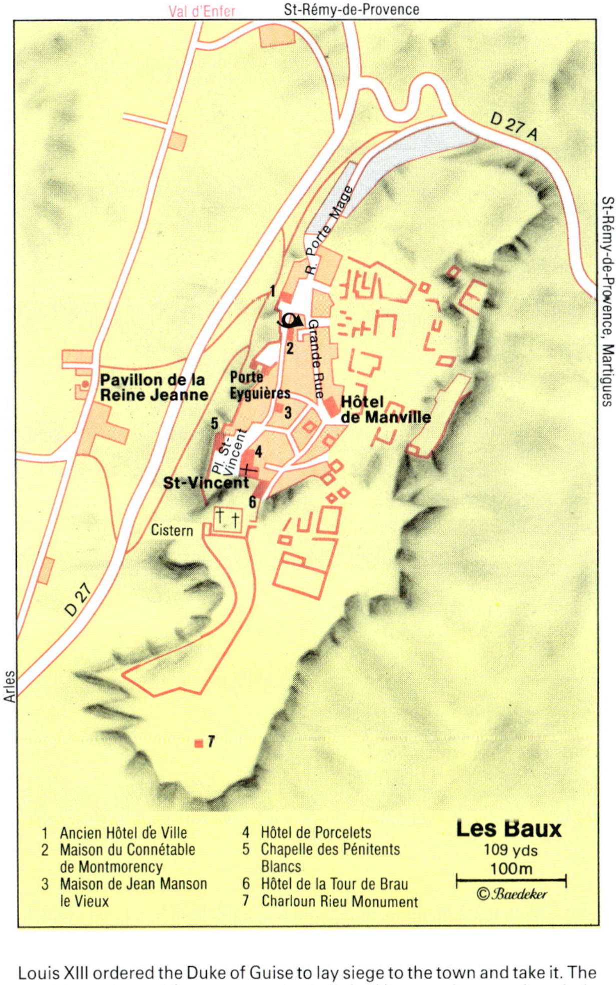


Louis XIII ordered the Duke of Guise to lay siege to the town and take it. The inhabitants longed for peace, and asked the king to take over the whole town and to tear down the fortifications at their expense, which was done two years later. In 1642 Les Baux was given as a gift to the Grimaldi family, who remained Dukes of Les Baux until 1791, when they were dispossessed during a revolution. Charles Maxime de Grimaldi, who died in 1880, was the last to hold the title of Marquis des Baux.
At the beginning of the Industrial Age another aspect quickly became important. In the surrounding countryside in 1821 rich deposits of a mineral were discovered which provides the main basic material for aluminium production, and which was named "bauxite" after the town.

L'Oustaù de Baumanière

This famous restaurant and hotel in the Vallon de la Fontaine – or, to be more exact, its founder Raymond Thulier – has an astonishing history.

*Les Baux-de-Provence in the evening light*

Having grown up in a railway restaurant at Privas in Ardèche run by his mother, Thulier entered the insurance profession in Paris. His hobby was cooking, but he was fifty before he devoted himself full-time to the culinary arts, and eighty when he became the doyen of French master chefs. In 1945 he came to Provence and built his own restaurant in an old oil mill. The official opening was performed by a young official from the Ministry of Tourism, the former grammar school teacher Georges Pompidou. In spite of its rather remote situation Thulier's cuisine was a success, and the Michelin Guide awarded him three stars as early as 1954. Since then the business has expanded further, the Dèpendance Cabro d'Or built and a wine shop added. Thulier was also mayor of Les Baux.

***Lower Town**

Passing the former 17th c. Town Hall and the Porte Eyguières, the ancient town gate, follow the Rue de L'Église to the attractive little Place St-Vincent, the south side of which is formed from rock-hewn walls. There is a fine view from this square towards the west.

St-Vincent

The sturdiness of the Church of St-Vincent, dedicated to St Vincentius, a 4th c. martyr, gives a surprising impression of space. Its present-day form dates from the Romanesque and Gothic periods. The chapels leading off the right-hand aisle have been hewn into the soft stone; in the centre one stands a font contrived from the actual rock. The right aisle is 10th c., from the Carolingian era. The 12th c. nave relects the Romano-Cistercian style. The left-hand aisle is 15th c., from High to Late Gothic; Immediately behind here the Marquis of Les Baux lie buried; their tombs in the subterranean gallery beneath the church are not open to the public.
All the windows of the church are modern and were the gift in 1962 of Prince Rainier of Monaco, the successor to the last Dukes of Les Baux.
At Christmas shepherds celebrate midnight vespers here, an event which already threatens to become a spectacle for the "initiated". As only a few seats are available, anyone wishing to attend is advised to come early and dress warmly.

*Lower town, with St Vincent's Church*

*Hôtel de Manville*

Chapel of the White Penitents

Opposite the church the square is closed off by the 17th c. Chapelle des Pénitents-Blancs; inside can be seen some modern paintings by Yves Brayer.

Hôtel des Porcelets

On the left near the church stands the Hôtel des Porcelets, a 16th c. building which now houses the Musée d'Art Moderne, which is open 8.30am–7pm, in winter until sunset; an entrance ticket for all museums and the Upper Town can be used here. On exhibition are works by contemporary artists, especially from the Provençal region.

Hôtel de Manville

A lane going gently uphill on the left of the museum passes on the right the former Protestant Church (Temple Protestant) and leads to the 16th c. Hôtel de Manville, with its beautiful inner courtyard. This now houses the office of the Mayor and the Office de Tourisme; on the ground floor is a picture gallery and on the second floor a permanent exhibition of modern masters, as well as documents and photographs dealing with Les Baux past and present. Open: summer, 8.30am–8pm; winter, 9am–5pm.

Hôtel de la Tour de Brau

Coming from the Hôtel de Manville, Rue des Fours and Rue du Trencat, the latter a chemin creux (sunken road) cut into the rock, lead to the entrance to the Upper Town. The 14th c. Hôtel de la Tour on the right houses the Musée Archéologique et Lapidaire, exhibiting remains of the fortress and archaeological finds from the surrounding countryside – especially from graves of a Celtic necropolis – as well as information concerning the mining of bauxite.

** **Upper Town**

The best time to visit the Upper Town is in the evening, in order to experience the special light when the sun goes down; the ticket office is open until 7pm, but visitors can of course stay in the Upper Town later than that.

Plateau

On the far side of the 14th c. Chapel of St-Claude-et-St-Blaise – which has been restored and contains an exhibition of olive production and processing – extends a large bare rock plateau, the edge of which falls almost

vertically to the foothills below. This steep slope should be approached with due caution, for it is completely unsecured and the often violent and gusty winds here can be dangerous.
Quite near to the end of the plateau stands a monument to the Provençal poet Charloun Rieu (1846–1924), who belonged to the circle of "Félibres" around Frédéric Mistral. This association was responsible for the renaissance of the Provençal language and culture. From here there is a grandiose panorama into the Valley of the Rhône, the Plain of the Crau and over the Alpilles.

Ruins

The way to the ruined edge of the town runs parallel to the eastern edge of the plateau. The phenomenon of wind erosion which can be observed everywhere on exposed surfaces is impressive.
Only scanty remains of the former castle have survived. Right on the edge of the rock at the highest point is where the keep was built, with its huge windows and spacious proportions; some remains of the foundations of the adjoining residential quarters still exist.
A comprehensive and highly impressive panorama can be enjoyed from the rocky crests which border the Upper Town and which can be climbed by narrow paths and steep steps.

The Lower Town can be reached by a direct path which passes the old Columbarium, or "dove-cote", an Early Christian burial-place with niches for the urns containing ashes.

**View

The best view of Les Baux is from the Plâteau des Bringasses; take the D27 road north, and turn right after 1km/½ mile. From here can be seen "half of Provence", as well as Mont Ventoux and Luberon, the Rhône Valley and Camargue, Aix and Arles.

Cathédrale des Images

About halfway the road to the above viewing point passes the former quarries, some of which were underground. In one such quarry the artist Albert Plécy installed his "Cathedral of Pictures", with slides on various subjects projected onto the giant stone walls some 400m/1300ft in length. Plécy's aim was to create a "total picture", where the observer actually stood within it rather than simply looking at it. Open: 10am–7pm, Nov. 10am–6pm, closed mid-Nov.–early Dec., Jan. and Feb.

## Surroundings of Les Baux

St-Rémy

See entry

Fontvieille

See Montmajour

## Beaulieu-sur-Mer — D5

Département: Alpes-Maritimes
Altitude: sea-level
Population: 4300

Location

Beaulieu-sur-Mer, highly regarded as a marina, lies in the eastern part of the Côte d'Azur, about halfway between Nice and Monaco. Protected from the north winds by ranges of hills, Beaulieu-sur-Mer is a popular summer and winter holiday resort. Abundant vegetation flourishes in the especially mild climate.

Baie des Fourmis

Villa Kerylos

The Baie des Fourmis (Bay of Ants), fringed by a palm-lined promenade, is picturesque. On a spit of land, which closes off the bay towards the north-east, stands the Villa Kerylos, an imitation of an ancient Greek mansion. This building, which since 1928 has been owned by the Institut de France, has a remarkably fine interior with marble and bronze work, mosaics and furniture of the finest materials. However, only a very small number of these objects are in fact antique.

From the Baie des Fourmis the Avenue des Hellènes, the Boulevard Maréchal Leclerc and the fine Boulevard Alsace-Lorraine lead north-east to the well-equipped yacht harbour which is one of the best of its kind on the French Mediterranean coast.

Petite Afrique

Not far east of Beaulieu the modern holiday seaside settlement of Petite Afrique (Little Africa) has been laid out. It is protected by steep cliffs up to 300m/985ft high and has a good pebble beach.

## Surroundings of Beaulieu

### Eze

Location

When travelling to Monaco on one of the Corniches de la Riviera (see Suggested Routes, 2b), the two-part settlement of Eze is to be found 4km/2½ miles north-east of Beaulieu.

*Eze-Village

Eze-Village, the old refuge settlement, has a picturesque situation 427m/1400ft up on a conical rock crowned by the ruins of a castle from which there are marvellous views; it is still surrounded by its 17th c. walls. In its narrow streets can be found many handicraft enterprises and perfumeries. This is where Nietsche drafted the third section of his "Thus spake Zarathustra" composition.
Of interest are the Musée d'Histoire Locale et d'Art Religieux (local and religious art) and the Chapelle des Pénitents Blancs with modern frescoes

*Eze-Village, with its exotic garden*

by J. M. Poulin. The Jardin Exotique (exotic garden) offers flowering shrubs, cacti and a good view.

Eze-Bord-de-Mer

On the coast, dominated by high cliffs, lies the fishing village of Eze-Bord-de-Mer. This place was already well known in ancient days and in more recent times has been developed into an important tourist centre.

## St-Jean-Cap-Ferrat

Location and sights

This friendly villa colony is situated 4km/2 miles south-west of Beaulieu on the promontory of the same name which extends far out into the sea. It has some excellent holiday residences and attractively laid-out gardens.
To the east of the picturesque village centre the Chapel of Ste-Hospice, with a bronze Madonna and a 16th c. tower, stands on the Pointe Ste-Hospice.

Musée Île-de-France

High above the sea in a magnificent park on the road towards Beaulieu can be found the Musée Île-de-France, founded by Ephrussi de Rothschild. It houses a ceiling fresco by Tiepolo, paintings, furniture and other works of art from the 14th to the 19th c. from Europe and the Far East. Guided tours only.

Cap Ferrat

The most southerly tip of the peninsula is Cap Ferrat with its lighthouse – well worth the climb – and a statue of the Virgin Mary.

# Cagnes-sur-Mer D5

Département: Alpes-Maritimes
Altitude: 77m/253ft
Population: 35,500

Location

Cagnes-sur-Mer, which consists of several sections, is situated about 12km/7 miles west of Nice on the far side of the River Var which flows into the Mediterranean at this point.

## *Haut-de-Cagnes

Inland on a conical hill lies the picturesque old village of Haut-de-Cagnes, with narrow little streets and houses built close together within the enclosing walls. It is overlooked by the 14th c. former Château Grimaldi. The castle was taken over in 1536 and rebuilt at the beginning of the 17th c. Since 1939 it has been owned by the town and furnished as a museum, the Musée Ethnographique d'Olivier, Musée d'Art Méditerranée Moderne and Musée Renoir de Souvenir, with an ethnographical collection, information about olive-growing, works by Chagall, Matisse, Renoir, etc. There is an extensive view from the tower. Closed Tues. and mid-Oct.–mid-Nov.
On the way towards the centre of the old village stands the Chapel of Notre-Dame-de-la-Protection, with fine 16th c. frescoes not discovered until 1936, and "Maison Les Colettes", the house in which Renoir (1841–1919) lived and died, a good example of Provençal architecture.

Cros-de-Cagnes

The old fishing port of Cros-de-Cagnes, about 2km/1 mile south of the old village at the mouth of the Cagne, is now a large seaside resort and yacht harbour.

## Surroundings of Cagnes

La Colle-sur-Loup

This place, which is popular with artists, lies 6km/4 miles north-west of Cagnes, amid the fertile foothills of Vence, the scene of vineyards and

*Marina Baie des Anges* ▶

flower-growing. Of interest are the restored 12th c. church and chapel dating from the same period, formerly owned by the monks of Lérins. Nearby stands the Château Le Gaudelet of King François I.

Villeneuve-Loubet

Situated 3km/2 miles south-west of Cagnes, Villeneuve-Loubet, originally a farming village and standing some 2km/1 mile from the coast high up on the left bank of the Loup, has a castle, built originally in the 12th c., with a 30m/98ft high defensive tower; the castle is not open to the public.
In the house where the famous chef Escoffier (1846–1935) was born there is a Museum of Cuisine, which is open Tues.–Sun. 2pm–6pm; displaying culinary objects of the 14th to 20th c.

Marina Baie des Anges

A chain of hills some 50m/165ft high separates the old part of the village from the coastal settlement which was begun in 1930. Here gigantic houses built in pyramids and the newly created Marina-Baie-des-Anges characterise the landscape.

Biot

See Antibes

## Camargue D2

Département: Bouches-du-Rhône
Area: 92,000ha/227,332 acres

Location and importance

The marshy area of the Camargue – so named after the Roman senator Camars who hailed from Arles – includes Grande Camargue, an area of some 720sq.km/280sq.miles between the Grand Rhône and the Petit Rhône, the two arms of the river which divide just short of Arles, together with the Petite Camargue which covers an area of about 200sq.km/77sq.miles west of the Petit Rhône. The river's western arm (Petit Rhône) here forms the boundary between the regions of Provence-Alpes-Côte d'Azur and Languedoc-Roussillon.

Agriculture

Camargue has been used for agriculture since medieval times. It was probably at the end of the 13th c. that the Arabs from Spain introduced rice to the marshy lands of the Camargue. After 1942 rice-growing intensified, but subsequently went into decline as a result of competition and increased draining of the land. In recent years it has been revived, mainly in an attempt to help neutralise the salty nature of the soil. In 1985 50,000 tonnes of rice were grown here, equal to eighteen per cent of France's requirements. The traditional rearing of beef-cattle and horses, together with wine-producing and of course tourism, all play an important part in the economy of the region.

**Landscape

In spite of the enormous amount of tourism, parts of the Camargue are still completely isolated and flat. The Camargue (Provençal Camargo) is an area with a thoroughly individual and often quite melancholy character. Over many centuries the Rhône has deposited detritus, sand and soil in its delta, pushing it ever further out into the sea. As a result, the old port of Aigues-Mortes has receded some 5km/3 miles from the coastline in the course of some 600 years. While this has been happening in the western part of Camargue, the very opposite has occurred in the south-east; Stes-Maries-de-la-Mer, which was some miles inland during the Middle Ages, is now on the coast!
The part nearest the sea, around the lagoon of the Etang de Vaccarès, consists almost entirely of lagoons and reed-infested marshes or dry salt expanses and dunes on which, in places, umbrella pines, juniper bushes and tamarisks thrive.
Waterfowl – in recent years there has been a considerably increased colony of flamingoes, heron, etc. – and even birds of prey are numerous; turtles and beavers can also be found. In winter especially, men on horseback

*La Camargue: horses feeding in the shallow water*

round up half-wild herds ("manades") of sheep, small black cattle and light grey horses. After spending much of their young lives in freedom these well-known Camargue horses are sold for riding or hired out in the holiday season – in many places there are centres with Promenades à Cheval (horse-riding centres).

## Drive through the Camargue

The most favourable starting points for a drive through the Camargue are Arles and St-Gilles (see entries). Road D570 coming from Arles – which is joined after 15km/9 miles near Albaron by the D37 from St-Gilles – leads south-west and ends in Stes-Maries-de-la-Mer (see entry). Initially the road runs through acres of sunflowers, rice-fields and vineyards; as it nears the sea the landscape becomes more steppe-like and halophytes – plants well suited to the salty soil – take over.

Parc Régional de Camargue

The Camargue Regional Nature Park was set up in 1970; covering an area of 820sq.km/320sq.miles, it takes in roughly the whole of Grande Camargue. The aim is to preserve the traditional landscape, provide natural surroundings for the flora and fauna and foster tourism. The southern part, the Etang de Vaccarès (see below) and the adjoining coastal area have been nature reserves since 1975.

Musée Camarguais

Some 10km/6 miles south-west of Arles, on the marshy Plaine de Meyran, by the D570 just before Albaron, lies the Mas du Pont de Rousty. An old sheep-farm now houses the Nature Reserve Centre and the Musée Camarguais, which provides information about the history of the region and way its inhabitants lived. A walk lasting some 1½ hours along a 3.5km/2 mile path will provide instruction on peasant life and rural conditions. Open: Apr. 1st–Sept. 30th 9.15am–5.45pm (July 1st–Aug. 31st to 6.45pm), Oct.

1st–Mar. 31st 10.15am–4.45pm; Oct. 1st–Mar. 31st closed on Tues. and public holidays.

Centre d'Information

At the Etang de Ginès, a small coastal lake (about 4km/2½ miles from Stes-Maries), the Centre d'Information de Ginès was established in 1976. It is dedicated to the first president of the Camargue Nature Park Foundation, François Huet (1905–72). Large projected slides show the flora and fauna of the area and explain the geology and ecology of the Camargue. Between the information centre and the lake large windows afford a panoramic view of the bird sanctuary; telescopes are provided. Open: 9am–12.30pm, 2–6pm; Oct. 1st–Mar. 31 closed Fri. and on public holidays.

Parc Ornithologique

The Pont de Gau bird sanctuary covers more than 12ha/30 acres of marshland. Numerous species of birds, either native to the Camargue or resting during migration, can be observed here. Keen naturalists can obtain information from a building which looks rather like a beach-hut. Many species which are difficult to observe in the wild can be seen here in aviaries constructed to be as near as possible to their native habitat. Open: daily 9am–sunset.

Etang de Vaccarès

Near Albaron (13th c. tower, remains of a fort; pumping station for freshwater irrigation) the D37 branches off from the D570; a signpost reads "Etang de Vaccarès". On the far side of Méjanes this road runs close to the Etang de Vaccarès surrounded by a girdle of reeds. This lake, which has an area of about 6000ha/14,800 acres – varying according to the water-level – is by far the largest in the Camargue, but its average depth is only about 50cm/20in.

Near Villeneuve the D36 B bears off to the right; this is a charming scenic stretch. It follows – often with fine views – the eastern shore of the lake which towards the south gives way to a number of level lagoons dotted with sandbanks.

La Capellière

Here the Ministry of the Environment provides information regarding the Camargue National Park. There are also walkways with instruction boards and hides and observation huts.

Digue à la mer

Near Le Paradis, some 16km/10 miles south of Villeneuve, a little road branches off to the right. The path to the lighthouse, the Phare de la Gacholle, has to be negotiated on foot. There is a fine view from here, with a telescope for bird-watching. From there the road leads past the dyke known as "Digue à la mer" as far as Stes-Maries-de-la-Mer (about 20km/12½ miles). To the south lie more than 30km/19 miles of beaches of fine sand.

*Salin-de-Giraud

Near Salin-de-Giraud lie giant "salt pans", where salt is obtained by the gradual evaporation of sea-water. South of the village huge white heaps of

*Salt in abundance – les Salins-du-Midi*

salt are deposited. From an artificial hill, which is signposted, there is an extensive panorama of the mountains of sea-salt and the huge evaporation basins, the water of which is coloured by microbes with shades of brown, red and violet. Some of the salt undergoes further processing in chemical factories to produce bromide and magnesium salts.

La Palissade

The road now runs south between the embanked Rhône and the salt-pans. Where the road leaves the river stands the La Palissade estate, a museum displaying flora and fauna from the Camargue. There are exhibitions, slide-shows, a herbarium and an aquarium; open 9am–5pm Sept. 1st–June 15th, closed Sat. and Sun. The road ends near the Plage de Piemançon, a broad beach of fine sand with no tourist facilities, forming the eastern end of the Golfe du Lion.
The return journey can be made considerably more quickly on the D36, the course of which is parallel to the Rhône and which shortly before reaching Arles joins the D570. Alternatively, the Grand Rhône can be crossed by ferry near Salin-de-Giraud on to the D35, or the road via Martigues (see entry) and the Chaîne de l'Estaque to Marseilles can be followed.

## Cannes

D4/5

Département: Alpes-Maritimes
Altitude: sea-level
Population: 73,000

Location and importance

The exclusive resort of Cannes marks the western end of the Côte d'Azur in its real sense. It enjoys a sheltered situation on the wide Golfe de la Napoule, with the island group of the Îsles de Lérins offshore.
Because of its exceptionally mild climate, averaging 9·8°C/50°F in winter, its rich subtropical vegetation and its fine beach, Cannes is a tourist centre at all times of the year. The International Film Festival held in April–May is of particular importance.

History

Evidence of an early setlement on Mont Chevalier is given by finds of the Celto-Ligurian Age. In the 2nd c. B.C. the Romans are said to have erected the Castrum Marsellinum here, and in the 11th c. a watch-tower was built, around which an unwalled town later developed. In the 14th c. the town became part of Provence and in 1481 formed part of France. It only became a famous resort after having been discovered to be a healthy place by the Englishman Lord Brougham (1778–1868) who had fled from Nice to Cannes to avoid a raging cholera epidemic. In 1838 the harbour was laid out, and 30 years later a beginning was made with a promenade along the shore.

## Sights

Old Town

The Le Suquet quarter, the Old Town, slopes up to Mont Chevalier (67m/220ft), the summit of which is crowned by the 11th c. watch-tower, from which there is a magnificent view. A few yards to the south stands the Musée de la Castre, which contains Egyptian, Phoenician, Etruscan, Greek and Roman antiques as well as art from the Far East and Central Americ.

North of the tower stands the Church of Notre-Dame de l'Espérance (1541–1648), with a notable 17th c. Madonna on the High Altar and a wooden statue of St Anne, *c.* 1500.

The Boulevard Jean-Hibert leads westward along the shore, passing the square of the same name, to the magnificent Square Mistral. From here the 3km/2 mile long Boulevard du Midi connects with the Corniche de l'Esterel (Corniche d'Or).

Quartier Anglais

Above the Boulevard du Midi extends the Quartier Anglais (English Quarter) with its sumptuous villas. The Boulevard Leader leads up to the Croix des Gardes. situated 164m/538ft above sea-level in a copse of mimosa which blooms in February and March. This is a fine viewpoint with the best light towards evening. 1km/½ mile to the north-west the Rocher de Roquebillière lies 130m/427ft above the little river of the same name.

*Vieux Port

To the east below the Old Town lies the Vieux Port, or Old Port, also known as Port Cannes I; at its north-eastern corner is the Gare Maritime (Marine Railway Station), built in 1957.

To the north the port is bordered by the pretty Allées de la Liberté which are lined with plane trees. In the mornings the fine Marché aux Fleurs (Flower Market) is held here. At the western end of the Allées stands the Hôtel de Ville, or Town Hall, built in 1874–76.

The Rue Félix-Faure, which runs parallel on the north, and its eastern extension, the Rue d'Antibes, are the town's main shopping streets.

Le Cannet

From the northern edge of the Inner Town the broad Boulevard Carnot winds northwards to the beautifully situated villa settlement of Le Cannet from which there are fine views.

*Palais des Festivals

On the east side of the Old Port, at Boulevard de la Croisette 1, stands the Palais des Festivals, opened in 1982. It is an impressive complex of buildings with three large auditoriums; the most modern technical apparatus includes sound studios, simultaneous translation arrangements, audio-visual equipment and large projectors. There are eleven conference rooms, two exhibition halls (one of which has 14,000sq.m/16,745sq.ft of undivided useable space), a casino, a night-club and a restaurant. This is where the annual film festival is held.

*Boulevard de la Croisette

The centre of tourist activity is the Boulevard de la Croisette which extends eastward from the new Palais des Festivals along the Rade de Cannes, with its fine sandy beach; from it there is a magnificent view of the gulf and the offshore Lerin Islands (Îles de Lérins; see below). The boulevard is dominated by luxury hotels – some from the Belle Epoque period – and high-class shops.

In the yacht harbour lies the pirate ship Neptune, built as the backdrop for an adventure film.

The eastern section of the boulevard bends south at the fine Parc de la Roseraie, skirts the new port layout of the Port Pierre Canto and ends at the

LEVEL 4

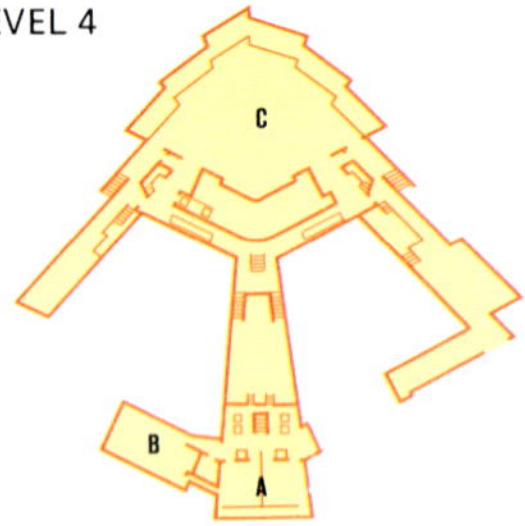


LEVEL 3

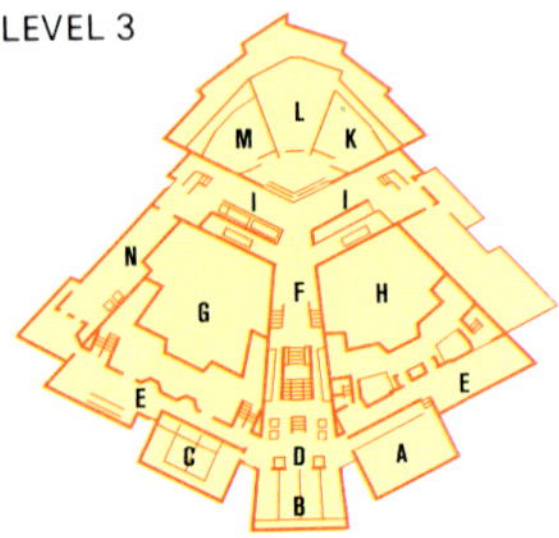


LEVEL 1/2

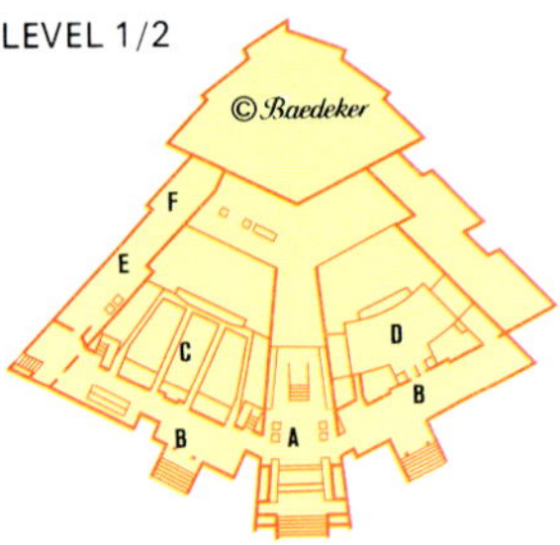


GROUND-LEVEL

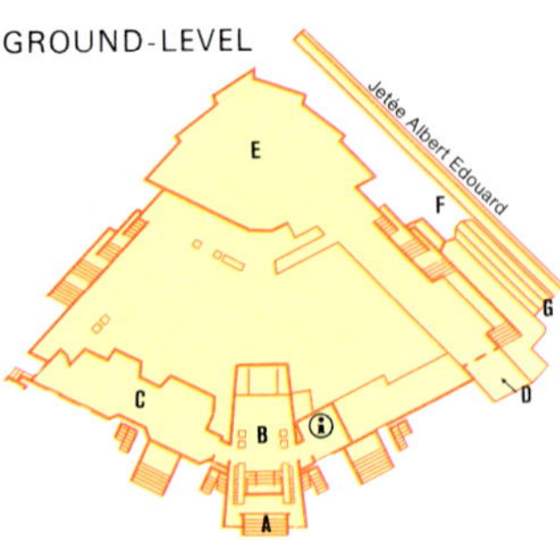


# Cannes Palais des Festivals

LEVELS 5 and 6 (no plan)
Roof Terrace 1700 sq. m (2033 sq. yd)

LEVEL 4
A Rooms I and J (each 80 seats)
B Room K (150 seats)
C Large Reception Hall ''Les Ambassadeurs''

LEVEL 3
A Room a (300 seats)
B Rooms b, c, d and e (each 40 seats)
C Rooms f, g and h (each 50 seats)
D Ante-room
E Foyers
F Internal Corridor (Rue Interieure)
G Grand Auditorium
H Claude Debussy Theatre
I Press Club
K Television Studio
L Press Conference Room (300 seats)
M Radio Studio
N Press Offices

LEVEL 2
F Organisers' Offices
Audio-Visual Production
Projection Rooms and
Interpreters' Booths

LEVEL 1
A Palais Corridor (Rue de Palais)
B Foyers
C Grand Auditorium (hall with 2400 seats)
D Claude Debussy Theatre (1000 seats)
E Administration of the Palais des Festivals

GROUND-LEVEL
A Main Entrance
B Entrance Hall
C Reception and Exhibition Hall
D Casino Entrance
E Casino
F Le Bistingo Restaurant
G Entrance to Car Park

(i) Information

BASEMENT LEVEL 1 (no plan)
Exhibition Area 14,000 sq. m (16,744 sq. yd)

BASEMENT LEVEL 2 (no plan)
Parking for 900 cars; lorry ramp, store, workshops

Cannes: Hôtel Carlton, the epitome of the Côte d'Azur

Cannes: le Vieux Port and Le Suquet, the old town

southern tip of the Pointe de la Croisette by the Port du Palm-Beach and the Palm Beach Casino. On the east side of the peninsula the pleasant Boulevard Eugène-Gazagnaire, with its fine beach, leads north to the Port du Moure Rouge.

La Californie

From the eastern part of the Boulevard de la Croisette the road leads northwards through the district of Cros-Veil on the far side of the railway – where the Église Russe, or Russian Church, on the Boulevard Alexandre-III is well worth seeing – to the especially charming part of the town known as "La Californie", where Picasso lived in 1955. This area is overlooked by the Observatoire de Super-Cannes, which is 325m/1067ft high and has an observation tower, orientation table and the terminus of the old funicular. Below, on the Boulevard des Pins, stands the notable Mémorial St-Georges, erected in memory of the Duke of Albany.

## Surroundings of Cannes

**Îles de Lérins**

The island group of the Îles de Lérins lies between the Golfe de la Napoule and the Golfe Juan. The two principal islands are Ste-Marguerite and St-Honorat. The ferry plies several times a day between Cannes and the islands 4km/2½ miles out.

History

As early as the 5th and 6th c. the islands were an important centre of ecclesiastical erudition and monastic life. In the year 660 the monastery assumed the Rule of St Benedict. Attacks by the Saracens and later by pirates from Genoa affected the monks very severely, and in the 16th c. the convent began to decline into obscurity.

Ste-Marguerite

Ste-Marguerite, 3km/2 miles long and up to 1km/½ mile wide, is the largest island of the group and is covered with eucalyptus and pine woods. On its northern side stands a 17th c. fort, fortified by Vauban, which served for a long time as a prison. Towards the end of the 17th c. the man known as the "Masque de Fer" (Man in the Iron Mask), who was surrounded in secrecy and whose identity has never been established, was held prisoner here.

St-Honorat

About 700m/765yds from Ste-Marguerite, and linked by ferry, lies the Île St-Honorat, 1·5km/1 mile long and up to 400m/438yds wide, and also covered with pine woods. On a tongue of land in the south lie the monastery buildings which were once fortified and, it is believed, were a foundation of St Honoratus, Bishop of Arles, who died in 429.

In the south by the sea stands the impressive Château St-Honorat, the tower built in the 11th c. as a refuge against pirates and later altered; there are beautiful cloisters on the ground floor and on the first floor, and extensive views.

There were formerly seven chapels scattered about the island, but today the only two remaining are the Chapelle St-Sauveur, an Early Christian smooth-walled building, with a diameter of almost 10m/33ft, and the Chapelle de la Trinité, an early medieval cemetery chapel.

**Mandelieu–La Napoule**

The twin villages of Mandelieu–La Napoule, which are bisected by the motorway, are situated 5km/3 miles west of Cannes between the mouths of the rivers Siagne and Argentier at the foot of the Massif du Tanneron.
Picturesquely situated by the sea and popular as a holiday resort, the village sector of La Napoule-Plage is overlooked by a restored 14th c. castle (art exhibition) standing on a porphyry rock. Open: July and Aug. only.
From the nearby hill of San Peire, rising to 131m/430ft above sea-level and with a ruined chapel, there is a view of the coast, with apartment blocks and marinas.

**Théoule-sur-Mer**

In the western part of the Golfe de la Napoule lies the resort of Théoule-sur-Mer, which has an 18th c. soap-works by the sea, remodelled into a manor

*Boulevard de la Croisette, the famous artery of Cannes*

house, and a harbour which dates from the 17th c. The slopes are lined with tiers of apartments in old Sardinian style; in the vicinity of the yacht harbours Port de la Rague and Port de la Galère to the south lies the Pointe de l'Aiguille, above which the settlement of Théoule-Supérieur is highly regarded as a place at which to spend holidays.

**Vallauris–Golfe-Juan**

The locality above the Golfe-Juan, 5km/3 miles north-east of Cannes, with the seaside estate of the same name, was originally called "Vallis Aurea" (Golden Valley). This little town with its potteries, vineyards and orange groves once belonged to the monks of Lérins.

Sights

The only relic of the Middle Ages is the Romanesque chapel, in the beautiful crypt of which Picasso painted between 1952 and 1959 his famous *picture "War and Peace". The monastery, which was fortified in the 12th c., was destroyed in 1569 and rebuilt during the Renaissance. Today it houses the Musée National d'Art Moderne (open: Wed.–Mon., Apr.–Sept., 10am–6pm; Oct.–Mar. 2pm–5pm). In front of the church – where there is a market in the morning – stands Picasso's sculpture "Man with a Sheep".

Pottery

Pottery has been important in Vallauris since the time of the Romans. After the Second World War the activity of Pablo Picasso gave the place a fresh impetus. It was here that in 1946 Picasso got to know the ceramic-artists Suzanne and Georges Ramié and became enthusiastic about this new material. Today there are about a hundred potters working in Vallauris and their products are sold in the streets. The biennial pottery fair assures the future of this craft. The Madoura workshop near Avenue Clémenceau, headed by Alain Ramié, still produces pottery based on Picasso's designs as well as some fine work of its own.

"Man with a sheep", by Picasso . . .

. . . and potters' workshops

## Carpentras

C3

Département: Vaucluse
Altitude: 102m/335ft
Population: 26,000

Location

The little industrial town of Carpentras lies between Mont Ventoux to the north-east and the Plateau de Vaucluse to the south-east, in a plain which is open to the Rhône. The River Alzon flows past the north of the town centre.

History

The town is descended from the ancient Carpentoracte which, from 1320 until the French Revolution in 1789, was the capital of the Papal county of Venaissin. From 1342 onwards it offered special protection to Jews and – as in Cavaillon and Avignon – they had their own quarter in the town.

### Sights

St Siffrein

In the town centre stands the former Gothic Cathedral of St Siffrein, started in 1405 and consecrated in 1519. The stump of a tower is to be seen on either side of the west façade which was altered in the 17th c. but which nevertheless remains incomplete; in more recent times another tower was added on the south side. The south doorway of 1470/80, the "Porte Juive" (Jews' Gate), revels the typical flamboyant style of Late Gothic. Jews who wished to be baptised would enter by this doorway.
The nave, without transepts, has six bays, the last two combined into a vault, and is flanked by chapels. The differing patterns of the walls bear witness to the long building period. The interior of the church is richly decorated and includes a number of remarkable panels as well as an altarpiece consisting of a radiant halo of gilded wood (1694) by Jacques Bernus. In a chapel to the left of the choir is a collection of religious art.

*St-Siffrein: Porte Juive, with Late-Gothic flamboyant decoration*

On the north side of the church are the remains of the Romanesque building and a Roman triumphal arch dating from the 1st c. A.D., which had been incorporated in the Romanesque church, and on the narrow side of which prisoners and trophies of war are represented.

Palais de Justice

Adjoining the north side of the church is the Palais de Justice which was built in 1640 in imitation of Italian Baroque style. It was formerly the episcopal palace. The interior has some magnificently furnished rooms including the Bishop's Room (18th c. prayer-desk), the Council Room and the Criminal Court (cartouches with views of the towns of the Venaissin). A permit to visit can be obtained from the Office de Tourisme.

Museums

The most important museums of Carpentras are housed in a large common complex (Boulevard Albin-Durand) in the west of the Inner Town.
The Musée Comtadin has collections of the ethnology of the surroundings. The Musée Duplessis possesses several notable panels created by local painters (Duplessis, Lebrun, etc.) as well as some of Italian and Dutch origin; the Musée Sobirats houses artistic handicraft. Open: Wed. to Mon. 10am–noon, 2–6pm.
The Musée Lapidaire, in the Chapel of the Grey Penitents (5 rue Ste Maries) has finds from the Iron Age to the early Middle Ages as well as a collection of Natural History. Visits by previous notification to the Musée Comtadin.

Bibliothèque Inguimbertine

The Bibliothèque Inguimbertine, the municipal library, is housed in the north wing of the museum complex. It is named after Bishop d'Inguimbert (in office 1735–57), a bibliophile who bought up numerous libraries. Later the collection was increased by donations, so that today there are about 220,000 volumes available as well as manuscripts, prints, etc. Open: Mon. 2–6.30pm, Tues.–Fri. 9.30am–4.30pm, Sat. 9.30am–noon.

Synagogue

The Synagogue of Carpentras (Place de la Mairie) is the oldest remaining in France. It was built in the 15th c. and restored in the 18th c. and again in

1958. On the ground floor and in the basement are the ritual baths, some partly dating from the 14th c., as well as the kosher bakery; on the first floor is the place of worship which received its present furnishings in the 18th c. Open: Mon.–Fri. 10 am–noon, 3–5pm, closed on public holidays.

Hôtel Dieu

The Hôtel Dieu (hospital; 1750) in the Place Aristide Briand also goes back to the time of Bishop d'Inguimbert. This two-storeyed Classical building at the southern end of the town centre comprises an inner courtyard with two fountains; a monumental staircase leads to the upper floor. On the ground floor the pharmacy with its original furnishings is of interest. Open: Mon., Wed., Thur. 9–11.30 am.

## Surroundings of Carpentras

Venasque

South-east of Carpentras (11km/7 miles) the village of Venasque has a picturesque situation on the Vaucluse. Here the 13th c. church and the baptistery (6th and 12th c.) are worthy of note.

*Gorges de la Nesque

The Gorge of the Nesque is reached from Carpentras by driving east along D942 to Villes-sur-Auzon (17km/10½ miles) or as a continuation of the drive over Mont Ventoux (see entry). The gorge with its grey and light-brown rock walls begins a few kilometres beyond the picturesque old village of Monieux (12th c. tower; medieval houses and gates). The road follows the right bank of the Nesque and in about 6km/4 miles reaches a viewpoint (Belvedère; marked by pillars). Opposite can be seen the deeply fissured Rocher de Cire (872m/2862ft). At the exit from the gorge there is a magnificent view of the intensely cultivated plain around Carpentras to the south of Mont Ventoux.

# Castellane D4

Département: Alpes-de-Haute-Provence
Altitude: 724m/2376ft
Population: 1400

Location

The township of Castellane lies in the south-east of Provence (54km/34 miles south-east of Digne) on the Route Napoléon (see Suggested Routes 3a) and on the River Verdon (see entry), which to the west of here flows through the well-known gorges. Castellane is, therefore, of touristic importance as the starting-point for a visit to the Grand Canyon du Verdon.

The town

On the northern edge of Castellane there are some remains of the old walls, the most important relic of which is the Tour Pentagonale (five-angled tower).

At the western edge of the Old Town with its narrow streets rises the picturesque Tour de l'Horloge (14th c. clock-tower). Of interest here are the Fountaine aux Lions (Lion Fountain; partly Romanesque) and the Church of St-Victor, originally 12th c. but altered later on several occasions.

"Roc"

Over the little town towers a mighty almost cubic block of rock, 184m/604ft high, on which stands the little pilgrimage chapel of Notre-Dame du Roc (1703). On the rock there was once a Celtic oppidum which later became Petra Castellana. In the 14th c. the settlement was moved into the valley and surrounded by a wall. To the rear of the parish church at the eastern end of the Old Town (not particularly important) a path leads to the rear of the limestone block and past the Stations of the Cross up to the top, from where there is a good view of Castellane and of the river as it flows into the gorge.

*The mighty rock of Castellane*

## Châteauneuf-du-Pape

C2

Département: Vaucluse
Altitude: 117m/384ft
Population: 2100

Location

The famous wine town of Châteauneuf-du-Pape lies between Orange and Avignon in a gently undulating landscape near the left bank of the Rhöne away from the main road.

Viticulture

Châteauneuf-du-Pape is the centre of an area exclusively devoted to the growing of vines, as the pebbly soil is unsuitable for any other form of agriculture. From some 3200ha/7907 acres of vineyards about 100,000 hectolitres (2,200,000 gallons) of wine are produced, 98% of which is red wine, considered to rank with the wines of Bordeaux and Burgundy as one of the best in France. According to the Appellation Controlée the wine must contain 12.5% of alcohol, the highest in France (it actually contains 13–14%). The wine is made from thirteen different varieties of grape, so that its character depends on the establishment in which it is produced.

Châteauneuf-du-Pape is a strong, full-bodied wine which takes at least four or five years to reach maturity. A lighter wine has been successfully produced which can be drunk when it is younger, but this is not the traditional Châteauneuf-du-Pape.

The impetus for the standardisation of the quality of wine and the corresponding grading originated in Châteauneuf (see Practical Information, Wine).

There are many opportunities to visit the wine cellars and to taste the wines ("visite du cave", "dégustation de vins"). The Caves du Père Anselme Museum, a completely tourist establishment (open: 9am–noon and 2–6pm) has interesting exhibits on the history of viticulture. The cellars and

*Vineyards at Châteauneuf-du-Pape*

bottling plant can also be visited. The wines on sale here, although not cheap, are not exactly of the highest quality.

The town

Châteauneuf-du-Pape lies on a gently sloping hill, clustered about the ruins of the castle which the popes built as a summer residence at the time of their exile in Avignon and which gave the place its name. Only the high tower and remains of the walls are still to be seen, but there are rewarding views of Avignon, the Dentelles de Montmirail and Mont Ventoux.
The new stretch of the TGV high-speed railway line is scheduled to run through the area of Châteauneuf-du-Pape. It will divide villages and vineyards and there is understandable opposition to the proposal.

## Corniches de la Riviera

See Suggested Routes 2b

## Digne C4

Département: Alpes-de-Haute-Provence
Altitude: 608m/1995ft
Population: 17,000

Situation and importance

Digne lies in the heart of Provence, approximately on a line joining Grenoble and Cannes, in the foothills of the Alps. It is a spa, the headquarters of lavender growing and the centre of the Hautes-Alpes nature reserve.

The Town

The 15th c. Cathedral of St-Jérome has an elevated situation in the Old Town. In the Romanesque former Cathedral of Notre-Dame-du-Bourg

(12th–13th c.) can be seen remains of wall-paintings of the 14th–16th c. as well as a Merovingian altar.

## Surroundings of Digne

Lac de Serre-Ponçon

There is a rewarding 60km/37 mile drive from Digne to the north (at first not on the direct road D900 but west of this on the D900A) through the Clue de Barles and the Clue de Verdaches, two romantic gorges; then over the Col de Maure (1347m/4421ft) to the Lac de Serre Ponçon (see Gap). After leaving Le Vernet on the return journey take the D900 instead of the D900A and cross the Col du Labouret (1240m/4070ft).

## Donzère-Mondragon C2

Région: Rhône-Alpes
Département: Drôme
Altitude: 64m/210ft

Location

The Rhône Dam was constructed to the north of Bollène on an arm of the Rhône between the two villages of Donzère and Mondragon (between Montélimar and Orange) and this gives it its name.

Rhône Dam

Between Donzère (in the north) and Mondragon (in the south) the 28km/13 mile-long Canal de Donzère avoids a very narrow stretch of the Rhône, into which flow the rivers Conche and Ardèche (see entry).
The Ursine de Collène, one of the river power stations, lies not far north of the village of the same name. As well as the buildings housing the turbines, it includes a lock for canal traffic. The construction, which was completed in 1952, is 240m/788ft long and 15m/49ft high. On the downstream side a road crosses the canal and on the west side of this there is a car park. The interior of the power station is not open to the public.
A short way downstream from Bollène there is a very good view of the canal from the suspension bridge, across which runs road D994 to St-Esprit (see entry).

Nuclear power station

About 2km/1¼ miles north of the dam lies the Complexe Eurodif, a diffusion plant for the enrichment of uranium, together with its associated installations. Its capacity is sufficient to produce some 25% of the world demand for enriched uranium and it is therefore of great importance for the economic development of the Tricastin area. Eurodif is a joint project of Belgium, France, Italy and Spain.
The four heavy water reactors of the Tricastin nuclear power station, each with a capacity of 900 MW, produce over 20 million kilowatt hours of electricity annually.

## Draguignan D4

Département: Var
Altitude: 181m/594ft
Population: 28,000

Location

Draguignan lies about 27km/17 miles inland of Fréjus, north of the Massif des Maures and the Valley of the River Artuby which borders these mountains.

History

In the 5th c. the area was Christianised by Hermentarius, the first Bishop of Antibes. According to legend the Bishop had won the confidence of the

inhabitants by killing a dragon which had threatened the whole countryside and laid it to waste. The name of the town also recalls this episode; it appears to be derived from "dragon" and the legendary monster figures in the arms of the town.
In the 17th c. when Anne of Austria was acting as a Regent for her under-aged son Louis XIV, the town was surrounded by a stout defensive wall. During the French Revolution Draguignan was the district capital and then the capital of the Département of Var.

Townscape

The old town centre of Draguignan is clustered about the Tour de l'Horloge (clock tower) which stands on a rock from which there is a fine view. Normally the tower is closed but the key can be obtained at the Office de Tourisme. The broad streets south of the Old Town, which are unusual in a small town, were laid out by Baron Haussmann who was largely responsible for the infrastructure of Paris (he was Prefect there from 1853 to 1870).

*Museums

Not far north-west of the clock tower, in the Rue de la République, stands a former 17th c. Ursuline convent which was later the summer residence of the Bishop of Fréjus. It now houses a museum (open: Tues.–Sat 10–11.30am and 3–6pm) which has a number of treasures (Rembrandt: "Child blowing soap-bubbles"; Franz Hals: "Kitchen Interior", as well as paintings by Van Loo, J. Parrocel and Ziem, and a sculpture by Camille Claudel. Also notable are ceramics (Moustiers, Sèvres), furniture, French and Flemish 17th c. painting, an illuminated manuscript (with pictures) of the "Roman de la Rose", the most important work of courtly poetry in France (12th c.) and an illustrated Bible in Latin with 2000 engravings which dates from 1493 and which came from a workshop in Nuremberg.

## Surroundings of Draguignan

Lorgues

The little town of Lorgues, 13km/8 miles south-west of Draguignan, is a centre for the production of olives and olive-oil; it has a beautiful Old Town and a fine boulevard lined with plane-trees. In the Classic Collegiale St-Martin (parish church; 17th c.) can be seen a statue of the Virgin which is attributed to Pierre Puget.

Le Thoronet

See entry

*Entrecastaux

Entrecastaux, situated to the west of Draguignan (31km/19 miles via Salernes, or about 20km/12 miles from Le Thoronet) has an impressive castle with severe architecture; this dates essentially from the 17th c. and was the seat of the Comte de Grignan, the stepson of Madame de Sévigné (see Grignan). The castle, which is open to the public, was renovated after the Thirty Years' War and contains furniture and objets d'art from many countries. The spacious park was laid out by Le Nôtre who was also responsible for the park of Versailles. Entrecastaux itself, a medieval, typical Provençal village, with narrow streets and house façades, is a protected monument. Worth seeing are the fortified church of St-Sauveur, the 17th c. washing place and Nôtre Dame de l'Aube which dates from the 12th c.

# Entrevaux D4

Département: Alpes-de-Haute-Provence
Altitude: 515m/1690ft
Population: 700

*The village

Amid the picturesque scenery of the upper reaches of the River Var, 43km/27 miles north-east of Castellane and 70km/43 miles north-west of Nice, lies the old town of Entrevaux on the left bank of the river. 135m/443ft

Draguinan: Tour d'Horloge

Entrevaux: Town Gate and Citadel

above the village towers a steep rocky crag crowned by a Citadel. The finest view of the township and the citadel is to be had from the road to the Col de Felines/Col de Buis, which winds its way up the valley above the village.

History

Entrevaux was founded in the 11th c. Because of its position Louis XIV ordered Vauban to build new fortifications during the war between France and Savoy. he linked the citadel with the village and had bastions and towers erected.
Entrevaux is the birthplace of Augustin Bonnetty (1798–1879) the founder of the "Annales de la Philosophie Chrétienne".

Sights

The Cathedral (built 1610–27) is richly decorated, partly Baroque partly Classical. The main altar has a fine retable depicting the Assumption of the Virgin Mary, which like the choirstalls dates from the 17th c. The "Descent from the Cross" (on the left) is ascribed to Jouvenet. On the left of the entrance stands the silver reliquary bust of St John the Baptist. Every year on the Saturday preceding June 24th this reliquary is taken to the Church of St-Jean-du-Desert, 12km/7½ miles away.
On the Sunday afternoon the solemn procession of the "St-Jeannistes", wearing local uniforms carries the bust back, running the last hundred metres through the town.
An old house in the Rue Serpente contains a small motorcycle museum. The oldest machine dates from 1901; all are in working order.

Steam trains

Entrevaux lies on the narrow-gauge railway Annot–Puget-Théniers, part of the line from Nice to Digne (see Practical Information, Railways). On some Sundays from the beginning of May until the end of October a special train operates on this line; it is hauled by a steam locomotive of the Mallet type, built in 1923 by Henschel in Kassel, and is made up of old carriages. Information – indispensible, since there is only one return journey – can be obtained from Chemins de Fer de la Provence, Gare du Sud, 33 Avenue Malausséna, F-06000 Nice; tel. 93 88 28 56.

## Esterel (Massif de l'Esterel) D4

Départements: Var, Alpes-Maritimes
Altitude: up to 618m/2028ft

Location

The Esterel Mountains rise immediately behind the coast between St-Raphaël in the west and Cannes in the east. They are bordered in the north by the Valley of the Argentière and in the west by the Valley of the Reyran.

Topography

The Esterel Mountains are formed of old volcanic rock, predominately of porphyry, the characteristic red colour of which is a feature of the landscape. The proliferation of conifers, cork-oaks and coriaceous trees which formerly covered the entire massif, has in recent years fallen victim to devastating forest fires.

*Mont Vinaigre

The highest peak of the Esterel Mountains is Mont Vinaigre (618m/2028ft) near to its northern escarpment. It can be reached from Fréjus (see entry) on road N7, from which in 11km/7 miles a narrow forest road branches off. There is an extensive panorama from the summit.

*Pic de l'Ours

From the coastal village of Agay (see St-Raphaël), situated on the Corniche de l'Esterel, a road leads inland and encircles (mostly as a single-track road) the Pic de l'Ours (496m/1628ft). This summit in the eastern part of the mountain range, from which there is an extensive view, is best reached from the nearby Col Nôtre-Dame, to which the mountain road climbs with numerous bends. From this stretch of road there are magnificent views of the deeply fissured rocky coast. It takes about half an hour's climbing to reach the summit of the Pic de l'Ours on which there is a radio and television transmitter. The panorama from here is highly impressive.

*Corniche de l'Esterel

The Corniche de l'Esterel (N98) is a charming road which winds its way along the rocky coast between St-Raphaël and Cannes. It runs through the

*The coast of the Esterel Massif*

resort of Boulouris, passes the impressive Cap du Drammont (lighthouse; offshore the little Île d'Or) and the village of Agay which has a fine situation on a bay; on the Pointe de la Baumette is a memorial to the aviator and writer Antoine de St-Exupéry. The road then continues through Anthéor with the Pic du Cap Roux (452m/1482ft; rewarding view) rising on the left, Le Trayas, Miramar (with a marina), La Galère (in the holiday complex of Port-la-Galère are some remarkable grotto-like houses) and Théoule-sur-Mer. Cannes is then reached via La Napoule.

## Etang de Berre — C3

Département: Bouches du Rhône
Area: 15,000ha/37,065 acres

**Location**

The Etang de Berre is a large lagoon to the north-west of Marseilles. It is connected to the Mediterranean by the Caronte Canal to the west; in the south is the Chaîne de l'Estaque, a ridge up to 279m/916ft high; to the west extends the Plain of the Crau.

**Topography**

The Etang de Berre is a popular recreation area for the people of Marseilles and district; nevertheless on the southern and eastern shores there is a great deal of industry as well as the large airport of Marseilles and its associated satellite towns. The northern shore, however, with its quiet little communities and gentle landscape is reminiscent of the atmosphere of the lakes in northern Italy.

(See also Suggested Routes, 1c)

**Martigues**

(see entry)

**Salon**

(see entry)

## Fontaine-de-Vaucluse — D3

Département: Vaucluse
Altitude: 80m/263ft
Population: 600

***Location**

The little village of Fontaine-de-Vaucluse, well known for its spring (the source of the River Sorgue) and for the Italian poet and humanist Petrarch, lies in the west of Provence about 30km/19 miles east of Avignon.

The village, although often thronged with tourists, is charmingly situated at the end of the valley. The surrounding hollow (*vallis clausa*) has given the place its name. Fontaine-de-Vaucluse can be reached on a by-road; there are extensive parking places near the village centre.

**History**

Fontaine-de-Vaucluse was made famous by the Italian poet and humanist Francesco Petrarca (Petrarch; 1304–74); he was born in Arezzo in Italy but took up residence in the former Papal town of Avignon and later withdrew to his country seat in the Vaucluse where he devoted himself entirely to his literary pursuits.

### Sights

**The Village**

In the centre of the village lies the pretty Place de la Colonne, shaded by plane trees; a column here commemorating Petrarch was erected in 1804 to mark the 500th year of his birth. Around the square are restaurants and bars, some with terraces by or above the river.

*Valley of Fontaine-de-Vaucluse*

*Water-wheel at Isle-sur-la-Sorgue*

On the right bank of the Sorgue, in the house in which Petrarch is reputed to have lived, there is a little museum devoted to the poet and his works. Open: Apr. 15th–Oct. 15th: Wed.–Mon. 9.30am–noon, 2–6.30pm; at other periods only on Sat. and Sun.

Leaving the car park and before reaching the Place de la Colonne there can be seen on the right the Romanesque Church of St-Véran, dating from the first half of the 12th c.; in the crypt is the grave of St Véran who was Bishop of Cavaillon in the 6th c.

Musée d'Histoire

The very interesting Musée d'Histoire was opened in 1990 in a former paper factory on the road to the source of the Sorgue. It is dedicated to the "dark years" of the German occupation and the Resistance in the Vacluse. Themes include the trauma of defeat, everyday life and its difficulties and the collaboration of the Pétain government with the Nazis.

Open: Sept. 1st–Oct. 15th and Apr. 15th–June 30th: Wed.–Mon. 10am–noon and 2–6pm; July 1st–Aug.31st: 10am–8pm, Oct. 16th–Dec. 12th: Sat. and Sun. 10am–noon and 1–5pm; Mar. 1st–Apr. 14th: Sat. and Sun. 10am–noon and 2–6pm.

Spring

The Fontaine de Vaucluse is a resurgent spring at the foot of a vertical rock wall 200m/656ft high. Here the water seeping through the limestone of the Plateau de Vaucluse emerges, and according to the amount of precipitation the level of the water and the force of the spring vary considerably. It is most impressive in the spring, when the snow is melting.

It is reached by a roadway 800m/875yds long which is generally only passable on foot because of the numerous stalls selling souvenirs of all kinds; there are no parking facilities. On the right at the edge of the village and by the river is a cave museum ("Le Monde Souterraine"; open: daily 10am–noon and 2–6.30pm; closed mid-Nov.–Jan., Mon., Tues. in low season; guided tours every 30 minutes) which provide information about the nearby spring.

Further along the path is a paper-mill with a great water-wheel and this has now been set up as a workshop open to the public in which paper is made according to 15th century methods.
On the mountain spur on the far side of the river, which appears turquoise green on acount of the water plants, can be seen the ruins of the castle built by the Bishops of Cavaillon. The roadway continues upwards into the narrowing valley beside the river which is fringed with ancient plane trees and which rushes down in foaming cascades (hidden beneath the rocks when the water level is low). Set into the rock on the left above a small spring can be seen a tablet, placed here in 1963 by the Dante Society in memory of Petrarch and his beloved Laura.

## Surroundings of Fontaine-de-Vaucluse

Branching of the Sorgue

Shortly before reaching the township of Isle-de-la-Sorgue the river divides into two arms. One winds its way northwards to Velleron, a typical Provençal village; the other flows through Isle to Thor, where the Romanesque Church of Nôtre Dame du Lac (12th c.) towers above the water like a shipwreck.

Isle-sur-la-Sorgue

After the "touristic attractions" of Fontaine-de-Vaucluse the atmosphere of the former little industrial town of Isle-sur-la-Sorgue (17km/10½ miles from Fontaine and 23km/14 miles from Avignon) comes as a welcome relief. By the Sorgue, which divides here into several canals and reminds the visitor of Venice, 70 water-mills used to provide power for papermaking, cereal poduction, oil pressing, woollen and silk mills and a tannery. Six of the water-mills still exist and have been restored, including those on the Avenue des 4 Otages (on the edge of the park), in the Place E. Char and the Place V. Hugo. The church dates from the 17th c. and has a richly decorated interior; during the Revolution the art treasures which had been confiscated were assembled here and formed one of the finest Baroque collections in Provence. Other buildings worth seeing are the public corn store of 1779 (now the Office de Tourisme), the Hôtel Donadeï de Campredon, an L-shaped palace of 1773/1775 (Rue Dr. Tallet; exhibitions of important artists) and the Hospital (Place des Fr. Bruns) with its wrought-iron gate of 1762 and the wood-panelled Apothacary's, which houses a collection of Moustiers vessels and a gigantic bronze mortar.

## Fréjus D4

Département: Var
Altitude: 21m/70ft
Population: 42,000

Location

The town of Fréjus is situated in the eastern section of the French Riviera between the Massif des Maures and the Massif de l'Esterel. Not far to the south-east the River Argens flows into the Mediterranean.

History

Whether the site of the Forum Julii, founded by Caesar, was already settled in pre-Roman times has not been conclusively proved. Under the Emperor Augustus the place became a royal port and was linked to the sea by a canal 1200m/1313yds long and 30m/33yds wide. In the 4th c. Fréjus became the see of a bishop, and in the 10th c. it suffered from attacks by the Saracens. From the 12th c. onwards the development was frequently influenced by epidemics of plague. The harbour had to be finally abandoned in the 18th c. because of silting up. In August 1944 Allied forces landed here.
The breaching of the Malpasset Dam in 1959 was a catastrophe. The mighty rush of water down the valley caused 421 deaths and buried the town under mud.

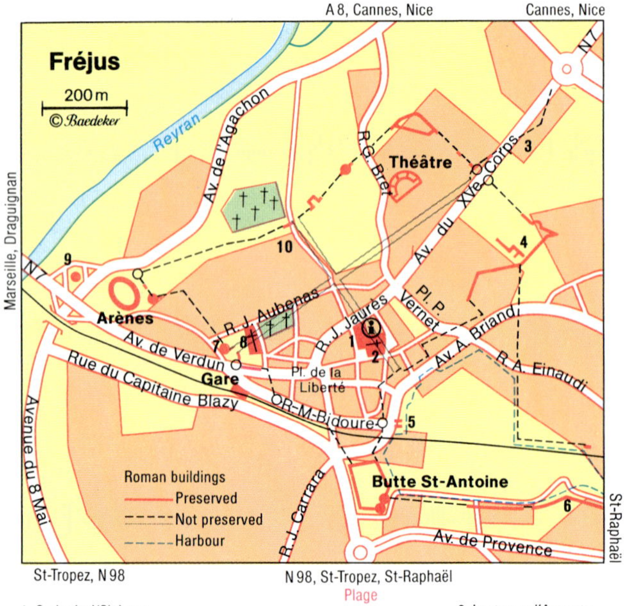


1 Cathedral/Cloister
2 Hôtel de Ville
3 Aqueduct
4 Platform (Praetorium)
5 Porte d'Oree
6 Lanterne d'Auguste
7 Porte des Gaules
8 St-François-de-Paule
9 Columns
10 Porte d'Agachon

## Cathedral

**Opening times**
Apr. 1st–Sept. 30th
Tues.–Mon.
9am–7pm;
Oct. 1st–Mar. 30th.
9.30am–noon,
2–5.30pm.

**Guided tours**

The cathedral, built in the 11th and 12th c. is almost completely surrounded by other buildings; only the doorway leading into the narthex (lobby) is visible from the outside. Above rises the tower with its spire, rectangular in the lower part but octagonal above.
The narthex of the cathedral is entered through the south doorway with its impressive Renaissance doors (1530), which, however, are usually protected by wooden shutters and are shown only on guided tours. Some of the carvings are ornamental, others represent scenes from the lives of the Virgin Mary, St Peter and St Paul; in the borders can be seen symbols of the Saracen wars.

*Baptistery

To the left of the narthex is the Baptistery, a pre-Romanesque octagonal building of the 4th or 5th c. The arcades are borne on eight pillars; six of these came from older buildings (three pairs of differing marble). In the centre stands the font. There were originally two doors to the chapel; the person to be baptised came in through the lower door and left by the higher one.

Interior

In the two-aisled cathedral can be seen, left of the entrance, two marble tombs (17th c.), a wooden Crucifix (16th c.) and a beautiful 16-part altarpiece (15th c.) by Jacques Durandi (died about 1470; school of Nice); in the chapel to the left of the High Altar are two other bishops' tombs (14th and 15th c.).

*Cloister

Steps from the narthex give access to the two-storeyed cloister. It is composed of delicate pillars and in the coffered ceiling can be seen a cycle of

*Fréjus: Cloister . . .* *. . . and gateway*

scenes from the Apocalypse, dating from the 14th and 15th c., not all of which have been preserved. In the middle of the cloister is a well, 16m/53ft deep.

Musée Archéologique

On the north side of the cloister is a double staircase, the steps of which were once used as seats for the nearby Roman amphitheatre. The upper storey of the cloister was originally also enclosed on all four sides, but a great deal was destroyed in the French Revolution, so that only one side of the gallery now remains. In the adjoining room can be found the Musée Archéologique with a Roman mosaic floor and other finds of the Greek and Roman eras.

## Other Sights

Amphitheatre

he Roman Amphitheatre (Arènes) in the Rue Henri Vadon dates from 1st–2nd c. AD. It measures 114m/125yds by 82m/90yds and once had accommodation for 10,000 spectators. To a great extent it is unrestored and also largely free of modern buildings. On the north side the oval leans against the slope, while on the south side an elaborate vaulted construction supports the steps from below. Open: Apr. 1st–Sept. 30th: Wed.–Mon. 9.30–11.45am and 2–6. 15pm; Oct. 1st–Mar. 31st: Wed.–Mon. 9–11.45am and 2–4.15pm.

Aqueduct

In the north-east of the town, on the N7, there are still some remains of the Roman aqueduct which brought water from the Esterel Mountains.

Roman Theatre

Not far west of the aqueduct are the remains of a Roman theatre laid out in a semicircle.

Pagoda

Outside Fréjus to the north, on the road leading to the Esterel Mountains, can be seen a pagoda, a somewhat unconventional sight with its vivid coloration.

Fondation Daniel Templon

This private museum in the Capitou industrial zone houses a collection of works by important artists of the last thirty years. Access is by the D37 to the junction with the A8 in the direction of Cannes; at the roundabout immediately before the tollbooth turn into the industrial zone, then along the A8. Open: July 1st–Sept. 14th: daily 10am–7pm; Sept. 15th–June 15th: Sat. and Sun. 10am–6pm.

## Surroundings of Fréjus

Barrage de Malpasset

Access: follow road D37 which leads to the A8 motorway, but just before the junction turn right and follow the valley of the Reyran upstream. The road, which is much used by heavy lorries and in its final part not made up, goes under the motorway and ends not far below the Barrage de Malpasset, the dam which burst in 1959. About 90 minutes should be allowed to wander around the remains of the dam; there is an explanatory diagram and a general sketch near the path.
Looking at the gigantic blocks of reinforced concrete which were torn away by the flood wave and which today lie strewn about everywhere, gives some idea of the enormous force of the water as it rushed towards the sea from the reservoir.

Le Muy

The lively community of Le Muy, 11km/7 miles west of Fréjus at the confluence of the rivers Nartuby and Argens, is situated in an area of intensive agriculture. The 15th c. church and the round Tour Charles-Quint (tower of Charles V) are notable.
Anglo-American parachute troops landed here on August 15th 1944.
About 2.5km/1½ miles south-west on the slope of the Montagne de Roquebrune (up to 372m/1022ft; fine views and peculiar rock formations) stands the Chapelle Nôtre-Dame-de-la-Roquette to which there are pilgrimages on March 25th, the second Monday after Easter and September 8th.

# Ganagobie (Abbaye de Ganagobie) C/D3

Département: Alpes-de-Haute-Provence
Altitude: 660m/2166ft

Location and importance

On a plateau which was already settled in prehistoric times, situated 350m/1149ft above the valley of the Durance, stands Ganagobie Abbey (12th c.) an example of Provençal Romanesque architecture. It is celebrated for its mosaics which were made between 1135 and 1170 and which are some of the rarest surviving works of art of this size and importance. The view from the plateau is equally fine. Ganagobie is reached from Manosque by taking N96 and D30 (27km/17 miles) and from Digne along N85, D4 and N96 (35km/22 miles).

**View

Going east from the church along the "Allee des Moines" which is bordered by holm oaks, we reach a rocky ledge from which – as if from a balcony – the view extends over the valley of the Durance and the Plateau of Valensole as far as the area of the pre-Alps around Digne; on clear days the Alps themselves (Pelvoux, Monte Viso) can even be seen.
From the western edge (in the opposite direction from the church), past prehistoric standing stones, presumably of astronomical significance, there is a prospect over the Forcalquier Depression to the Montagne du Lubéron.

## *Abbey

History

After the foundation of a monastery by the Bishop of Sisteron, Jean III, and the assimilation of this monastery into the already powerful Cluny in 935, it

## Ganagobie Abbey

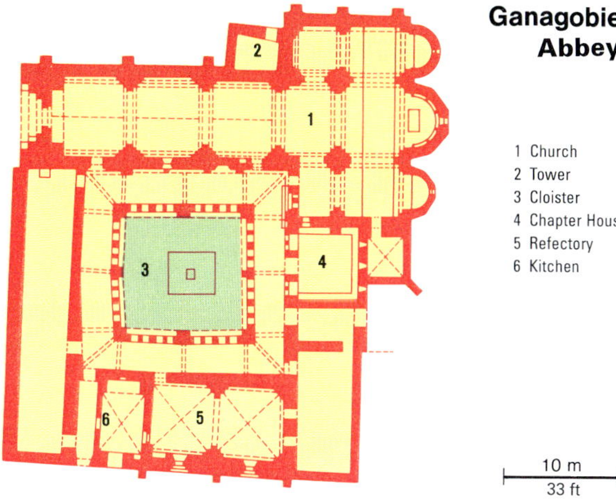


1 Church
2 Tower
3 Cloister
4 Chapter House
5 Refectory
6 Kitchen

is presumed – although there is no documentation – that the present buildings were erected in the 12th c. In good times there were more than a dozen monks in the community; the prior later acquired the title of Baron and had a seat in the state council. Decline set in about 1400 and at times the office of prior was held by laymen and even by Protestants. At the Revolution the abbey was secularised and sold. In 1881 it came into the possession of Benedictines who began the rebuilding; meanwhile restoration (including the mosaic) was concluded.

Church

The exterior is simple, with well-jointed masonry and wall pillars on the long sides as the only articulation. The doorway is both unusual and remarkable; in its archivolts and even in the door-frames round-toothed decoration was inserted at a later date and for this, stone from ribbed pillars was used. The somewhat archaic representation and iconography of the tympanum is remarkable for the period, including as it does temporal power, Christ in the Mandorla, the four evangelists among the twelve apostles. The interior has a single nave and consists of three square bays articulated by rectangular surrounding arches and buttresses. Adjoining the twin bays of the transepts is the choir with a main apse and side apses. The northern one is externally circular and probably belongs to an earlier building. The gallery in the west wall is reminiscent of Cluny and its liturgy, in which the singing of the choir is antiphonal. The sculptural decoration is modest, since it was accompanied by frescoes (traces of which remain) and the mosaics in the eastern bay of the transept and in the apses (see below).

Cloister

The cloister, largely reconstructed with preserved medieval material, probably dates from the second half of the 13th c. It was later joined to the church and chapter-house. Its barrel vault is higher on the outside than on the inside, in order to minimise the weight on the arches. The eight arches of the garden front are divided by double and multiple pillars and separated by an intermediate pillar; the leaf decoration is similar to that in Notre-Dame, Vaison (see entry) which is under Burgundian influence. Each four arches are held together by a large relieving arch.

**Mosaics

The mosaics in the choir and transepts were made between 1135 and 1170 and with their area of almost 70 sq.m/84 sq.yds form the largest Romanesque floor mosaic in France. Dating was made possible by an inscription which names both the client, a certain Prior Bertrand, and the artist Petrus

Trudbert. The themes and representation point to the influence of antiquity (especially in the ornamentation) and to the time of the crusades; incorporated with this is the overlying theme of good and evil which are given their "traditional" sides – good on the right, evil on the left. In addition to magical symbols (signs of the zodiac) fables are the principal subjects; in the left apse a galloping rider pursues a monster, there are centaurs, unicorns and elephants. Of especial note in the right transept is the fight between St George and the dragon and the stag as the symbol for Christ.

## Gap C4

Département: Hautes-Alpes
Altitude: 733m/2406ft
Population: 35,000

*Location and importance

The busy Département town of Gap is an important traffic junction on the Route Napoléon; it lies on the River Luye in the north of Provence and in about the same latitude as Montélimar. Gap has a charming situation, with a backdrop of the Alps to the north of the town. Its pleasant climate has led to its becoming a popular health resort and it has a good reputation as a base for winter sports.

History

The place was already populated when the Romans penetrated into this region. Almost every trace of the Roman settlement of Vapincum disappeared during the succeeding centuries, especially as the place lay on the crossing of important north–south and east–west routes and was always much sought after and consequently fought over. In 558 the Lombards sacked the town; in 1650 plague removed two-thirds of the population, and in 1692 Savoy troops burned down almost all the houses. In March 1815 Napoleon arrived on his way back from Elba and passed through Gap on his march to Paris.

Sights

In the Avenue du Maréchal Foch, a little to the east of the town centre, can be found the Musée Départmental which houses Gallo-Roman antiquities, ceramics from Moustiers, furnishings from the Queyrasa and exhibits illustrating the history of the town and its surroundings. Its principal attraction is the mausoleum of François de Bonne, Duke of Lesdiguières, constructed from black marble from Campsaur with an alabaster statue by Jacob Richier (1585–1640).

The Cathedral in the town centre has a tower 77m/253ft high; occupying the site of several previous buildings, it was constructed between 1866 and 1898 according to Romanesque and Gothic models. The decoration is in Byzantine style and is noteworthy for the use of local black, red and grey stone.

### Surroundings of Gap

*Serre-Ponçon

By driving east for about 20km/12 miles on road N94 or on D900 B in a south-easterly direction we come to the Lac de Serre-Ponçon with its 120m/394ft high barrage, built in 1955–61, which dams the River Durance and creates a large lake covering some 2700ha/6672 acres.
The best excursion is a circular drive: from Gap take the above road as far as Chorges then turn right on to the D3 which winds its way south, with beautiful viewpoints, to the dam; the best general view of the dam is from the Belvédère a little way north on the road. The D3 continues to the junction of the D900 B. Take this road, cross the Durance and then, at varying distances from the water, follow the southern bank of the reservoir. In about 20km/12 miles turn west on the the D954. A little way from the road

*Gap, with a backdrop of the Massif des Ecrins*

can be seen the Demoiselles Coiffées (ladies with head-dresses) a group of earth pyramids. Still following the bank of the lake we reach the N94 near Savines-le-Lac and once again cross the lake and return to Gap via Chorges.

Demoiselles Coiffées

## La Garde-Adhémar

C2

Région: Rhône-Alpes
Département: Drôme
Altitude: 185m/607ft
Population: 1100

*Location

In the 13th c. La Garde came into the possession of the Adhémar family who also had a castle at Grignan (see entry) in the 11th c. Since the 13th c. La Garde has borne their family name. Situated on the edge of the heights of the Tricastin above the Rhône valley (about 20km/12 miles south of Montélimar and 17km/10½ miles west of Grignan) its beautiful position is best appreciated if it is approached from Grignan through the Val-des-Nymphes (see below).

### Sights

Townscape

Outside the town on the north there is a car park from which the modest little town can be explored. Parts of the medieval town wall have been preserved in the north-east, including two town gates. From the main door of the Church of St-Michel, one of the important monuments of the district, there is a fine view of the Rhône valley and the outlying hills of the Viverais, with the Dent de Rez (719m/2360ft) among them.

*St-Michel, Provençal Romanesque*

*View over the Rhône valley*

*St-Michel

A chapel dedicated to St Michael is mentioned as early as 1105, but the present church was certainly not built until forty years later (at the same time as the church in Bourg-St-Andéol on the other side of the Rhône, and the Cathedral in St-Paul-Trois-Châteaux). The church was restored in 1849/50 at the instigation of Prosper Mérimée.

With its simple clear architectural forms St-Michel, although situated in the extreme south of the Dauphiné, is typical of Provençal Romanesque – a lack of figure-decoration, little articulation and masonry precisely shaped and assembled. Its three aisles form a square, on the east side are three apses but no transept. The nave has a barrel-roof and the side aisles a quarter-barrel which relieves the weight of the vault. Only the south wall and the apses have embrasure-like windows, so that practically the only light entering the building comes through the door. The west apse is an extremely rare feature in French Romanesque. In constrast to the rest of the church the tower bears on a massive square base a delicate octagon (the arches of the arcades have ovoid decoration and rest on pilasters with capitals modelled on those of antiquity). The west front, too, has bands of relief work, but these were probably added in the 19th c.

Chapelle de Val-des-Nymphes

Two kilometers east, on the D572 A are the ruins of the 12th c. Chapelle de Val-des-Nymphes set in a green valley abounding in water. In Gallo-Roman days this spot was probably a pagan shrine, as the name implies. The roof and arches of the single-aisled Romanesque chapel are lacking. The west front is remarkable; above simple wall surfaces – the arch of the doorway has keystones from a Roman building – the tympanum has three niches, separated by fluted pilasters with imitation Classical capitals. The arches which support the corner pilasters are later additions. Of interest is the articulation of the choir apse by blind arcades on two levels.

# Gordes

D3

Département: Vaucluse
Altitude: 373m/1224ft
Population: 1600

**Location and scenery

Gordes, some 40km/25 miles east of Avignon, is world-famous for its extremely picturesque situation on the steep slope down from the Plateau de Vaucluse to the valley of the Coulon. In the 1950s Gordes was often neglected, but today it is one of the most visited places in Provence. This "village perché" is dominated by its 16th c. castle. The best view of Gordes is to be had from the the road leading up from Cavaillon.

## Sights

Castle

The fortified castle, flanked by corner-towers, was erected in 1540 and served as a medieval fortress. Features of that time are the doorway and windows, as well as the richly decorated fireplace (one of the finest Renaissance fireplaces in France) in the Great Hall.

*Musée Vasarély

The castle was made available to Victor Vasarély for his "Didactic Museum" (Musée didactique) in appreciation of his having met the costs of restoration. The Hungarian painter (born 1908) is one of the most important artists of Constructivism and Op-art (see Aix-en-Provence). As well as abstract paintings which consist primarily of flat geometric forms, there are also kinetic objects on view. The development of Vasarély from the thirties to the present day is well illustrated. Open: Wed.–Mon. 10am–noon and 2–6pm; also on Tues. in July and Aug.

*Village des Bories

The Village des Bories lies 2km/1 mile south of Gordes. From the main road a narrow carriageway branches off to the west, it is enclosed in places by

*The classical face of Gordes*

*A Renaissance fireplace and Op-art in Gordes Castle*

walls made of boulders and in spite of stretches of one-way operation cannot be used for large motor or towed caravans. Open: daily 9am until sunset.

Bories are built of flat stones without mortar, that is in drystone work, and are generally without windows. The slope of the roof consists of a kind of false vaulting whereby each layer of stone overhangs the one immediately below on the inside, until the slopes coincide in the middle of the roof. These constructions which are quite common in Provence used to serve generally as herdsmen's huts but, as in the case here, rural farms and whole settlements could consist of bories. Examples of this curiously archaic construction had their precursors in the New Stone Age and were built in Provence until the beginning of the 20th c.; they could be put up by an experienced craftsman with no other tool than a hammer.

The settlement of bories near Gordes was thoroughly restored in the 1960s. It is probably the largest and most complete of its kind still remaining. The village is surrounded by a wall, scarcely as high as a man, enclosing the five groups of huts. Beside houses and stables there are a winepress, bakery, etc.; in a few of the bories farming implements of several periods are exhibited. In a two-storey 17th c. house there is instructive literature about this method of construction and its corresponding forms in other countries.

The view to the south over the hills covered with maquis (evergreen shrubs) is charming.

Glass painting

In Moulin des Bouillons (5km/3 miles south on D148) can be found the Musée du Vitrail in which glass painting and the art of stained glass church windows in Europe is documented.

## Surroundings of Gordes

*Roussillon

The little town of Roussillon lies 10km/6 miles east of Gordes in the well-known ochre area between the Plateau de Vaucluse and the Montaine du Lubéron. The whole town reveals the intensive colour of ochre which was mined here and which brought prosperity to the citizens as a raw material much in demand for the manufacture of paint, until the competition from synthetic pigments became too great.
At the entrance to the town on the left is a car park which is often full (there are other parks on the road from Apt in the west on the Rue des Bourgades and in the north on the road leading to D2). From the main car park there is a signposted tour of Roussillon.
The town is entered through a charming clocktower. Further uphill cross the narrow steps of the Rue de l'Arcade and the very pretty Place de la Mairie and go past the church to the "Castrum", an observation platform with an orientation panel. To the north can be seen the Plateau de Vaucluse and further on the broad shape of Mont Ventoux. All around among the woods are ochre rocks, the colours of which vary from violet to light yellowish brown.

Ochre Rocks

Impressive ochre formations, the "Chaussée des Géants" (street of the giants) can be seen from the entrance to the town, to the south of the car park mentioned above. It takes some 30 minumtes to reach them; the path is waymarked and provided with explantory material on tablets. Also very impressive is the "Val des Fées" (view from the Rue des Bourgades to the south). Those with a special interest in ochre rocks are recommended to visit the "Colorado of Rustrel" (see Lubéron)

Sénanque

See entry

Fontaine-de-Vaucluse

See entry

*Roussillon, the hill-village of ochre rocks*

# La Grande-Motte

D2

Région: Languedoc-Roussillon
Département: Hérault
Altitude: sea-level
Population: 4000

Location

The modern holiday centre of La Grande-Motte lies on the Golfe du Lion, 10km/6 miles west of Aigues-Mortes and 20km/12 miles south-east of Montpellier. It is actually not part of Provence but of the adjoining région of Roussillon.

Townscape

La Grande-Motte came into being in 1974 as the first of the modern holiday centres which are essentially "drawing-board foundations" in the lagoon and dune country west of the Camargue; these centres include Port-Barcarès, Port-Leucate, Valras-Plage and Port-Camargue (see below). It has developed into a huge holiday town, with a sophisticated infrastructure of accommodation, and entertainment and sporting facilities.

The town

The place is grouped around the well-equipped marina, on both sides of which stretches a beach of fine sand. The typical silhouette is formed by pyramid-shaped blocks of apartments. On the east side of the harbour is a fine aquarium with more than 30 tanks. There is a casino in La Grande-Motte.
To the north and east of the main road through the town are holiday houses, various sports centres and a holiday village.

In the nearby lagoons, Etang du Ponant and Etang de Mauguio, fairly large groups of flamingoes can be observed. Here there are also opportunities for water sports and fishing.

## Surroundings of La Grande-Motte

Le Grau-du-Roi

Le Grau-du-Roi (3km/2 miles south-east), a more conventional place than La Grande-Motte, is in the Département of Gard. It has developed around a fishing village which, however, has already been almost swallowed up by the usual concrete skyscrapers. To the north-west on the horizon can be seen the skyline of La Grande-Motte.

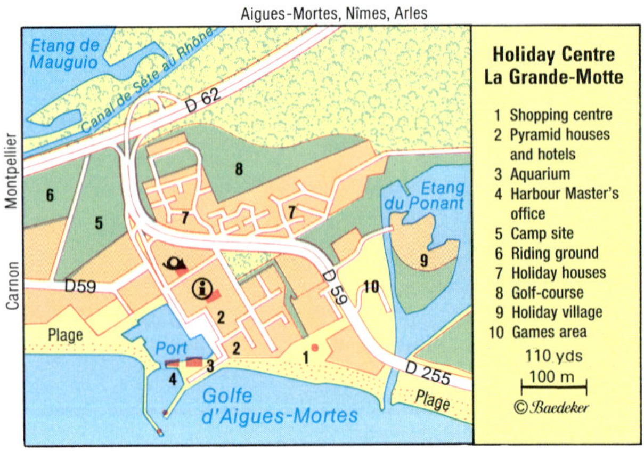

La Grande-Motte

Le Grau-du-Roi with its old lighthouse

The lagoons, lying to the south-east, which extend into the countryside of the Camargue are used mainly for obtaining sea salt.

Port-Camargue

South of Le-Grau-du-Roi lies Port-Camargue, the newest and most easterly of the holiday towns on the coast of Languedoc-Roussillon. Port-Camargue has excellent boating facilities and broad sandy beaches. The complex of holiday homes and apartment blocks, generally only one or two storeys high, are built out into the lagoon so that boats can often be tied up right outside the front door. Two broad roads run round the edge of this attractive place and finish on either side of the harbour keeping traffic away from the residential area.

Camargue

See entry

## Grasse D4

Département: Alpes-Maritimes
Altitude: 333m/1093ft
Population: 43,000

Location and importance

Grasse, at heart still an ancient little town and Sous-Préfecture of the Département of Alpes-Maritimes, lies about 18km/11 miles north of Cannes. It has a sheltered situation on the slope of the Roquevignon some distance from the coast on the Route Napoléon. Even before the Côte d'Azur, Grasse was known as a winter health resort, on account of its mild climate. The town is famous as the centre of the perfume industry.

History

The area of Grasse is rich in finds from pre- and early historical times, especially of the late Neolithic era. It is believed that the place existed in

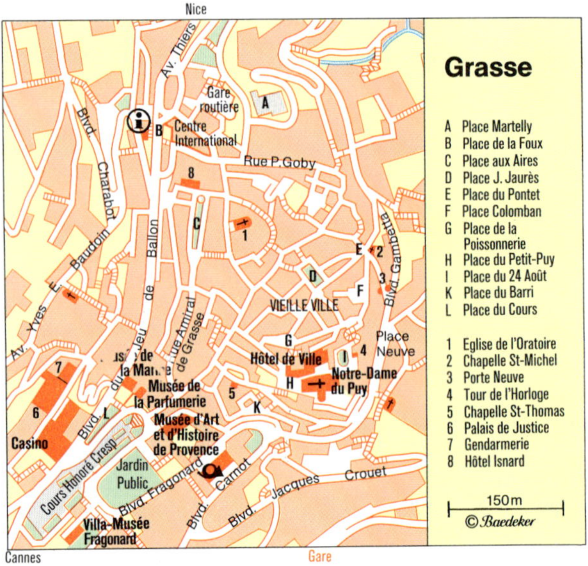


Merovingian times (5th/6th c. A.D.). In the 12th c. Grasse gained its independence but in the 13th c. came under the control of the Dukes of Provence. It was the seat of a bishop from 1244 until 1790. The perfume industry, which has made Grasse world-renowned, was introduced in the 16th c. by Catherine de' Médici. The Rococo painter Jean Honoré Fragonard (1732–1806) was born in Grasse. Pauline Borghese, the sister of Napoléon Bonaparte, lived in Grasse (garden above the town, Boulevard Jeu-de-Ballon 2; from here the view extends from Nice to Cannes).

*Perfume industry

Grasse is the most important centre of the perfume industry, not only in France but also in the whole of Europe. The material from which the perfume is extracted is provided by the large flower plantations and lavender fields of the surrounding area. In and around Grasse about 30 large firms process throughout the year several million kilograms of blossoms (orange, rose, jasmine, thyme, rosemary, mignonette, violet, etc.). For the manufacture of perfume from natural raw materials three main methods are used: the first is the old-fashioned distillation process by means of steam; the second is an extraction process in which the perfumes together with fatty deposits are extracted by using alcohol; the third is a method of solution whereby the scents are extracted by chemical means. In order to obtain 1kg of ethereal oil 1000kg of orange-blossom, for example, are necessary. To obtain oil of lavendar the plants are picked (either by machine or by hand), allowed to dry for a week and then treated with steam in vats. After the mixture is cooled the particles of lavender oils, which have a lighter specific gravity, float to the top of the brew and can be removed. About 40kg of lavender plants are necessary to obtain 1 litre of oil of lavender.

Most of the perfume factories in Grasse (e.g. Fragonard, Molinard, Galimard) have set up sales rooms and operate guided tours.

Musée de la Parfumerie

The Perfumery Museum (8 Place du Cours) was opened in 1989 and has many exhibits – from ancient times until the present day – illustrating the history and production of perfumes. Adjoining is a research and documentation centre and on the roof a garden of scented plants has been laid out. Open: June 1st–Sept. 30th 10am–7pm; Oct. 1st–May 31st Wed.–Sun. 10am–noon and 2–5pm; closed in Nov.

## Sights

Because of the narrow thoroughfares in the Old Town, Grasse can only be visited on foot.

The tour begins at the Office du Tourisme (Tourist Office) in the Place de la Foux; not far east of here lies the Centre International de Grasse, a modern congress and conference centre. From the southern end of the square a double set of steps enclosing a fountain leads down into the Old Town.

Place aux Aires

The first place to be reached is the elongated Place aux Aires where the lively market is held every morning which also has a fountain; on the north side of the square stands the elegant Hôtel Isnard which was built by the wealthy Gerber Isnard (1781).

Place du Cours

From the Place aux Aires follow the Rue Amiral de Grasse southwards to the Place du Cours, from where there is a pleasant view over the parts of the town lower down and into the valley. In a curve of the street can be seen the pretty red façade of the Perfumery Museum (see above) and to the south the Parfumerie Fragonard, on the ground floor of which is a very interesting museum about the history of the perfumery industry since ancient times, and a collection of perfumes of Grasse. The basement houses part of the production process and can be visited.

Musée Fragonard

A little to the south at 23 Boulevard Fragonard is the Villa Musée Fragonard (a 17th c. town house). It was here that J-H. Fragonard withdrew in 1791

*Grasse: Hôtel Isnard, in the Place aux Aires*

*Museum of Fragonard Perfumerie*

after he had lost his aristocratic customers through the French Revolution. On the staircase can be seen Grisaille pictures by Alexandre-Evariste, Fragonard's son, good copies of paintings by J-H. Fragonard which were done for the Countess du Barry, the mistress of Louis XV (the originals are now privately owned and in the USA), and other members of the family. Open: June 1st–Sept. 30th 10am–1pm and 2–7pm; Oct. 1st–May 31st Wed.–Sun. 10am–noon and 2–5pm; closed in Nov. and on public holidays.

Musée d'Art et d'Histoire de Provence

To the east opposite the observation terrace in Rue Mirabeau stands the former Hôtel de Clapiers-Cabris, a stately palace of 1771. It now houses the Musée d'Art et d'Histoire de Provence (Museum of Provençal Art and History; opening times as for the Musée Fragonard) with historic furniture, ceramics and a collection devoted to the history of the town.

Notre-Dame du-Puy

To the north-east behind the museum and right in the centre of the Old Town stands the three-aisled Cathedral of Notre-Dame, originally 12th–13th c. and extended in the 17th and 18th c. The architecture shows influence by Lombardy and Liguria. Inside the church, which looks ancient because of its walls of great ashlar blocks, can be seen three paintings by P. P. Rubens (1601) – "Christ crowned with Thorns", "The Crucifixion" and "St Helena", a remarkable representation of the "Washing of Feet" by J-H. Fragonard, one of the rare religious paintings by this master of Rococo, and the Altar of St Honorat which has been attributed to Bréa.

To the north, opposite the church, stands the Ancien Evêché, the former bishop's palace, built in the 13th c. and later considerably altered; it is now the Town Hall (Hôtel de Ville). From the Place du 24 Août which adjoins the church there is a fine view over the valley.

## Surroundings of Grasse

Cabris

Cabris is a picturesque village, once poplar with artists, above the Grasse basin (8km/5 miles west). Of interest are the ruins of the 12th c. castle, a church (1606–50) and the Chapel of Ste-Marguerite with a winged altar of about 1500. At the western edge of the village stands the 16th c. Chapel of St-Jean Baptiste.

*Gourdon

About 16km/10 miles north-east the little village of Gourdon is situated on a ridge. The fortress, built in the 13th and 17th c. on Saracen foundations, houses a museum (Oriental and French weapons, pictures of the Cologne school of about 1550, primitive painting). The park-like terraces laid out by Le Nôtre partly belong to a botanical research station. From here there is a fine view of Cap d'Antibes and Cap Roux.

*Gorges du Loup

The gorge which the River Loup has cut deep into the rock is reached from Grasse via Bar-sur-Loup and the D2210. The road (D6) through the gorge runs below rock walls up to 400m/1313ft high, past the Cascade de Courmes (altogether 70m/230ft high) and near the 25m/82ft-high Saut du Loup. Near a winding stretch of the D3 which returns to Grasse there is an observation point (signed "Surplomb des Gorges du Loup"), from which there is an almost vertical view down into the gorge and up to the 1248m/4096ft high Pic des Courmettes.

## Grignan

C2

Région: Rhône-Alpes
Département: Drôme
Altitude: 197m/647ft
Population: 1100

Situation and *Townscape

The township of Grignan lies in hilly terrain east of the Rhône Valley about 30km/17 miles south-west of Montélimar. The little town nestles below the castle and around the church, forming a charming picture. The town must be explored on foot; there are car parks in the lower town.

History

Grignan, which was a barony in the Middle Ages in the possession of the old Provençal aristocratic family of Adhémar-Castellane, was made famous by the Marquise de Sévigné (1626–96). The letters which she wrote to her daughter, the wife of the last count of Grignan, and to other contemporaries were published in 1726 and became celebrated for their vividness and for the details they give of contemporary life. The Marquise died in the castle at Grignan.

## Sights

*Chateau

The castle which dominates the whole town was originally a modest building of the late Middle Ages. About the middle of the 16th c. it was completely rebuilt by Louis Adhémar, a diplomat and officer, after the collegiate church had already been erected. At the time of the French Revolution a considerable part of the castle had to be pulled down by order of the authorities. The fixtures which were still available and the remains of the castle were purchased at the turn of the century by a descendant of the Adhémars. The present aspect is largely the result of a thorough but not particularly successful restoration at the beginning of the 20th c.

The castle complex is entered by a gateway flanked by towers. To the south extends a large courtyard adjoining a terrace, with the Church of St-Sauveur which was built about 1660. From here there is an excellent view of Mont Ventoux in the south-east, of the Rhône plain and of the mountains of Viverais in the north-west.

The principal attractions of the interior of the castle include the apartments of the Marquise de Sévigny and several rooms with old furniture (Louis XIII,

*Grignan and the Castle of Madame de Sévigné*

Louis XV) as well as Gobelins; an "audio-visual" guiding system, with acoustic and lighting effects and projected slides accompanies the visitor. Open: April 1st–Oct. 31st 9.30–11.30am and 2.30–5.30pm (July and Aug. until 6pm). Closed January and Tues. and Wed. mornings from Nov. 1st–Mar. 31st.

St-Sauveur

Below the castle stands the Church of St-Sauveur, built 1535–39 on the order of the above-mentioned Louis Adhémar by Jehan Delanche for the canonry founded in 1654. The left-hand wall of the nave abuts the hillside. A gallery in the single-aisled church has a direct entrance (17m/56ft above the ground) to the castle; during the French Revolution it was walled up. With its ribbed vaults and traceried windows the building reveals elements of Late Gothic (Flamboyant). To the left of the gilded High Altar, with its altarpiece showing the "Transfiguration", can be seen the tomb of the Marquise de Sévigné beneath a marble slab. The panelling dates from the second half of the 17th century.

Place Sévigné

On the northern edge of the Old Town lies the Place Sévigné with a fountain commemorating the Marquise. The little square is dominated by the 12th c. belfry (a defensive civic tower). Continuing past this tower, the road leads to the Upper Town and the castle; below on the right can be seen a Classical pumproom.

## Surroundings of Grignan

Valréas

The lively little town of Valréas, 9km/6 miles south-east of Grignan, was until the French Revolution the property of the Pope and is still called "Enclave des Papes". Although in the Département of Drôme, it belongs historically to the Département of Vaucluse. Agriculture, commerce and packaging are important factors in the economy.

The Old Town is surrounded by spacious boulevards with plane-trees and parking places which follow the line of the former town walls. Although of modest size the fine Hôtel de Ville, once the town house of the Marquise de Simiane (15th–18th c.), is impressive. The keep dates from the 12th c. The Church of Notre-Dame-de-Nazareth has a fine south door.

La Garde-Adémar

See entry

# Hyères D4

Département: Var
Altitude: 40m/131ft
Population: 42,000

Location

Hyères, an important agricultural centre (wine, flowers, early vegetables) and the oldest winter health resort of the French Riviera, lies only 20km/12 miles east of Toulon at the foot of the 2204m/670ft high Castéou, 4km/2½ miles from the sea.

History

Near the town lay the Greek foundation of Olbia. The Romans fortified the settlement and the fortifications were subsequently extended, first by the Lords of Fos and afterwards by Charles of Anjou. During the Wars of Religion (16th c.) the town suffered considerably; after a siege lasting a year the Duc de Guise had the walls pulled down. At the beginning of the 17th c. the keep was destroyed (the remains have been preserved). Hyères was "discovered" in the 19th c. as a health resort.

## Sights

Old Town

The heart of the Old Town is the Place Massillon, where the lively daily market is held and where the 12th c. Tour St-Blaise can be seen, the remains of a residence of the Knights Templar.

In the Rue Rabaton can be found the birthplace of the great preacher Massillon, court minister to Louis XIV and Bishop of Clermont. Continue along Rue Ste-Cathérine to the Place St-Paul (orientation table; extensive view), with the church of the same name, originally built in the 12th c. and restored in the 16th when the side chapels were added. On the right of the steps leading to the main door stands a charming little Renaissance house with little corner turrets, beneath this extends the Rue St-Paul.

A few yards to the west stands the Porte des Princes, part of a former monastery. To the north of the square in the Rue Paradis are some pretty 13th c. houses (No. 24 on the left; No. 6).

South-east of the Place Massillon, on the edge of the old town centre, stands the 13th c. Porte de la Rade, the former main gate of the town which gives access to the Place Clemenceau. To the north lies the Place de la République with a monument to Massillon, and the 13th c. Church of St-Louis, (Romanesque/Early Gothic) which formerly stood outside the town walls. East of the apse of the church, on the Cours Strasbourg, is the theatre and behind it the attractive Jardin A. Denis.

The busy Avenue du Général-de-Gaul leads west from the Place Clemenceau and forms the boundary of the New Town to the south.

New Town

The impressive Avenue Gambetta leads south from the Place du Portalet into the New Town. To the east lies the Place Lefèbvre and here can be found the interesting Musée Municipal with archaeological, local and natural history collections. Open: Mon., Tues. Thur. Fri. 10am–noon and 3–6pm; Sat. and Sun. only during special exhibitions 3–6pm.

*Jardins Olbius-Riquier

To the south of the inner town can be found the Jardins Olbius-Riquier, a fine garden layout of 6.5ha/16 acres with a great many exotic plants and birds.

Notre-Dame-de-Consolation

The suburb of Costebelle lies 3km/2 miles south of the town centre on a 98m/322ft high hill. On the top of the hill there was a place of pilgrimage as early as the 11th c. There is a fine view from the Chapel of Notre-Dame-de-Consolation, the tower of which is surmounted by a statue of the Madonna. A pilgrimage to this spot takes place on August 15th and 16th. From the chapel the 306m/1004ft high Mont des Oiseaux (view) can be climbed in about 1½ hours.

St-Pierre d'Almanarre

Still farther south are the ruins of the Monastery of St-Pierre d'Almanarre (Arabic al-manar = lighthouse).

Hyères-Plage

By the sea south of Toulon-Hyères Airport lies the resort of Hyères-Plage with a racecourse and the harbour of Port St-Pierre-de-la-Mer (marina).

L'Ayguade-Plage
Le Ceintruon-Plage

North-east of the airport and on the far side of the mouth of the River Capeau are the seaside settlements of L'Ayguade-Plage and Le Ceinturon-Plage which have beaches of fine sand. This was one of the places from which the Crusaders set sail.

## Surroundings of Hyères

### Presqu'Île de Giens

Location

Near Toulon-Hyères Airport the Presqu'Île de Giens juts out into the Mediterranean. To the east of this narrow tongue of land stretches the wide bay of Rade d'Hyères and to the west extends the Etang des Pesqueirs, closed off on the west by a dike along which runs the Route du Sel (Salt Road); here are the Salins Neufs (new salt-pans; 500ha/1236 acres). These two spits of land link the coast to the Giens Peninsula, 6.5km/4 miles long and up to 1.5km/1 mile wide, which only became joined to the mainland in Roman times.

On the eastern spit, which is covered with pines, are long sandy beaches, with opportunities for surfing, and the settlement of La Capte. The central point of the peninsula is Giens with its castle ruins (52m/171ft above sea-level; good view). In the west near the village of La Madrague rises the highest point of the peninsula (118m/387ft; signal station).

Some 2km/1 mile east of Giens the road from Hyères ends at the ruins of the former Fort de la Tour-Fondue, built in the time of Richelieu. Immediately adjoining is the mooring-place of the motor-boats for Porquerolles (see below). To the south of the Giens Peninsula lies the Île du Grand-Ribaud, a rocky island with a lighthouse.

## *Îles d'Hyères (Îles d'Or)

Location and character

The Îles d'Hyères, Porquerolles, Port-Cros and the Île du Levant (as well as other islands) continue the peninsula of Giens to the east. Geologically they form part of the Massif des Maures (see entry) and are called – probably on account of their glistening mica-bearing rocks – the Îles d'Or (golden islands). The islands are for the most part wooded, with steep fissured slopes; they have fine natural harbours and are popular not least because of their beaches which are ideal for bathing. In the time of King François I the islands were used as a base by pirates.

Ferry services

From Toulon, Hyères-Plage and La Tour-Fondue to Porquerolles; from Port-de-Miramar, Le Lavandou and Cavalaire.

Île de Porquerolles

The Island of Porquerolles, almost 8km/5 miles long and about 2km/1½ miles wide, is the largest of the archipelago. It has vineyards extending over some 200ha/494 acres and beautiful beaches with clear water which are especially popular with visitors. The beaches on the north coast are predominantly flat; the entire southern and eastern part falls steeply into the sea.
The principal place is Porquerolles on the main bay of the north coast. From here there is a rewarding walk (about 45 minutes) through beautiful Mediterranean vegetation south to Phare de l'Ousteau, the southernmost tip of the island (96m/315ft above sea-level; lighthouse).
Going north-east from Porquerolles through the woods along the Plage Notre-Dame the Cap des Mèdes is reached in just over an hour. About half-way a path branches off on the right which leads past the Fort de la Repentance to the Sémaphore (signal station; 142m/466ft; view).

Île de Port-Cros

East of the Île de Porquerolles lies the Île de Port-Cros (about 4km/2½ miles long, 2km/1 mile wide). Since 1963 it and the surrounding off-shore area has been a Parc National (nature reserve); only a few people live on this island.
The luxuriant Mediterranean fauna and flora (primeval forests, nesting sites of rare birds, fishing grounds) and the former Fort du Moulin (17th c.) at the entrance to the harbour of Port-Cros are of considerable interest. West of the harbour lies the little Île de Baguad (up to 59m/194ft high). From Port-Cros a particularly rewarding walk (1½ hours) leads from the harbour south-east into the Vallon de la Solitude (Valley of Loneliness) and to the imposing Falaises du Sud (almost 200m/654ft high steep cliffs). Also worth while is a 3 hour walk eastwards to the charming Pointe de Port-Man. The highest points are Mont Vinaigre (196m/643ft) and La Vigne (207m/679ft). The island is at its best during blossom time from March to May.

Île du Levant

Still farther east lies the geologically interesting lonely rock island, the Île du Levant (8km/5 miles long and up to 1.5km/1 mile wide). It was formerly the possession of the Abbots of Lérins. It has become well known through the naturist colony of Héliopolis set up in 1932. Large parts of the island are military territory.

## La . . ., Le . . ., Les . . .

See main name

## Le Lavandou D4

Département: Var
Altitude: 0–483m/0–1585ft
Population: 4700

Le Lavandou lies at the foot of the Massif des Maures, about half-way between Toulon and St-Tropez (40km/25 miles east of Toulon), on a broad bay facing south-east. Location

This pretty former fishing village, now popular as a holiday resort, may owe its name to the large amount of lavender which grows in the surrounding area. Extensive areas of holiday homes and numerous high-rise buildings are prominent features of the town. From the harbour, in the eastern part of which spacious mooring facilities for yachts have recently been established, ferries leave for the Îles de Hyères (see Hyères). Townscape

West of the harbour stretches the Rade de Bormes, a bay with fine sand, and along it runs the Boulevard-de-Lattre-de-Tassigny; from the boulevard there is a comprehensive view of the sea and the islands of Port-Cros and Levant (part of the group of the Hyères Islands). In the south the bay is enclosed by the wooded slopes of Cap Bénat. Far to the east Cap Lardier rises from the sea.

Road N559 running east from Le Lavandou, gives access to sandy beaches, interspersed with rocky stretches.

South of Le Lavandou the wooded Cap Bénat extends out into the sea. The road leading to it comes first to the resort of La Favière (yacht harbour, beach) before reaching the settlement of holiday homes at Cap Bénat. On the highest point, Les Fourches (205m/673ft), stands a castle and, on the extremity of the cape, a lighthouse. Cap Bénat

### Surroundings of Le Lavandou

The old township of Bormes-les-Mimosas, 2km/1 mile north-west, is picturesquely situated on the flank of a hill. The best view is from the terrace near the castle ruins. In the Place de la Liberté stands the handsome 16th c. Chapelle St-François-de-Paule (illuminated in summer), flanked by two cypress trees. A statue commemorates the beneficent deeds of St Francis of Paula during the plague of 1481. In the cemetery can be seen a memorial to the landscape-painter Jean-Charles Cazin (1841–1901); some of his work is to be seen in the Hôtel de Ville. Also of interest is the Tour de l'Horloge, an 18th c. clock-tower, and the Church of St-Trophime (also 18th c.; fine winged altar). Below the church extends old Bormes, a typical Provençal town with steep streets (known as "rompi-cuou"=breakneck). With La Favière Bormes-les-Mimosas has a good yacht harbour. Bormes-les-Mimosas

See Massif des Maures Collobrières

## Lubéron (Montagne du Lubéron) D3

Département: Vaucluse
Altitude: up to 1125m/3692ft

## Lubéron (Montagne du Lubéron)

Location and geography

The Montagne du Lubéron rises in the interior of the region to the east of Cavaillon. On the south the mountain range is bordered by the River Durance, the plain of which is intensively cultivated (vineyards, cereals, orchards) and in addition there are some green areas; in the north the valley of the Coulon divides it from the Plateau de Vaucluse. The Montagne du Lubéron is a mountainous area of chalk which reaches a height of 1125m/3692ft in the Mourre Nègre. Usually a distinction is made between the Petit Lubéron in the west and the Grand Lubéron in the east, which are separated by the gorge of the Combe de Lourmarin.

History

A dark chapter of history was the massacre in 1545, which the Baron of Oppède perpetrated in 24 villages (including Cadenet, Lourmarin, Ménerbes and Mérindol). Because his beloved, the Baroness of Tour d'Aigues, would not marry him he had over 2000 inhabitants of her villagers killed in every conceivable manner; he sold 800 men to be galley-slaves and plundered and burned the houses. These people had the misfortune to be Waldenses (Christian followers of Peter Waldo), who had been threatened since the Parliament of Aix; the persecution lasted from 1524 until the Baron obtained approval from King Francis I for his act of revenge.

Parc Régional du Lubéron

A large part of this mountainous area is taken up by the Parc Régional du Lubéron (nature park), established in 1977, which has an area of about 120,000ha/296,520 acres and which extends into the neighbouring Département of Alpes-de-Haute-Provence.

Bories

In several places in Lubéron can be seen the characteristic so-called "bories", huts built of boulders without mortar (see Gordes).

Rustrel

A good 10km/6 miles north-east of Apt (see below) is the village of Rustrel. Like Roussillon (see Gordes) it is known for its deposits of ochre. Here the little River Dôa has cut a gorge, called the "Colorado de Rustrel". This picturesque gorge can be reached by two roads going south from Rustrel. Footpaths lead to the ochre rocks.

## Drive through the Lubéron Mountains

Apt

The best starting point for a drive through the Lubéron is Apt, situated in the basin of the same name, the Bassin d'Apt on the little River Calavon. Of interest is the former Cathedral of Ste-Anne, originally Romanesque but considerably altered in the 14th and 17th c. In the Baroque Chapelle Ste-Anne is the reliquary of the patroness of the church. The treasury contains reliquaries from Limoges and illuminated manuscripts. The archaeological museum has, in addition to Gallo-Roman antiquities, a considerable collection of ceramics.

From Apt Road D943 runs south to the Lubéron. It passes through a varied and scenically beautiful landscape with vineyards and orchards; ahead rises the mountain range of the Lubéron with the old village of Bonnieux and, on the right, the village and castle ruin of Lacoste. The castle is associated with the notorious Marquis de Sade to whom it belonged; he withdrew here after the Arcueil affair in 1771.

*Bonnieux

100m/330ft separate the highest and lowest parts of this little town on the north slope of the Lubéron. The upper church (12th and 15th c.) is reached by a flight of steps from the Place de la Liberté; it is surrounded by mighty cedars (in the 1860s cedars from the Atlas Mountains were planted in the Lubéron). From here the view extends across the Bassin d'Apt to Gordes and Roussillon and across the Plateau de Vaucluse to Mont Ventoux which dominates the landscape. The Musée du Tourisme (Rue de la République) houses the Musée de la Boulangerie. The lower church contains four

*In the "Colorado de Rustrel"*

*Bonnieux: the upper church*

panels by a 15th c. German master (St Veronica; representations of the martyrdom of Jesus).

Combe de Loumarin

Road D934 leads to the dense, relatively low forest of holm oaks, sweet-chestnuts and gorse in the Gorge of the Aigue Brun, below impressive, partly overhanging rock walls.

*Mourre Nègre

Just short of Lourmarin a narrow forest track branches off to the left, climbs up to the crest of the Grand Lubéron and in about another 15km/9 miles reaches the Mourre Nègre, the highest point of the range. The last short stretch must be made on foot; from the top there is a magnificent panorama.

Loumarin

At the southern end of the Combe lies Loumarin, overlooked by its 15th/16th c. hilltop château; from the tower there is a good view of the Lubéron, the plain of the Durance and the Montagne Ste-Victoire (half-hour guided tours morning and afternoon). The writer and Nobel prizewinner Albert Camus (1913–60) who had settled here is buried in the churchyard.

Cucuron

There is a worthwhile excursion from Loumarin to Cucuron, about 10km/6 miles distant. The Romanesque and Gothic church is in poor condition; it has a pulpit with various coloured marble intarsis work and an 18th c. altarpiece of the Resurrection by Puget. The Regional Museum in the Hôtel des Bouliers has exhibits illustrating pre- and early history as well as Gallo-Roman finds. Mourre Nègre (see above) can also be climbed from Cucuron.

Cadenet

The plain of the Durance and the Abbey of Silvacane (see entry) are reached via Cadenet, which is dominated by the ruins of an 11th c. castle.
In Cadenat stands the statue of the "Drummer of Arcole". According to legend this 19-year-old boy, who was a soldier in Napoleon's army, swam

*In the Combe de Lourmarin*

*The "Drummer of Arcole" in Cadenet*

*Marcoule: the nuclear research centre of 1956*

the river during the battle and beat his drum so loudly that the Austrians, thinking they were surrounded, surrendered. In the 14th c. church a Roman sarcophagus serves as the font.

## Marcoule

C2

Région: Languedoc-Roussillon
Département: Gard
Altitude: 50m/164ft

Location

The nuclear research centre of Marcoute lies in the west opposite Orange on the right bank of the Rhône.

Usine Nucléaire

The extensive complex of this nuclear research centre, where 2200 people are employed, is situated right by the river, the water of which is used for cooling the reactors. The principal task of the centre is, however, not the production of electrical energy but nuclear research and the obtaining of radio-active substances for medicine, science and industry, of tritium for military purposes and of nuclear fuel (plutonium) for power stations. For this purpose the reactor "Phénix", the first fast breeder in the world, on the edge of the area, was started up in 1973. In Marcoule the fuels from French and Spanish gas-graphite reactors are also reprocessed.

Belvédère de Marcoule

The best view of the complex is from the Belvédère (observation point) which is reached along a private road (open: 8am–7pm). A large panoramic display gives a general view of the complex; in an exhibition the layout and working of nuclear power stations and uranium enrichment are explained and the atomic industry of France is documented.

## Marseilles

D3

Département: Bouches-du-Rhône
Altitude: 0–160m/0–525ft
Population: 880,000 (conurbation 1,104,000)

Location and importance

Marseilles (Marseille in French), the oldest and second largest city, after Paris, and the most important port of France, is situated on the Mediterranean east of the Rhône delta. Marseilles is the chief place in the Département of Bouches du Rhône, a university town and the seat of an archbishop.

Marseilles has a charming situation on a broad bay which is enclosed on the north by the Chaîne de l'Estaque towards the Etang de Berre (see entry) and rises on bare limestone hills. It is dominated by the Church of Notre-Dame-de-la-Garde, the landmark of the city and the port. Although the oldest city in France there are few remains of ancient or medieval buildings.

Economy

The economic situation of the town is primarily determined by the importance of the port. A third of French maritime trade is handled by the independent Port Autonome de Marseille. The annual turnover of goods amounts to about 100 million tonnes (almost 90% imports), of which the greatest part (over 90%) is handled by the new installations of Fos-sur-Mer and Lavéra which extend a long way to the west (transport of mineral oil, mineral oil products and ores). With some 1.2 million passengers annually Marseilles is the third passenger port of France; a great proportion of this traffic is attributable to the busy ferries across the harbour basins.

Raw materials and heavy industry characterise the area of Marseilles/Etang-de-Berre/Fos; four refineries produce 30% of national capacity, steel production amounts annually to 1.3 million tonnes. The traditional industries of Marseilles – shipping, the production of cooking-oil and the manufacture of soap – have suffered from recession, and both steel and

petro-chemical production have declined, with the result that Marseilles has the highest unemployment in France. The position has been intensified by the significance of Marseilles as a "bridge" between Europe and North Africa, that is as the principal place at which emigrants from Africa arrive. Over 100,000 arabs live in Marseilles; the Belsunce quarter north of the Canebière is also known as the "Marseilles Beirut"; few European faces are to be seen in this part of the city.

Marignane, the airport of Marseilles, is the third largest in France, (after Paris and Nice) a symbol of the economic area.

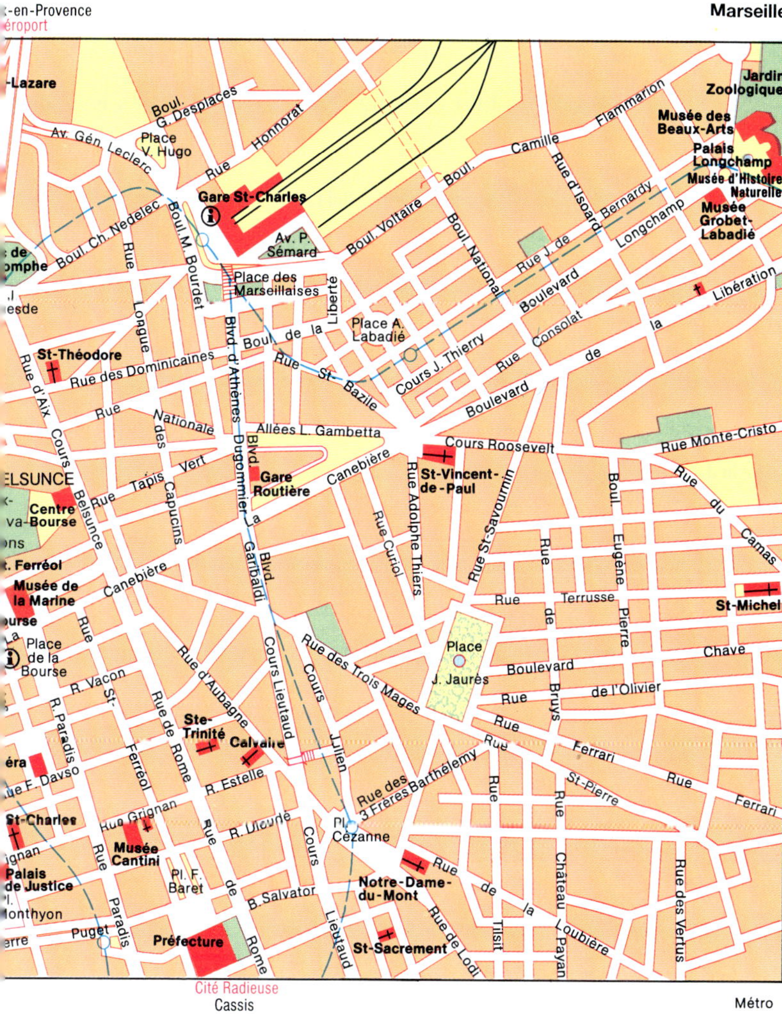


The town was founded in the 7th c. B.C. under the name of "Massalia" by Greeks from the town of Phocaea in Asia Minor. Until well into the time of the Roman Empire it was a centre of Greek culture. The town experienced its first flowering in the middle of the 6th c. B.C. after Phocaea had been destroyed by the Persians, and the population was soon increased by streams of refugees. Massalia expanded to the north-east towards the present-day Butte des Moulins. Trade flourished, especially with the Ligurians who, it is generally believed, had their principal settlement in the nearby Oppidum of Entremont (see Aix-en-Provence).

History

The intervention of the Romans after the Second Punic War in favour of the Greeks culminated in the destruction of the Saluvian tribe in 124, whereupon Aquae Sextiae Saluviorum (Aix), the first Roman town on Gallic soil was founded. The quarrel between Caesar and Pompey led to a fateful clash with the Romans, when the people of Massalia sided with Pompey. Caesar conquered the town, added to it the extensive territory of the Province of Arles and promoted the development of the Forum Julii (Fréjus).

Already in the 1st c. A.D. an extension of the now Roman town of Massalia was carried out by draining the extensive marshes to the east. The wall which had been built in the Imperial Age enclosed the settlement until well into the 11th c.; at that time the town was composed of an Upper Town (temple, forum and other public buildings) and a Lower Town (port, dock installations, etc.).

After the fall of the Roman Empire the town came under the domination of the Western Goths, then of the Franks and finally passed to the Kingdom of Arles. After its destruction by the Saracens it was rebuilt in the 10th c. and was subject to the Vicomtes de Marseille; in 1218 it became free until 1250 when Charles of Anjou conquered Marseilles which was united to France in 1481. The importance of the harbour increased enormously at the time of the Crusades. In the Middle Ages defences were constructed as opportunity offered, for example the Tour St-Jean on the north side of the harbour entrance, erected by the Knights of the Order of St John, a bastion near the present-day Pilgrimage Church of Notre-Dame-de-la-Garde by François I and extensions to the Château d'If. Under Mazarin the Forts of St-Jean and St-Nicolas were reinforced at the harbour entrance.

During the French Revolution which led to violent clashes between the Jacobins and the merchants, the most unruly elements withdrew to Paris where they made popular the "Marseillaise" which had been written and set to music by the army officer Rouget de Lisle, in Strasbourg.

In the 19th c. there were large-scale extensions to the town as there were in Paris, where Baron Haussmann had laid out broad boulevards through whole quarters of the city. Notable among the improvements were the Rue de la République between the Old and New Harbours, numerous examples of prestigious architecture, including the Triumphal Arch in the Place d'Aix and the Palais Longchamps, all of which bear witness to the economic prosperity at the time of the Industrial Revolution.

The increase of French influence in North Africa from 1830 and the opening of the Suez Canal resulted in a great demand for accommodation, etc. (many new dwellings; "bidonvilles"=tin-can towns; extension of the harbour), a trend which has continued until the present day and which had led to a similar townscape to that of other European centres of population.

## Around the Canebière

La Canebière

The principal traffic artery of the extremely busy inner city is the Canebière (Provençal Canebiero), a broad highway which begins at the harbour. This street, about 1km/½ mile long, carries a great deal of traffic and is lined with shops and offices. The name is derived from Cannabis (hemp) and means "ropewalk". Fields of hemp could once be seen near the Old Harbour to which the raw material was delivered to the rope-makers.

The former boulevard – it was once compared to the Champs-Elysées – now forms a social and cultural boundary, separating the poor Belsunce quarter in the north from the more affluent southern part of the city. Various redevelopment programmes are atempting to ameliorate the situation.

Bourse

Coming from the harbour, on the left of the Canebière stands the Bourse (Stock Exchange), an impressive building of 1852–60, with the Musée de la Marine de Marseille (marine museum; collection of pictures and other artistic exhibits of the Marseilles Chamber of Trade; many drawings and plans of 17th c. ships).

*Fish-market in the Old Port*

*The Bourse (Exchange)*

Musée d'Histoire de Marseille

The redesigned Centre de la Bourse (Stock Exchange Centre; department store, etc.) gives access to the excavation site where remains of the Greek fortifications of the port of Massalia (3rd–2nd c. B.C.) were uncovered, and which has been laid out as a park (Jardin des Vestiges) and open-air museum. On the ground floor of the Stock Exchange Centre can be seen a collection of the finds, including the hull of a 3rd c. Roman ship. Open: Mon.–Sat. noon–7pm.

*Musée Cantini

South of the Canebière, at Rue de Grignan 19, which is reached by way of Rue Paradis, is the Musée Cantini. As well as old porcelain the museum has an important collection of 20th c. applied art (there are also temporary exhibitions). Open: 10am–5pm; Sat. and Sun. in summer noon–7pm.

Not far to the east of the Stock Exchange the Canebière crosses the broad Cours St-Louis (on the right) which leads into the Rue de Rome and on the left the Cours de Belsunce which is continued by the Rue d'Aix. This crossing is the intersection of the main roads leading east to west and north to south and is also the south-western corner of the arab quarter which extends to the north as far as the Porte d'Aix and the Gare St-Charles. About 250m/275yds farther on is the intersection with the Boulevard Dugommier (to the left) and the Boulevard Garibaldi (to the right). At the end of the Canebière stands the neo-Gothic Church of St-Vincent-de-Paul.

## Around the Boulevard Longchamp

*Palais Longchamp

At the eastern end of the Boulevard Longchamp, which runs parallel to the Boulevard de la Libération, the continuation of the Canebière, stands the Palais Longchamp with stately museum buildings on either side of a pillared hall (fountains). It was built by Espérandieu in 1862–69 at the end of the canal from the Durance to Marseilles. On the left is the Musée des

Beaux Arts with 16th and 17th c. paintings (Perugino, Rubens), works by Provençal masters (Puget, Serre, Mignard), modern sculptures and works by the caricaturist Honoré Daumier, born in 1808 in Marseilles. (Opening times as for the Musée Cantini.) On the right is the Musée d'Histoire Naturelle (Natural History Museum). Behind the Palais lies the large Zoological Garden.

Musée Grobet-Labadié

The Boulevard Longchamp terminates in a circular open space, where stands the Musée Grobet-Labadié, a mansion with beautiful furniture, given to the town by Madame Grobet. On display are musical instruments, medieval sculpture and tapestries, 18th c. furniture and ceramics (opening times as for the Musée Cantini).

## Around the Old Harbour

*Vieux Port (Old Harbour)

In the west of the town, where the Canebière begins, lies the picturesque Vieux Port (Old Harbour; 25ha/62 acres, 4–7m/13–23ft deep), which is now used only by fishing boats and sports craft. From here boats leave for the Château d'If and Calanques, near Cassis (see Surroundings of Marseilles). The lively waterfront, especially the Quai des Belges on the east side (fish market every morning), is a focal point for tourists. At the harbour entrance two forts stand sentinel, on the left the Fort St-Jean and on the right the Fort St-Nicolas (17th c.; viewpoint).

Basilique St-Victor

To the east of Fort St-Nicolas is the fortress-like Basilique St-Victor, which once belonged to an abbey founded in the 5th c. In its present form, with its turreted towers, it is of 11th and 14th c. date; the foundations go back to Early Christian and Carolingian times. In the crypt can be seen the original catacomb chapel and the Grotto of St Victor, and in the basilica a 13th c. Black Madonna. Open: 8am–noon and 2–6pm.

*Marseilles: the Vieux Port, with Notre-Dame-de-la-Garde*

Parc du Pharo

On a hill to the south of the harbour entrance, below which runs a road tunnel, the Tunnel St-Laurent, lies the Parc du Pharo, with the former great castle of the Empress Eugénie (the wife of Napoleon III) and a naval memorial. In summer open-air plays are performed outside the castle. From the park there is an extensive view of the port installations and of the town.

*Notre Dame-de-la-Garde

The 154m/505ft high limestone hill in the south of Marseilles was used in ancient times at least as an observation point or guard post. In the 15th c. it was the official relay-station for the royal intelligence network (smoke and light signals). Today the Basilique Notre-Dame-de-la-Garde on its summit is the landmark of the city, visible from afar. It was built on the site of a medieval pilgrimage chapel in 1853–64 by Espérandieu in neo-Byzantine style of light and dark natural stone. A gilded Madonna crowns the 46m/151ft high belfry.
The whole of the interior of the church is clad in white and dark marble. In the crypt can be seen many votive tablets and model aircraft given by aviators. Open: summer 7am–7.30pm; winter 7.30am–5.30pm. Access by bus 60.

**View

From the terrace encircling the church there is a marvellous panorama including the offshore islands of Pomègues and Ratonneau and the Château d'If (see Surroundings of Marseilles). At the north-west bastion is an orientation table.

## Old Town

The Old Town with its steep crooked streets lies to the north of the Old Harbour. On the north side of the harbour basin is the Quai du Port, with the Hôtel de Ville (Town Hall) built in the second half of the 17th c. on a Genoese model.

*Notre-Dame-de-la-Garde*

*"Unité d'Habitation" by Le Corbusier*

Museums

The Musée du Vieux Marseille (history of the town, Provençal furniture and costumes, utensils of the 17th–19th c.) is housed in the Maison Diamantée to the north of the Old Harbour. The house is so named because of the diamond-shaped stone blocks of which it is built; it is a good example of bourgeois architecture of the end of the 16th c. Further west in the Place Vivaux is the Musée des Docks Romains (Musée du Commerce Antique) which is equally worth a visit. It is the only museum in Provence to be erected right above the excavations; on view is one of the few remaining Roman trading places. Opening times of both museums as for the Musée Cantini.

St-Laurent

Near Fort St-Jean (see page 150) stands the Romanesque Church of St-Laurent which was severely damaged in the Second World War. The side chapels date from the 15th and 16th c. and the octagonal tower from the 18th c.

Cathédrale de la Major

On a terrace in the north-west of the Old Town, above the new port installations, stands the mighty Cathédrale de la Major, with two domed towers and a 16m/53ft high dome over the crossing. It was built between 1852 and 1893 in a mixture of Romanesque and Byzantine styles of alternate courses of white and green limestone. With a length of 141m/463ft it is the most spacious ecclesiastical building of the 19th c. The interior is richly decorated with marble and mosaic; in the crypt can be seen the tombs of the Bishops of Marseilles.

St Lazare

Near the Cathédrale de la Major the Church of St Lazare, the old cathedral (4th–12th c), almost disappears. Here in the Chapel of St-Severinus is a reliquary altar; another (of St-Lazarus) is in the left-hand aisle. In the chapel on the left of the fine apse is a Romanesque reliquary of 1122 and an Emtombment of the school of della Robbia.

*Vieille Charité

Musée d'Archéologie Méditerranée

Not far north-east of St-Lazare is the Vieille Charité, a hospice for the poor, built between 1671 and 1749 to plans by Jean and Pierre Puget (the latter is little known as an architect). This masterpiece of French hospital architecture of the end of the 17th c., with its chapel designed by Pierre Puget, is now a scientific and cultural centre; the Musée d'Archéologie Méditerranée, formerly in Borély Castle, is now housed here. It has a notable Egyptian department and pottery, bronzes and glass dating from Etruscan, Greek and Roman times. Also on display are drawings and paintings by a number of masters (Fragonard, Ingres, Boucher) and a collection of regional archaeology. Opening times are as for the Musée Cantini.

South of here is the Cour des Accoules, with a 19th c. Calvary chapel, overlooked by the Clocher des Accoules (bell-tower), the remains of one of the oldest churches in Marseilles. In the immediate vicinity in the Place Daviel stands the Hôtel-Dieu, which is reputed to have been founded towards the end of the 12th c. The plans for the construction of the new building were largely the work of the architects Portal and Mansart. In the front courtyard is a monument to the designer Honoré Daumier of Marseilles, with a bronze by A. Bourdelle. Also in the Place Daviel is the fine Palais de Justice (old lawcourts; 1743–47).

## The northern part of the city

Port Moderne

Downhill from the cathedral, about 1km/½ mile from the Old Harbour, the Port Moderne (New Harbour; over 200ha/494 acres; 25km/16 miles of quais) was laid out from 1844. Most passenger ships (including ferries for Corsica) tie up in the Bassin de la Grande Joliette which is 20ha/49 acres in extent. At the Quai de la Joliette, opposite the end of the Boulevard des Dames, lies the Gare Maritime (Marine Railway Station) immediately above the harbour basin. From the Jetée (mole) 5km/3 miles long (access only at week-ends), there is a good view of the New Harbour. Going east from the port along the Boulevard des Dames we come to the Place Jules-Guesde, where stands the Arc de Triomphe (Triumphal Arch), erected in 1825–32 to commemorate the capture of Fort Trocadéro at Cadiz.

Arc de Triomphe

## The southern part of the city

Avenue du Prado

The broad Avenue du Prado (called the "Prado" for short), expansively laid out and shaded by plane trees, is the southern continuation of the Rue de Rome and leads to the Rond-Point du Prado. On the left are the Parc Amable Chanot and the exhibition grounds with the Palais des Congrès.

*Parc Borély

From the Rond-Point the Avenue du Prado continues in a south-westerly direction to the shore. On the left is the Parc Borély where the film of the tales of Marcel Pagnol (director Yves Robert, première 1991) was shot, and the mansion which was built for a rich merchant called Borély in 1767–78.

*Unité d'Habitation (Cité Radieuse)

About 1.3km/1 mile south of the Rond-Point, on the right side of the Boulevard Michelet, extends the Unité d'Habitation, also called the Cité Radieuse, a residential complex designed by Le Corbusier and intended to "show the way ahead". The huge rectangular construction, 165m/180yds long and 56m/184ft high, comprises on eight double storeys 337 flats of 23 different types. There are communal rooms, shops (also the "Le Corbusier" hotel), a kindergarten, a bar, a theatre, etc., and on some floors "rues intérieures" complete the internal facilities. The "House", which is supported by seventeen pairs of concrete stilts – these also contain the supply services – represents a whole town for some 1600 inhabitants. The basic idea behind this construction was to provide accommodation for many people in the smallest possible area and to leave room for green open spaces. Le Corbusier has nevertheless sought to realise harmonious proportions and forms. Today this experiment is criticised for not permitting the spontaneity and individuality of modern city life.

## Surroundings of Marseilles

*Château d'If

About 2km/1¼ miles south-west of Marseilles, the fortified rock island in the Bay of Marseilles with its Château d'If is famous on account of the novel "The Count of Monte Cristo" (1844–45) by Alexandre Dumas the Elder. The fortress, built in 1524, was once used as a prison. There is a fine view from the top of the cliff.

Ratonneau
Pomègues
Le Planier

West of the Château d'If lie the two fairly large islands of Ratonneau and Pomègues, linked by a causeway which encloses the Port de Frioul (yacht harbour; quarantine station). Farther out to sea can be seen the little island of Le Planier.

Europort Sud

See Martigues

Rove-Tunnel

From the Anse de l'Estaque in the north of the bay the Rove Canal used to run in a tunnel under the Chaîne de l'Estaque to the Etang de Berre. 22m/72ft wide and 15.4m/50ft high it was the tunnel with the largest cross-section and ships with a draught of up to 4.5m/14ft could use the 7km/4 mile long canal. In 1963 it collapsed and has since been closed. From the N568 a path under the railway line leads to the tunnel entrance.

Château Gombert

On the northern edge of the city, at the end of the Place des Héros, with its rows of plane trees, stands the Château Gombert. Here is housed the Musée des Arts et Traditions Populaires du Terroir Marseillais, a collection of Provençal art in the house of a pupil of Mistral.

Grotte Loubière

About 1.5km/1 mile north-west in the Massif de l'Etoile is the Loubière Grotto, a cave system with impressive karst phenomena.

Allauch

The health resort of Allauch is situated amid magnificent hill scenery on the outskirts of Marseilles about 10km/6 miles north-east. In the Church of St-Sébastien can be seen a fine painting of the Ascension by Monticelli. To the south lies the attractively laid-out square, Allée des Grands Vents, with four 16th c. windmills, one of which has been restored and now houses the Tourist Office. In the Place Pierre Bellot is the Musée du Vieil Allauch (local history).
Above the village to the east stands the 12th c. Chapel of Notre-Dame-du Château, from where there is a rewarding view.

Cassis

The little port of Cassis, 22km/14 miles south-east of Marseilles, lies on a semicircular bay, framed by mountains. It was once the haunt of painters, including Vlaminck, Dufy and Matisse; nowadays it is an important recreation centre for the people of nearby Marseilles. The white wine of Cassis is renowned (Appellation Controlée).
Of interest are the old settlement centre with remains of 12th and 14th c. fortifications, a castle (1381) and the beautiful Fontaine des Quatre Nations. In September 1991 a cave with important pre-historic painting was discovered. The entrance is under water.

**Calanques

Between Marseilles and Cassis lie the magnificent Calanques, narrow fiord-like coves cutting deep into the land between clear vertical rock-walls. They are partly used as natural yacht harbours and are popular with climbers for rock ascents. The large Calanques, Port-Miou, En-Vau and Port-Pin, are particularly impressive; they are also accessible from the land and can be reached by boat from Cassis (trips according to demand).

Warning

During the holiday season cars are often broken into and thefts committed; visitors are, therefore, strongly urged to leave no valuables behind in their vehicles.

La Ciotat

**Corniche des Crêtes

The port and industrial town of La Ciotat, south-east of Marseilles, can be reached via Cassis (see above). Given sufficient time, the visitor should not use the inland route D559 from Cassis but the somewhat narrow and winding Corniche des Crêtes which runs just below the Falaises, the tallest

*View from Cap Canaille towards the Calanques*

cliffs in France, high above the sea to Cap Canaille (362m/1118ft). In the afternoon especially there is a splendid view of the coast from the Calanques to Cap Croisette. The whole stretch, barely 15km/9 miles long, leads via the Grande Tête to La Ciotat.
La Ciotat, a pretty fishing village with a once important shipyard (now closed; dry dock for ships up to 300,000 tonnes) lies on the western side of the bay of the same name, dominated by the bold crags of the Bec de l'Aigle (eagle's beak), 155m/509ft high. Offshore is the little Île Verte (Green Island) with a fortress. In the attractive Old Town are many 17th and 18th c. houses, and near the Town Hall (1864) a turreted keep. Notable paintings are to be seen in the parish church at the Old Port. A visit to the Musée d'Histoire Locale (local history) is recommended.
Following the new harbour northwards we reach the district of La Ciotat-Plage, with hotels and a beach.

## Martigues

D3

Département: Bouches-du-Rhône
Altitude: sea-level
Population: 42,000

Location

The picturesque old town of Martigues lies on the western edge of the Etang de Berre, about 30km/19 miles north-west of Marseilles.

Sights

The character of the surroundings of Martigues has been strongly influenced by the construction of the motorway and industrial plants; nevertheless the town, which because of its situation on the Canal de Caronte is also called the "Venice of Provence", has still retained to a considerable extent its atmosphere of bygone days. The Canal St-Sébastien and the picturesque corner – Miroir aux Oiseaux (Mirror of the Birds) – of the Île, the central part of the town, are given a particularly attractive appearance by fishing-boats with their nets hanging up to dry. The canal is overlooked by the square tower of the 17th c. Church of La Madeleine with its wrought-iron bell-cage.

*The Old Harbour and wharves in La Ciotat*

In Jonquières, in the southern part of the town, near the Church of St-Genest (17th c.), is the Chapelle de l'Annonciade with 17th c. sculpture and paintings.
In Ferrières, in the north of the town, can be found the Musée du Vieux Martigues with local history collections, and the Ziern Museum (Félix Ziern 1821–1911, landscape painter).

## Surroundings of Martigues

Europort Sud

With the petroleum harbour of Lavéra there begins the largest port and industrial complex in area of southern Europe. It comprises refineries, steelworks, production of man-made materials and oil storage installations. In this coastal zone, known as "Europort Sud", more than 80 million tonnes of oil are handled every year. The 782km/486 mile long pipeline to Karlsruhe starts from here.

Cap Couronne

9km/5½ miles south of Martigues and pleasantly situated on a hill above the Anse du Verdon lies the resort of La Couronne. 2km/1 mile south rises Cap Couronne, from which there is a good view of the sandy bays to the east.

Sausset-les-Pins

On a little bay, protected by the southern escarpment of the Chaîne de l'Estaque (which was one of the subjects of Paul Cézanne) lies the fishing port and resort of Sausset-les-Pins, 6km/4 miles east of La Couronne. It is popular as a recreation area for the people of Marseilles.

Carry-le-Rouet

The fishing port and resort of Carry-le-Rouet, another 4km/2½ miles east on the southern foot of the Chaîne de l'Estaque, is a popular resort and yacht anchorage. The sector of Le Rouet-Plage at the end of the charming Vallon de l'Aigle is especially attractive. Just to the east lies the beautiful Calanque des Anthénors (yachting and bathing) and the little bay of Méjean.

*Martigues: bridge over the Canal Baussengue*

Châteauneuf-les-Martigues

The largely agricultural community of Châteauneuf-les-Martigues, some 10km/6 miles east of Martigues, lies at the foot of the northern flank of the Chaîne de l'Estaque. The beach, the Plage du Jaï, is situated on the spit of land cut off by the Etang de Balmon.

Marignane

The township of Marignane, 16km/10 miles east of Martigues and 18km/11 miles west of Marseilles, is considerably affected by traffic using the nearby Aéroport Marseille-Marignane, within which are situated the installations of Aérospatiale (air and space industry, Airbus).

## Maures (Massif des Maures) D4

Département: Var
Altitude: up to 780m/2560ft

Location and importance

The Massif des Maures, on the coast between Hyères in the west and Fréjus in the east, is a hilly area some 60km/37 miles long and 30km/18 miles wide; it is composed of primitive rocks – granite, gneiss and slate (reddish or dark grey in colour, with metallically glistening mica). It represents the remains of a land mass which once covered the whole of the western Mediterranean. The deeply fissured afforested uplands are still relatively isolated. The name has nothing to do with the Moors who in these parts were always called "Sarrasins", but is derived from the Provençal "maure" or "moure", meaning dark, uncanny.

*Corniche des Maures

The Corniche des Maures for the greatest part of the way is road D559 along the coast and, with its many bays and cliffs between Le Lavandou and St-Tropez (see entries), has exceptionally fine scenery. It passes a considerable number of resorts; just beyond Cavalaire it skirts Cap Nègre (120m/394ft) and, via Canadel-sur-Mer and Rayol, reaches the resort and port of Cavalaire (castle ruin) situated on a sheltered bay. To the north-west rises the 528m/1733ft high summit of Les Pradels. The Corniche continues around the peninsula of Cap Camarat near St-Tropez and ends near St-Tropez Bay.

Collobrières

Reached by road D41 going north from Bormes-les-Mimosas (see Le Lavandou) for about 22km/13 miles, Collobrières lies in a hollow in the heart of the Massif des Maures. It is well known for its marrons glacés and Provençal joinery. Good fossils and minerals have been found in the vicinity.

La-Garde-Freinet

Also inland lies La Garde-Freinet, reached from Port-Grimaud along roads D14 and D558 (16km/10 miles). Situated on a pass with fine views, the village was a major strongpoint of the Saracens, but had already been a Roman military post. Of interest are the ruins of the former Saracen fortress of Freinet on a hill to the north-east (about 30 minutes' walk), from where there is an unusually extensive panorama.

Grimaud

See Port-Grimaud

## Menton D5

Département: Alpes-Maritimes
Altitude: sea-level
Population: 25,500

Location

Menton (Italian Mentone), at the eastern end of the Côte d'Azur on the border between France and Italy, lies on the Golfe de la Paix which is divided by a rocky promontory into the Baie de Garavan on the east and the

*The italianate harbour and Old Town of Menton*

Baie de l'Ouest on the west. The situation and climate of Menton makes possible the cultivation of citrus fruits.

## Lower Town

Casino

*Jardin Biovès

The focus of the town is the Casino (1932) on the west bay, and from here the Promenade du Soleil leads north to the harbour. On its landward side in the valley of the River Carei (now diverted underground) is the fine Jardin Biovès with its exotic trees. In the park (Avenue Boyer) stands the Palais d'Europe, a building of the Belle Epoque housing the Congress and Cultural Centre and the Tourist Office.

*Musée Jean Cocteau

In the 17th c. harbour bastion at the beginning of the mole can be found the Musée Jean Cocteau, with pictures, drawings, stage designs, etc.
From the end of both the moles of the Vieux Port there are fine views of the Old Town. From the Casino the Avenue Félix-Faure, the principal shopping street of the town, runs north east parallel to the promenade.

*Hôtel de Ville

In the next parallel main street, the Rue de la République, stands the italianate Hôtel de Ville (town hall). Of particular interest is the Salle des Mariages which was decorated by Cocteau (guided visits).

**Musée Municipal

The Musée Municipal, in Rue Henri Greville north of the Town Hall, has paintings by Chagall, Dufy, Modigliani, Picasso, Vlaminck and others from the Wakefield-Mori Collection. There is also a comprehensive collection of local and prehistoric exhibits (including the negroid skull discovered in 1884 in the caves of Baoussé-Roussé, Italian Balzi-Rossi).

## Old Town

Harbour

The Old Town is reached by way of the Rue St-Michel, the continuation of the Avenue Félix-Faure. On the east side are the Harbour and the Plage des

Sablettes, the principal beach which has been artificially improved and is well maintained.

Farther north along the Montée des Logettes and the narrow Rue Longue, the former main street of the Old Town, the atmosphere of which is thoroughly Italian (a tunnel now runs under this area), we pass the remains of the town fortifications. On the left an imposing flight of steps (Rampes St-Michel) leads up to an observation terrace. Here on the left side of the Place de la Conception stands the Parish Church of St-Michel (17th c.; winged altar by Manchello 1569) and higher up is the Eglise de la Conception of 1685. Both churches are in the Italian Jesuit style. On the old castle hill, reached via the Rue du Vieux Château or the Montée du Souvenir, lies the Old Cemetery (altitude 46m/151ft; fine view) which was laid out in the 19th c. and has become the last resting place for rich foreigners of various faiths.

## Outer districts

*Jardin Botanique

From the cemetery the Boulevard de Garavan runs above the east bay to the Jardin Botanique on the right. This exotic garden on the site of the former Villa Val Rameh, contains many tropical and sub-tropical plants which flourish in the warm climate of Menton. From the terrace there is a view of the town and the sea. Above the Boulevard de Garavan lies the Jardin des Colombières, a park adorned with Mediterranean flora and ancient statues. The road now reaches the Pont St-Louis on the French–Italian frontier. From here it is possible to drive back to the town centre along the Quai Laurent which follows the east bay.

Monastère de l'Annociade

The Monastère de l'Annociade (Capuchin monastery) lies outside the town to the north-east, high above the road to Sospel, with a marvellous panorama. Continuing under the motorway, there is a good view on the right of the typical Provençal village of Castellar.

Castillin Neuf

By following the road up the Valley of the Careï we reach Castillin Neuf, a village which was exemplarily rebuilt after the Second World War.

## Surroundings of Menton

Ste-Agnès

A narrow winding mountain road leads north-west to Ste-Agnès (11km/7 miles), a "village perché", in a most attractive situation with picturesque stepped streets. The hamlet is the starting-point for fine walks in the mountains, including the ascent of the Pic de Baudon (1264m/4148ft; 2–3 hours), a climb which in places is very arduous but which rewards the climber with good views.

*Villa Hanbury

There is a worthwhile excursion to the Villa Hanbury, near Mortola Inferiore 4km/2½ miles inside Italy. The 18ha/45 acre park, originally laid out by an English merchant's family named Hanbury, contains 8ha/20 acres of typical Mediterranean vegetation with Aleppo pines, and 10ha/25 acres of gardens in which, since 1898, 7500 different species have been planted (today it is estimated that there are still about 2000). Open: Thur.–Tues. Oct.–May: 10am–4pm; June–Sept.: 9am–6pm.

# Mercantour · Gorges des Alpes-Maritimes

C/D4/5

Départements: Alpes-Maritimes, Alpes-de-Haute-Provence
Altitude: up to 3143m/9994ft

Location

The Massif du Mercantour is situated in the extreme south of the Alpine chain, about 50km/31 miles north of Nice as the crow flies. The Franco-

Italian frontier runs over its principal crest. A considerable part of this mountainous region forms the Parc National du Mercantour, 200,000ha/494,200 acres, founded in 1979, which is continued on the Italian side by the Parco Nazionale della Argentera. Information: Parc National du Mercantour, 23 rue d'Italie, B.P. 316, F-06006 Nice Cedex.

Vallée des Merveilles

The attraction of the Mercantour has in some places caused problems, especially on Mont Bego in the Vallée des Merveilles. More than 100,000 figurative symbols, which the Bronze Age people carved in the rock here (1800–1500 B.C.) are under severe threat. The messages to the gods repeat over and over again a few motifs: the celestial bull which brings thunder and lightning; the three-edged dagger, typical of the Bronze Age; the scythe and geometric figures. "Friends of nature" contribute their own messages or help themselves to souvenirs and so certain areas have been closed and educational trails laid out. In Tende there is a museum devoted to research and documentation of the history of the herdsmen and the Vallée des Merveilles from the Bronze Age to the present day.

Access

The best route to the National Park from the Mediterranean coast is the N202 west of Nice which leads inland up the valley of the Var. From the north the stretch from Gap via Barcelonnette to Auron crosses the highest pass in the Alps, the Col de la Bonette (2802m/9196ft).

**Gorges des Alpes-Maritimes**

The following description of the route through the gorges to the south of the Mercantour National Park is given from south to north.

*Gorges de la Vésubie

About 23km/14 miles north of Nice airport the D2565 branches off near Plan-du-Var into the Gorges de la Vésubie, the impressive ravines of the

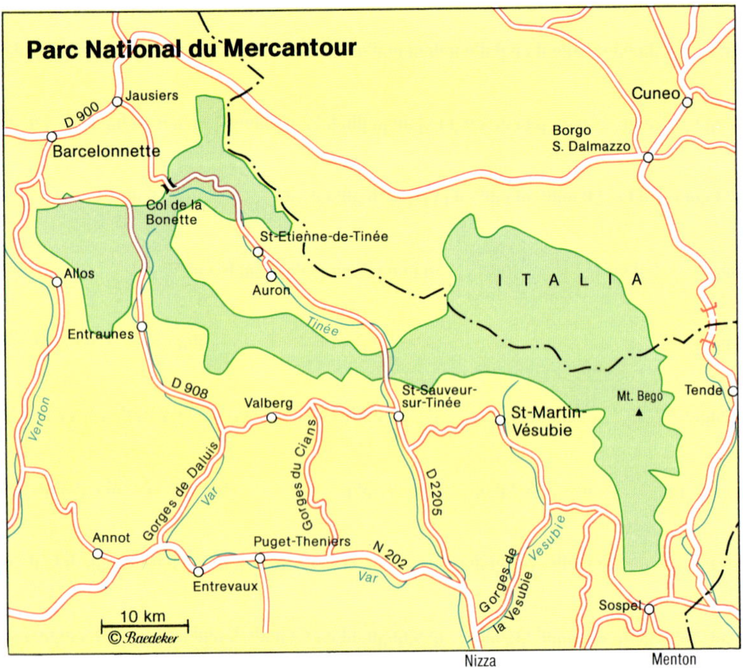

*St-Jean-la-Rivière in the valley of the Vésubie*

river of the same name. Follow the road through the narrow lower part of the valley for 10km/6 miles to the village of St-Jean-la-Rivière. From here a narrow winding road on the left comes, via the village of Utelle, to the Pilgrimage Church of Notre-Dame-des Miracles (Madone d'Utelle) which was founded in the 9th c. From the church, which is at a height of 1174m/3855ft, the view extends over the mountains to the Mediterranean.

After the diversion near Plan-du-Var mentioned above, the main road continues along the river which, not far to the north, rushes through the Défilé du Chaudan, a picturesque gorge framed by vertical cliffs. At the far end of the gorge the Route Nationale crosses the river by the Pont de la Mescla. The sloping strata of limestone at the narrow part of the gorge near the place where the D2205 turns off on the right, just short of the bridge, make a very impressive sight. We now follow D2205 into the valley of the Tinée. *Défilé du Chaudan

The river Tinée, which is now followed, flows through the Gorges de la Mescla just before its confluence with the Var. The gorges are a scenic highlight of this magnificent stretch. The valley is quite wide as far as Bancairon, then the road again hugs the rock face. We pass the villages of Clans and Marie, which are built high up on outcrops and are worth making a detour to see (very narrow winding streets). *Gorges de la Mescla

Beyond Bolinette the scenery changes. The white and grey limestone with its huge and often dramatically folded rock strata gradually is replaced by dark porphyry, a uniform brittle volcanic rock, which can also be seen in the Gorges Supérieures du Cians (see page 162). The harmony of rocks and luxuriant vegetation is very beautiful.

About 21km/113 miles after leaving the Route Nationale, the D2565 turns right over the 1500m/4923ft high Col St-Martin into the beautiful upland

Valley of the Boréon, the starting point of many mountain footpaths. The D2205 continues to follow the main valley to the high mountain region which is popular both in summer and in winter for walking, mountaineering and skiing.

Beyond St-Sauveur (belfry of 1333, altarpiece of 1483) the D30 branches off and winds along amid a gentle alpine landscape, with terraced meadows and deciduous and coniferous forests, through the following small mountain resorts: the village of Roure (16th c. church of St-Laurent with 13th c. belfry) perched boldly on the mountainside; Roubion (alt.1200m/3938ft; on the left of the D38 before reaching the village are the 16th c. Chapel of St-Sébastien; wall paintings); and Beuil with a 15th c. belfry, a 17th c. church with interesting paintings and a 16th c. Chapel of the White Penitents with trompe-l'œil paintings on the façade. Finally the road leads west to the winter sports village of Valberg, but by turning south we enter the Gorges du Cians.

**Gorges du Cians

By following the N202 from the Pont de la Mescla (see above) for about 19km/12 miles we reach a junction on the right, the D28, which leads to the Gorges du Cians. The cleft which the River Cians has cut into the rock is up to 80m/263ft deep, but in places only a few metres wide. The road runs alongside the river at the bottom of the gorge.

The road first traverses the Gorges Inférieures, the 5km/3 mile long stretch dominated by 450m/1477ft high chalk pinnacles, to the Moulin de Rigaud. Then the road winds upwards into the more rugged and deeper Gorges Supérieures 7km/4 miles long, which are entirely cut into the dark red porphyry.

*Gorges du Daluis

Still fully 20km/12 miles farther up the Valley of the Var, beyond the village of Entrevaux (see entry), the D902 diverges from the N202 which climbs towards the top of the pass – the Col de Toutes Aures (1124m/3689ft) – 18km/11 miles to the west. The D902 follows the upper course of the Var and reveals another rewarding landscape. The Gorges du Daluis are an impressive 6km/4 mile long ravine, with the road up to 200m/644ft above the Var. Curious red porphyry walls, in places flecked with green, line the road which is led through them in tunnels or around them.

Lac de Castillon

By driving over the Col de Toutes Aures and past the attractive reservoir of Castillon, we reach Castellane (see entry) and continue into the magnificent gorges of the Verdon (see entry).

## Monaco D5

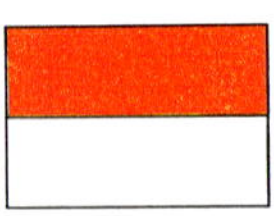

*Flag*

**Principality of Monaco**
Area: 1.95sq.km/¾sq.mile
Altitude: sea level to 65m/213ft
Number of citizens: 4500
Number of inhabitants: 28,000
Car identity letters: MC

*Coat of arms and International Licence Plate*

The old town of Monaco, at the eastern end of the Côte d'Azur, close to the Italian border, is a principality. It was founded in 1297 by the Genoese noble family of Grimaldi and until 1861 also took in Menton and Roquebrune. To this day it is still ruled by princes belonging to the Grimaldi dynasty (since 1949 Prince Rainier III). Monaco is important today not only as an economic centre, but also as an inexhaustible topic of interest for the world's popular press.

Monaco, formally the Principality of Monaco, has an area of 1.95sq.km/¾sq.mile, making it the second smallest European state after the Vatican City. The population, which is predominantly Catholic, consists of indigenous Monégasques (around 17%, with their own local dialect,

Monegasco, which is a mixture of Provençal and Ligurian), French (about 50%), Italians (about 20%) and the remainder made up of other nationalities. Residence on the rock of Monaco itself is reserved for the local Monégasques.

Two famous motor-racing events are closely associated with the principality: the Monaco Grand Prix (the week-end following Ascension Day), the only Formula One race in the world to be held on public roads, and the Monte-Carlo Rally, the route of which in fact lies almost completely on French soil.

History

Prehistoric finds in the area now occupied by the present-day town of Monaco indicate that there were settlements here before the Stone Age. Around 900 B.C. Phoenicians dedicated a rock to the Baal of Tyre (the Melkart cult). After its development as a trading centre by the Greeks it became a port under the Romans and was given the name "Herculis Monoeci Portus". Its subsequent history was influenced by the effects of population migrations and Saracen rule. From the 8th c. A.D. Monaco found itself under Genoese authority. The fief of Monaco was provided with a fortress in 1215, remains of which are still recognisable today, and since 1297 has been ruled by the Genoese noble family of Grimaldi, which in 1612 was granted the title of prince. After a period under Spanish protection Monaco came under the control of the French line of Goyon de Matignon-Grimaldi and in 1793 was united with France. In 1814 it was returned to Prince Honoré IV and between 1815 and 1860 came under the protection of the kingdom of Sardinia, only to be transferred back to France in 1860. Prince Charles III protested at this and in return for ceding Mentone (Menton) and Roccabruna (Roquebrune) to France, the principality was given its independence. In 1866 the town of Monte-Carlo was founded. In 1911 Albert I drew up a constitution for the principality and in 1918 relations with

*Monaco: panorama from the Tête du Chien*

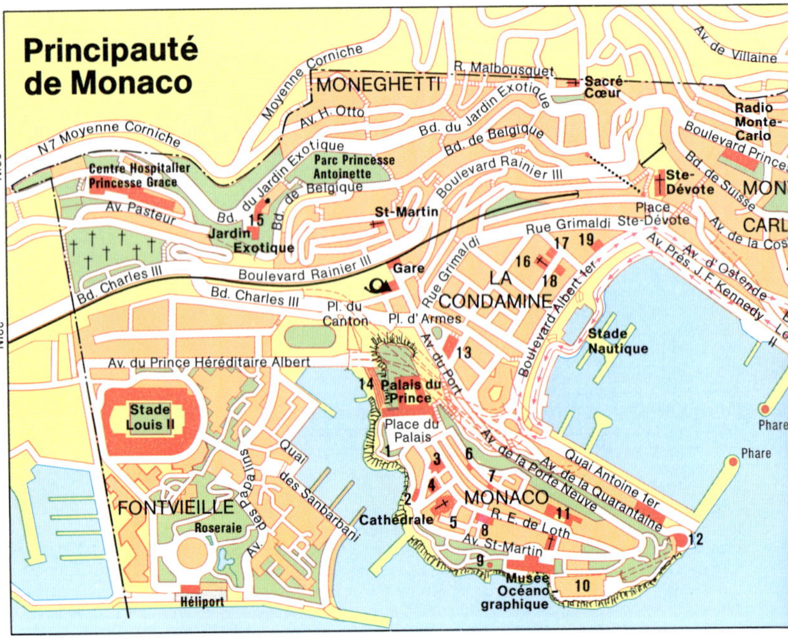


France were put on a new footing. In 1949 Rainier III succeeded Louis II, who had reigned since 1922, and in 1956 he married the American film actress Grace Kelly (Princess Gracia Patricia; d. 1982).

Government

The 1962 constitution defines the state as a constitutional hereditary monarchy. The reins of government are formally invested with the Prince and are delegated by him to the Minister of State. Apart from budgetary questions, the Head of State has an absolute right of veto within the government.

The government is made up of a minister of state (Ministre d'État) and three government councils (Conseils de Gouvernement) for Home Affairs, Finance and Economics, and Public Works and Social Services. In addition there is also a council of state and a trade council.

Representation of the people consists of the National Council (Conseil National), elected for five years, with 18 members, and a Community Council (Conseil Communal) elected for four years. The actual parliament is the Conseil National, which meets twice a year.

In internal as well as external affairs, the government has close links with France, both in terms of customs and monetary union (dating from 1865 and 1925 respectively) as well as in taxation laws.

Stamps

The principality is part of France for the purposes of customs administration, but since 1885 it has issued its own stamps, which are used for letters sent from Monaco. The Office des Emissions de Timbre-Poste (2 Avenue St Michel; open: Mon.–Fri. 8.30am–4.30pm) has set up a collectors' service, which can supply stamps (also by subscription).

Economy

Gambling has made Monaco rich and famous. Today the receipts from the casino, the Café de Paris and the gambling room of the Hotel Loews

represent a mere 4% of the budget; nevertheless, apart from high taxes on consumer spending, which make up 55% of its income, the state levies no other taxes, either on income, capital growth or wealth. The largest items of expenditure are culture and science.

Besides the Monaco of gambling and casinos, there is also an industrial and commercial Monaco which is of great importance. More than 2700 firms employ over 21,000 people, of whom half live in France. In the narrower industrial sector the number of firms has risen from 162 in 1949 to close on 400 at the present time. These industries include electrical and electronic goods, publishing, chemical and pharmaceutical products, perfume and synthetic materials. Monaco also plays an important role today as a financial centre. In less than 15 years three urban areas have been created by building out into the sea and the land area of the town has thereby been expanded by 20% with the addition of nearly another 2sq.km. The principality sees its role today very much in the service sector. The number one money earner is tourism; in 1989 there were almost 250,000 overnight stays (28% from Italy, 22% from France, 12% from the USA, 9% from Great Britain, 4.5% from Germany). The tourist organisation whose presence is felt throughout Monaco is the Société des Bains de Mer (S.C.B.), founded in 1856, whose brief was to bring money into the tiny and impoverished principality. The most important hotels and restaurants belong to it, as do the casino, the opera house, the golf club and other sporting facilities. The largest hotel is the 636-room Loews Monte-Carlo, which also can boast a casino, night-club, cabaret and swimming-pool, and which on the 1350sq.m/1615sq.yds of its "Grand Salon" can welcome up to 1500 guests. In general Monaco has completely adapted itself to its role as a conference, convention, exhibition and festival centre. Besides the Centre de Congrès–Auditorium Monte-Carlo (in the Les Spélugues complex)

*The Palais du Prince in Monaco town*

whose amphitheatre will hold 1100 guests, there is the Centre des Rencontres Internationales and the Monte-Carlo Sporting Club with its famous Salle des Étoiles. And in 1994 the Centre Culturel et des Expositions, which surpasses all the others in terms of size and facilities, is due to come into operation.

Organised events

The cycle of organised events, of whatever kind, never halts in Monaco, from traditional festivals such as that of Ste Dévote (January 27th, when a boat is set on fire), car rallies, television festivals and flower parades, to the International Circus Festival in December (see Events). The Monte-Carlo Opera and Philharmonic Orchestra are also renowned, with outstanding conductors and orchestras from all over the world giving guest performances here. In Monaco Diaghilev founded his world-famous "Ballet Russe" in 1909.

## Monaco-Ville

Location

With its narrow streets Monaco-Ville, the oldest district and seat of the Bishop, dominates a broad picturesque peninsula jutting out into the sea. Here much evidence of earlier fortification is to be seen.

*Place du Palais

In the western part of Monaco lies the Place du Palais with its bronze cannons dating from the time of Louis XIV; from here there is a beautiful view of Monte-Carlo. Dominating the square is the Palais du Prince, built in the 13th c. as a Genoese fortress. The changing of the guard takes place every day at 11.55am. Apart from providing this display, the Prince's Guard is also responsible for the security of the Prince and his family and also appears at major events.
In the Palais there are splendid apartments, including the throne-room in Empire style, the York bedroom (18th c.) and beautiful 17th c. frescos

*"Grand Prix de Monaco" – the "Ancien Gare" curve*

(Genoese work). Tours take place when the Prince and his family are absent (in which case the Prince's flag on the Tour Ste-Marie is not raised) June 1st–Sept. 30th, 9.30am–6.30pm; October 10am–5pm.
In the Palace Museum (officially Musée Napoléonien et des Archives Monegasques; opening times as for the Palais; additionally Dec.–Mar., Thur.–Sun. 10.30am–12.30pm, 2–5pm) can be seen many mementoes of Napoleon I, a stamp collection and a rock sample from the moon.
During the summer months concerts take place in the palace courtyard.

Cathedral

The Rue du Tribunal leads from the palace to the cathedral, built between 1875 and 1884 in the Romanesque-Byzantine style. A chapel to St Nicolas, dating from 1252, was pulled down to make way for the building of the cathedral. Inside can be seen an altarpiece by Louis Bréa (*c.* 1500), other works of the Nice School, as well as tombs of the princes (burial place of the Princes of Monaco) and bishops. The grave of Princess Grace is also to be found here.
Opposite stands the Palais de Justice (lawcourts) and nearby the Historial des Princes (historical collection), as well as the notable Chapelle de la Miséricorde of 1639; the first provost of the penitential monks resident here was Prince Honoré II. Inside there is a wooden statue of Christ, by François-Joseph Bosio, official sculptor of Napoleon, born in 1769 in Monaco (d. 1845 in Paris).

*Musée Océanographique (Plan p. 168)

The Jardins de St-Martin extend along the coast round the peninsula with a steep cliff on the seaward side, near which stands a statue commemorating Prince Albert I, celebrated as a marine researcher. At the end of the gardens is the Musée Océanographique (marine museum); the façade facing the sea is 87m/286ft high and rests on massive foundations. The museum, which was opened in 1910 and took eleven years to build, houses valuable scientific collections (objects from Prince Albert's journeys of exploration, finds, submarines and diving equipment of Jacques-Yves Cousteau, slides

## (Museum of Oceanography)

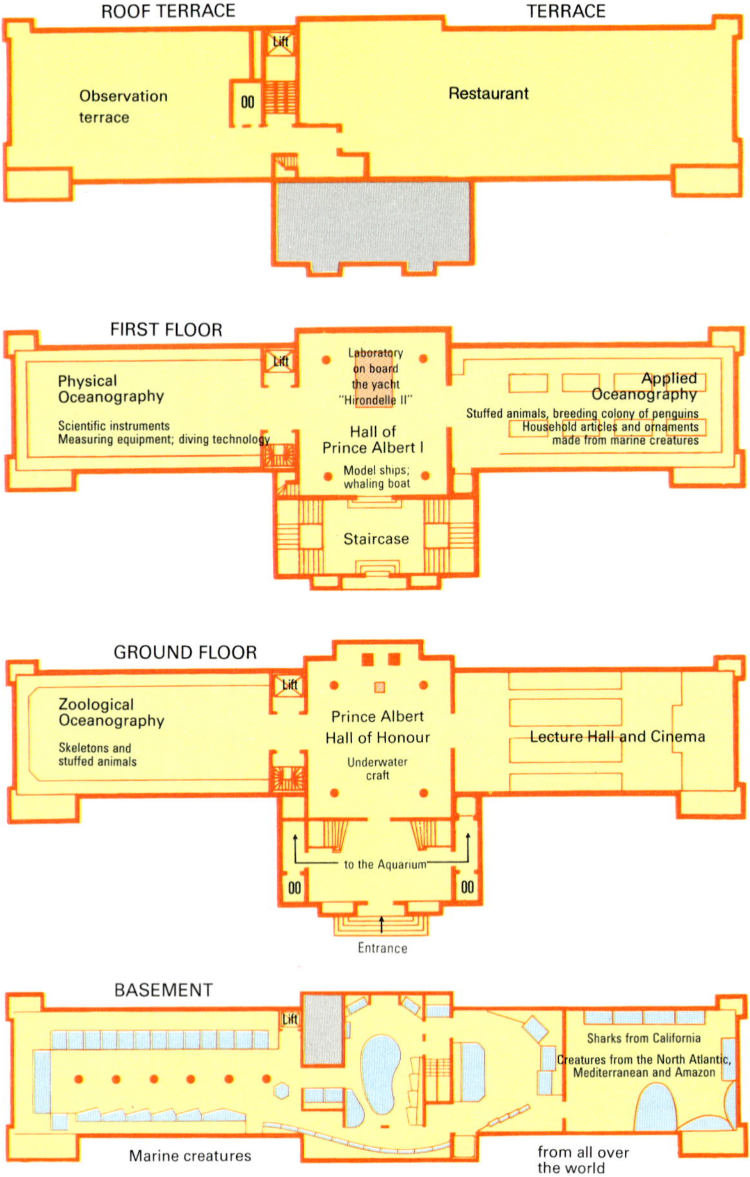

of marine plants and animals), also an important aquarium, laboratory and library and exhibits of model ships and educational film shows, especially about Jacques-Yves Cousteau. From the roof terrace (restaurant) it is possible to enjoy a superb view of the Italian Riviera as far as the Esterel Massif (also visible from Fort Antoine on the east of the peninsula). Open: July, Aug. 9am–9pm; Apr.–June, Sept. 9am–7pm; Oct.–Mar. 9.30am–7pm. On the western slope of the cliff is the Centre d'Acclimatation Zoologique (a centre for animal acclimatisation, a kind of zoo with tropical and African fauna), established in 1954.

## The Old Town

Fontvieille

A 222,000sq.m/265,500sq.yd area was laid down and protected from the sea by a dam 30m/98ft deep in order to create the district of Fontvieille. To the west, underneath the rock, on which the old town rises, is the newly laid-out Port de Fontvieille. Behind the harbour the Stade Louis II was opened in 1985, a modern sports stadium with 20,000 roofed seats. There are guided visits, daily 3pm and 4.30pm.

Harbour

To the north, at the foot of the cliff, lies the busy, almost square-shaped, harbour which was constructed between 1901 and 1926. Large numbers of yachts, including from time to time the Prince's private vessel, are to be seen here. On the western side of the harbour, near the Boulevard Albert I, is the modern Stade Nautique Rainier III, a stadium for water sports.

Centre de Rencontres

Near the northern mole of the harbour in the Avenue d'Ostende can be found the Centre de Rencontres Internationales, an international meeting-place with a roof terrace.

La Condamine

The Boulevard Albert I is the main street of the district of La Condamine. In this quarter of the town there are a large number of businesses, shops and

*View across the harbour of Monte-Carlo*

public buildings (railway station, library, market). In the ravine-like valley cleft on the northern edge of the town, below a road bridge stands the little Church of Ste-Dévote, dedicated to the patron saint of the town. The church has a fine 18th c. marble altar.

Moneghetti

Seemingly endless steps and roads with hairpin bends climb up the eastern slope of the Tête de Chien to the Moyenne Corniche (actually on French territory, N7; see Recommended Routes). These roads give access to the district of Moneghetti in the west of the principality, a part of the town which is built on terraces with fine villas and gardens.

**Jardin Exotique

The Jardin Exotique (Exotic Garden) is one of the most impressive of its kind. Because of the favourable climate, with little variation in conditions on the constantly warm and damp steep slope, a great variety of the most delicate, and in some cases unique, tropical plants thrive in the Exotic Garden. In the grottoes, beautiful fossils can be seen. In the park there is also the interesting Musée d'Anthropologie Préhistorique (Museum of Prehistory and Anthropology), which not only exhibits bones discovered in the area but also a collection of coins, ornamental objects, etc. from the pre-Roman and Roman periods in particular. Open: May 1st–Sept. 30th 9am–7pm; Oct. 1st–Apr. 30th 9am–6pm.
To the north of the museum lies the Parc Princesse Antoinette.

## Monte-Carlo

Location

The district of Monte-Carlo occupies a rocky promontory to the north of the Port of Monaco. Its most elevated part is crossed by streets with shops and offices, including the Boulevard Princesse Charlotte (in the west, the headquarters of Radio/Télévision Monte-Carlo), the Boulevard des Moulins (pavilion of the Office de Tourisme at its south-western end; a short distance to the north is the Church of St-Charles of 1883), and the Avenue de la Costa with its many luxury shops.

Casino

To the north of the harbour stands the magnificent Grand Casino, which was built by the architect of the Paris Opéra, Charles Garnier, between 1877 and 1879. It houses the legendary gaming-rooms, opened in 1861, of the Société Anonyme des Bains de Mer et du Cercle des Etrangers (S.B.M.). The company's full name makes reference to the fact that, to begin with, it was only allowed to open the doors of its casinos to non-Monégasques.
From the marble-covered atrium, surrounded by Ionic columns of onyx, one reaches the "Salle Garnier", the red and gold opera theatre, and the various gaming-rooms. There is a room with games machines (open from 10am, admission free), the American room with American roulette and Black Jack (open from 4pm, admission free) and the "European" salons with roulette, trente-et-quarante and baccarat (open: from 3pm, admission fee). The doormen insist on appropriate dress.

*Les Spélugues

Below the casino extends the large-scale complex of the Congress Centre (called Les Spélugues), which was opened in 1978. The Boulevard Louis II runs under the massive building which has been constructed of elements on a hexagonal plan and includes the 636-room Hotel "Loews", 100 apartments and a casino. On the highest roof-level, of which there is an excellent view from the terrace in front of the casino, there is a striking mosaic composed of coloured tiles, which was designed in 1979 by Victor Vasarély and has the title "Hexagrace–Le Ciel, la Mer, la Terre". The Fondation Vasarély in Aix-en-Provence (see entry) was responsible for its execution.

Larvotto

In the south-west of the district of Larvotto stands the Centre Culturel et des Expositions. In the Avenue Princess Grace can be found the "Musée National des Automates et Poupées d'Autrefois (museum of mechanical toys and dolls), housed in a villa of the Belle Époque. On view are several

*The Casino of Charles Garnier, the landmark of the Principality*

hundred dolls, more than 80 automatons and over 2000 miniature objects, the purpose of which is to depict life in the 18th and 19th c. In the garden there are sculptures by Zadkine, Maillol, Rodin and Bourdeille.

## Surroundings of Monaco

Cap d'Ail

At the foot of the Tête de Chien amid sparse pine-woods lies the holiday resort of Cap d'Ail (2km/1 mile to the south-east of Monaco). Of interest are the ruins of the Tour d'Abeglio and the open-air theatre, designed by Jean Cocteau and decorated with mosaics. Several rocky promontories jut out into the sea near Cap d'Ail.

La Turbie

The picturesque old township of La Turbie is situated on the saddle between a ridge of the Tête de Chien and the Mont de la Bataille, 8km/5 miles to the north-west of Monaco. In the Baroque church of St-Michel-Archange (St Michael Archangel; 2nd half of 18th c.) there is a most remarkable communion-rail made of agate and onyx, two paintings by Jean-Baptiste van Loo, a pietà of the school of Bréa and a fine High Altar of coloured marble, which was used during the French Revolution in Nice. Both town gates are relics of the fortification begun in the 13th c.

*Trophée des Alpes

La Turbie is dominated by a feature visible from afar, the Trophée des Alpes, also called the "Trophée d'Auguste". This is a monument which was erected to the Emperor Augustus by the Roman Senate in 6 B.C. as a memorial to the suppression of the alpine tribes (14–13 B.C.). In the 14th c. the monument was converted into a fortress and in 1705 blown up (with little success) by Louis XV during the War of the Spanish Succession. About 1930 restoration was begun to which the monument owes its present appearance. The funds were provided by an American and his wife. The grounds around the monument have been laid out as a park and from the steep south and south-eastern sides offer a marvellous view of the coast.

The "Trophée des Alpes" in La Turbie

Peillon, "village perché" par excellence

*Peillon

Peillon, situated at an altitude of 376m/1234ft in the hinterland of Monaco (5km/3 miles as the crow flies), is probably one of the finest examples of a Provençal "nid d'aigle". In the Chapel of Notre-Dame de la Madone-des-Douleurs (Chapel of the White Monks) there are frescos by Canavesi (15th/16th c.). In August the Fêtes du Vieux Village take place.

Peille

Another beautiful "village perché" (perched on a rock) is Peille, situated 630m/2067ft high above the River Peillon. The Romanesque church dating from the 12th c. boasts a rose martyry (16th c.) as well as beautiful naïve paintings. Over the village tower the ruins of a 13th c. castle.

## Montélimar C2

Région: Rhône-Alpes
Département: Drôme
Altitude: 81m/266ft
Population: 30,000

Location

Montélimar lies not far to the east of the Rhône, which is dammed in this section, some 150km/93 miles south of Lyon. The River Roulion flows past the town centre.

Montélimar, which derives its name from its castle (Mont Adhémar), is known for its nougat industry, which uses locally grown almonds and honey from Provence. The confectionery comes in many varieties, hard or soft, white or coloured, "normal" or in various flavours or "perfumes": vanilla, honey, lavender . . . Shops selling it are to be found on Allées Champs de Mars and Boulevard A. Briand (ring-road, car parking).

Castle

To the east of the old town rises the castle, built by the powerful Adhémar family (see Grignan) in the 12th c. From 1340 to 1383 the castle, together

*The castle of the Adhémar family in Montélimar*

with the town, came into the possession of the Popes, who were responsible for enlarging it. In the 16th c. it formed the north-east corner of the fortified town. From 1791 the castle was used as a prison (until 1926) – a role which it had fulfilled on and off since the 15th c. Still preserved are the massive square Tour de Narbonne, the donjon (keep), logis (tower with living quarters) and the St-Pierre chapel, probably the oldest building in the complex, which displays the early Southern French Romanesque style (11th c.) and has 14th c. frescos in its main apse.
From its terraces and tower the castle offers a vantage point; in the north the cooling towers of the atomic power station at Cruas on the Rhône can be seen.

## Montmajour · Fontvieille D2

Département: Bouches-du-Rhône
Altitude: 15m/49ft

### *Abbaye de Montmajour

Location and History

The former Benedictine Abbey of Montmajour (Mont-Major), perched on a rocky hill 5km/3 miles north-east of Arles, rather like a fortress, was founded in the 10th c. and throughout the Middle Ages was an important place of pilgrimage. This pilgrimage could lead to the "Pardon of Montmajour" and provided the monastery with a plentiful source of income. Other monasteries were founded by the monks from this abbey. The plain surrounding the hill was originally marsh and alluvial land and was not drained until the abbey was founded. At the start of the 18th c. the Baroque buildings were begun, as the original 12th c. buildings had largely fallen

## Former Benedictine Abbey

# Montmajour

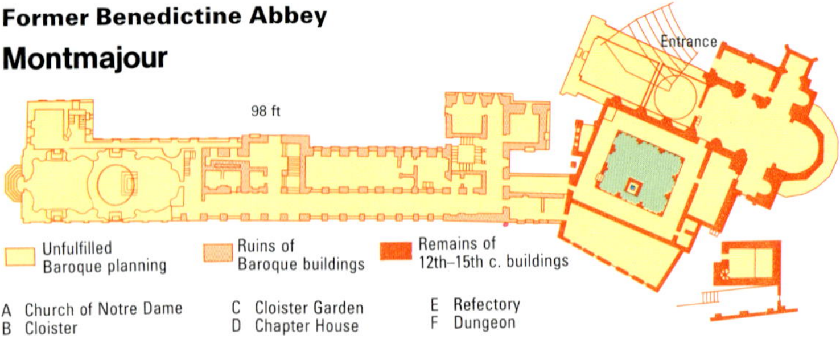


into disrepair; however in 1785/86 the abbot, Cardinal Rohan, was implicated in the famous "necklace" affair and the monastery was closed. In 1791, together with most church property, it was confiscated and sold.

**Visit**

The large plan drawings in the lobby of the ticket office offer an initial overview of the abbey; other sketches are to be found in the parts of the abbey open to the public. Open: Apr. 1st–Sept. 30th 9am–6.30pm, otherwise 9–11.30am, 2–4.30pm; closed on public holidays.

**Crypt**

The first part of the monastery to be visited is the huge Romanesque crypt, dating from the 12th c., which forms the load-bearing foundation of the church above, and which is partly built into the rock. The central space is surrounded by a vaulted corridor with apses in a semicircle, with which round-arched openings in the walls connect.

**Church**

From the crypt the single-aisled church above can be reached; this is a short, rugged, austere building with only two bays in the nave, a semicircular main apse and two side apses; at the end of the left transept is the square Chapelle Notre-Dame-la-Blanche. In the 18th c. plans were made to extend the nave considerably to the west, but the plans were never realised.

**Cloister**

The cloister is entered from the second transept and adjoins the church on the south-west. It was probably built at the same time as the church, though only the east wing shows the original Romanesque outline. The rounded arches are divided by double pillars in threes or fours; rich ornamentation (comparable to that at St-Trophime at Arles; see entry) can be seen on the corbels which support the ribbed vaults. The cloister, in the middle of which stands a well mounted on a pedestal, is overlooked by the battlemented defensive keep, 26m/85ft high, which was built in 1369 and boasts a superb view from its roof.

**Baroque ruins**

To the west of the Romanesque buildings are the ruins of extensions to it which date from the Baroque period and which are not open to the public. This enormous construction – a length of 135m/443ft was planned, whilst a further 90m/295ft were added during the building – was undertaken in 1703 by the architect Pierre Mignard. In 1726 a fire destroyed those parts which had been completed. Restoration of the damaged parts and further building under Jean-Baptiste Franque came to a halt in 1736.

**Ste-Croix**

On the right of the road about 200m/220yds east of the monastery stands the little Chapelle Ste-Croix (Chapel of the Holy Cross), dating from the 12th c. It was once the cemetery chapel of the monastery as is indicated by the tombs which were hewn into the rock.

Montmajour Abbey: the cloister and keep

Moulin de Daudet, a symbol of Provence

## Fontvieille

*Moulin de Daudet

To the north-east of Montmajour (5km/3 miles), near Fontvieille, stands one of the most popular attractions of Provence for the French – the windmill made famous by the writer Alphonse Daudet in his book "Lettres de mon Moulin". Daudet did not live in the mill, however, and the "Lettres" were not written here but in Paris. Nevertheless it is a fact that Daudet derived the inspiration for a great part of his literary output in this region. In the base of the windmill there is a small museum with mementoes to the poet (open: 9am–noon, 2–7pm; Sun. only in Jan.). There is a good view down the valley to the Rhône, with two old watch-towers in the distance.

Aqueducs Romains (Roman Aqueducts)

On either side of the D33 road, about 3km/2 miles south of Fontvieille, the visitor will find the remains of two Roman aqueducts, which once provided water for Arles. The ruins have not been restored, but have been left uncovered and are easily accessible.

## Montpellier D1

Région: Languedoc-Roussillon
Département: Hérault
Altitude: 50m/164ft
Population: 202,000

Location and importance

Montpellier, university city, diocesan city and capital of the region of Languedoc-Roussillon and of the département of Hérault, is situated some distance west of the Camargue on the River Lez, some 10km/6 miles from the coast of the Golfe du Lion. With its three universities, national élite schools (Grandes Écoles), agricultural college (the "Agropolis" agrarian

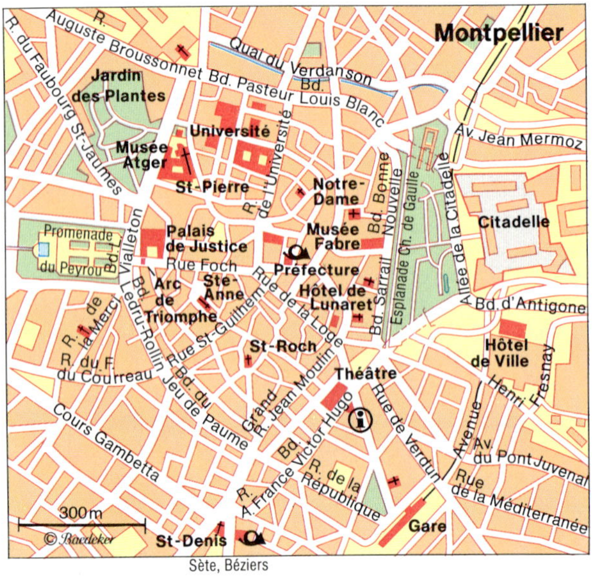


research centre), libraries, conservatoire, etc. it is an economic and cultural centre for the region.
Although Montpellier is not actually in Provence, it is an attraction for visitors touring the western part of the region and is therefore included in this book.

History

The town came into being after the second destruction of the nearby settlement of Maguelone by Charles Martel (737). In the 13th c. it belonged to the Kings of Aragon, then until 1349 to the Kings of Mallorca as vassals of the French. As early as 1289 Montpellier had a university, where Francesco Petrarch studied from 1316 to 1319 and François Rabelais from 1530 to 1532 and from 1537 to 1538. At the end of the 16th c. the city was a headquarters of the Huguenots. In 1622 it was conquered by Louis XIII.

## Sights

Place de la Comédie

The Place de la Comédie with its Fontaine des Trois Grâces, a fountain dating from 1776, is the heart of the Inner City. On the south-western side of the square stands the theatre (opera-house). From here the great boulevards radiate around the area of the Old Town (the greater part a pedestrian precinct), which extends to the north-west on a hilltop. In the Old Town the 50 or so patrician and merchants' mansions from the 17th/18th c. testify to the former wealth of the city.

*Promenade du Peyrou

From the Place de la Comédie the visitor can take the Rue de la Loge (pedestrian area) and the Rue Foch, impressive with its splendid 19th c. buildings, to reach the Promenade du Peyrou, an elevated park on two levels, dating from the 17th and 18th c., which offers a beautiful view as far as the Cévennes and the sea. At the intersection of the promenades stands an equestrian statue of Louis XIV, dating from 1828, while at the western end of the terraces is a water-tower. The water is led through a channel

14m/46ft wide which was constructed between 1753 and 1766 and which terminates in an imposing aqueduct 800m/875yds long and up to 21.5m/71ft high. On both sides of the water-tower steps lead down to the Boulevard des Arceaux where the market is held.

Arc de Triomphe

Forming the gateway to the Old Town, the Arc de Triomphe, a 15m/49ft high triumphal arch in honour of Louis XIV, stands at the east end of the Promenade du Peyrou, on the northern side of which is the stately Palais de Justice (lawcourts). Rue Foch, which goes east from here, is impressive for its fine 19th c. buildings.

Jardin des Plantes

Flanking the Boulevard Henri IV, just to the north of the Arc de Triomphe, lies the Jardin des Plantes; laid out in 1593, it was the first botanical garden in France and has a large number of exotic plants.

Musée Atger

The Musée Atger (Boulevard Henri IV) has drawings by French and Italian masters from the Baroque period on display. The impressive building was originally a bishop's palace belonging to the Abbey of St-Bênoit (14th and 16th c.); since the French Revolution it has been the seat of the Faculté de Médicine, founded in 1221. The Maison d'Heidelberg (Centre Culturel Franco-Allemand) is also housed here.

To the north of the museum stands the Tour des Pins, a relic of the medieval city fortifications.

Cathédrale de St-Pierre

To the east of the Faculté de Médicine (Rue de l'École de Médicine) stands the Gothic cathedral of St-Pierre, founded in 1364 after the Wars of Religion and restored in 1867. The severe double-towered façade has a high-vaulted canopied portico.

*Musée Fabre

At the eastern edge of the Old Town, diametrically opposite the Promenade du Peyrou, lies its simpler counterpart, the Esplanade Charles de Gaulle. On the west side (Rue Montpellieret) stands the Musée Fabre, which includes a picture gallery with works by old Italian and Dutch painters, as well as older and more modern French masters and fine 18th c. sculptures.

Corum

At the northern end of the Esplanade Charles de Gaulle Corum, the opera hall and conference building by Claude Vasconi, was opened in 1990 (Opéra Berlioz, 2000 seats). From its roof terrace there is a beautiful view across the Old Town to the sea.

To the east of the Esplanade stands the former citadel, built in 1624, which is today used for educational purposes (Lycée Joffre).

Antigone

To the east of the Polygone department store, between Bd. Antigone and Allées du Nouveau Monde, Ricardo Bofill has constructed the Antigone district, which stretches as far as the River Lez, and which is a shining example of post-modern architecture.

## Mont Ventoux

C3

Département: Vaucluse
Altitude: 1909m/6265ft

Location

Mont Ventoux is situated in the north-west of Provence in the latitude of Orange to the east of the Rhône, from which it is separated by the Valley of the Ouvèze.

Landscape

Mont Ventoux (Provençal Mont Ventour = windy mountain), which takes its name from the frequent and violent storms that are experienced in the area, is a long limestone ridge, geologically a continuation of the Pyrénées. It towers in impressive isolation over the surrounding countryside, its summit completely bare and devoid of vegetation, evidence of the drastic deforestation which the whole mountain has undergone. Above 1500m/4923ft there are extensive ski-slopes.

History

According to tradition, on April 24th 1336, the poet Francesco Petrarch climbed Mont Ventoux. This first ascent of a mountain for its own sake – albeit totally from religious and spiritual motives – reflects the increasing feeling for nature of a new age.
From 1902 until the 1960s the present road (D974) on the southern slopes of Mont Ventoux was a motor-racing course of international repute.

## **Drive over Mont Ventoux

North side

A typical starting-point for a drive over the mountain is Vaison-la-Romaine (see entry) to the north-west of the Ventoux Massif. Follow the D938 as far as Malaucène, then turn left on to the D974. This stretch, which traverses exceptionally beautiful scenery with magnificent views on both sides, climbs fairly steeply through coniferous forests. Some 16km/9 miles beyond Malaucène, at an altitude of about 1400m/4595ft, there is a junction where a narrow road leads to the viewpoint of Le Contrat. Beyond the junction the D974 is closed in winter, and even in early summer the availability to traffic of this road, which in any case is not particularly wide, may be further restricted by snow on the northern flank of Mont Ventoux. For the last 6km/4 miles the road winds upwards, the vegetation becoming increasingly scanty, until at 1829m/6001ft the highest point of the road is reached at the Col des Tempêtes (literally Pass of Storms), where there is an orientation table. From here there is a magnificent view over the Valley of the Toulourenc and the mountains rising beyond it. At this point the pass is fully exposed to the frequent storms which roar violently over the crest.

Summit

On the summit of Mont Ventoux an observatory and a television transmitter have been erected, with a radar station a little lower down. Near the

*Sunrise on Mont Ventoux*

observatory can be found an observation platform facing south, from where the view extends to the Montagne du Lubéron (see Lubéron).

South side

The road downhill on the southern side is less steep, has fewer bends and is also wider than the road on the northern flank. It descends to the valley amid gravel slopes completely bare of vegetation. After 6km/4 miles there is a junction; the turning on the right, which formed part of the former racing circuit, goes to Bédoin and on to Carpentras. To the left the D164 goes via Sault to Aps. From Sault, though, the trip through the Gorges de la Nesque (see Carpentras) is definitely not to be missed.

## Nice

D5

Département: Alpes-Maritimes
Altitude: sea level to 20m/66ft
Population: 400,000

*Location

Nice, capital of the département of Alpes-Maritimes and diocesan city, lies on the Baie des Anges (Bay of Angels), surrounded by the foothills of the Maritime Alps, in the eastern part of the Côte d'Azur, about 30km/19 miles from the Franco-Italian border. Its sheltered location and mild climate made Nice one of the classic winter resorts of the Côte d'Azur and right up to the present time it has remained one of the most popular places of all for holidays.

History

Proof of prehistoric settlement has been found in the caves of the castle hill and in those of Mont Boron further to the east. Phocaeans from Marseilles in 4 B.C. founded the strongpoint Nikaia Polis (town of Victory) on the castle hill, in what is now the Old Town. Later the Romans settled on the Hill of Cimiez on the far side of the River Paillon farther inland in order to protect the Via Julia.

Incursions by Saxons and Saracens wreaked havoc in the town, the former in the 6th c. and the latter in the 9th c. In the Middle Ages Nice formed part of the lands of the Count of Provence and from 1388 – after it had failed to recognise Louis of Anjou as heir to Provence – belonged to the dukedom of Savoy. In 1543 Nice, a Savoyard–Hapsburg city, was besieged by French and Turkish ships. In 1720 Savoy gained possession of Sardinia and it was at this period that the harbour and fortress were built (providing the only access to the sea for Piedmont). In 1792 Nice became part of France, in 1814 it was incorporated into the Kingdom of Sardinia, but in 1860 as a result of a referendum it was returned to France.

Nice is the birthplace of the Italian freedom fighter Giuseppe Garibaldi (1807–82). The painters Dufy and Matisse are buried here, and Paganini died in a house in the Rue de la Préfecture.

Max Gallo, writer and first government spokesman of President Mitterand, comes from Nice. Since 1966 Nice has also been a university city.

Economy and tourism

Its mild climate (average winter temperature 9°C/48°F) enabled Nice to become a popular winter health resort in the second half of the 19th c. and one of the earliest centres of tourism – the initial British "invasion" having been triggered off as far back as 1776 by the travel diaries of the Scottish doctor, Tobias Smollett. Until the 1920s Nice was merely a winter resort for rich elderly English gentry and Russian aristocrats, who whiled away their time at the gambling tables. After the First World War, in the wake of visits by American soldiers, artists and writers, the Riviera became well-known as an area for holidays and when in 1926 over 8000 American visitors spent July here, it could be said that modern mass tourism as we know it today had arrived. Yet for many years after that the income from the winter months far exceeded that of the summer season; this situation did not change until 1936, when French workers started to be given holidays with pay for the first time.

Today tourism to a large extent lives on the myth of previous times: the "wedding-cake" style architecture of the luxury hotels is now juxtaposed with concrete apartment blocks; the magnificent promenade round the bay is now a six-lane motorway; corruption, property speculation, organised crime, casino violence – these are the labels used to describe Nice these days. Since 1928, under the "rule" of the mayors Jean and Jacques Médecin, father and son, a "Mediterranean Chicago" has evolved over the years

(Jacques Médecin fled to Uruguay in September 1990) – "La Côte, c'est fini", was the cry . . . However, with the impact of "conference tourism" and the establishment of high-tech industry (especially in Sophia-Antipolis, a European "Silicon Valley") new fields of activity are being opened up for capital to be invested in. It should be noted that the Nice–Côte d'Azur airport, which was opened in 1962, is the second most important in France, even ahead of Marseilles.

*Nice: Hôtel Negresco*

In spite of all this Nice has remained a city with its own individual dynamism: a walk through the Old Town is sufficient to make that clear.

Carnival

The famous carnival, which has existed in Nice since the 14th c., begins 12 days before Ash Wednesday. During this period various performances and festivities succeed one another on a 2km/1 mile stretch of the town. The focus is near the Place Masséna of the Jardin Albert I. Processions of floats, cavalcades, masked balls, floral processions, showers of confetti and dancing in the streets are just a few of the highlights. The main Battle of Flowers is on the day after Ash Wednesday. The conclusion of the carnival is marked by a grand firework display on Shrove Tuesday which lights up the whole of the Baie des Anges. At Micarême (mid-Lent) a second celebration takes place.

## Colline du Château

The first part of the city to be settled was the Colline du Château (castle hill, 92m/302ft high), which can be reached by lift from the shore promenade (Quai des États-Unis) at the end of the Baie des Anges. The area at the top has been laid out as a park and offers an impressive panorama (orientation table). The citadel which once stood here was destroyed in 1706. Worth seeing are the remains of two churches built one above the other in the 11th and 15th c., which have now been excavated. Just to the east of the remains there is a good view of the harbour below.

Tour Bellanda

From the Colline du Château steps lead down to the promenade, passing the Tour Bellanda, a massive round tower built in the 16th c. on the site of the Bastion St Lambert, and in which Hector Berlioz composed his opera "King Lear". The tower houses the Musée Naval (maritime museum).

## Vieille Ville

**Location**

The lively and picturesque Old Town, with its maze of tiny alleyways and streets, in which one could be forgiven for imagining oneself transported to Italy, is popularly known as "Babazouk". It opens out at the western end of the Colline du Château and in the north-west is bounded by spacious boulevards and parks, which extend over the Paillon (Jardin Albert I, Place Masséna, Promenade du Paillon). In the south it is bordered by the Ponchettes, in which fishmongers and grocers supplement the wares on display at the market on the adjoining Cours Saleya.

**Galerie de Malacologie**

Near the eastern end of the Cours Saleya (no. 3), a short distance to the west of the steps descending from the castle hill, can be found a department of the Musée d'Histoire Naturelle (Musée Barla, see below) with an aquarium and an interesting collection of molluscs. Open: Tues.–Sat. 10.30am–1pm, 2–6pm; Nov. closed.

**Cours Saleya**

An Italian atmosphere – Nice did not become French until 1860 – pervades the Cours Saleya, a long plain square without any real "sights" (even if in 1796 Napoleon, then Chief Commander of the Italian army, resided in the house on the south-western corner). Known for its flower market (Tues.–Sun. mornings), its attraction really lies in the richness of Nice's daily life. The market offers all the things which go to make up the cuisine of the Côte d'Azur, from Nice olives, sheep's cheese and home-gathered mushrooms to fish. The obligatory junk market is held on Mondays. Here fashionable young people and peasant women converge and it is again possible to hear the "lenga nissarda", a mixture of French and the Italian dialect of the Riviera, which is once again being taught in the schools.
The flat roof of the "Ponchettes" (the double row of houses between Cours Saleya and Quai des États-Unis), which is several hundred metres long, is unfortunately not accessible; from there it would be possible to look across

*The Cours Saleya, the heart of Nice*

the Baie des Anges over to Antibes, and even to make out Corsica on a clear day.
The trilogy "The Bay of Angels", in which Max Gallo describes the story of an Italian immigrant family in Nice, was written in the yellow Baroque-style house on the east side of the Cours. On the north side stands the baroque Chapelle de la Miséricorde of 1736; inside there is an altar with the "Vierge de la Miséricorde" (Virgin of Mercy) by Jean Maralhet, dating from the early 15th c., and a picture of the Madonna ascribed to Bréa. This, the most beautiful church in Nice, is closed because of damage to the fabric of the building; a visit would only be possible at the discretion of the Palais Lascaris.

Palais Grimaldi

Adjoining the chapel to the north is the former Palais Grimaldi, built in 1611–13 and restored in 1907. Today it is the seat of the Préfecture (government administration). Nearby stands the Palais de Justice (lawcourts), completed in 1892.

*St-Jacques

On the Rue Droite, to the north-east of the Préfecture, stands the former Jesuit church of St-Jacques (also known as the Église du Gésu, after the Il Gesù church in Rome), which dates from the 17th c. and has a richly adorned interior and colourful stucco decorations. The Corinthian pilasters extend sufficiently far out into the nave for it to be possible to lay an ambulatory on top of them.

Ste-Réparate

The Cathedral of Ste-Réparate in the Place Rossetti is the episcopal church and was built in the 17th c. It contains elaborate ornamental plasterwork, fine choir-stalls and wooden panelling in the Sacristy.

*Palais Lascaris

Further north on the Rue Droite, the Palais Lascaris is well worth a visit. This sumptuous Baroque building dating from the middle of the 17th c. was the palace of the Lascaris-Vintimille family, Counts of Castellar and since 1963 restoration has been taking place. On the ground floor are the fine entrance hall and a 18th c. apothecary's premises. In the rooms on view there are furnishings from the 17th and 18th c., Flemish tapestries, rich stucco work and ceiling paintings of the Italian school. Regular temporary exhibitions show the cultural tradition of the region. Open: Tues.–Sun. 9.30am–noon, 2.30–6pm; Nov. closed.

Quai des États-Unis

The Quai des États-Unis, the eastern part of the boulevard flanking the Baie des Anges, was called the Quai du Midi until 1917. Its change of name was a gesture of thanks to the USA on the occasion of that country's entry into the First World War.

*Galerie des Ponchettes

On the Quai des États-Unis, a few steps from the western end of the Cours Saleya, the Galerie des Ponchettes (Musée Dufy) is housed in the former arsenal of the Sardinian Navy. The gallery displays an outstanding collection of the works of Raoul Dufy (1877–1953), a gift from his widow to the city of Nice. Open: Tues.–Sat. 10.30am–noon, 2–6pm; Sun. 2–6pm.

Musée Mossa

Also to be found on the Quai des États-Unis (no. 59) is the Musée Alexis et Gustav-Adolf Mossa. Alexis Mossa (1844–1926), who conceived the idea of the Nice carnival procession, painted remarkable landscapes in water-colours. His son Gustav-Adolf (1883–1971) continued this theme; his early work is however distinguished by a surrealistic kind of symbolic universe.

Additional sights

To the west of this point is the opera-house, and beyond it the church of St François-de-Paule (1736, Italian Baroque) with a "Communion of St Benedict", ascribed to Van Loo. In the courtyard of the Hôtel de Ville (city hall, a little further to the west) there is a representation of Orestes in front of the statue of Athene.

## Ville Moderne

The buildings in the Ville Moderne include those situated on top of the covered-in River Paillon.

The Jardin Albert I is the park-like area between the Avenue des Phocéens and the Avenue de Verdun; here is situated the Théâtre de Verdure (open-air theatre). The gardens extend north as far as the busy Place Masséna, where the Fontaine du Soleil, a fine fountain, and the Casino Municipal (1883) are to be seen. To the north extends the busy Avenue Jean Médecin, one of the principal shopping streets in the city, in which further north still stands the neo-Gothic Church of Notre-Dame.

*Jardin Albert I

To the west of the Avenue de Verdun, the Quai des États-Unis leads into the Promenade des Anglais and continues along the shingle beach of the Baie des Anges. This highway, which was laid down between 1822 and 1824 on the initiative and with the financial contribution of English visitors, and which has subsequently been widened on several occasions, is lined with numerous opulent buildings, among them the Palais de la Méditerranée (theatre and gambling casino), the Palais Masséna and the famous Hôtel Negresco, which is under a conservation order. The old Casion Ruhl, however, was replaced in 1970 by a commonplace concrete building. Before the end of the century it is intended that the Promenade des Anglais should become a pedestrian area with gardens. Road traffic will be diverted into two tunnels, one on top of the other, each with three carriageways, which will run under the sea just off the coast. The shingle beach is to be replaced with sand.

*Promenade des Anglais

The Musée d'Art et d'Histoire is housed in the Palais Masséna (65, Rue de France). It contains relics of the Roman era, works of the Nice school of painting (Bréa, Durandi, etc.), Italian and Provençal porcelain, a collection devoted to regional history and culture and including the Nice water-colourists of the 19th c. A large collection of arts and crafts and the Félix Joubert collection of weapons can also be seen. Open: Tues.–Sun. May 1st–Sept. 30th 10am–noon, 3–6pm; Oct. 1st–Apr. 30th 10am–noon, 2–5pm; Nov. closed.

*Musée d'Art et d'Histoire

"Acropolis" Palais des Congrès et Musique

Private beaches, Promenade des Anglais

## Les Baumettes

*Musée des Beaux-Arts

In the university district of Les Baumettes, which adjoins to the west, is situated the Musée des Beaux-Arts Jules Chéret (33 Avenue des Baumettes; open: Tues.–Sun. May 2nd–Sept. 30th 10am–noon, 3–6pm; Oct. 1st–Apr. 30th 10am–noon, 2–5pm; closed first 2 weeks of Nov.). This important art collection includes works by Chéret (d. 1932 in Nice), Fragonard, Braque, Carrière, Chagall, Degas, Monet, Sisley, sculptures by Carpeaux and Rodin as well as pottery by Picasso.

Musée d'Art Naïf

Even further to the west, in the Avenue Val-Marie, is the Musée International d'Art Naïf (Museum of Primitive Art), which originated in a bequest by the art critic Anatole Jakovsky and provides an excellent overview of primitive art throughout the world. Adjoining it there is a research and information centre. Open: Wed.–Mon. May 1st–Sept. 30th 10am–noon, 2–6pm; Oct. 1st–Apr. 30th 10am–noon, 2–5pm.

## St-Barthélemy

Prieuré du Vieux Logis

From the eastern side of the university quarter the dead-straight Boulevard Gambetta and its continuation the Boulevard de Cessole lead north to the district of St Barthélemy. In a 16th c. building, the Prieuré du Vieux Logis, on the Avenue St-Barthélemy (no. 59), objects from the 14th to 16th c. have been assembled in order to represent what the interior rooms of houses would have looked like from towards the end of the Middle Ages: study, dining-room, a complete fitted kitchen, etc.; French artisans' work and paintings of the French and Flemish schools are also to be seen. Open: Wed., Thur., Sat., 1st Sun. in the month 3–5pm.

## Cimiez

*Roman Settlement
Plan p. 187

On a plateau in front of Mont Gros in the district of Cimiez can be seen the considerable remains of the Roman settlement of Cemenelum. The amphitheatre (over 5000 seats) and the baths, the largest complex in Gaul, are well preserved. The existence here of an early Christian church has also been proved.

Musée d'Archéologie

The Musée d'Archéologie (Archaeological Museum) is located within the area of the ancient settlement. Exhibited are finds from the excavations – coins, jewellery, Greek, Etruscan and Roman pottery – which are displayed according to thematic principles.
Opening times for excavation and museum: Tues.–Sun. May 2nd–Sept. 30th 10am–noon, 2–6pm; Oct. 1st–Apr. 30th 10am–noon, 2–5pm; closed Sun. mornings and November.

*Musée Matisse

The Musée Matisse, recently extended, is to be found in a Genoese villa on the same ancient site. Its contents (paintings, graphic designs, almost all his sculptures, pottery) derive from a gift by the family to the city of Nice. Especially interesting are the sketches for the decorations of the Chapel in Vence (see entry).

Monastère Notre-Dame-de-Cimiez

To the east, lying above the Roman ruins, stands the Monastère Notre-Dame-de-Cimiez, originally a Benedictine foundation which was taken over by the Franciscans in the 16th c. and extended in the 17th. Its present appearance is characterised by the restoration carried out according to Gothic models in 1850. The museum shows the life of the Franciscans in Nice from the 13th to the 18th c. and the general spiritual and social work of the Franciscan order. Inside the church there are fine altarpieces of the Nice school, including a Crucifix by Bréa dating from 1475. Open: Mon.–Sat. 10am–noon, 3–6pm.
In the square outside, from which there is a fine view, stands a marble cross dating from 1477.

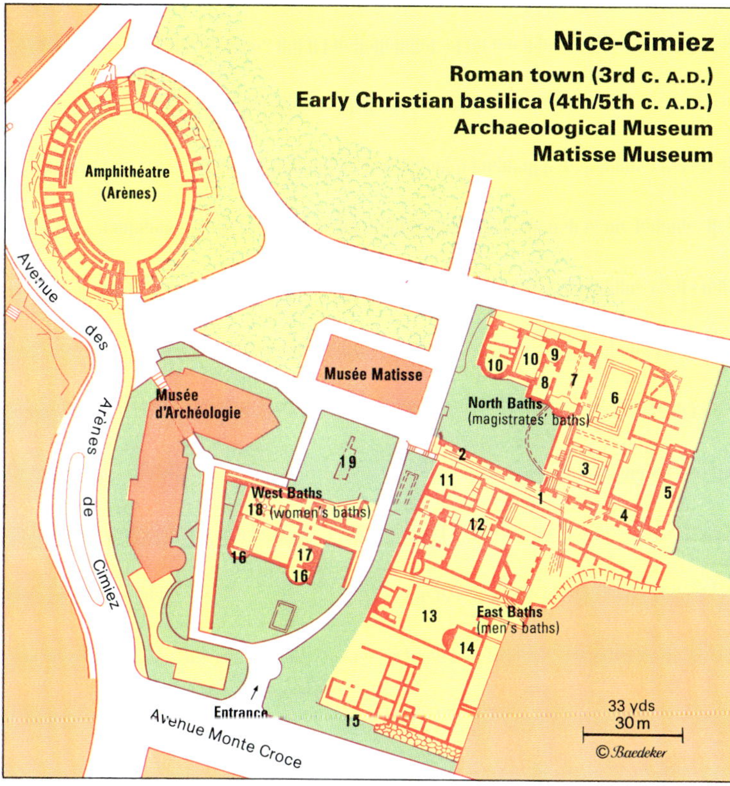


1 Decumanus I
2 Early boundary wall 1st c. A.D.
3 Natato (swimming bath)
4 Latrine
5 Reservoir
6 Courtyard (entrance)
7 Frigidarium
8 Tepidarium
9 Laconicum (sweat bath)
10 Caldarium
11 4th c. A.D. building
12 Praefurnium (stove)
13 Great courtyard (Palaestra)
14 School
15 Decumanus II
16 Foundations of baths (3rd c. A.D.)
17 Choir of early Christian basilica (5th c.)
18 Baptisterium
19 Cardo

## Carabacel

The Avenue de Flirey and the connecting Boulevard de Cimiez lead south from the amphitheatre and baths. At the crossing with the Avenue du Docteur Ménard stands the Musée National Message Biblique Marc Chagall, the most important exhibition of Chagall's works (paintings, etchings, lithographs, sculptures, stained glass, mosaics, wall tapestries on Biblical themes). Works by other artists are also displayed in the temporary exhibitions which are mounted. Open: Wed.–Mon. July 1st–Sept. 30th 10am–7pm; Oct. 1st–June 30th 10am–12.30pm, 2–5.30pm. *Musée Chagall

Continuing along the Boulevard de Cimiez and then taking the Boulevard Carabacel to the south-west, the visitor will once again arrive at the area where the River Paillon has been covered in. Here stands the Acropolis, which is the name given to the Palais des Congrès et de la Musique (centre Acropolis

*Museum of Modern Art, with a mobile by Calder*

for conventions and other events); the Office du Tourisme also has its office here.

Musée Barla

To the south of the Acropolis in the Boulevard Risso stands the Musée Barla, a branch of the Muséum d'Histoire Naturelle. It includes collections dealing with fungi, biological evolution, palaeontology, geology and mineralogy. The information displays give current information about endangered species. Open: Wed.–Mon. 9am–noon, 2–6pm; closed mid-August–mid-September.

*Musée d'Art Moderne et d'Art Contemporain

Opposite the theatre, with which it has been conceived so as to form an architectural unity, is the newly built museum for modern and contemporary art, which was opened in 1990. The architects were Yves Bayard and Henri Vidal. Its four towers, faced in Carrara marble, show a representative cross-section of fine arts during the 1960s and 1970s: new realists and pop art, American abstracts, minimalists, the flux movement. In particular, are works on display by Yves Klein, the main representative of the Nouveaux Réalistes, who was born in Nice in 1928. A whole room is devoted to his work, and on the roof terrace, which has an exceptionally beautiful view across Nice, two "immatériels" stand, which were created for the museum in 1990. Open: Wed.–Sun. 11am–6pm, Fri. until 10pm; closed on public holidays.

A short distance to the south-east is the Place Garibaldi, with its statue of the Italian freedom-fighter who was born in Nice. The Rue Cassini leads from the square down to the harbour.

## Harbour area

At the foot of Mont Boron (178m/584ft), which bounds the Baie des Anges to the east, lies the harbour area with Port Lympia and the Avant-Port (outer harbour). Three- and four-storeyed plain residential buildings in the Italian style characterise the scene. Adjoining on the north is the district of Riquier, developed in a chequer-board plan after 1780.

## Surroundings of Nice

Observatory

In the north-east of Nice, on the edge of Mont Gros (375m/1230ft) and accessible by the Grande Corniche D2564, stand the white buildings, visible from a long distance, of the Observatory built by Charles Garnier. The dome, which at 24m/79ft in diameter is the largest in Europe, was constructed by Gustave Eiffel in 1885. The observatory can be visited on Saturdays at 3pm and 3.30pm.

Villefranche

On the far side of Mont Boron, 6km/4 miles to the east, lies Villefranche, a beautiful natural harbour developed in the early 14th c. by Charles II of Anjou. The town is surrounded by olive-clad hills and has such a mild climate that even bananas ripen here. In the south of the picturesque Old Town stands the Citadel (1580; fortifications on the seashore). In the Church of St-Michel, built in the Italian Baroque style, is a figure of Christ carved in elm and another of St-Rochus (16th c.).
The remarkable Rue Obscure runs beneath huge shaded arches. By the harbour stands the fishermen's Chapel of St-Pierre (often closed) – the interior of which was decorated by Jean Cocteau – and the Palais de la Marine. Cocteau often stayed at both Villefranche and St Jean Cap Ferrat and a scene from his film "Le Testament d'Orphée" is set in the Rue Obscure.

Cap Ferrat

See Beaulieu

Phénix

In the south-west, opposite the airport, is the newly built Arénas shopping centre. Between it and the Promenade des Anglais there is a large park with various attractions, an artificial lake and aviaries. Of particular interest is a glass greenhouse (110m/361ft long, 25m/82ft high) with tropical plants divided into seven climatic zones.

Parc des Miniatures

Halfway between the city centre and the airport, on the Boulevard Impératrice Eugénie, lies the Parc des Miniatures. In a parkland setting it displays – on a scale 1:25 – episodes and monuments from the history of Nice from prehistoric times to the present day.

# Nîmes

D2

Région: Languedoc-Roussillon
Département: Gard
Altitude: 39m/128ft
Population: 145,000

Location and importance

Nîmes, which has the greatest wealth of ancient buildings in France, is strictly speaking not part of Provence, but is described here, as it is one of the principal attractions in this region.
The town is attractively situated in the foothills of the Cévennes, to the north-west of the Rhône Delta between Avignon and Montpellier. It is the capital of the département of Gard, a diocesan town and the birthplace of the writer Alphonse Daudet (1840–97). Nîmes has an important textile industry (in particular, silk; the name "denim" used for jeans material comes from the words "de Nîmes") as well as a thriving wine and spirits industry.

History

The old Nemausus was the capital of the Volcae Arecomici, who had built their town around a spring, the spirit of which was worshipped under the

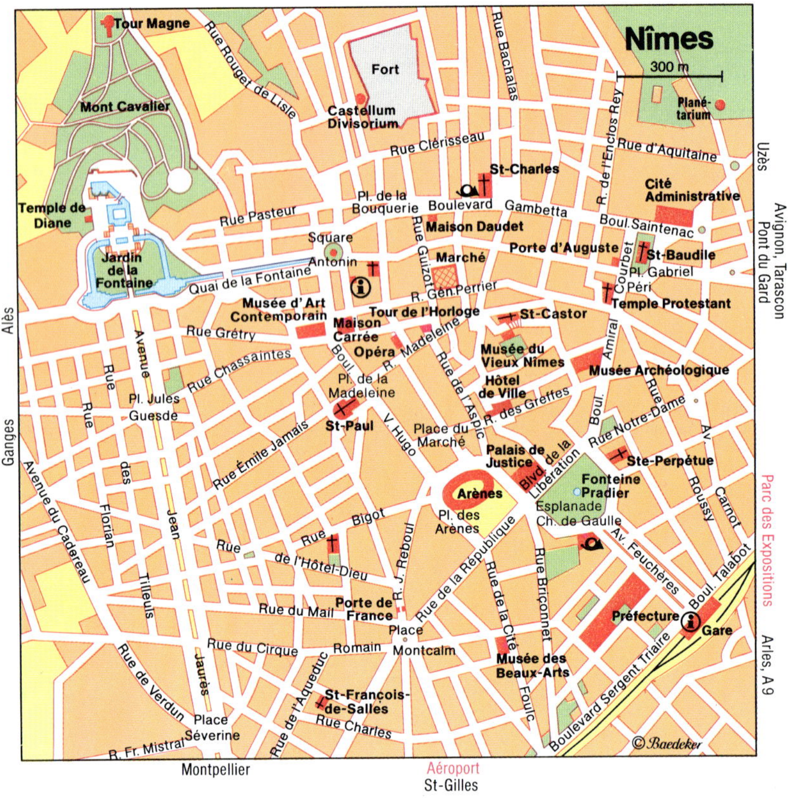


name Nemausus. In 121 B.C. Nemausus submitted to the Romans and soon became one of the most important towns in Gaul, situated on the main route between Italy and Spain. The old buildings and extensive town walls bear witness to its eminence.

In the Middle Ages until 1185 Nîmes had its own viscount and then passed to the Counts of Toulouse. In the 16th c., since three-quarters of its inhabitants were Calvinist, the town suffered greatly during the Wars of Religion, and again in 1704 at the time of the uprising in the Cévennes. From the middle of the 18th c. the inexpensive "Indiennes" material was produced on a large scale in the town, initially by hand, and then machine-printed, and this was to ensure Nîmes' prosperity. Today the town has had to yield importance to Montpellier as an economic and administrative centre.

*Townscape

In the last few years extensive renovation work has been carried out, in particular in the Old Town. In addition, modern architecture has made its appearance in Nîmes. Raysse designed the Fontaine au Crocodile (the town coat of arms of Nîmes shows a crocodile tied to a palm-tree) on the Place du Marché, while Starck designed the Abribus (bus-stop), including the seats and lighting, in the Avenue Carnot. On the Esplanade a shopping centre by Valle has been opened, Foster is building a museum for contemporary art, while the roofing of the amphitheatre was produced by Michelin and Geipel. Those buildings planned, or already under construction, by such architects as Hendricks, Gregotti, Kurokawa, Balladur and Nouvel will turn Nîmes into a favoured destination for lovers of architecture.

Été de Nîmes

In July/August the theatre, music and dance festival "Été de Nîmes" takes place, with performances in the Arènes and in the Jardins de la Fontaine. The emphasis is on jazz, rock and folk music. Information: tel. 66 67 28 02.

## Sights

**Arènes (Amphitheatre)

**Opening times:**
May 1st–Oct. 31st 9am–6.30pm, other times 9am–noon, 2–5pm

The chief monument in Nîmes is the Amphitheatre, which is located in the town centre. It dates from the 1st century A.D. and is 133m/146yds by 101m/110yds in area and up to 21m/69ft high. With a seating capacity of 21,000 it is admittedly not one of the largest, but it is one of the best preserved of all the 70 known Roman amphitheatres, especially in the upper part. The 60 arches of the exterior circuit are embellished in the lower part with pilasters and in the upper part with Doric half-columns. Brackets for the wooden masts of the awning can be seen on the top. The richly decorated main entrance faces north-west. The crowds thronging the theatre were able to leave by 124 exits in a few minutes.
In the 5th c. the Western Goths turned the arena into a fortress. In the Middle Ages it served as a knight's castle, then as dwellings for about 2000 people, who had their own chapel.
Since 1989 the amphitheatre has been covered with a 4800sq.m/5740sq.yd plastic roof, supported on 30 metal pillars, which are fixed in the non-Roman part of the building fabric. In this way cultural events can be held here even in winter, while in summer the roof is removed.

Esplanade de Gaulle

To the east of the amphitheatre extends the Esplanade Charles de Gaulle, a spacious square busy with traffic. Here stands the Fontaine Pradier, a marble fountain of 1848 representing a personification of Nîmes.

*The Arena of Nîmes, a theatre yesterday and today*

**Maison Carrée

The Maison Carrée is situated in the Place de la Comédie and is reached from the amphitheatre by going north-west down the Boulevard Victor Hugo. Standing on a podium, it is a splendidly maintained Roman temple which was erected at the time of Augustus between 20 and 12 B.C. In the Middle Ages the building was used on occasions as a convent; in the 18th c. it was thoroughly restored, then during the French Revolution sold to the Département as national property. An art museum was established here back in 1824.
Tall Corinthian columns bear the richly ornamented entablature with a frieze finely decorated with acanthus (front section missing). Fifteen steps lead up to the pronaos (antechamber) and the cella on the same level, which today serves as an exhibition room.

On the west side of the Maison Carrée, where the former theatre stood, is the Musée d'Art Contemporain, the architect of which is Norman Foster.

*Jardins de la Fontaine

West of the Maison Carrée, at the end of the Avenue J. Jaurès and on the edge of the Inner City, lie the beautiful Jardins de la Fontaine (Gardens of the Source). They were laid out in the 18th c. in the area of the former fortified ramparts and include the ruins of an ancient sanctuary of a sacred spring. The gardens extend over several levels, the lowest forming the water-basins and the waterways joining them. Groups of life-size Baroque statues give atmosphere to this attractive feature.

Temple de Diane

On the western edge of the park under old trees stands the so-called temple of Diana (it was in fact not a temple), a partly ruined, but harmoniously proportioned square building, which presumably formed part of the Roman baths and has been dated to the first half of the 2nd c. on account of its decorations. The three aisles formerly had barrel-vaulting. As the building had been used as a church since the Middle Ages, it was severely damaged during the Wars of Religion and its ruins later used as building stone.

*Maison Carrée, a relic of the Roman era*

*The market*

Tour Magne

Above the Jardins de la Fontaine rises the 114m/374ft high Mont Cavalier, with subtropical plants and shady footpaths. On its summit stands the Tour Magne, a 30m/98ft high Roman monument, dating from the year 15 B.C. The tower is the largest feature of the wall which surrounded the town in the Roman era. From the top an extensive view of the city and surroundings may be enjoyed.

Castellum Divisorium

To the west, beyond the fort, on the Rue de la Lampèze, the remains of an ancient water-tower (Castellum Divisorium, Château d'Eau Romain) were discovered in 1884. Its purpose was to distribute the water-supply for the town, which flowed over the Pont du Gard (see entry). The remains consist of a collecting basin, 6m/20ft in diameter, from which ten supply channels (lead pipes 40cm/15in. in diameter) led off to the individual areas of the town.

Notre-Dame et St-Castor

The Cathedral of Notre-Dame et St-Castor stands on the Place aux Herbes in the centre of the Old Town, almost due east of the Maison Carrée and reached from the latter along the Rue de l'Horloge with its 14th c. clock-tower. Originally built towards the end of the 11th c. and consecrated in 1096 by Pope Urban II, the cathedral has been renewed several times, in particular during the 19th c. in the Romanesque-Byzantine style. On the gable of the west front is an interesting Romanesque relief frieze, with scenes illustrating the story of the Creation, which is stylistically related to St Gilles and may date from the second half of the 12th c.

*Musée du Vieux Nîmes

Opposite the cathedral to the south stands the former Bishop's Palace, in which is housed the Musée du Vieux Nîmes with its collection of regional history and also the adjoining Musée Taurin (Bullfighting Museum). Of interest in the museum, which developed from the private ethnological collection of Henri Beaucquier, are products of local textile manufacture no longer carried on in the town, as well as furniture from Provence and Languedoc, arts and crafts, etc.

*Musée Archéologique

In the Boulevard Amiral Courbet which borders the Old Town in the east is the Musée Archéologique (officially Musée Lapidaire/Musée d'Histoire Naturelle). Its exhibits include Gallo-Roman finds and inscriptions, sculptures up to the Middle Ages and an exceptional collection of coins. In the former chapel can be seen a beautiful mosaic.

Porte d'Arles (Porte d'Auguste)

Near the northern end of the Boulevard Amiral Courbet stands the Porte d'Arles, also known as the Porte d'Auguste, after Augustus, who was instrumental in having the town surrounded by walls. This town gate, which was the starting-point of the road to Rome, dates from 15 B.C. and in the 14th c. was incorporated into the walls of a fortress. It was not uncovered again until 1752 when the fortress had suffered damage. Today a bronze statue of Augustus (a modern copy) stands near the gate. The position of the side wings of the gate, which were destroyed during the French Revolution, are marked on the pavement.

Musée des Beaux-Arts

The Musée des Beaux-Arts (Museum of Art) can be found in the Rue de la Cité Foulc which leads south from the amphitheatre. Its collection of paintings mainly includes works by old masters of the 16th to 18th c., especially of France, Germany and the Netherlands, but also of Italy and Spain. On the ground floor there is a remarkable ancient mosaic. Open: 9am–12.30pm, 2–6pm (admission fee).

## Surroundings of Nîmes

Source Perrier

At Codognan, about 20km/12 miles south-west of Nîmes, is the bottling plant of the Perrier mineral water firm (with its own glass factory). Conducted tours take place Mon.–Fri. at 9am, 10am, 1.30pm, 2.30pm, 3.30pm, and between June 1st and Sept. 30th also at 5pm; closed on public holidays.

Pont du Gard

See entry

Beaucaire

See Tarascon

St Gilles

See entry

## Orange

C2

Département: Vaucluse
Altitude: 46m/151ft
Population: 27,500

Location and Importance

Orange lies in the Lower Rhône Valley, its fertile alluvial lands being used for intensive fruit and vegetable cultivation. The town is famous above all for its famous buildings dating from the Roman era.
The Rhône flows past, about 6km/4 miles distant from the town, at the point where the River Aigues flows into it. The motorway coming from the north divides near the town into two branches, one in the direction of Marseilles and the other in the direction of Nîmes.

History

It was in front of the walls of Orange, or as it was known in ancient times, Arausio, that the first encounter took place between the Roman army and the Cimbri and Teutons – an encounter in which 100,000 Romans lost their lives. Three years later Marius carried out the counter-attack at Aix. In the period of the ensuing "Pax romana", Orange had four times as many inhabitants as it has today. Later it was to become the capital of the tiny princedom of Orange and in 1531 came under the control of the Dutch House of Nassau. For this reason the Queen of the Netherlands even to this today carries the title of Princess of Orange-Nassau. In 1713 Orange was ceded to France under the Treaty of Utrecht.

## Sights

**Théâtre Romain

The Roman Theatre, in the south of the Inner City, is the best preserved and one of the finest of antiquities. It was set up at the beginning of the Imperial era (1st c. A.D.), but was probably renewed in the next century. With its back wall, composed of massive stone blocks, several storeys high, towering over every other building to a height of 38m/125ft and a width of 103m/338ft, with some of the rich decorations still intact, and its circles and tiers of stepped seats, supported against the hillside, providing seating for 7000 people, it gives a good idea of a Roman theatrical auditorium. As the only Roman theatre, Orange has retained the statue of the Emperor Augustus; it is 3.55m/11½ft in size. Open: Apr. 1st–Sept. 30th 9am–6.30pm; Oct. 1st–Mar. 31st 9am–noon, 1.30–5pm; closed on public holidays.

Festival performances

During the summer months festival performances take place in the Roman Theatre, the "Chorégies d'Orange" (concerts, operas), generally with above-average attendance. The exceptional acoustics of the building contribute greatly to their success. The overall impression of the auditorium and stage is only marginally affected by the technical installations. Information and tickets from Chorégies d'Orange, B.P. 205, F-84107 Orange Cedex; tel. 90 34 24 24/90 34 15 52.

Temple

Adjoining the theatre on the west are the ruins of a great Roman temple which was situated at the end of a 400m/438yd long stadium. Directly

*Orange: the Roman Theatre* ▶

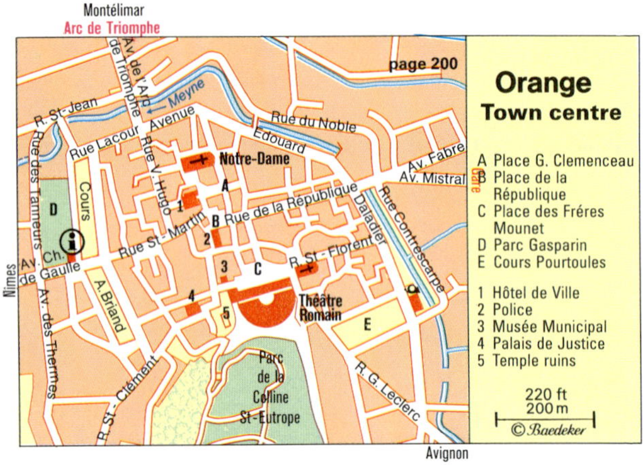


opposite is the interesting Musée Municipal (Town Museum), which contains antique fragments and can furnish information about the architecture and techniques of the Roman theatre. Open: Apr. 1st–Sept. 30th Mon.–Sat. 9am–6.30pm, Sun. 9am–noon, 1.30–5.30pm; closed on public holidays.

Colline St Eutrope

Above the Theatre to the south a beautiful park has been laid out on the Colline St Eutrope; from its northern side there is a wonderful view of the theatre auditorium, town and whole way across towards Mont Ventoux.

Old Town

The Old Town lies to the north of the Roman Theatre. In the Place Clemenceau stands the Hôtel de Ville (Town Hall), dating from 1671, and nearby the Cathedral of Notre-Dame (1083–1126) which was severely damaged during the Wars of Religion.

*Arc de Triomphe
(picture, see p. 54)

The arterial road (N7, Avenue de l'Arc de Triomphe), which leaves Orange in a northerly direction leads to the Arc de Triomphe (Triumphal Arch), situated outside the town and sited on a circular space framed by plane trees. It was erected after Caesar's victory in 49 B.C. In spite of severe weathering it is the finest of its kind in France. Three arches with coffered vaulting form the gateways. Once there were a bronze Quadriga (four-horse chariot) and four statues on the top, while there is a representation of a Gallic battle on the frieze; below on either side are trophies from Gallic vessels.

## Surroundings of Orange

Sérignan

At Sérignan-du-Comtat, 8km/5 miles to the north of Orange (on the N7 and the D976; then right at the entrance to the village), the biologist and ethologist J.-H. Fabre retired to his "Harmas" estate, where he lived and researched for 36 years in almost total seclusion. The house has been turned into a museum and the study and a room with drawings and water-colours can be visited. (Open: Wed.–Sat., Mon. 9–11.30am, 2–6pm; Oct. 1st–Mar. 31st until 4pm; closed on public holidays.) The statue of Fabre on the market square in Sérignan shows him with his most important tool, his magnifying glass.

Châteauneuf du Pape

See entry

Marcoule

See entry

## Pont du Gard

**D2**

Région: Languedoc-Roussillon
Département: Gard

Location

The Pont du Gard, an outstandingly well-preserved Roman aqueduct, bestrides the River Gard near the village of Remoulins about 25km/16 miles west of Avignon. In summer access from Remoulins is only possible along the left bank of the Gard (one-way street).
Cars are often broken into and thefts committed in and around the large car parks near the Pont du Gard.

**Pont du Gard

The Pont du Gard is a 49m/160ft high and 275m/300yd long aqueduct, spanning the deeply incised Valley of the Gard or Gardon. Probably built about 19 B.C. by Agrippa, the son-in-law and co-regent of the Emperor Augustus, the three-tiered construction is one of the greatest and best-preserved Roman monuments. With the exception of the topmost row, the arches are of varying widths (getting narrower from the middle outwards) and the whole structure is asymmetrical, because of the differing gradients of the two banks. In this way any kind of dull monotony is avoided. It is possible and well worth while to walk along the covered channel on the topmost row of arches, though this is only advisable for those with a head for heights. Through this channel ran the pipeline (some 50km/30 miles long) taking water to Nîmes. A height difference of only 17m/56ft was possible between the water-source and the distribution pipes. It is estimated that 20,000cu.m/700,000cu.ft of water flowed across the aqueduct each day. The road bridge at the same height as the first storey was added in 1743.
The plan to build a "theme park" around the aqueduct has been halted, thanks to campaigns in the press and from public pressure-groups. Hotels,

*Pont du Gard, a marvel of Roman architecture*

restaurants, reconstructions of Roman buildings and car parks were to have been built at great expense. Instead plans have been restricted to creating the necessary minimum infrastructure for the two million visitors, who come each year (a cultural-historical trail, car parks at wide intervals), in order to counteract uncontrolled parking and a profileration of souvenir stalls and snack stands.

Garrigue

Vast areas of land around the Pont du Gard are covered with garrigue. Garrigue, also "garigue", in Provençal "garoulia", is mainly to be found on rocky chalk soil. This thorny scrub does not grow much over 50cm/20in. high and consists of box, thistles, oak, gorse and aromatic herbs such as thyme, lavender, sage and rosemary; hyacinths, irises, tulips and orchids also grow alongside.

## Port-Grimaud D4

Département: Var
Altitude: sea level

Location

Port-Grimaud is situated at the south-western corner of the Bay of St-Tropez at the foot of the Massif des Maures; behind it stretches a plain which the Rivers Garde and Giscle have filled up with their deposits.

Townscape

The very attractive modern holiday resort of Port-Grimaud is reminiscent of a Venetian fishing and lagoon settlement, with its maze of channels. When the resort was translated from the drawing-board to reality in 1966, great importance was laid on creating a townscape typical of the region. The resort is free of traffic; there are car parks outside the town for holidaymakers and visitors. As well as motor-boats plying regular routes, there are four-seater electric boats for self-drive hire on the canals.

By the canals, on which there are many fine sailing-ships and cabin cruisers, there are boutiques, shops and restaurants; the market is held in the main square. Many of the apartment houses have their own mooring-places outside their front doors. Facing the sea stands the ecumenical Church of St-François d'Assisi, designed according to Romanesque models; a coin-operated turnstile gives access to the tower from which there is an exceptional panorama of the little town, the lagoons and the mountainous hinterland.

## Surroundings of Port-Grimaud

Cogolin

Cogolin, situated on the south-western edge of the coastal plain of Port Grimaud, is a centre of artisan and industrial wood and textile production. The main products are bamboo and cane furniture, carpets and pipes made out of bruyère (heather roots). In the village there is a pretty 16th c. church and a clock-tower – the remains of an earlier fortification.

To the south of Port-Grimaud lies the yachting harbour of Les Marines de Cogolin.

*Grimaud

Grimaud is situated inland on the site of a settlement which was used by the Ligurians; it is a "village perché", high above the Plain of Cogolin and with a particularly picturesque townscape. Of interest are the ruins of the fortress (11th c.; view) and the Church of St-Michel, also dating from the 11th c. Also well preserved is the Maison des Templiers (House of the Templars) with its Gothic arcades. Some 2km/1 mile east on the road from Port-Grimaud stands the charming Chapel of Notre-Dame-de-la-Queste.

La Garde-Freinet

See Massif des Maures

St-Tropez

See entry

*Port Grimaud*

## Roquebrune-Cap-Martin

D6

Département: Alpes-Maritimes
Altitude: sea level to 300m/985ft
Population: 12,500

Location

The municipality of Roquebrune-Cap-Martin is situated close to the Franco-Italian border, due west of Menton (see entry).
The old inland-lying community of Roquebrune is built like an eyrie on a greyish-brown conglomerate hill. Most of the narrow little streets are vaulted and are full of atmosphere; going uphill through these streets we reach the castle, which dominates the whole town. It dates from the 10th c. and from its fortified tower there is a fine view.

*Vista Palace

To the west above Roquebrune on the Grande Corniche stands the luxury hotel the Vista Palace (owned by the Grundig group), which has a breath-taking situation right on the mountainside and from which there is a marvellous view.

Cap Martin

Cap Martin, stretching like a tongue into the sea, offers beautiful walks; along the west shore runs the Promenade Le Corbusier (the architect was drowned here in 1965), which has splendid views. At the foot of the Sémaphore (signal station) can be seen the ruins of the Church of St-Martin, built by the monks of Lérin in the 11th c. In the midst of olive groves and pine woods there are many villas.

A steep street in Roquebrune

Rocquebrune, Monaco and Vista Palace

## Route Napoléon

See Recommended Routes

## Saint-Gilles

D2

Région: Languedoc-Roussillon
Département: Gard
Altitude: 7m/23ft
Population: 11,000

Location and Importance

St-Gilles lies not far beyond the western border of Provence on the northern edge of the Camargue, 16km/10 miles from Arles. The town is primarily important because of its 12th c. church, one of the most important Romanesque buildings in Southern France.
St-Gilles is a starting-point for trips into the Camargue (see entry).

**Church

In the heart of the Old Town stands the church, erected in the 12th c. and restored on a smaller scale in the 17th c. The west front is exceptionally fine (the light at its best in the late afternoon) with its three doorways and wealth of decorative figures, which include the first detailed representation of the Passion in Western sculpture. The damage inflicted on the church during the French Revolution makes the importance of its architecture all the more significant.
The entrance to the crypt is on the right of the façade. The interior of the church, which has three aisles but no transepts, is characterised by Gothic forms which are surprisingly broad for this period.

*Vis de St-Gilles

To the left of the façade a narrow lane leads to the ruins of the old Choir, which was destroyed in the 17th c. Here is the Vis de St-Gilles (Screw of St

*Saint-Gilles, a perfect example of Romanesque in southern France*

Gilles), a now free-standing staircase dating from the 12th c. The complicated shape of the spiral staircase in the interior of the building is an incredible masterpiece of the stonemason's art. Also to be seen here are the remains of the old apse (the bases of pillars, etc.)

Maison Romane

From the open space in front of the church (Place de la République) a narrow lane leads to the charming little Place de l'Olme. Here stands the Maison Romane (Romanesque House) which has capitals decorated with figures to be seen on its first and second storeys. Inside there is a museum with an early Christian sarcophagus, relief fragments and a natural history collection. From the hall on the second floor there is a fine view across the roofs of St-Gilles. Immediately adjoining is the tourist office.

## Saint-Maximin-la-Sainte-Baume D3

Département: Var
Altitude: 303m/994ft
Population: 8000

Location and Importance

St-Maximin-la-Ste-Baume lies at the northern foot of the Massif de la Ste-Baume in the basin of a dried-up lake, about 50km/31 miles north-east of Marseilles and 40km/25 miles east of Aix-en-Provence on the A8 autoroute.
The little basin was already settled at the time of the Roman occupation. The town became famous, not only for its church, but also as the place where, it is said, the bones of St Mary Magdalene were discovered.

History

Mary Magdalene is supposed to have landed by boat at Saintes-Maries de la Mer, accompanied by her sister Martha, her brother Lazarus, Maximin,

*Sainte-Madeleine, the finest Gothic church in Provence*

Sidonius, her servant Sara and others, after their expulsion from Palestine. While Maximin and Sidonius went into the country as missionaries, Mary Magdalene, at God's behest, spent thirty years without earthly nourishment as a penitent in a grotto ("Sainte-Baume", see below). She was buried, it is said, in a mausoleum, which has been preserved as the crypt of the church. Just as Mary Magdalene represents a synthesis of many Biblical figures (the sinner, Mary of Bethany, Maria of Magdala), so the story of the legend and its sequels is equally strange. In Vézelay in Burgundy St Magdalene was worshipped as long ago as the 11th c. It was maintained that her bones had been brought there at the end of the 9th c., from St-Maximin. Political quarrels – territorial conflicts, conflicts between Pope and King – caused Charles II of Anjou in 1279 to search for the "real" relics at St-Maximin and he was "successful"; four handsome sarcophagi were discovered in the crypt which had apparently been left unprotected by the Saracens. In the controversy over the authenticity of the relics Pope Bonifatius VIII decided in favour of Charles of Anjou; at a stroke Vézelay forfeited its pre-eminence.

## **Ste-Madeleine

History of the building

The new church and the Dominican convent were begun in 1295 and intended for the waves of pilgrims who were passing by. The choir and the first bay on the eastern side were finished in 1316, another five nave bays were not completed until 1404. In the last building period between 1508 and 1532 the western parts were added, while the façade and central doorway remained unfinished or temporary. A planned bell-tower to the right of the doorway was not built. The staircase tower at the southern end was not completed until later and serves as a bell-tower.

The French Revolution drove out the Dominicans; however Lucien Bonaparte, president of the local Jacobin club, set up a reinforcement camp here

## St-Maximin-la-Ste-Baume
### Ste-Madeleine

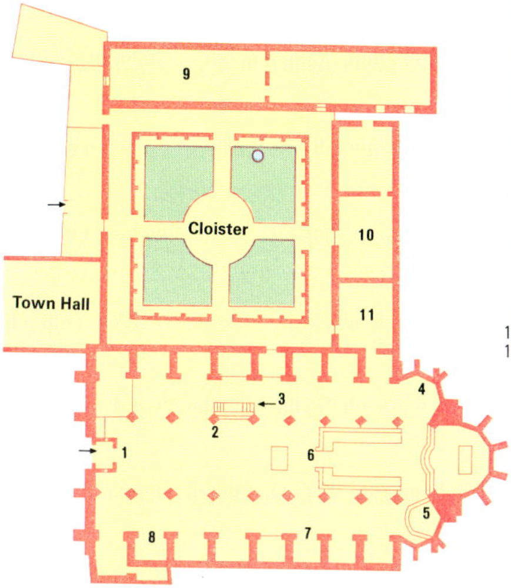


1 Organ
2 Pulpit
3 Crypt
4 Altar of the Passion by F Ronzen
5 Rosary altar
6 Choir screen and choirstalls
7 Pluviale (robe of St Louis of Anjou)
8 Altar (15th c.), with four saints: Laurence, Anthony, Sebastian and Thomas Aquinus
9 Refectory (later a chapel)
10 Chapter House
11 Sacristy

and thereby saved the building. Even the preservation of the huge organ can be attributed to Lucien; when the pipes were due to be melted down, he is supposed to have demanded that the Marseillaise should be played on the organ (although there is no mention of this in his memoirs).

**Exterior**

The tranquil little town is dominated by the massive structure of this, the largest and important Gothic church in Provence. The building, which measures 79m/259ft along its external length, is completely unified in its conception, despite the many years which it took to construct. Immediately striking are its flat silhouette, which is barely interrupted by any vertical lines, the enormous buttresses which flank the nave and the choir, and the complete absence of the usual Gothic decorations. The austere simplicity might be explained by the building regulations of the Dominicans, but also by the country's Romanesque tradition.

**Interior**

Just as simple, but at the same time giving an enormous impression of space, is the interior of the church (Measurements: width 37.2m/122ft, length of the central nave 72.6m/238ft, maximum height: central nave 28.7m/94ft, side aisle 17.5m/58ft, chapels 10.25m/34ft). Even here there are unusual features: there is no transept, nor does the choir have an ambulatory. Instead between the last bay of the central nave and the side aisles, polygonal chapels have been built in diagonally, though they are scarcely recognisable as such at first glance. The bays of the side aisles are continued into those of the chapels.
The interior, which is divided into three levels and is well lit by what were originally 66 windows, is of balanced proportions, both vertically and horizontally. The keystones of the ribbed vaults are decorated with the coats of arms of the founders. The choir bay has no windows because of the staircase towers, with the result that the choir itself seems particularly light with its high, narrow windows.

**Fittings**

In contrast to the architecture the Baroque fittings are very opulent: the splendid main altar (end of 17th c.), choir-stalls and screens made of walnut

Sainte-Madeleine: the organ of 1773

The Crypt

(1692), chancel (1756) with representations of the conversion and ecstasy of St-Mary Magdalene, the organ (by Isnard, 1773; one of the finest French organs of the 18th c.). In the left apse there is a special item of interest, the Passion Altar of 1520 by the Fleming François (Antoine) Ronzen, who had earlier worked in Italy (Rome, Venice). The 22 panels depicting the Passion of Christ are also of interest because of their precise details of places and buildings (Venice, Rome; oldest known picture of the Papal Palace in Avignon).

Pluviale

The chasuble (pluviale) of St Louis of Anjou (1274–97, son of King Charles II of Naples, Bishop of Toulouse) shows in silk embroidery on a gold background 30 scenes from the life of Christ and the Virgin Mary. It is stored in a display cabinet (generally kept covered) in the third side-chapel on the right.

Crypt

The "germ-cell" of the church is reached by a staircase (16th c.) from the north aisle (light-switch on the wall). This low room with barrel-vaulting (4.24×4.48m/14×14½ft; formerly covered with marble), dating from the end of the 4th c./beginning of the 5th c., contains the sarcophagi, dating from the same period, of Mary Magdalene (made of fine-grained marble from the Sea of Marmara), St Maximin, Sidonius and Marcel and St Susanne. Their reliefs show scenes from the Old and New Testaments and are some of the oldest Christian documents in France. The reliquary bust of gilded bronze (1860) contains a skull, supposedly that of Mary Magdalene.

Convent

The building of the convent was begun at the same time as the basilica in 1296. The cloister, full of atmosphere, with its simple massive forms, dates from the 15th c. The chapter house and sacristy (ribbed vaults), which connect the cloister to the church, today house the Collège d'Échanges Contemporains (a cultural centre; venue for concerts, etc.) Prior to this, between 1859 and 1966 the Dominicans were again resident here. Open:

Apr. 1st–Oct. 31st 10–11.45am, 2–4.45pm; Nov. 1st– Mar. 31st, Mon.–Fri. 10–11.45am, 2–4.45pm.
The cloister hostel dating from the 17th c. is today the town hall.

## Surroundings of St-Maximin

Nans-les-Pins

The wine village of Nans-les-Pins, 12km/7½ miles to the south, lies in the northern foothills of the Chaîne de la Ste-Baume and is dominated by the ruins of a medieval castle.

*Massif de la Sainte Baume

Beyond Nans-les-Pins road D80 leads up into the mountains. Some 8km/5 miles along this road, where it is joined by the D95 (a second route from the Hostellerie de la Ste-Baume, 1km/½ mile further), a footpath begins, which leads to the Ste-Baume (Holy Grotto), an opening in the calcareous rock face which has been converted into a chapel (return journey 1 hour). Ste Mary Magdalene is supposed to have lived there and since olden times it has been visited as a place of pilgrimage. On July 22nd the saint's festival is celebrated with a midnight mass in the grotto.
The word "Sainte-Baume" is derived from the Provençal word for grotto, "baoumo". The forest has retained a primeval character, unusual for the region, as a result of its earlier being considered sacred and to this day it has not been exploited commercially. The shady environment with a damp, cool microclimate enables deciduous trees, such as limes, beeches and maples, and a dense undergrowth to flourish.

**St-Pilon

From the Carrefour de l'Oratoire the path (part of the GR9, red and white markers) brings the walker in 30 minutes to the summit of St-Pilon (994m/3262ft) with a splendid view in clear weather (orientation panel); looking inland from Mont Aurélien and the Montagne Ste-Victoire as far as Mont Ventoux, southwards to the sea.

Tourves

Tourves, at a road junction in an area of intensive agriculture (5km/3 miles south-east of St-Maximin), has the impressive remains of the uncompleted Château de Valbelle (18th c.). Nearby there are grottoes with prehistoric paintings.

# Saint-Raphaël

D4

Département: Var
Altitude: sea level
Population: 24,000

Location

The port of St-Raphaël, half-way between St-Tropez and Cannes, has a charming situation on the north side of the Gulf of Fréjus at the foot of the Esterel range.

Townscape

In the old heart of the town stands the 12th c. Eglise des Templiers (a Templar church), with a tower which was built as protection against pirates. Adjoining the church on the north side is the Musée d'Archéologie Sous-Marine (Museum of Underwater Archaeology) with a notable collection of amphorae which were mostly rescued from ancient wrecks. Parallel to the shore runs the Promenade René-Coty, which is beautifully laid out and extremely popular in the season. From here and also from the pleasant Avenue de Gaulle there is a good view of the strange rock formations, the Lion de Terre (Lion of the Land) and Lion de Mer (Lion of the Sea) near Port Santa-Lucia.

## Surroundings of St-Raphaël

Agay

The very charming winding road along the red rocky coast leads (9km/5½ miles eastwards) to the delightful resort of Agay on the bay of the same name, which is enclosed by Cap Drammont and the Pointe de la Baumette. At the latter there is a lighthouse and a memorial to the French airman and author Antoine de Saint-Exupéry.

Agay is a good starting-point for trips to the Esterel mountain range (see entry).

## Saint-Rémy-de-Provence D2

Département: Bouches-du-Rhône
Altitude: 60m/197ft
Population: 8,500

Location and Importance

St-Rémy-de-Provence is situated about 20km/12½ miles south of Avignon to the east of the Rhône in the northern foothills of the Alpilles. The town became famous because of Glanum, an important Graeco-Roman town, and as the place where Vincent van Gogh lived.

Van Gogh

Between May 1889 and May 1890 the painter Vincent van Gogh lived – not entirely willingly – in St-Rémy. In 1888 he had settled in Arles, where the scenery and the light of Provence led him to his new style of painting with bright vibrant colours. Gauguin, who was very close to him, visited him there in the December. A row between the two of them sparked off a crisis in van Gogh. He cut off his ear and was taken to the asylum of St-Paul-de-Mausole in St-Rémy, which is today the Van Gogh Dr Berron clinic. After Arles St-Rémy was the most important place for van Gogh as a creative stimulus and the images for many of his pictures came to him here.

Nostradamus

In the same way that the light and colours of Provence cast a spell over van Gogh, so Nostradamus, born in St-Rémy in 1503, like the ruined town of Les Baux (10km/6 miles to the south), represents all that is cryptic and mysterious in what we associate with Provence.

*The Mausoleum and Municipal Arch of Glanum*

Maillane, 7km/5 miles to the north-east of St-Rémy, is the birthplace of the "Homer of Provence", Frédéric Mistral. His house, in which he lived from 1876, has been turned into a small museum.

Frédéric Mistral

## *Glanum (Excavation Site)

South of the little town, on the road into the Alpilles, lie the remains of the Graeco-Roman settlement of Glanum Livii (2nd c. B.C. and 1st–3rd c. A.D.) which was destroyed in the year 480 by the Western Goths.

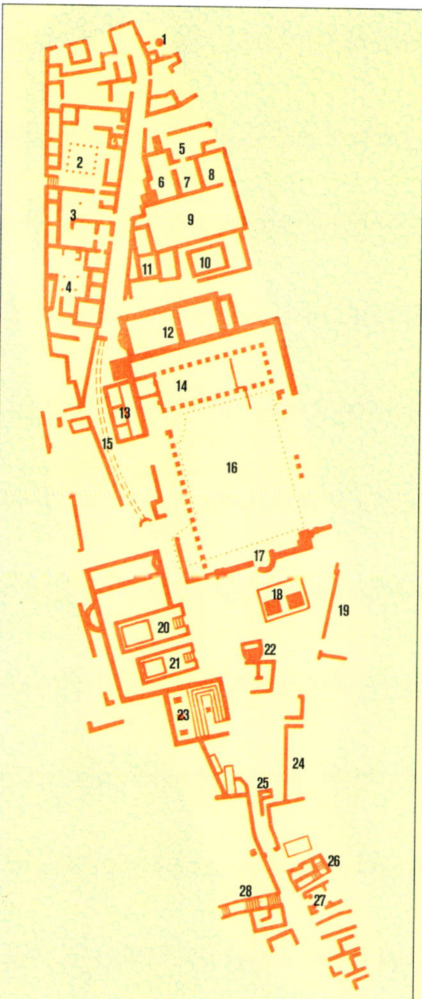


**Glanum**

**near St-Remy-de-Provence**

**Burial ground of the Graeco-Roman town (2nd c. B.C.–3rd c. A.D.)**

1 Basin of fountain

GREEK PERISTYLE HOUSES
2 Maison des Antes (House of the Antes)
3 Maison de Cybèle (Shrine of Cybèle
4 Maison d'Atys (House of Atys)

ROMAN BATHS
5 Heating chamber
6 Caldarium (hot water)
7 Tepidarium (tepid water)
8 Frigidarium (cold water)
9 Palaestra (courtyard)
10 Natatio (swimming pool; cold running water)

OTHER EXCAVATIONS
11 Maison de Capricorne (House of the ibex; mosaics)
12 Building with apse
13 Basilica
14 House of Sulla (mosaics)
15 Covered water-channel
16 Forum
17 Wall with apse
18 Monument or altar
19 Roman theatre
20/21 Roman temple (perhaps dedicated to Caius and Lucius, grandsons of Augustus)
22 Well
23 Buleuterion (council chamber ?)
24 Hall with Doric columns
25 Fortified gate
26 Nympheum (presumably above the sacred well of Glanum)
27 Altars (dedicated to Hercules)
28 Celtic shrine

55 yds
50 m

© Baedeker

*Glanum: excavations at the foot of the Alpilles*

Les Antiques

To the right of the road, in an open space surrounded by plane trees stands the impressive group of monuments known as "Les Antiques"; here stand the Monumental Gate, a souvenir of the foundation of the town, and the 18m/59ft monument in memory of Julius Caesar's two adopted sons, both dating from the 1st c. B.C. The lower part of the square base of the latter is decorated with reliefs of battle scenes; above the base rises a temple-like upper part borne on columns. The reliefs on the frieze of the archway of the Monumental Gate and the coffered internal vaulting are notable but the reliefs on the outside of the walls (trophies, prisoners) are severely damaged.

Excavations

The extensive excavation site can be entered via the new exhibition room with its vivid and informative illustrations and models of the way of life in ancient times. Open: Apr. 1st–Sept. 30th 9am–7pm, Oct. 1st–Mar. 30th 9am–noon, 2–5pm.

St-Paul-de-Mausole

Close to the excavation site and on the east side of the road is the former Monastery of St-Paul-de-Mausole with its Romanesque church and beautiful little cloister dating from the 12th c. Today it is, as it was a hundred years ago (since 1807), when van Gogh lived here, a psychiatric hospital.

## Saint-Tropez D4

Département: Var
Altitude: sea level
Population: 6300

Location

The little port and well-known resort of St-Tropez lies on the southern shore of the gulf of the same name at the foot of the eastern part of the Massif des Maures. There is a large car park to the west of the town at the Nouveau Port.

History

The settlement was known to the Greeks as Athenopolis; it was named Heraclea Cacabaris by the Romans. The present name is said to go back to St Tropez or Torpes, who was beheaded by the Romans and whose remains were discovered here. In the time of the Saracens the little coastal village was hard pressed but was able to recover and in the 15th c. became a republic.

Very early on St-Tropez was a meeting place for artists: Liszt and Maupassant stayed here; Paul Signac bought a house here (La Hune) and as a result a whole string of painters moved to St-Tropez, so that at the beginning of the present century the village became rather like an artist's centre (Matisse, Bonnard, Utrillo). From 1924 to 1938 the writer Colette lived in her villa "La Treille Muscate" in St-Tropez.

After the Second World War St-Tropez developed into an extremely popular resort, particularly with prominent people, film stars and the newly-rich. In 1955 Roger Vadim made the film "Et Dieu créa la Femme" ("And God created Woman") with Brigitte Bardot in the principal role, while in the 1960s Gunter Sachs made "The Girls of St-Tropez". However, it must be said that the gloss which the wealthy brought with them has paled somewhat in the face of mass tourism, even if St-Tropez is still a magnet for the rich and beautiful.

## Sights

Citadel

High over the town towers the Citadel, which was built between 1590 and 1607. In the gateway is a large modern relief by Paul Landowski, depicting a ship's cannon being made ready for action. Within the six-cornered fortress is the Musée de la Marine et de l'Histoire Locale (Museum of Shipping and Local History), in which there is a good reproduction of a Greek galley to be seen. Open: Wed.–Mon. June 16th–Sept. 14th 10am–6pm; Sept. 15th–June 15th 10am–5pm; closed Nov. 15th–Dec. 15th. From the battlements there is a good view of the Gulf of St-Tropez and the Massif des Maures.

Old Town

The Old Town of St-Tropez is situated to the west below the citadel and is bordered on the other side by the harbour basin. Part of it has been laid out as a pedestrian zone where shops, boutiques and restaurants abound.

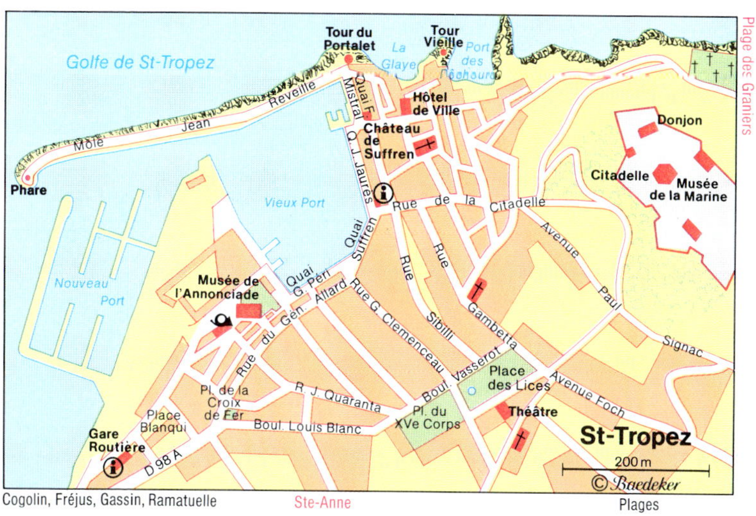

St-Tropez, once a fishing village

Rue de la Citadelle leads down into the centre; on the right in Rue du Portail-Neuf stands the 18th c. church, in Italian Baroque style, in which can be seen a bust of St-Tropez and beautiful woodcarving (at Christmas time there is a fine Provençal crib).

North-west of the church near the harbour and the Hôtel de Ville (Town Hall) stands the former Palais des Bailli Pierre-André de Suffren (1729–88), Bailiff of the Order of Malta and one of the most important admirals of the French fleet ("Scourge of the English"; his statue stands on the east side of the harbour). From here it is not far on the right to the Mole Jean-Réveille, enclosing the harbour on the north, from where there is a good view of the town's seafront. Luxury yachts in the harbour provide a splendid spectacle, especially when the regatta "La Nioulargue" is being held at the end of September and beginning of October.

*Musée de l'Annonciade

At the southern corner of the harbour basin (Quai de l'Epi) stands the former Chapel Notre-Dame de l'Annonciade (Chapel of the Annunciation, the Church of the White Penitents of 1510). It now houses the Musée de l'Annonciade, which contains the very remarkable collection of the Lyons industrialist Georges Grammont, pointillist and Fauvist paintings, the creators of which have worked in St-Tropez – artists such as Signac, Derain, van Dongen, Rouault, Braque, Bonnard, Matisse and Maillol. Open: Wed.–Mon. June 1st–Sept.30th 10am–noon, 3–7pm; Oct. 1st–May 31st 10am–noon, 2–6pm; closed November.

## Surroundings of St-Tropez

Ramatuelle

On the hilly and for the most part wooded peninsula 12km/7½ miles to the south of St-Tropez, lies the picturesque hill village of Ramatuelle, which has many superb views, besides its fortified houses with imposing gates,

*View from Cap Camarat over the beaches of St-Tropez*

surrounded by vineyards and pine woods. In the tiny cemetery is the grave of the actor Gérard Philipe (1922–59).

To the north-west towers the 326m/1070ft high Moulins de Pallas, named after the former mill situated on its southern flank. A narrow road leads to the top, from which there is a fine view across the whole peninsula of Cap Camarat, westwards to the Massif des Maures, south-westwards to the Bay of Cavalaire and northwards to the Bay of St-Tropez. 5km/3 miles beneath Ramatuelle Cap Camarat extends into the sea; from its lighthouse there are more views over to the beaches of the bay of Anse de Pampelonne (to the north) and Plage de l'Escalet (to the south).

La Croix-Valmer

Coming from St-Tropez and passing Ramatuelle the D93 road enters a scenically very rewarding but winding stretch over the Col de Collebasse to the resort of La Croix-Valmer which lies like an amphitheatre on the Bay of Cavalaire.

Ste-Maxime

On the far side of the bay to the north of St-Tropez (14km/9 miles) lies the port of Ste-Maxime, a popular holiday resort. In the church to the west of the harbour is a striking marble altar (18th c.) from the Carthusian Monastery of La Verna (in Italy). To the north-east of the little town there is the Sémaphore (signal station, 127m/417ft) with fine views. The Musée de la Photographie et de la Musique (on the road to Muy, 10km/6 miles; open: Easter–Oct. 10am–noon, 2–6pm) has on display a collection of over 300 musical instruments and phonographs.

Cogolin

See Port-Grimaud

Grimaud

See Port-Grimaud

## Les Saintes-Maries-de-la-Mer D2

Département: Bouches-du-Rhône
Altitude: sea level
Population: 2000

Location

Les Stes-Maries-de-la-Mer is situated in the extreme west of Provence, in the flat country of lagoons and salt steppes of the Camargue (see entry).

History

The place owes its name to the legend, according to which the three Marys – Mary (sister of the Virgin Mary), Mary Salome (mother of the Apostles James and John) and Mary Magdalene (the penitent) — in A.D. 45, with their black servant, Sarah, having been set adrift in a boat without equipment or supplies, landed here and converted Provence to Christianity (see St-Maximin-la-Ste-Baume).

Townscape

In recent years the place has been extensively remodelled into a holiday centre. In general the conversion has been successful, the erection of tall buildings having been avoided.

Warning

Stes-Maries is one of the places in Provence most visited by tourists, especially at the time of the gipsy pilgrimages. In and around Stes-Maries-de-la-Mer there are many thefts and cars are frequently broken into.

## Sights

*Church

The fortress-like church in the heavily commercialised town centre (pedestrian zone) dates from the 10th, 12th and 15th c.; inside is a well for use in case of siege. In a chapel above the apse are the reliquaries of the first two Marys, in the crypt those of their black servant Sarah. Gipsies come from far and wide to worship Sarah (pilgrimages on May 24th, 25th and at the weekend after October 22nd). From the roof of the church (admission fee) there is a fine view.

Musée Baroncelli

The Musée Baroncelli is in the former Town Hall, a few yards south of the church (Rue Victor Hugo). It has collections dealing with local history and

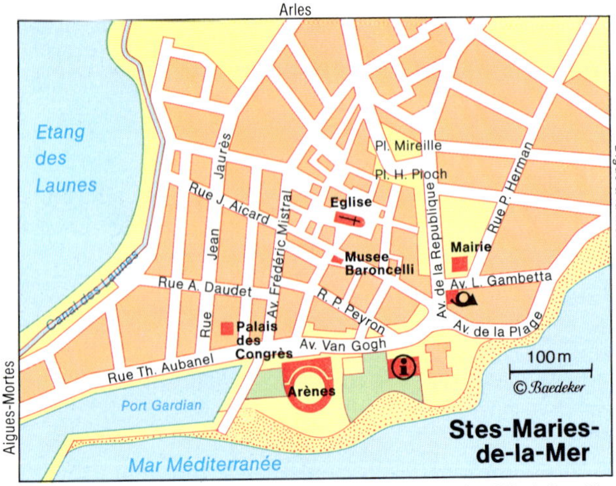


*Les Saintes-Maries-de-la-Mer: a gipsy pilgrimage to the "Black Sara"* ►

folklore from the Gallo-Roman era up to the beginning of the 20th c.; there are also slides and dioramas of the animal and plant life of the Camargue and archaeological finds from the vicinity. Open: Apr. 1st–Sept. 30th 9am–noon, 2–7pm, at other times Wed.–Mon. 9am–noon, 2–5pm.

Arènes

On the southern edge of the town between the Place du Marquis de Baroncelli and the beach, stands the Arena, which is used for bullfights and similar events which take place during the season.

Musée Tsigane

The open-air Musée Tsigane (Pioch Badet, on the D570, 10km/6 miles to the north of Stes-Maries) is devoted to the history of Rome. Old caravans and other historical objects are on display; in one exhibition photos, maps, etc. are used to document over 1000 years of Roman history. Connected to the museum is an archive. There are video showings and guided tours. The museum is open all the year round.

## Salon-de-Provence D3

Département: Bouches-du-Rhône
Altitude: 82m/269ft
Population: 36,000

Location

Salon-de-Provence is situated on the edge of the Plaine de la Crau, north of the Etang de Berre and north-west of Marseilles.

History

Once on this site, on the Hill of Valdemech, stood the Roman Castrum Salonense. The present-day town had its origins in the time of Charlemagne, after the salt-marshes were drained. Salon was the native town of Adam de Craponne, who in 1554 built the canal named after him linking the lower Durance to the Crau and thereby laying the cornerstone of the drainage and canal system between the Durance, the Rhône and the Etang de Berre. Nostradamus, who lived in Salon between 1547 and 1566 and here composed his "Centuries astrologiques", is buried in the Church of St-Laurent.

### Sights

*Château de l'Empéri

From its central position, the 170m/558ft long fortress Château de l'Empéri dominates the town. Built by the Archbishops of Arles between the 12th

*Les Stes-Maries silhouetted above the sand dunes of the Camargue*

and 15th c., it is one of the best preserved and largest fortifications in Provence. The present site in essence goes back to Archbishop Jean des Baux (1233–58). The name "Emperor's Castle" stems from the fact that Salon had fallen to the German emperors in 1032 with the rest of the kingdom of Provence and actually become part of the Empire. Of note is the beautiful Chapel of Ste-Cathérine (12th c.). Open: Wed.–Mon. 10am–noon, 2.30–6.30pm.

Musée de l'Empéri

The Musée de l'Empéri is housed in the castle. It traces the history of French weaponry from the time of Louis XIV to the end of the First World War and includes uniform, equipment, firearms, swords, etc.

St-Michel

East of the castle in the Rue St-Michel stands the 13th c. Church of St-Michel with its characteristic two-storeyed bell-wall with five apertures. The Romanesque doorway has an unusual tympanum, which is made up of relief panels; in the middle at the top is the Archangel Michael, patron of the church, with two snakes (devil), and underneath a lamb with the cross, a symbol of the risen Christ. The other sections show stylised floral ornaments based on ancient models.

A short distance to the east the visitor passes through the Porte Bourg-Neuf, the remains of the town fortification from the 13th c., which had to make way for the ring of boulevards which now surrounds the town. To the right stands the fountain with the statue of Adam de Craponne and the attractive town hall, built in 1655–58.

Maison de Nostradamus

In the former house of the cosmologist Nostradamus (Michel de Nostre-Dame, 1503–66) – he spent the last 19 years of his life here – the noteworthy Nostradamus Museum is housed (2 rue Nostradamus). It includes historical editions of his prophecies, mementoes, and a reproduction of his study. During the period of renovation (until 1992) the Nostradamus Gallery is open (Boulevard Jean Jaurès, open Wed.–Mon. 4–7pm).

*Salon-de-Provence: the typanum of St-Michel*

Place Crousillat

The town gate Porte D'Horloge (dating from the middle of the 17th c.; bishop's arms over the gateway) leads to the Place Crousillat with its completely moss-covered fountain.

*St-Laurent

To the north of the town centre, on the Square St-Laurent, stands the Dominican church St-Laurent (14th/15th c.), which in its total simplicity is an outstanding example of the Provençal Gothic style. Inside there is an alabaster statue of the Madonna (16th c.), a stone relief of the Descent from the Cross (15th/16th c.) and the tomb of Nostradamus which in its present form is a modern work.

## Surroundings of Salon

La Barben

The little village of La Barben is charmingly situated in the Valley of the Touloubre 8km/5 miles east of Salon. About 1km/½ mile east of the village stands the Château La Barben on a steep rocky height. It is surrounded by beautiful parkland with an animal compound and an aquarium.

Cornillon-Confoux

The picturesque village of Cornillon-Confoux, noted for its wine (Appellation Controlée), lies on a spur from which there is a fine view of the Etang de Berre. Of interest are the 17th c. castle and the 12th c. church.

St-Chamas

The little fishing and yachting port of St-Chamas lies some 3km/2 miles south-west of Cornillon-Confoux on the Etang de Berre (see entry). The village is separated from the water by a narrow mountain ridge, on top of which runs a canal. There is an aqueduct with a clock-tower where the canal crosses a gap in the sea-barrier. Well worth seeing are the prehistoric dwelling-caves, the single-arched Pont Flavien (a bridge over the Touloubre, to the west of the village, with triumphal arches as gateways, dating from the 1st c. A.D.) and the 17th c. church with its Baroque façade.

# Sénanque (Abbaye de Sénanque) D3

Département: Vaucluse
Altitude: 480m/1575ft

Location

The abbey of Sénanque, with those of Silvacane and Le Thoronet (see entries), form a group of important Romanesque Cistercian monasteries in Provence – the "three sisters of Provence", as they are called. Sénanque is situated on the southern edge of the Plateau de Vaucluse in the valley of the Sénancole, to the north of Gordes (see entry). The name is derived from the Latin words "sine aqua" ("without water"), as very little water flowed in the river.

On the approach from Gordes, 4km/2 miles on the D177, a narrow road with passing places which traverses dense garrigue, there is a good view of the monastery, deep down in the valley cleft amid fields of lavender. The picture is at its most beguiling in July and the beginning of August, when the lavender is in flower.

Visit
Cultural events

The monastery, which is today the home of a Cistercian community, can be visited Mon.–Sat. 10am–noon, 2–6pm, Sun. 2–6pm, Oct.–Mar. 2–5pm. Visitors may take part in the monks' services; the times are displayed at the entrance. In the monastery buildings exhibitions on regularly changing themes, cultural events, seminars and concerts (also church music, especially Gregorian Chant) take place.

History

Sénanque was set up in 1148 by the Cistercian monastery at Mazan (Ardèche). Building of the church was begun in 1160 and finished by the early 13th c. The monastery buildings were erected during the years 1180–

1210 (the buildings at Silvacane were begun in 1175, Le Thoronet in 1160). The heyday of the abbey was during the 14th c., when the Cistercian Benedict XII was Pope in Avignon. Because of its growing wealth – Sénanque owned a vast amount of land between Mont Ventoux/Montagne de Lure and the Montagne de Lubéron – its strict discipline slackened, leading to its decline. In 1544 it was a victim of an uprising during the Wars of Religion, from which it never recovered. During the French Revolution the estate was confiscated and sold to a private owner who maintained the monastery. In 1854 a community of Cistercians moved back in but after setbacks during the anti-clerical Third Republic the last monks transferred to Lérin. Later Paul Berliet, the lorry and bus manufacturer, started up a cultural centre and in October 1988 a group of monks returned to Sénanque from Lérin.

## *Monastery buildings

Exterior

Sénanque's external appearance is defined by the way the most simple and geometrically assembled parts form a whole which, with its harmonious proportions and the characteristically seamless joins of its perfectly crafted stonework, creates a monumental impression. The north front, which dominates the scene, with its continuous sloping roof over transepts and monastic rooms, is accentuated on the left by the rounded main apse and the crossing tower, on the right by pilasters. The side apses end in straight lines and lie under sloping roofs. The cupola is surrounded by a walled octagon, the narrow sides of which are strengthened by small pilasters. To the right there are two medieval chimneys.
According to the rules of the Cistercian order, the rooms which were used for all the activities connected with day-to-day living were to be by the river, whilst the church should occupy the most elevated position. At Sénanque this could only be achieved by having the church aligned to the north.
Except for the south wing, which was destroyed and then later rebuilt during the 18th c., and the refectory, Sénanque is preserved today in its original state.

Dormitorium

The monastery buildings are entered from a wing connected to the northwest side of the abbey (19th c.; ticket office, books, souvenirs). The circular route is signed by arrows and leads first to the dormitorium (sleeping quarters) situated on the upper floor, an austere room, the Gothic pointed arches of which are a continuation of the vaulting which covers the tran-

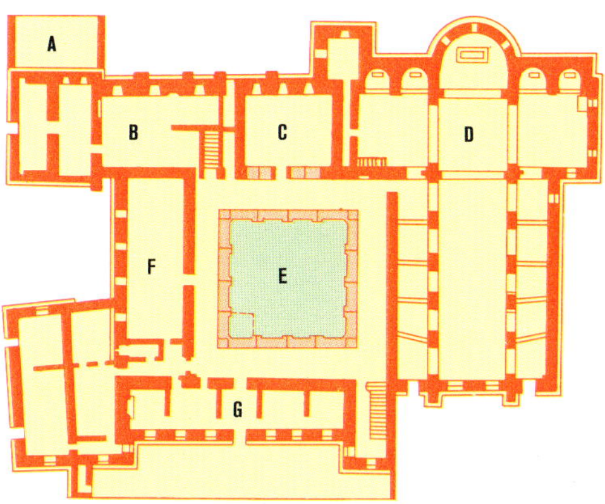


**Sénanque**

**Cistercian Abbey**

A West wing (entrance)
B Monks' Hall (scriptorium)
C Chapter House
B & C Upper storey Dormitory
D Abbey church
E Cloister
F Refectory
G Lay brothers' building

septs of the monastic church. The monks used to sleep here in their clothes on sacks of straw. Today there is an excellent set of displays here providing information about the building techniques (architecture, stonemasonry). From the dormitorium there is direct access to the church; the monks assembled seven times a day for worship, including twice during the night. Thus there is one flight of stairs leading to the church, another leading down to the cloister.

Cloister

The cloister is barrel-vaulted; the arcades leading to the garden consist of four relieving arches on square pillars for each wing. In each of these there are two decorative pillars supporting three small round arches (hence twelve arches in all, a "holy" number). The rhythm of this sequence affords a picture of great harmony; the cloister at Le Thoronet, which is only slightly older, is far more archaic. On the capitals the decorations, which are copious for a Cistercian monastery, as they are also in comparison with the church, show palm-leaves, petals and water-lilies; they are simple and beautifully crafted. Of the well which is situated in the south-west corner there remain only the pillars which supported the vaulting.

Chapter house

Below the dormitorium are the chapter house and the monks' hall. Together with the church, the chapter house was the centre of the abbey. Here matters pertaining to the day-to-day life of the monastery and the monastic order were discussed and decided. The monks sat on the steps around the sides of the room. The ribbed vaulting of the six pointed arches (inserted at a later date) converge in two pillars with lavishly worked capitals.

Monks' Hall

On the same level as the cloister is the monks' hall, the only room in the monastery which could be heated. While in other monasteries belonging to the order the monks' hall was only used for purposes which required a warm environment (care of the sick, writing work), in Sénanque it also served as a general day-room. It possessed two chimneys; the one which has been preserved also passes through the dormitorium, where it gave off some heat. The cross vaults of the roof ridge are supported in the middle of the room by a thick column resting on a square base.

Refectory

The refectory, which was destroyed in the 16th c. and rebuilt in the 19th, has regained its original appearance as a result of recent restoration work. Today it is used by the monastic community as a chapel and during the week most of the services are conducted here. Consequently visitors to the abbey cannot visit it.

Church

The building of the three-aisled monastery church was begun in 1160 with the chancel and the transverse wings, and completed in the 13th c. with the nave. The alteration of the nave arcades (first bay a rounded arch) to a pointed arch and the irregularity of the side aisle girder arches probably came about as a result of alterations to the plan. The height of the nave was also raised to that of the highest point of the cupola, so that windows could be put in. Apart from these windows, the walls of the nave are totally bare right up to the ledge where the roof vaults come across. On the south wall there is no central doorway, merely two small doors leading through to the side aisles (with cut-out pointed barrel vaults). The crossing is unusual in that it is vaulted by an octagonal cupola; most Cistercian churches only have a ridge turret.
Connected to the broad transept with its pointed barrel-vaulting is the equally high choir section with a semi-circular main apse and two side apses on each side, to right and left, which are set into the massive choir wall. The altars, of which one dates from the Romanesque period and served as a model for the others, are original. In the right-hand transept arm there is a radial window in ten sections.

As a whole the bright airy building impresses by its feeling of space, which is in no way spoilt by any decorative excrescences. It represents a reali-

*The Abbey of Sénanque, impressive in its simple architecture*

sation of the Cistercian concept of monastic living: seclusion, poverty and simplicity, prayer and hard physical labour – those qualities which Bernhard von Clairvaux prescribed when he renounced the worldly splendour of Cluny.

## Silvacane (Abbaye de Silvacane) D3

Département: Vaucluse
Altitude: 230m/755ft

Location

The former Cistercian Abbey of Silvacane lies near the little village of La Roque-Anthéron on the left bank of the Durance, below the Montagne du Lubéron (see entry), 25km/15½ miles north-east of Salon and 26km/16 miles north-west of Aix-en-Provence.
Open: Apr. 1st–Sept. 30th 9am–7pm, Oct. 1st–Mar. 31st Wed.–Mon. 9am–noon, 2–5pm; closed on public holidays.

History

The name of the abbey comes from the Latin "silva cannorum" (forest of reeds) and signifies that the area was formerly marshland. The monastery was founded in 1144 by Raymond des Baux and transferred to the Cistercians. Unlike other Cistercian monasteries, Silvacane does not lie far from civilisation, but is situated where important transport routes meet. Previously there had been a monastic community here which had cared for the spiritual well-being of travellers crossing the Durance. Work on the building was not begun until 1175 and the church was finished in 1230, during which period the Gothic style of architecture had already established itself in the north of France. The cloister and monastery buildings followed around 1250–1300, while the refectory was not erected until the 15th c., during a short new burst of activity. In 1443 Silvacane then came under the

*Silvacane Abbey, on the threshold of Gothic*

cathedral chapter of Aix-en-Provence and became the parish church of nearby La Roque-Anthéron, long after it had become completely insignificant as a monastery. Like many other ecclesiastical properties it was sold during the French Revolution and was intended to have been torn down to provide building materials. However in 1846 the government acquired the estate and this resulted in extensive restoration work being carried out.

## *Monastery buildings

Church

Although Silvacane has a very simple design (only rectangular elements), the delayed and protracted period of its construction has meant that a certain watering-down is discernible in the strict building principles of the Cistercian Romanesque style (see Le Thoronet). The powerful buttresses on the façade, transept and choir, initially designed for static reasons, convey a certain unity of structure; the outer windows in the east and west fronts (especially the round window over the main doorway) are not cut straight into the wall, but show a varyingly profiled outline. The main doorway is stepped with pillars and capitals, the latter decorated with flower-buds. The top of the tower has a charming effect with its round-arched sound arcades (and a four-sided pyramidal roof to complete it). Over the doorway on the west façade the coat of arms of the cathedral chapter of Aix is to be seen; it was put up on the occasion of the transfer of Silvacane to the diocese in the 15th c.

Interior

The nave with its three bays and ogival barrel-vaulting is linked to the long reaches of the transept; the main and side choir chapels are barrel-vaulted. The slope from south to north is hidden from the eye by means of a wall at base level running along the northern side aisle. The ribbed vault of the crossing was probably inserted at a later date, as it assumes a knowledge of Gothic building methods. As a whole the interior of Silvacane is stronger

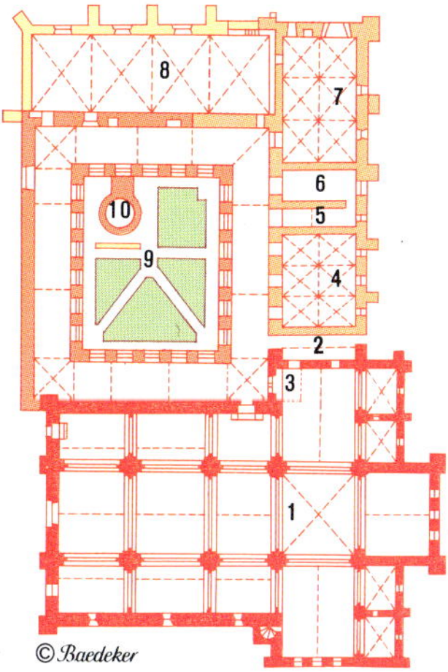


## Silvacane
### Cistercian Abbey

1 Church
2 Sacristy
3 Armarium
4 Chapter house
5 Monks' staircase
6 Consulting room
9 Cloister
10 Well

1175 – 1230
1210 – 1230
1250 – 1300
1420 – 1425

and fashioned less sparingly than Sénanque or Le Thoronet; the rectangular girders of the vaults and side aisles, and of the arcades running lengthways, are all lined with half-pillars (in the central aisle resting on consoles which have several steps). The capitals of these half-pillars are embellished with leaf decorations (partly very archaic, partly sophisticated and revealing Gothic forms). A progression in both building techniques and in aesthetics can be detected in the varied vault shapes of the side aisles.

Cloister

As was usual in Cistercian monasteries, there was direct access from the church to the cloister and to the monastic buildings. A staircase leads down from the northern side aisle to the small cloister, at a level 1.6m/5¼ft lower, and full of atmosphere. It has barrel-vaults which in the corners penetrate through to a cross-ridge vault. The very simple, Romanesque-looking round-arched arcades which lead through to the garden were originally subdivided with a double pillar (which in some cases has been retained), which carries two pointed arches, and a round window (oculus). The fact that the building was erected during the Gothic period is discernible in the shapes of the girders, consoles and capitals; the whole impression is significantly more "Gothic" than that created by the church.

Conventual buildings

The conventual buildings are situated lower down. The chapter house has six cross-vaulted bays, which inside are supported by two contrasting and elaborately shaped pillars. The chapter house is connected to the dormitorium on the upper floor by a staircase. The monks' hall was fitted with a fireplace (as a heated room) and also served as a writing-room. The refectory, which because of the natural slope of the land, was built at cellar level, dates from the 15th c. and has four-bay ribbed vaults. Its windows shows the Gothic influence in their pointed arches and tracery and the capitals have Late Gothic leaf embellishments; of special interest is the rose window in the eastern bay.

A converse building (building for the lay brothers), which was a normal feature of Cistercian monasteries, has not been preserved.

## Sisteron C3

Département: Alpes-de-Haute-Provence
Altitude: 482m/1582ft
Population: 6500

Location

Sisteron lies in the extreme north of the area covered in this guidebook on the Route Napoléon and to the north of the Montagne de la Lure; it is not far from the confluence of the Buëch with the Durance.

History

It is believed that the caves in the vicinity were lived in from very early times, but there is no actual proof of this. Augustus subdued the tribes of the Avantici and Vocones which were settled here and built Segustero at an important narrow point of the Durance on the Roman Via Domitia. In the 5th c. Sisteron became the seat of the Bishop and remained so until the French Revolution. In the 9th and 10th c. the Saracens held the town; in 1348 half the population died of the plague. About the middle of the 14th c. a beginning was made with the defence works, most of which can still be seen today. In 1481 Sisteron fell to the Kingdom of France, but the Wars of Religion caused great devastation. On his journey from Elba to Paris Napoleon passed through the Defile of Sisteron without much difficulty. In August 1944 the town and citadel were bombed by US planes (over 300 casualties) in order to drive out the German troops.

### Sights

*Townscape

Situated high above the place where the Durance breaks through its mountain ridge the Citadel of Sisteron crowns an unusually impressive landscape. In summer a little tourist railway (starting-point at the Place de la République) runs up to the citadel.

*Citadel

Above the town to the north on a high rocky hill, through which the N85 road runs in a tunnel, stands the Citadel, built in the 12th and extended in the 16th and 19th c. It is a fortified barrier on several levels from which not only the narrows of the river but also the entire north and south hinterlands could be controlled. The greater part of the fortifications was the work of the architect Jean Erard (16th c.). From the highest turrets and the "Guérite du Diable" outwork there is an unusually impressive view to the north over the Alpine region and eastwards across to the other side of the narrows where the Rocher de la Baume rises, a steep rock face on which the almost vertical faulting due to erosion can clearly be seen. On the north side of the citadel an open-air theatre has been constructed.

Notre-Dame-des-Pommiers

In the centre of the Lower Town stands the former Cathedral of Notre-Dame-des-Pommiers which was built between 1160 and 1220. Like many churches in this area of the Alps it reveals the influence of Lombardy. Of special interest are the figural decoration on the entrance, the capitals of the half-pillars in the nave and the two Baroque altars.

Town Walls

To the south of the church in the Allée de Verdun can be seen three well-preserved towers of semicircular plan which were once part of the town walls.

Old Town

In the Old Town of Sisteron are a number of fine 16th and 17th c. houses; a walk through the picturesque streets, which in places lead beneath flying buttresses, is marked by arrows.

*Sisteron: Rocher de la Baume, a visual lesson in geology* ▶

# Tarascon D2

Département: Bouches-du-Rhône
Altitude: 9m/30ft
Population: 11,000

Location

Tarascon is situated on the left bank of the lower course of the Rhône about half-way between Avignon and Arles.

Legend and Fable

Tarascon gets its name from the Tarasque, a fabulous man-eating creature of wild appearance said to have dwelt here and which only St Martha was successful in pacifying. It has become the heraldic animal of the town celebrated by a festival in June, the Fête de la Tarasque, when a terrifying effigy of the creature is led through the procession.

No less romantic is the second notability, Tartarin de Tarascon, the hero of the novel by Alphonse Daudet. Short and somewhat stocky with a black beard and quite warlike in his behaviour, he is nevertheless more inclined to dream his adventures rather than carry them out in reality; in the long run he values physical well-being more highly than war and deprivation, and with his lovable humanity he is, for many, the embodiment of the Provençal character.

## Sights

Château du Roi René

Immediately north of the road bridge (Boulevard du Château), on the banks of the Rhône, stands the massive fortress-like castle. (Open: daily 9am–4pm, conducted tours on the hour; closed on public holidays.) Its origins go back to the late 14th c. and it was named after René, Duke of Anjou and former King of Naples (called "le Bon Roi René"), who ordered the completion of the castle in the middle of the 15th c. and who provided for artists and scientists a comfortable and courtly existence.

Protected on one side by the river and on the other by a deep moat, the solid castle resisted every siege and attack right up to the bombardment by Allied forces in 1944. The building includes a court of honour; from the battlements there is a fine view.

Ste-Marthe

Diagonally opposite the castle stands the Church of Ste-Marthe, originating in the 10th c., but now predominantly Gothic. The doorway to the south aisle is interesting, in spite of damage to the figures in the decoration. Inside the church is a panel by Pierre Parrocel, a less well-known member of the family of painters; in the crypt can be seen the Sarcophagus of St Martha, whose remains were found in Tarascon.

Hôtel de Ville

Not far from the castle (Rue des Halles) stands the Hôtel de Ville (Town Hall) dating from the 17th c.; in the Old Town there are a number of fine old buildings.

## Surroundings of Tarascon

Beaucaire

The little town of Beaucaire lies on the right bank of the Rhône opposite Tarascon and is in the Région of Languedoc-Roussillon and the Département of Gard. It was once famous in the whole of the Western World for its market (Foire de Beaucaire), which has existed since 1217 and which takes place from July 21st to 28th. Today it includes a historical procession, wine festival, concerts and bullfights. Noteworthy is the beautiful Town Hall (1679–83), built by J. Hardouin-Mansart. Above the town are the ruins of a castle of the 13th–14th c. from which there is a rewarding view.

Abbaye St-Roman

About 5km/3 miles to the north of Beaucaire, on the other side of the Rhône, is the Abbaye (Troglodytique) of St-Roman, which is built into the rocks

*Tarascon: the Castle of "Good King René"*

(5th c.). Access is by following the road parallel to the D986L; 15 minutes' walk from the car park. Open: July 1st–Aug. 31st Tues.–Sun. 10am–7pm, Apr. 1st–June 30th Wed.–Sun. 10am–6pm.

*View

From the top of the hill (go straight up the mountain from the turning off the D986L) there is a superb view across about 40km/25 miles of the Rhône Valley from Avignon to Arles (Fourques Power Station), the mountain chains of the Montagnette and the Alpilles, as well as Tarascon and Beaucaire.

## Le Thoronet (Abbaye Le Thoronet) D4

Département: Var
Altitude: 142m/466ft

Location and Importance

The Abbey of Le Thoronet (26km/16 miles to the south-west of Draguignan on the D562) is the oldest and smallest of the three Cistercian monasteries in Provence (see Sénanque, Silvacane) and has a secluded position in a wooded, hilly area to the south of the Argens.

Le Thoronet is the epitome of the Provençal Romanesque style and represents a perfect embodiment of Cistercian building principles, which derive from the strict rules of the order – absolute simplicity, clear lines and proportions, a complete absence of decoration. The severe exterior is tempered by the reddish hue of the building materials (stone from the Esterel Massif), the bright Provençal light and the beautiful setting.

Open: Apr. 1st–Sept. 30th Mon., Wed.–Sat. 9am–7pm, Sun. 9am–noon, 2–7pm; Oct. 1st–Mar. 31st 9am–noon, 2–5pm.

History

The convent and church were built, like Sénanque, by the monks of Mazan (Ardèche) between 1160 and 1190, after they had settled near there in 1136

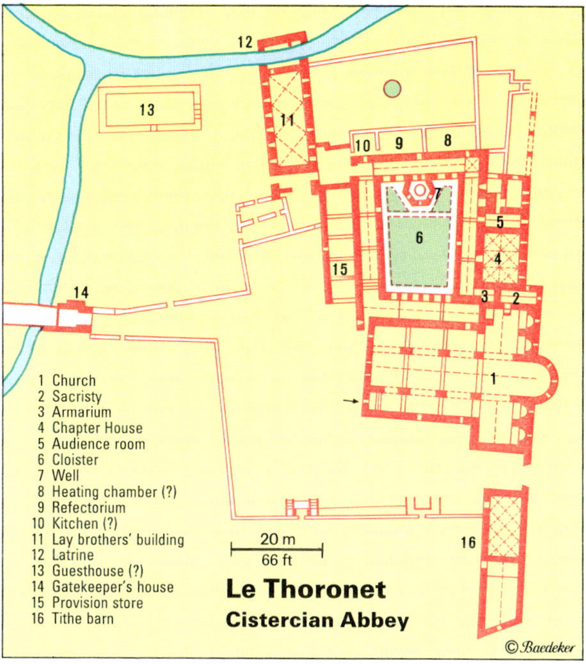


at the instigation of Raymond Bérenger, Count of Barcelona and Toulouse. Raymond also ensured that the foundation should have a secure basis for its existence by transferring land to its ownership. One of the first abbots, Folco or Folquet (from 1201), had been a famous troubadour before he renounced worldly and amorous concerns and became a Cistercian monk in 1196. After a period of decline during the 14th c., the monastery was abandoned and in 1791 during the Revolution was confiscated by the state and sold off. That it was bought back by the state in 1840 and preserved from dilapidation is thanks to the French writer Prosper Mérimée. The Baroque additions which the building acquired in the 18th c. were removed during restoration work which took place after 1873.

## **Monastery buildings

Church

The stone belfry is unusual for a Cistercian church – normally only roof turrets were permitted. The masonry is impressive by virtue of the exactness with which the slabs of stone have been cut and laid; the slightly sloping saddle-roofs rest directly on the vaults. The façade does not have a central doorway – as there was no "congregation" – but merely two side doors (the left one was assigned to lay brothers).

Interior

The nave is built with four bays and pointed barrel-vaulting; they are separated from one another by simple rectangular girders which rest on simple ledges made up of a quarter-circular bar and a straight strip. The

◀ *Le Thoronet Abbey: the east end and bell-tower*

lower arms of the transept do not form a crossing with the nave, but are merely attached to it. Set in the eastern wall of the transept, to the left and right of the choir, there are two apses, while the choir, even from the outside, appears to the eye to form a semicircle.

The transition to the Gothic style is heralded by the ogival barrel-vaulting in the nave and transept and the rising half-barrels in the side aisles, which divert the weight from the vaulting on to the exterior walls. The eastern bay of the northern side aisle, which was the first to be built, still possesses a quarter-barrel; similarly the chronological succession of the various building elements can be traced in the development and refining of the ledges. The only subdivision on the walls is provided by semicircular articulated columns, which rest on a console at a height halfway up the arcades, as well as a perimeter ledge which marks the base of the vaulting. Light reaches the interior through a few small windows in the west, south and east walls and in the apses; the north side has no windows.

Cloister

The cloister is reached from the northern side aisle. The noticeably irregular shape of its ground-plan (a trapezium with unequal sides, the longest 37m/121ft) and vertical plane is caused by the shape of the land on which it is built. The walls and vaults appear even more massive than when seen from inside the church, because of the almost total absence of any subdivisions. The history of building is also documented here in the various shapes of the ledges and vaults; the early south wing (*c.* 1160–70) has barrel-vaulting, while the vaulting in the east wing is slightly broken. In the north-east and north-west corners the Gothic ribbed vaults which have been placed there are very evident. The round-arched arcades leading to the garden rest on rectangular buttresses and are filled out with a pair of rounded arches, which sit on circular pillars with simple capitals and soften the heavy impression made by the 1.50m/5ft thick wall. Here it is possible to trace the tradition of Romanesque building forms (cf. the Temple of Diana in Nîmes).

*View from the south transept towards the lay-brothers' doorway*

The terrace above the cloister, which is reached from the dormitorium, offers the best view across the site.

Wellhouse

The wellhouse on the north wing of the cloister is the only remaining example in Provence to have survived. The hexagonal building has hinged ribbed vaulting and round-arched windows and is provided with a separate entrance and exit. The fountain itself is modern.

Monks' buildings

Next to the northern transept arm on the same level is the 3m/10ft wide sacristy and the tiny library (the Cistercians restricted themselves to only the most essential of reading matter), which, like the conventual buildings is situated at a lower level. Connected to it is the 9.5×8m/31×26ft chapter house, the six ribbed vaults of which rest on two free-standing pillars. The sculptures on the capitals (leaves, palm branches, volutes) represent the only building decorations in the whole complex; probably it was felt fitting not to deny a certain degree of embellishment to what was, after the church, the most important room for monastic life.
The parlatorium (speaking-room) is situated between the cloister and the monastery garden. Other buildings in the north of the site (warming-room, refectory, kitchen and monks' hall) have not been preserved, although their ground-plan is still discernible.

Following the Cistercian tradition, a staircase leads from the northern arm of the transept directly into the dormitorium, the monks' sleeping room, which is situated above the chapter house.

Converse building

The converse building (lay brothers' building), which dates from the early 13th c., is connected to the north-west end of the cloister. On the ground floor is the refectory with a double-bayed hinged ribbed vault; on the upper floor the dormitorium with ogival barrel-vaulting. The door in the north wall led to the latrine, now in ruins, which was directly above the stream.

Cellar

On the west side there is a store-room built on to the cloister, which, like the latter, dates from the end of the 12th c. It is a long room with ogival barrel-vaulting and arcades on the west wall. Here there are walled containers for oil and wine, the remains of an oil-press and an exhibition dealing with the restoration of the monastery and the building activities of the Cistercians.

Outbuildings

In the north-west corner of the site the foundation walls of the guest house have been uncovered; in the south stands the former tithe barn.

## Toulon — D3

Département: Var
Altitude: sea level to 10m/33ft
Population: 181,500

Location and importance

The port of Toulon lies about 70km/43 miles south-east of Marseilles near the most southerly point of the French Riviera. The Bay of Toulon forms an outstanding natural harbour; it consists of the inner "Petite Rade" (little harbour roads) and the outer "Grande Rade" (large roads) and is protected by the off-shore promontory of St-Mandrier. Toulon is the most important military port in France with appropriate dock and supply facilities.

History

The settlement, called Telonion by the Greeks, Telo Martius by the Romans, was of importance in ancient times primarily because of the purple dye which could be obtained from the purple snails which lived in the sea. The conversion to a naval port did not occur until recent times. In 1487 Toulon passed into French hands under King Louis XI and became an important base by virtue of its strategic position (the largest natural harbour in the

Mediterranean). The Tour Royale, which controlled the access to the "Petite Rade", was built in 1514. The fortifications, which were installed towards the end of the 16th c. and strengthened by Vauban in 1660, withstood in 1707 the combined forces of Prince Eugene, Holland and England. In 1793, during the Revolution, the royalists delivered the town to the English Admiral Hood; it was reconquered by the revolutionary army after a six-week siege, during which the 23-year-old batallion commander Napoleon Bonaparte (later Napoleon I) gained particular distinction and was as a result promoted to brigadier-general. In the 19th c. it was from Toulon that the French troops left to go to war: to the Crimea, Italy, Mexico, Indo-China, Madagascar, Africa. Until 1939 the naval fleet constituted the only employer in the town worth naming. In the Second World War Toulon was occupied by German troops in November 1942 and half-destroyed by bombing; the French fleet went down on November 27th. When the Allied forces landed in August 1944 Toulon was one of the first towns to be liberated (see below Mont Faron). In 1974 Toulon became (after a lapse of 181 years) a prefecture again and capital of the département of Var.

## Sights

**Old Town**

The Vieille Ville (Old Town), which was severely damaged during the Second World War, lies by the Darse Vieille (Old Harbour), on the north-west of which stands the Préfecture Maritime; every day after sunset the "Cérémonie des Couleurs" takes place here. The fronts of the row of houses along the Quai Stalingrad, which leads south-east to the Rond-Point Bonaparte, were rebuilt after the Second World War and are dominated by the tower of the new Town Hall. The caryatides by Pierre Puget (1620–94), originally in the Old Town Hall, which was also destroyed in the war, today adorn the entrance to the Municipal Information Centre. They have been copied over and over again all over Provence (for instance at Cours Mirabeau in Aix-en-Provence), but here remain, unsurpassed in the vividness of their effect. Just to the west from here the narrow, but very busy Rue d'Alger runs north and leads into the Rue Hoche, at the end of which is the Place Puget with the Fontaine des Trois Dauphins (1782, by Chastel), which, like many fountains in Provence, is overgrown and covered with deposits of lime.

Musée de la Marine

To the north of the Préfecture Maritime stands the Musée de la Marine (Naval Museum), which houses a collection of old models of ships, etchings and drawings and an exhibition about the development of artillery. Open: Wed.–Mon. 10am–noon, 1.30–6pm.

Ste-Marie-Majeure

South-west of the Place Puget in the centre of the Old Town stands the early Gothic cathedral of Ste-Marie-Majeure (11th/12th c.; rebuilt in the 17th c.) with an 18th c. belfry. Nearby is the colourful Marché (market; vegetables, flowers) and (on the Cours Lafayette) the Musée du Vieux Toulon with local history collections and sacred art. Open: Mon.–Sat. 2–6pm.

Other sights

The Bibliothèque du Vieux Toulon is also situated on the Cours Lafayette. At the east end of Rue Garibaldi, which branches off here, stands the impressive Porte d'Italie, a 16th c. bridge. Farther on, to the south of the cathedral, is the Place de la Poissonnerie, the fish market.
Leaving the Place Puget, the busy centre of the Old Town, by Rue Muraire (also called "Raimu") we come to the noteworthy Opera House (1862–64). North-west lies the Place de la Liberté with the Monument de la Fédération by Allard. Farther to the west, on the Boulevard Leclerc, is the Musée d'Art et d'Archéologie (Museum of Art and Archaeology; pictures from the 13th to 20th c., prehistoric and ancient finds; open: 1–7pm). In the same building is the Musée d'Histoire Naturelle (Natural History Museum; geological and palaeontological collections; open: 10am–noon, 2–6pm). Adjoining is the attractive Jardin Alexandre-I with magnolias, palms and cedars and to the south of this the large Palais de Justice (lawcourts).

Port

At the west end of the Quai Stalingrad along the Darse Neuve (New Harbour) begin the workshops, docks and stores of the Arsenal Maritime behind the fine Porte de l'Arsenal (1738).

**Mourillon**

Beyond the Rond-Point Bonaparte lies Mourillon, the quarter in the south-east. From the Tour Royale, an impressive fortified building of the time of Louis XII at the southern end of the roadstead, there is an exceptional panoramic view. The contents of the "Musée Naval Tour Royale", which was once housed here, have now been transferred to Paris. To the north-east stands Fort St-Louis (1707), which guards a small harbour.

*Corniche Mistral

Probably the finest street in Toulon is the Corniche Mistral, which leads along the Grande Rade de Vignettes of Mourillon past the Jardin d'Acclimatation (botanical garden) to the charming residential district of Cap Brun

Toulon: Fontaine des Trois Dauphins

Signes: market place and Tour d'Horloge

(103m/338ft; fort, view). Below the coast road runs the Sentier des Douaniers ("Customs Officers' Path"), a winding footpath along the coast, which leads across the Batterie Basse du Cap Brun to the romantic bays of Méjean and Magaud.

## **Mont Faron

Corniche du Mont Faron

The Corniche du Mont Faron (Corniche Marius Escartefigue), a panoramic road half-way up Mont Faron, borders the district of Ste-Anne (with the spacious Hôpital Maritime) and Super-Toulon. The last named has only been opened up relatively recently and is characterised by fine villas situated on the slope. There are magnificent views early in the morning and shortly before sunset.

Summit

Mont Faron (542m/1779ft) dominates the city in the north; from Super-Toulon a cableway 1437m/1572yds long (Boulevard Amiral-Vence, dep. every 10mins; closed Mondays) goes up to the Mémorial du Faron and the Tour Beaumont (493m/1618ft). From here there is a very rewarding but narrow, steep and winding road (Route du Faron; mostly one-way traffic and certainly not suitable for large motor or towed caravans), which starts in the west and climbs up past the Fort du St-Antoine to the Musée.

Mémorial du Débarquement

Mémorial du Débarquement en Provence. This martial building contains a collection and documentation about the landing of the Allied forces from August 15th 1944 (weapons, articles of equipment; diorama; film presentation). Open: Tues.–Sun. 9.30–11.30am, 2.30–4.30pm; duration of visit 1 hour.

From the roof of the fort (orientation table, telescope) there is a superb panorama of the city and the port and mountains rising all round.

*Toulon and its harbours, seen from Mont-Faron*

On the plateau on the summit, which is charming because of its great variety of flowers, there is also a small zoological garden. Open: 2pm–sunset.

From the Mémorial the road leads eastwards past Fort Croix Faron and Fort Faron and back down to Super-Toulon.

## Surroundings of Toulon

Cuers

Cuers, situated 22km/14 miles to the north in the country, is a well-known wine-producing and cork-processing centre. On the south-eastern edge of the Barre de Cuers (696m/2284ft) there are extensive areas of flower cultivation.
The centre of the village is picturesque with its fine parish church (great organ of 1669), the medieval gateway and pretty little streets. Above the village stand the ruins of a former castle from which there are good views.

Ollioules

Ollioules, on the southern slope of the gorge of the same name (8km/5 miles to the west), is well-known for its flower-growing (auctions). There is a ruined castle in the village.

**Gorges d'Ollioules

Not far north of the village one reaches the Gorges d'Ollioules, which has been cut by the River Reppe with strange rock formations. Above the gorge on a sheer volcanic rock lies the village of Evenos, a "village perché" with the remains of a castle, the keep of which, like the old houses, is built of blocks of basalt.

La Seyne-sur-Mer

La Seyne-sur-Mer, 4km/2 miles to the west of Toulon on the other side of the bay, is an industrial town with several parts; it has important shipyards, mussel-beds and works for the processing of olive-wood. Of interest are the 17th c. Church of Notre-Dame-du-Bon-Voyage, the former Fort Balaguier, also 17th c., and the Musée de la Seyne (local history). To the east lies the pleasant yacht and fishing harbour with a movable bridge.

Tamaris

Tamaris, which gets its name from the tamarisks which grow here, is a popular resort with a yachting harbour which is reached by following a beautiful coastal road around the promontory of Fort Balaguier. To the west above the resort stands Fort Napoléon, and behind it along the Rade du Lazaret is the district of Les Sablettes which lies on a sandy spit between Cap Sicié and Cap Cépet. From here there is a particularly fine view of the roadsteads of Toulon and the sea.

Signes

The quiet old vine- and fruit-growing village of Signes lies 30km/19 miles to the north of Toulon in a hollow on the edge of the headwaters of the Gapeau. It is reached either via Ollioules (west, N8, D402 and D2) or via Solliès-Pont (east, N97, D554 and D2). Here in the Place St-Jean stands a beautiful chapel which was restored in the 17th c.; inside can be seen pictures, votive tablets and penitents' garments. The square is embellished by an 18th c. fountain. In the Church of St-Pierre, which was also restored (16th c. belfry), the beautiful wooden altar of the 14th and 17th c. is worthy of note.

Autodrome Paul-Ricard

On the western route to Signes, at the junction of the D402 with the N8, is the motor-racing track of Paul-Ricard, which until 1990 was the venue of the Grand Prix de France (Formula One). Since 1991 the race has been held at Magny-Cours, near Nevers in Burgundy.

Six-Fours-la-Plage

See Bandol

# Uzès C2

Région: Languedoc-Roussillon
Département: Gard
Altitude: 138m/453ft
Population: 8000

Location and Townscape

The little town of Uzès is actually situated beyond the boundaries of Provence, some 40km/25 miles west of Avignon. It has a picturesque situation above the wooded valley of the Alzon. The town centre with its narrow streets and alleys is surrounded by a ring of boulevards shaded by plane trees.

The best facilities for parking are on the broad Esplanade on the western edge of the Old Town.

## Sights

*Place aux Herbes

A short way east of the Esplanade is the Place aux Herbes, the beautiful main square of the town, shaded by plane trees and adorned by its fountain, which is mainly overgrown. All round the square are medieval houses with arcades. On Saturdays the market takes place here.

Hôtels

In Rue de la République further north stands the Hôtel de Joubert with a pretty staircase and inner courtyard. From here we turn east and on the far side of the small Place Dampmartin (arcades with ribbed vaults) reaches the equally interesting Hôtel Dampmartin. To the north stands the great complex of buildings of the Château Ducal (Ducal Castle; entrance from the Place du Duché).

Château Ducal

The former castle of the Dukes of Uzès was built in various stages from the 11th to the 17th c., but was again altered in the 19th c. In the inner courtyard

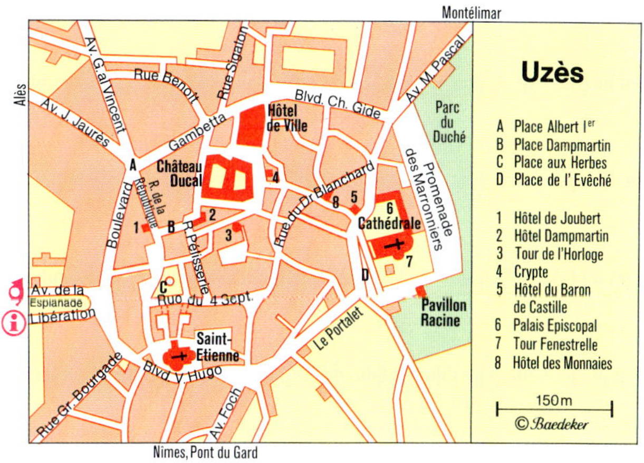


the Renaissance façade between the keep and the chapel tower deserves particular attention; it is divided by pillars and decorated with relief medallions. There is a good panorama from the Tour Bermonde (the tower was certainly built in the 11th c. but did not receive its balustrade until 1839). Open: Apr. 1st–Sept. 30th 9.30am–noon, 2.30–6.30pm; Oct. 1st–Mar. 30th Tues.–Sun. 10am–noon, 2.30–5pm.

Hôtel de Ville

Opposite the castle gateway stands the Hôtel de Ville (Town Hall) which was erected in 1773 under Louis XVI. The façade facing the castle still shows the elegance of the time when it was built, while the north front, where the main entrance is situated, was renewed about 1900. The façades of the courtyard are broken up by pillars. The view of the ducal castle through the wrought-iron grille is delightful.

Crypte (Crypt)

Opposite the north-east corner of the castle is the entrance to the so-called "crypt", an Early Christian cult chamber hacked out of the rock. On the walls in half relief are the figures of John the Baptist and an Orans (a figure praying with outstretched arms).

Palais Episcopal

From the castle and the town hall going east past the Ancien Hôtel des Monnaies (former Mint) we reach the Palais Episcopal, the former Bishop's Palace (Place de l'Evêché). Today the lawcourts and the library are situated here and in the second storey is the Musée d'Art et de Tradition de l'Uzège (Museum of Art and History of the region of Uzès) with exhibits of art, ethnology, prehistory and natural history, as well as mementoes of the writer André Gide, whose family originated from Uzès. Open: 3–6pm, in winter Sat., Sun. 2.30–5.30pm.

Cathedral

To the south by the bishop's palace stands the Cathedral of St-Théodorit dating from the 17th and 19th c.; the previous building was destroyed during the Wars of Religion. The present façade was not added until the 19th c.

Tour Fenestrelle

The most interesting part of the medieval cathedral is the round Tour Fenestrelle ("Window Tower"), a 42m/138ft high belfry, erected in the 12th c. on a Lombardian model. Its six storeys, which seem to become lighter as they ascend, are divided up by varyingly shaped arches, which from the second floor upwards have windows. Since it served at that time as a watch-tower, the building escaped destruction by the Albigenses.

Uzès: the elegant Tour Fenestrelle

Fountain on the Place aux Herbes

Hôtel du Baron de Castille

On the far side of the square opposite the bishop's palace stands the Hôtel du Baron de Castille, a classical building with an elegant pillared façade (18th c.).

St-Etienne

On the southern edge of the Old Town, in the Boulevard Victor-Hugo, is the Church of St-Etienne, a large Baroque building (1765–78). The tower standing alongside, with a square design, dates from the 13th c.

## Surroundings of Uzès

Musée 1900

The small museum at Arpaillargues (4km/2 miles to the west, D982) displays an attractive collection of old cars, motor-bikes, carriages, agricultural tools and machines, as well as cameras and toys.

Haras (stud-farm)

Founded in 1972, the Haras d'Uzès (about 4km/2 miles to the west, D407; signed) is one of 23 French national stud-farms and has in excess of 70 horses of different breeds, including Arab and English. It is also used as a Gîte d'Étape by long-distance horse-riders. Conducted tours through the stud-farm: July 1st–Aug. 31st Tues., Fri. 3pm.

Pont du Gard

See entry

# Vaison-la-Romaine C3

Département: Vaucluse
Altitude: 200m/656ft
Population: 6000

Location

Vaison-la-Romaine lies to the north-west of the foot of Mont Ventoux, about 30km/19 miles north-east of Orange. To the south of the town extend the wine-producing regions of Séguret and Gigondas and the Dentelles de Montmirail.

History

In the 4th c. B.C. this was the chief place of the Celtic Vocones. Later the Romans founded Vasio Vocontiorum in the fertile region of the Valley of the Ouvèze and in five peaceful centuries this developed into a flourishing community. As early as the 3rd c. A.D. Vaison was the seat of a bishop and in 442 and 529 ecclesiastical councils were held here; in the 11th and 12th c. it was resolved to build a cathedral. However, a little later, Raymond, Count of Toulouse, laid siege and conquered the town, robbed the Bishop of his property and had a castle built on the highest spot of the mountain which rises above the town. The Upper Town was surrounded by a wall and not until the 18th c. was the territory of the former Roman city settled again.

## *Roman Excavations

Location

To the west and the east of the Place du 11 Novembre can be found the two separate sites with Roman excavations. The eastern part corresponds to the Quartier de Puymin and the western to the Quartier de la Villasse.

## Vaison-la-Romaine

Opening times

Excavations and Notre-Dame: April, May 10am–12.30pm, 2–5.45pm; June–Aug. 9am–12.30pm, 2–6.45pm. Conducted tours: 11am, 2.30pm, 4pm.
Museum: April/May 10am–1pm, 2.30–5.45pm; June–Aug. 9.30am–1pm, 2.30–6.45pm.
The combined entrance ticket to all the sights is valid for five days.

Quartier de Puymin

The extensive gently sloping Quartier de Puymin is laid out like a park with oaks, cypresses, etc. In the lower part foundations of walls have been uncovered including those of the House of the Messii, the Portico of Pompey (pillared hall), the Nymphaeum, etc. The statues which have been set up on the excavation site are copies of the ancient originals which can be seen in the museum.
In addition to a large and very well arranged lapidarium (Roman tombstones, statues, etc.), the museum in the centre of this site includes a model of the theatre. Other specialised subjects concern the Roman dwellings and Gallo-Roman pottery. Of interest is a showcase containing urns for ashes, some of which are made of glass. Immediately by the entrance there is a historic map on the wall showing the Province of Gallia Narbonensis.

Theatre

Just above the museum a tunnel leads to the ancient theatre which was somewhat smaller than those at Arles and Orange. It has been comprehensively restored and now serves its original purpose once more as an open-air theatre.

Quartier de la Villasse

Extending to the west on the far side of the square (Information pavilion of the Office de Tourisme) and the park is the Quartier de la Villasse, the second large excavation site of Vaison-la-Romaine. It has not been so thoroughly restored as the Puymin site and provides, as it were, a more original impression. Of interest here are the great arch of the former basilica and the carefully paved Roman street which was provided with

*Vaison-la-Romaine: Roman bridge over the River Ouvèze*

gutters. In some places mosaic floors can be seen under a protective covering.

## Other sights

Notre-Dame

On the western edge of the Quartier de la Villasse stands the Church of Notre-Dame, the former cathedral. Its origins go back to Merovingian times, but the present building was erected between the 11th and 13th c.; its plan is smaller than that of its predecessor as can be seen from the former foundations which have been uncovered near the church. Adjoining on the north of the church is the cloister dating from the 12th c. but which had to be extensively renovated in the 19th c. Of interest are the beautifully decorated capitals of the pillars of the arcades.

Upper Town

South of the River Ouvèze the Upper Town rises up the castle hill. The river is crossed by a bridge originally built by the Romans and the path then passes through a medieval gate-tower. In the romantic narrow streets of the Upper Town which, protected by the castle, had developed from the 14th c., artists and craftsmen have settled in recent times, producing pottery, olive-wood carving, etc. At the eastern edge of the Old Town stands the church and, from the open space in front of it, there is a good view of the valley below. The cube-shaped ruin of the castle (the interior is not open to the public) stands right on the top of the Old Town and can be reached by a narrow, meagrely signed footpath. From the rocky plateau which in the south and west falls sharply and is completely unprotected (caution!) there is a rewarding panorama.

## Surroundings of Vaison

Mont Ventoux

Vaison-la-Romaine is the northern starting-point for the drive over Mont Ventoux (see entry).

*The idyllic Place du Vieux Marché*

*The cloister of Notre-Dame*

Dentelles de Montmirail

The western foothills of Mont Ventoux between Malaucène and Gigondas are appropriately called "Dentelles de Montmirail" (dentelles = lace). The chalk rocks with their vertical strata give more of an impression of the Alps than Mont Ventoux does and in spite of their modest height (Pic St-Amand 734m/2408ft) they are a paradise for climbers; it is also a popular area for walkers.

Gigondas

In Gigondas, 15km/10 miles to the south-west of Vaison, the best vines in the area grow, equal to those of Châteauneuf-du-Pape, with their own Appellation Controlée. In the village square there are sales stands with wine-tasting.

# Vence D5

Département: Alpes-Maritimes
Altitude: 325m/1067ft
Population: 13,500

*Location

Vence is a superbly situated "village perché" in the east of the Côte d'Azur slightly inland between Nice and Antibes.

## Sights

Townscape

In the centre of the Old Town stands the former cathedral (St-Véran; 10th –15th c.). The interior has fine choir-stalls and a Roman sarcophagus which serves as an altar. In the baptism chapel there is a mosaic by Marc Chagall which depicts the rescue of Moses from the Nile. The choir and the tower chapel are decorated with Carolingan interlace work. On the façade of the cathedral there are two Roman inscriptions which are dedicated to the Emperors Heliogabalus and Gordianus.
East of the church, in the Place Godeau, stands an ancient column; also of interest are the battlemented belfry and the charming Renaissance gate. In the west on the edge of the Old Town lies the attractive Place du Peyra with the fountain of the same name. Also to the west, outside the town centre, in the Avenue Henri Isnard, stands the 15th c. Chapelle des Pénitents-Blancs.

*Chapelle du Rosaire

On the northern edge of the town, to the right of the road D2210, can be found the inconspicuous Chapelle du Rosaire (Rosary Chapel; open: Tues., Thur.10–11.30am, 2.30–5.30pm, or 4–5pm), which belongs to a Dominican convent. It can be recognised by the severely linear representation of Mary, Jesus and St Dominic, by Henri Matisse, to be found over the doorway. The interior was also designed by Matisse (between 1947 and 1951) with bold graphics (black outlines on white ceramic tiles) based on Biblical themes. These include the birth of Christ, St Dominic and the Passion of Christ (Way of the Cross). Kept completely white, the simple room only receives colour through its glass window. The economy of form and the drama thereby expressed are very impressive. The altar furniture and various chasubles were also designed by Matisse; they are kept in the Matisse Museum at Cimiez in Nice (see entry).

## Surroundings of Vence

St-Paul-de-Vence

The little town of St-Paul-de-Vence, which has managed to retain its medieval character, is attractively situated on a hill 3km/2 miles to the south. The well-preserved circle of rampart-walls, dating from the 16th c., is provided with sturdy reinforcing supports on the steep slopes; there is also a government defence tower. In the early 13th c. church can be seen a fine treasury

Vence: Place du Peyra

Fondation Maeght, centre of modern art

Fondation Maeght: the comical fountain by Miró

with silver-work, reliquaries and a ciborium dating from 1439. In the Place de la Fontaine (with a fountain) stands the Musée Provençal. In the 1920s St-Paul was "discovered" by painters such as Signac, Modigliani and Bonnard.

**Fondation Maeght

On the Gardettes hill, 1km/½ mile to the north-west of St-Paul-de-Vence, lies the Fondation Maeght, a foundation established by the art dealers Aimé and Marguerite Maeght (husband and wife) and opened in 1960, which offers a very interesting combination of nature, architecture (Josep Lluis Sert) and modern art. Alongside mosaics by Braque, Chagall and Tal-Coat, the ceramic sculptures of Miró are of special note, as well as the bronze figures of Giacometti and the stabile by Calder. The chapel was created by Braque and Ubac. In the museum there are works by artists such as Arp, Bonnard, Chagall, Giacometti, Kandinsky and Miró.
The Fondation Maeght also organises temporary exhibitions, concerts and symposia; there is also an interesting bookshop for art lovers and an extensive archive. Opening times: July 1st–Sept. 30th 10am–7pm, Oct. 1st–June 30th 10am–12.30pm, 2.30–6pm. Visitors should allow at least two hours to tour the foundation.

Tourette-sur-Loup

The charming former defence village of Tourette-sur-Loup with its medieval towers lies on a rocky plateau 5km/3 miles west of Vence above the Valley of the Loup, surrounded by olive groves, pine woods and fields of violets. In the 14th c. church is a notable ancient altar and an altarpiece of the school of Bréa. Also of interest is the Musée d'Artisanat Local (Museum of Local Industry).

## Verdon (Grand Canyon du Verdon) D4

Département: Alpes-de-Haute-Provence

Course and scenery

The Verdon, 175km/109 miles in length, is the most important tributary of the Durance. Between Castellane and the man-made Lac de Ste-Croix it flows through the Grand Canyon du Verdon, a 21km/13 mile series of magnificent wild gorges in the fossil-filled chalk beds of Haute-Provence. At their deepest they descend to 700m/2297ft, the water of the river falling 153m/502ft over this stretch.

Timetable

The round trip described below is about 120km/75 miles long. To have sufficient time to appreciate to the full the numerous scenic beauties, at least six hours should be allowed, and if possible a whole day.

### **Drive through the Grand Canyon du Verdon

Access

The best starting-point for a circular tour of the Grand Canyon du Verdon is the little town of Castellane (see entry) on the Route Napoléon.

Take the road D952 in a south-westerly direction downstream through the Defile of Porte St-Jean and Clue de Chasteuil. At the fork (in about 12km/7 miles) bear left on the D955, cross the river (Pont de Soleils; signposted "Rive Gauche") and continue south over attractive uplands. Some 6km/4 miles beyond the fork, near the picturesquely situated village of Trigance with its dominating castle on the right, take road D90 as far as the D71 which is followed north-west.

Balcons de la Mescla

The Balcons de la Mescla (mescla=mixing, referring to the nearby confluence of the Artuby with the Verdon), provide the first high spot of the drive. Here there is a fine view into the gorge 250m/821ft below. A little farther on cross a boldly curved bridge over the Artuby, which joins the Verdon at this point.

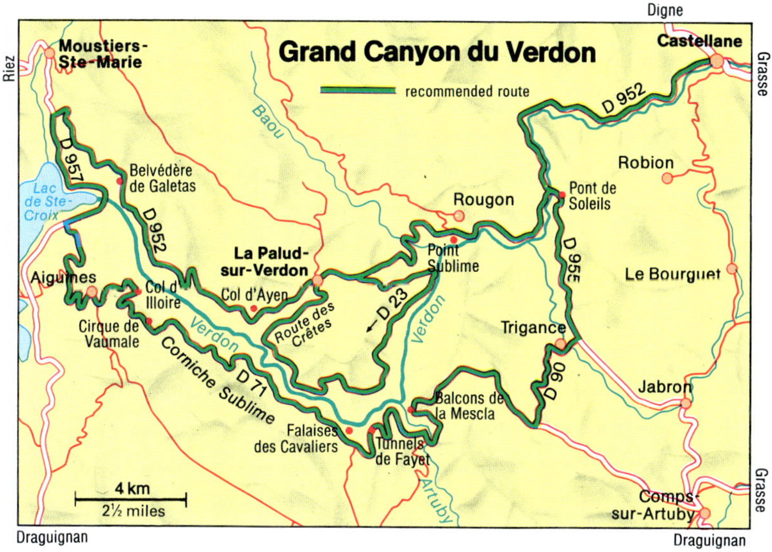


**Corniche Sublime**

The road continues its winding course, with breathtaking views high above the Verdon and through the Tunnels de Fayet (views between the tunnels).

**Falaise des Cavaliers**

There is a viewing platform near the restaurant at the Falaises des Cavaliers, then the road continues along a 10km/6 miles long magnificent stretch up to 400m/1313ft above the river as it rushes along the ravine.

**Lac de Ste-Croix**

After driving round the impressive cwm of Vaumale and crossing the 964m/3164ft high Col d'Illoire, the road winds its way down to the deep turquoise-green Lac de Ste-Croix (about 2500ha/6178 acres), a lake formed by the damming of the Verdon. On the shore of the lake is a popular leisure centre (sailing, wind-surfing, camping, etc.). Here the D19 joins the D957 which is followed to the right. At the point where the Verdon leaves the gorge and enters the reservoir cross the river by the bridge (fine view of the gorge on the right).

Some 7km/4 miles beyond the junction of the D19 with the D957 the D952 bears right just before Moustiers. This road borders the northern (right) bank of the Verdon. Passing the Belvédère de Galetas (viewpoint) and crossing the Col d'Ayen (1032m/3287ft) we reach Palud-sur-Verdon.
To drive along the winding Route des Crêtes first continue along the D952 and then turn right on to the D23; part of this road is one-way and can only be used in this direction.

***Route des Crêtes**

The 23km/14 mile long Route des Crêtes draws close to the edge of the Grand Canyon, and on its course passes several viewpoints – the Belvédère de Trescaire, the particularly impressive Belvédère de L'Escalès and the Belvédères du Tilleul, des Glacières and de l'Imbut before leading back to La Palud.

****Point Sublime**

The D952 heads for probably the finest viewpoint of the tour, Point Sublime. From the car park it is about ten minutes' walk to the viewing platform, from which the visitor can enjoy the classic view of the Gorge of the

Verdon. The platform stands 180m/591ft above the confluence of the Baou with the Verdon; there is a magnificent prospect of the resurgence of the river near the Couloir Samson.

Passing below the "Eagle's Nest" of Rougon, with the romantic ruins of a castle (rewarding detour) and through the defile of the Clue de Carejuan we reach, about 5km/3 miles beyond Point Sublime, a road junction near the Pont de Soleils and return to Castellane.

## **Sentier Martel

Martel Footpath

The Sentier Martel is named after the great French speleologist Edouard Martel (1859–1938) who was the first in the 20th century to explore the entire length of the Gorge of the Verdon. The path runs along the bottom of the gorge and can be reached from the road at Point Sublime or at the Chalet de la Maline on the Route des Crêtes.

A walk along the entire length of this section is not particularly easy and will require from six hours to a whole day. Stout footwear, provisions, drinking-water and suitable clothing (including a sweater and a waterproof of some kind) are essential; a pocket torch is desirable, as in places the path leads through tunnels.

**Warning**

Loitering in the immediate vicinity of the river is dangerous, as depending on the operation on the dam and the sluices, the water-level can rise considerably in a very short time and a strong current can result. Therefore walkers should not linger in places where there is no escape path up the cliff.

◀ *Point Sublime: the classical view of the Gorges du Verdon*

# Practical Information

## Accommodation

See Camping, Holidays for Young People, Holidays in the Country, Hotels, Private Rooms, Youth Hostels.

## Airlines

International routes are flown by Air France, the national airline; inland traffic is handled by Air Inter. Both airlines are represented at all French airports. Abroad information for both companies is provided at the offices of Air France.

**Air France**
1 Square Max Hymans, F-75741 Paris Cèdex 15
Tel. (1) 43 23 81 61

Head office

158 New Bond Street, London W1Y 0AY; tel. (071) 499 9511

United Kingdom

666 Fifth Avenue, New York N.Y. 10019

USA

1 Place Ville-Marie, Suite 3321, Montreal H38 3N4, P.Q.

Canada

## Banks

See Currency

## Bicycle Rental

See Cycling

## Bus Tours

Europabus

Europabus, a subsidiary of eight European railway companies, operates a number of one-day tours from Avignon; these include "Roman Provence", "The Wine Road", "The Wild Camargue" and "The Heart of Provence". Information can be obtained from Avignon railway station.

Bus network

France has an extensive network of bus routes operated by private firms. Timetables and details of routes can be obtained from local information offices.

Pass Côte d'Azur

The "Rapides Côte d'Azur" bus company operates inclusive tours between Cannes and Menton and also inland (Grasse, Aspremont, Peille, Sospel) which are good value. Information from the bus and rail stations in Cannes and also from the bus stations in Grasse, Antibes and Nice.

◀ *Autumn in Haute Provence (near Séderon)*

## Business Hours

See Opening Times

## Camping

Camping plays a more prominent role in France than in other European countries. Almost every place of touristic interest has one or often several camp sites (terrains de camping). Sites are classified by one to four stars. During the height of the season sites along the coast and on the main holiday routes are generally full (complet), but as a rule space can be found inland.

Information

Space does not permit the inclusion of a detailed list of camp sites. Information can be obtained from regional and local "Offices de Tourisme" and also from:
Féderation Française de Camping et Caravaning
78 rue de Rivoli
F-75004 Paris
Tel: (1) 42 72 84 08

Camping à la ferme

The French themselves are very fond of "camping à la ferme" (camping on a farm), where an informal holiday can be spent, usually for an extended period. Visitors from abroad who have a good knowledge of French may well find a farm holiday an enjoyable experience.
Information from "Gites de France" (see Rural Holidays).

Camping au château

Of particular interest are camp sites which have been set up in the grounds of châteaux. Information:
Castels & Camping Caravaning B. P. 301,
F-56007 Vannes; tel. 97 42 55 83

Note

In high summer in Provence drinking water can be in short supply. Therefore economy in the use of water is necessary, and in many places attention is drawn to this by notices.

## Car Rental

Booking

Visitors who wish to rent a car during their stay in Provence can make a booking before leaving home. During the high season (July, August) prior booking is recommended.
Local firms are often cheaper than international undertakings, but the latter will often permit the vehicle to be returned to a different place from where it was initially rented. Weekend or weekly rental are the norm, usually with unrestricted mileage. Visitors are recommended to book their vehicle as a package together with air or rail travel. (See also Railways, train + car.)

A passport and a driving licence (held for at least one year) must be produced. Personal liability insurance is included in the rental; other types of insurance can also be included.

**Avis**

Aix-en-Provence

11 Cours Gambetta; tel. 42 21 64 16
Gare SNCF; tel. 42 21 64 16

Antibes

32 Boulevard Albert-1er; tel. 93 34 65 115
Gare SNCF; tel. 93 34 65 15

Arles

12 bis Avenue Victor-Hugo; tel. 90 96 82 42
Gare SNCF; tel. 90 96 82 42

| | |
|---|---|
| Impasse Ruer; tel. 42 84 36 06 | Aubagne |
| 34 Boulevard St-Roch; tel. 90 82 26 33<br>Avignon Airport; tel. 90 82 26 33<br>Gare SNCF; tel. 90 87 17 75 | Avignon |
| 1 rue Georges Clemenceau; tel. 93 01 00 13 | Beaulieu-sur-Mer |
| Gare SNCF; tel. 93 34 65 15 | Cagnes-sur-Mer |
| 69 la Croisette; tel. 93 94 15 86<br>Gare SNCF; tel. 93 94 15 86 | Cannes |
| 110 Boulevard Crillon; tel. 90 71 59 46 | Cavaillon |
| c/o Garage Volkswagen; tel. 90 63 28 64 | Carpentras |
| Garage Peugeot, Route de Marseille; tel. 92 31 06 11 | Digne |
| 9 Avenue du Commandant Dumont; tel. 92 51 26 09 | Gap |
| 2 Boulevard du Maréchal Leclerc; tel. 93 70 80 49 | Grasse |
| Pont de la Villette; tel. 94 38 98 02 | Hyères |
| Gare SNCF; tel. 93 34 65 15 | Juan-les-Pins |
| Gare SNCF; tel. 94 95 60 42 | Les Arcs |
| 17 Avenue Jean Giono; tel. 92 72 18 18 | Manosque |
| 267 Boulevard National; tel. 91 50 70 11<br>Gare SNCF; tel. 91 64 71 00<br>Aéroport Marignane; tel. 42 89 02 26 | Marseilles |
| 11 Boulevard Lucien Degut; tel. 42 07 07 96 | Martigues |
| 9 rue Victor Hugo; tel. 93 35 50 98 | Menton |
| 9 Avenue d'Ostende; tel. 93 30 17 53<br>Gare SNCF; tel. 93 30 17 53 | Monaco |
| 84 Boulevard St-James; tel. 75 51 86 20<br>Gare SNCF; tel. 75 51 86 20 | Montélimar |
| 900 Avenue des Prés d'Armée; tel. 67 92 51 92<br>Gare SNCF; tel. 67 92 92 00<br>Aéroport; tel. 67 92 94 00 | Monpellier |
| 2 rue des Phocéens; tel. 93 80 63 52<br>Aéroport Nice-Côte d'Azur; tel. 93 21 36 33 | Nice |
| 1 bis rue de la République; tel. 66 21 00 29<br>Aéroport Nîmes-Garons; tel. 66 29 05 33<br>Gare SNCF; tel. 66 29 05 33 | Nîmes |
| Gare SNCF; tel. 90 82 26 33 | Orange |
| Avenue Gargarine; tel. 94 94 55 47 | La Seyne-sur-Mer |
| Capitainerie du Port; tel. 94 49 09 09 | Ste-Maxime |
| Place de la Gare; tel. 94 95 60 42 | St-Raphaël |

**Car Rental**

| | |
|---|---|
| St-Tropez | 13 Boulevard Louis Blanc; tel. 94 97 03 10 |
| Toulon | Carrefour Léon Bourgeois; tel. 94 36 20 01 |
| **Budget** | |
| Aix-en-Provence | 16 Avenue des Belges; tel. 42 38 37 36 |
| Antibes | 40 Boulevard Albert 1er; tel. 93 34 36 84 |
| Avignon | 89 Route de Montfavet; tel. 90 82 03 00<br>Gare SNCF; tel. 90 82 09 00 |
| Cannes | 1 rue André Chaude; tel. 93 99 44 04 |
| Draguignan | 24 rue Carnot; tel. 94 68 60 96 |
| Marseilles | 40 Boulevard des Plombières; tel. 91 64 40 03<br>232 Avenue du Prado; tel. 91 71 75 00 |
| Monaco | 9 Quai Prés J. F. Kennedy; tel. 92 16 00 70 |
| Montélimar | 7 rue Ducatez; tel. 75 51 90 07 |
| Montpellier | 4 rue J. Ferry; tel. 67 92 69 00 |
| Nice | 23 rue de Belgique; tel. 93 16 24 16 |
| Nîmes | 6 bis Avenue Général Leclerc; tel. 66 29 88 08 |
| Orange | 42 Boulevard Deladier; tel. 90 34 00 34 |
| Port Grimaud | 26 Place du Sud; tel. 94 43 48 64 |
| St-Raphaël | 40 rue W. Rousseau; tel. 94 96 62 00 |
| St-Tropez | 19 Avenue du Général Leclerc; tel. 94 54 86 54 |
| Ste-Maxime | 12 bis Avenue du G. Clemenceau; tel. 94 96 62 00 |
| **EuropCar** | |
| Aix-en-Provence | 55 Boulevard de la République; tel. 42 27 41 27 |
| Antibes | 26 Boulevard Foch; tel. 83 34 79 79 |
| Arles | 2 bis Avenue Victor-Hugo; tel. 90 93 23 24 |
| Avignon | 27 Avenue St-Ruf; tel. 90 82 49 85 |
| Bandol | Station Total; tel. 94 06 66 06 |
| Beaulieu-sur-Mer | c/o Garage Total, Port de Beaulieu; tel. 93 01 13 78 |
| Cagnes-sur-Mer | 2 Avenue de Nice; tel. 93 20 99 66 |
| Cannes | 3 rue du Commandant Vidal; tel. 93 39 75 20<br>Palais des Festivals; tel. 93 39 75 20<br>Aéroport Mandelieu; tel. 93 90 40 60 |
| Carpentras | 32 Boulevard Albin Durand; tel. 90 63 17 85 |
| Cavaillon | 70 Cours Carnot; tel. 90 71 20 44 |
| Digne | 2 A. St-Christophe R. N. 85; tel. 92 32 19 42 |

| | |
|---|---|
| Draguignan | 35 Avenue Carnot; tel. 94 68 16 94 |
| Fréjus | 308 Avenue de Verdun; tel. 94 51 53 88 |
| Gap | 6 bis Avenue de Commandant Dumont; tel. 92 53 71 71 |
| Grasse | 2 Boulevard Victor Hugo; tel. 93 36 37 36 |
| Hyères | Aéroport Le Palyvestre; tel. 94 58 06 22 |
| Le Lavandou | 7 Avenue des Commandos d'Afrique; tel. 94 71 19 68 |
| Manosque | Les Alpilles, Boulevard Ch. de Gaulle; tel. 92 72 54 34 |
| Marseilles | 93 Avenue du Prado; tel. 91 79 05 29<br>Aéroport Marignane; tel. 42 78 24 75 |
| Martigues | Résidence La Venise, Quai Alsace-Lorraine; tel. 42 07 36 80 |
| Menton | 9 Avenue Thiers; tel. 93 28 21 80 |
| Monaco | 47 Avenue de la Grande-Bretagne; tel. 93 50 74 95 |
| Montélimar | 9 Place de la Gare; tel. 75 01 99 70 |
| Montpellier | 6 rue Jules Ferry; tel. 67 58 16 17<br>Aéroport Fréjorgues; tel. 67 64 77 33 |
| Nice | 6 Avenue de Suède; tel. 93 88 64 04<br>Aéroport Nice-Côte d'Azur; tel. 93 21 36 44 and 93 21 42 53 |
| Nîmes | Centre Atria, 5 Boulevard de Prague; tel. 66 21 31 35 |
| Orange | Cours Aristide Briand; tel. 90 51 67 53 |
| Salon-de-Provence | 284 Allées de Craponne; tel. 90 42 31 11 |
| St-Raphaël | Place de la Gare; tel. 94 95 56 87 |
| St-Tropez | Résidence du Port; tel. 94 97 21 59 |
| Ste-Maxime | 1 rue de la Plage; tel. 94 96 00 07 |
| La Seyne-sur-Mer | Rd. Point 8 Mai 1945; tel. 94 87 75 98 |
| Sophia Antipolis | Sophia Country Club; tel. 93 65 44 55 |
| Toulon | Rue Sylvain; tel. 94 41 09 07 |

**Hertz**

| | |
|---|---|
| Aix-en-Provence | 43 Avenue Victor Hugo; tel. 42 27 91 32 |
| Arles | 4 Avenue Victor Hugo; tel. 90 96 75 23 |
| Aubagne | Avenue de Verdun; tel. 42 10 20 14 |
| Avignon | 6 Route de Lyon; tel. 90 82 37 67<br>Aéroport Châteaublanc; tel. 90 88 99 43 |
| Beaulieu-sur-Mer | Port; tel. 93 01 62 30 |
| Cagnes-sur-Mer | 35 Boulevard du Maréchal Juin; tel. 93 20 33 57 |

**Consulates**

| | |
|---|---|
| Cannes | 147 rue d'Antibes; tel. 93 99 04 20<br>Hôtel Carlton, 59 Boulevard de la Croisette; tel. 93 39 94 39<br>Aéroport Mandelieu; tel. 93 90 40 20 |
| Gap | 1 Avenue des Alpes; tel. 92 53 97 77 |
| Hyères | 6 Avenue Geoffroy St-Hilaire; tel. 94 57 63 16<br>Aéroport Le Palyvestre; tel. 94 58 06 44 |
| Juan-les-Pins | 129 Boulevard Wilson; tel. 93 61 18 15 |
| Le Lavandou | Avenue des Ilaires; tel. 94 64 48 11 |
| Manosque | Route de Marseille; tel. 92 72 13 50 |
| Marseilles | 16 Boulevard Charles Nédelec; tel. 91 91 26 55<br>27 Boulevard Rabatau; tel. 91 79 22 06<br>Aéroport Marignane; tel. 42 89 00 45 |
| Monaco | 27 Boulevard Albert 1er; tel. 93 50 79 60<br>Hôtel Abela, 23 Avenue des Papalins; tel. 93 50 79 60 |
| Montélimar | 1 rue André Ducatez; tel. 75 01 60 61 |
| Montpellier | 18 rue Jules Ferry; tel. 67 58 65 18<br>Aéroport Fréjorgues; tel. 67 65 16 45 |
| Nice | 12 Avenue de Suède; tel. 93 87 11 87<br>Aéroport Nice-Côte d'Azur; tel. 93 21 36 72 |
| Nîmes | 39 Boulevard Gambetta; tel. 66 76 25 91<br>Aéroport Garons; tel. 66 70 19 96 |
| Orange | 42 Boulevard Edouard Daladier; tel. 90 34 19 08 |
| Ste-Maxime | Le Victoria, Rue Georges Clemenceau; tel. 94 96 46 60 |
| St-Raphaël | Place de la Gare; tel. 94 95 48 68 |
| St-Tropez | Route de la Nouvelle Poste; tel. 94 97 22 01 |
| Toulon | 18 Avenue François Cuzin; tel. 94 41 60 53 |
| **Train + Auto** | See Railways |

## Consulates

See Diplomatic Representation

## Currency

The unit of currency is the French franc which is made up of 100 centimes. There are banknotes for 10, 20, 50 100 and 500 francs and coins for 5, 10, 20 centimes and ½, 1, 2, 5 and 10 francs.

In Monaco the French franc is officially used but a few coins, ranging in value between 1 centime and 10 francs are also minted; however, these are only accepted in Monaco and its immediate surroundings.

Currency exchange

Foreign currency, travellers' cheques, Eurocheques, etc. can be exchanged at official bureaux de change, banks and savings banks ("Caisses d'Epargne Ecureuil"). For business hours, see entry.

These fluctuate daily and often differ according to whether francs are obtained before leaving home or actually in France. Current rates of exchange can be obtained from banks, tourist offices, travel agents and are published in the principal national newspapers. Rates of exchange

There are no restrictions on the import of French or foreign currency. However, cheques, etc. with a total value of more than 50,000 francs must be declared to French customs officials on arrival in or departure from the country. Currency regulation

For the sake of security visitors are advised to take travellers' cheques or Eurocheques. When travellers' cheques are encashed a commission is charged. Eurocheques can be made out to a maximum of 1400 FF. Cheques

Many hotels, shops, car rental firms, etc., accept credit cards (Eurocard, Visa, Diners Club, American Express, etc.). Tolls on motorways can be paid by using Eurocard, Mastercard or Visa International. Credit cards

If credit cards or cheques are lost or stolen the issuing office must be informed immediately. Loss of credit cards, etc.

## Customs Regulations

Personal effects, sports equipment, etc., can be taken in without payment of duty. Video equipment must be declared on entry. Entry into France

For goods obtained duty-free in the EC or on a ship or aircraft, or bought outside the EC, the allowances are 200 cigarettes or 100 cigarillos or 50 cigars or 250 grams of tobacco; one litre of alcoholic drinks over 22 per cent volume (33·8° proof), or two litres of alcoholic drinks not over 22 per cent volume or fortified or sparkling wine, plus two litres of still table wine; 50 grams of perfume; 250 cc of toilet water; and other goods to the value of £28 sterling. The allowances of tobacco goods is doubled for visitors from outside the EC.

For goods obtained duty-paid in the EC the allowances are 300 cigarettes or 150 cigarillos or 75 cigars or 400 grams of tobacco; one and a half litres of alcoholic drinks over 22 per cent volume or three litres of alcoholic drinks not over 22 per cent volume or fortified or sparkling wine, plus four litres of still table wine; 75 grams of perfume; 375 cc of toilet water; and other goods to the value of £120.

In January 1993 for citizens of any EC country the allowances of goods permitted to be imported for personal use into any country of the EC will be considerably increased. For citizens of non-EC countries the allowances will remain as at present. The sale of duty-free goods will be discontinued.

## Cycling

Provence is an ideal region for exploring by bicycle and traffic is mercifully light on most of the smaller roads. However a cycling tour can be quite strenuous; the hilly and often mountainous terrain, the intensive sunlight from early spring and (especially in the Rhône valley) the often strong or even stormy wind (see Climate) should be taken into account when planning. If possible the coastal roads of the entire Côte d'Azur, which are very busy practically throughout the year, should be avoided.

The French Tourist Office with the help of other organisations concerns itself with the increasingly popular cycling holidays (brochure "Cycling in Information

France"; suggested tours; booking facilities). In addition special cycle paths have been constructed. Details can be obtained from French cycling clubs.

Bicycle Club de France
8 Place de la Porte-Champerret
F-75017 Paris

Fédération Française de Cyclotourisme
8 rue Jean-Marie-Jégo
F-75010 Paris

Organised Cycling Tours

Various holiday organisations offer cycling tours of differing types (duration, route, sporting standard) with accommodation ranging from tents to comfortable hotels (many of the latter as a gourmet-tour). Access by plane or bus. Information from travel agents.

Gîtes d'Etape

Cyclists, for whom contact with the country and its people is more important than comfort, may find the Gîtes d'Etape interesting.

Cycle rental
train + bicycle

Cycles can be rented even in small places.
The French National Railways (SNCF) keep bicycles for rental at about 250 stations (train + bicycle). The stations of places described in this guide are: Antibes, Arles, Bandol, Cagnes-sur-Mer, Cannes, Gap, Le Grau de Roi, Hyères, Juan-les-Pins, Montpellier, Nîmes, St-Raphaël. Cycles can be returned to any station.

## Diplomatic Representation

United Kingdom

Embassy
35 rue Faubourg St-Honoré
F-75008 Paris; tel. (1) 42 66 91 42
Consular section; tel. 42 60 33 06

Consulate-General
24 Avenue du Prado
F-13006 Marseille
tel: 91 53 43 32

There is also a consulate at Nice

United States of America

Embassy
2 Avenue Gabriel
F-75008 Paris
Tel. (1) 42 96 12 02 and 42 61 80 75

Consulate-General
12 Boulevard Paul-Peytral
F-13286 Marseille
Tel. 91 54 92 00

There is also a consulate at Nice

Canada

Embassy
35 Avenue Montaigne
F-75008 Paris
Tel. (1) 42 25 99 55

Consular section
35 Avenue Montaigne
F-75008 Paris
Tel. (1) 47 23 01 01

Consulate-General
24 Avenue du Prado
F-13006 Marseille
Tel. 91 37 19 37 and 91 37 19 40

## Electricity

France is committed to introducing the international norm (adopted in 1983) of 230 volts AC by the year 2003. In the meantime there is no difficulty with British equipment using 240 volts AC. An adaptor to accommodate British or American type plugs is necessary.

## Emergencies

Motoring breakdowns

There are emergency telephones on all motorways and on some national roads, permitting help in the case of breakdown or other motoring emergency.

On country roads and in built-up areas the Police de Secours may be contacted by dialling 17. The fire-brigade can be reached by dialling 18.

In the case of an accident without personal injury it is sufficient to contact a notary (*huissier*) for an assessment of the damage (see Motoring).

AA Continental Emergency Centre

The AA (in association with G. A. Gregson & Sons) operates an emergency centre at Boulogne. This is open day and night from April 1st to September 30th and during other months from 9am to 6pm. The address is:
F-62201 Boulogne-sur-Mer
Tour Damremont (18ième)
Boulevard Chanzy
Tel. 21 30 22 22

## Events

| | |
|---|---|
| Monaco: Rallaye Monte-Carlo; International Circus Festival | January |
| In many places (especially in Nice): Carnival<br>Menton: "Golden Fruit" Parade<br>Monaco: Television Festival<br>St-Raphaël: Mimosa Festival | February |
| Cagnes: Flower Show<br>Hyères: Flower Parade; horse-racing<br>Monaco: International Tennis Tournament; art festival<br>Toulon: Spring Festival | March |
| Cannes: International Cat Show | March–April |
| Arles: Provençal bull-running | Palm Sunday |
| Roquebrune-Cap-Martin: procession | Good Friday |
| Arles: Corrida | Easter |
| Antibes: Antiques Fair; "Old Timer" Rallaye<br>Le Lavandou: Flower Parade<br>Marseilles: International Boating Week<br>St-Tropez: Watersports<br>Toulon: Flower Parade | April |
| Cannes: International Film Festival<br>Arles: Festival of Cowherds | April–May |

## Events

| | |
|---|---|
| May | Antibes: Festival of young musical soloists; International Bridge Tournament<br>Cavaillon: Grand Parade<br>Grasse: Rose Festival<br>Monaco: Grand Prix de Monaco (car race)<br>Nice: May Fair<br>Stes-Maries-de-la-Mer: Gipsies' Pilgrimage (May 24th/25th)<br>St-Tropez: Second-hand Fair<br>Sisteron: Patronal Festival<br>Toulon: Cartoon Film Festival; Veteran Car Rally |
| June | Antibes: Flower Festival<br>Cavalaire-sur-Mer: St Peter's Festival<br>La Ciotat: Midsummer Eve Bonfire<br>Le Lavandou: Midsummer Eve Bonfire; Venetian Festival<br>Menton: Festival Parade<br>Nice: Fishermen's Festival; St Peter's Fair<br>Nîmes: Bullfights<br>Sanary-sur-Mer: Fishermen's Festival<br>St-Tropez: Spanish Bravado<br>Stes-Maries-de-la-Mer: Votive Festival<br>Tarascon: Festival of the Tarasque (heraldic animal of the town)<br>Toulon: Festival of the Sea |
| July | Everywhere: events for the national holiday<br>Antibes: "Golden Rose" Song Festival; Jazz Festival<br>Arles: Dance and Folklore Festival<br>Avignon: Festival productions (theatre, music)<br>Cannes: International Folklore Festival<br>Hyères: Festival of St Mary Magdalene; Garden Festival<br>Martigues: Folklore Festival with Fishermen's Festival<br>Menton: Torchlight Parade<br>Nîmes: Jazz Festival<br>St-Tropez: Fishermen's Festival<br>Toulon: Music Festival; St Peter's Festival |
| July–August | Aix-en-Provence: International Music Festival<br>Cagnes-sur-Mer: Horse-racing<br>Cannes: Theatre and Music Festival<br>Monaco: Concerts in the courtyard of the Prince's Palace; Fireworks Festival<br>Nice: Flower Festival; International Summer Academy<br>Orange: performances in Roman Theatre<br>St-Rèmy: Music Festival<br>Sènanque: Medieval Music |
| August | Antibes: Concerts in the Château<br>Bandol: Fishermen's Festival<br>Beaulieu-sur-Mer: Torchlight Parade<br>Cagnes-sur-Mer: Antiques Fair<br>Digne: Lavender Festival<br>Frèjus: Feria, Wine Festival; bullfights<br>Gap: Summer Festival; Flower Parade<br>Grasse: Jasmine Festival<br>Menton: Procession of Lanterns<br>Monaco: International Biennale of antiques, jewellery and art<br>Roquebrune-Cap-Martin: Votive Procession<br>St-Jean-Cap-Ferrat: Venetian Festival<br>St-Raphaël: Sea Procession<br>St-Rèmy-de-Provence: Provençal Costume Festival |
| August–September | Digne: Lavender Market<br>Monaco: International Festival of the Amateur Theatre |

| | |
|---|---|
| Cannes: International Amateur Film Festival<br>Le Lavandou: Arts and Crafts Fair<br>Nîmes: Wine Festival<br>Peille: Fête des Baguettes | September |
| La Ciotat: Michaelmas Fair; Fishermen's Festival<br>Nîmes: Vintage Festival; bullfights | September–October |
| Antibes: International Car Rally<br>Montpellier: Wine Festival | October |
| Cannes: International Amateur Golf Championship | October–November |
| Marseilles: Nativity Market<br>Monaco: Monegasque National Festival (Nov. 19th)<br>Toulon: Nativity Market | November |
| Les Baux: Christmas Midnight Mass | December |

## Food and Drink

French cuisine is world-famous, both for its quality and for its variety. Great importance is paid to a varied menu. Undue haste in serving and eating is unknown and at least one hour should be allowed for a meal. Even modest, unpretentious country inns often have a remarkable cullinary standard – this is even reflected in the way in which the table is set (clean tablecloths, polished cutlery, sparkling glasses, flowers, etc.) – in which regional dishes play an important role.
White bread, cut from long crusty baguettes, is always provided, as is fresh drinking water.

Gastronomy

Places providing food and drink are called variously restaurants, rotisseries, bistros (usually simple hostelries, but can also be places offering high-class service), and brasseries (originally the small bars of breweries, but now more generally restaurants). Snacks (sandwiches, etc.) are also served in cafés, tea-shops and bars. In the larger towns there are reasonable self-service restaurants ("self") and at railway stations and airports quick-service buffets.

Prices

At first glance prices may seem high, but when the quality and variety are taken into account this impression will generally be revised.

Prices on the menu are usually inclusive of service and taxes. For exceptionally good service a tip of about 5–10% of the bill is the norm.
It is customary to round-up the bill in any case.

Meals

The various meals are: *petit déjeuner* – a simple breakfast of coffee, bread, butter and jam and/or the popular croissants; *déjeuner* (lunch) is served from about midday to 2.30pm and *dîner* or *souper*, served from 7 until 9pm. In most restaurants there are one or more "menus" (set meals), with starters, main courses and sweets, or a customer can choose from an "à la carte" bill of fare.

Provençal cuisine

Provençal cuisine makes use of the wide range of local produce and seafood. It is charcterised by the freshness and quality of its ingredients, among the most common of which are olives and olive-oil, garlic (*ail*) and rosemary, thyme, sage and basil, called "herbs of Provence".

The classic collection of Provençal recipes is "Le Cuisinier Durand", published 1830 and compiled by Charles Durand. Durand (Alès 1766–Nîmes 1854), the "carême" of Provençal cuisine, was chef to the bishops of Alès,

Nîmes and Montpellier and his work made the cuisine of his home region famous throughout the region.

Soups

Among soups fish soup occupies a special place. One of the best known is *bouillabaisse*, originally a simple fishermen's dish which they prepared after returning to port, throwing the poorest fish of their catch into a large pot. Bouillabaisse is prepared from various kinds of fish, even mussels and crustaceans, with olive oil, garlic and various herbs, especially saffron, together with dried orange peel. The seafood and the soup are served separately, the latter poured over slices of white bread (in Marseilles there is a particular bread called "marette"). However there were and are so many different recipes that in 1980 a Marseilles chef published the "Real Bouillabaisse".

*Bourride* is similar but this contains green beans, carrots and potatoes in addition to fish, and is enriched with *aïoli* (garlic mayonnaise). *Aigo-Saou* is a soup prepared from white fish and potatoes.
Another soup which should be mentioned is *soupe au pistou*, consisting of beans and tomatoes and served with "pistou", a herbal mixture of garlic, olive oil, bacon and basil.

Meat

A typical Provençal method of cooking meat is to cut it into small pieces and braise it with a great variety of additional ingredients; the whole dish is then called *daube*, which may consist of beef, lamb or poultry with tomatoes and olives. Lamb is the principal meat eaten and is sometimes cooked over a charcoal fire. Connoisseurs appreciate "pieds et paquets", lamb's feet braised with tomatoes and olive oil and little packets of lamb cutlets. *Saucisson d'Arles* (sausage from Arles) is a popular delicacy; the original recipe included pork and also donkey-meat.

Fruit and vegetables

The valleys of the Rhône and the Durance are the largest vegetable and fruit-growing areas of France, and it is not surprising that vegetables of all kinds feature largely in the menu. "Salade Niçoise" consists of radishes, tomatoes, peppers, beans, olives, anchovies and tuna fish. *Tomates à la Provençale* are tomatoes with olive oil, parsley and garlic, baked or grilled; aubergines and courgettes are similarly prepared. *Fleurs de courge farcies* (stuffed marrow flowers) are an exotic speciality. *Ratatouille* consists of onions, courgettes, aubergines, tomatoes, peppers, garlic and herbs, stewed in olive oil. Also popular are artichokes, fennel and beet, often grilled or fried.
In Tricastin, in the north of Provence, truffles are harvested; their marketing centres are Valrèas and Carpentras.

Seafood

Fish and crustaceans play a major part in Provençal cuisine, even though fish has tended to become relatively expensive. In addition to the soups already mentioned, popular fish dishes are *brandade*, a mousse of cod (sometimes dried), olive oil, cream, garlic and lemon, as well as grilled barbel, sole, bream and other sea fish. The visitor should also try cuttlefish or squid (*calmar, seiche*) which are prepared in various ways, mussels (*moules, coquilles*), oysters (*huîtres*), crayfish (*langoustes*), shrimps (*crevettes*) or crabs (*tourteaux*).

Pasta

Pasta is often served as a side-dish, especially as an accompaniment to braised meat, such as daube. Noodles (*pâtes*), differing from Italian pasta in being usually made with eggs are designated as "fresh" or "speciality of the house". As well as the different varieties of pizza and *pan bagnat* – a kind of bread filled with olives, tomatoes and anchovies and baked in oil – there is *pissaladière*, a popular spicy flan of onions, olives and sardine fillets. In Nice, with its Italian past, pasta such as ravioli, tortellini, cannelloni, lasagne and gnocchi is frequently served.

Cheese

The numerous varieties of Provençal cheese (*fromage*) are for the most part made from sheep's or goat's milk. They bear such names as Annot,

Banon (prepared from sheep's milk in winter and from goat's milk in spring), Brousse, Claqueret (a soft cheese served with diced onions), Poivre d'Ane (with Provençal herbs) and Sospel.

Desserts

There is a great variety of fruit from the huge plantations along the Rhône and Durance and the coastal plains, where oranges and lemons also thrive. The figs of Solliès are renowned. Cakes and pastries are available in many kinds, for example *torte bléa* (a cake with raisins and pine seeds), *beignets de fleurs d'acacia* (pancakes with acacia blossoms), *calissons d'Aix* (biscuits made from almond paste with melon and honey), as well as white nougat (especially around Montélimar) and dried or candied fruits (Apt, Grasse).

Drinks

The French national drink continues to be wine (see entry), but beer (*bière*), mostly from breweries in Alsace, is growing in popularity. There are many brands of mineral water, either carbonated (*gazeuse*) or still (*plat*). The springs and filling plants of the well-known Perrier water are situated to the west of the Rhône delta between Nîmes and Montpellier.

The fiery distillate called *marc*, a by-product of wine-making, is excellent. From the region around Nice comes a popular grape brandy called *branda*. *Lérinade* is a liqueur formerly made by monks. The aniseed liqueur *pastis*, which is second only to wine as a national drink, is generally drunk diluted with ice-cold water; it is also pleasant when mixed with mint or grenadine syrup.

## Getting to Provence

By air

The most important airports for the area covered in this guidebook are Marseille-Marignane and Nice, but there are good services to Nîmes and Montpellier which are also served by local airlines as are Toulon/Hyères and St-Raphaël/Fréjus. There are direct flights from British airports to Marseilles and Nice and numerous charter flights in connection with package holidays. From the United States and Canada most visitors first fly to Paris and use connecting flights from there.

By rail

The principal route from the north of France to Provence is via Lyon and Marseilles to Toulon, Cannes and Nice. The journey time can be shortened by taking the TGV (*Train à Grande Vitesse*) from Paris to Lyon. The service is being extended to the Riviera. Details of services and fares can be obtained from:
French Railways (SNCF)
179 Piccadilly
London W1V 0BA; tel. (071) 493 9731

610 Fifth Avenue
New York N.Y. 10020; tel. (212) 582 2110

1500 Stanley Street
Montreal H3A 1R3. PO. Q.; tel. (514) 288 8255/6

By road

From the channel ports to the Riviera is a distance of some 1125km/700 miles and, even if the motorway (*autoroute du soleil*) is used, at least two days should be allowed for the journey. The motorway is subject to tolls which are certainly not low. The alternative *routes nationales* are good but liable to be crowded during the holiday season.
Visitors wishing to avoid the long journey by road from the Channel ports can use one of the motorail services to Avignon, Fréjus/St-Raphaël, Toulon and Nice.

## Guided Tours

Many secular buildings and certain parts of churches (crypt, treasury, etc.) can only be visited with a guide. As the majority of tourists are French, commentary in English is infrequent. However, explanatory texts in English are sometimes available on loan. The guide expects a tip at the end of the visit.

Recorded commentary

In many places of interest a coin-operated tape recorder *guide parlant* is frequently encountered. This provides a commentary in French and sometimes in other languages as well.

## Help for the Disabled

In the brochure "Touristes quand même! promenades en France pour les voyageurs handicappés" the French association for the disabled (*Comité National Français de Liaison pour la Réadaptation des Handicappés – C.N.F.L.R.H.*), 38 Boulevard Raspail F-75005 Paris, gives details of 90 French towns which are suitable for disabled visitors. It also contains a great deal of information concerning accommodation, transport, public institutions, etc., for visitors who are disabled or who have hearing or visual difficulties.

Rail travel

The brochure "Guide pratique voyageur: supplément à l'intention des personnes à mobilité réduite", published by French Railways SNCF (see Railways) gives information concerning facilities and reduced fares for disabled passengers.

## Holidays for Young People

France could be described as the classic country for young people's holidays; the school holidays are chiefly spent by the sea, in the countryside or in other towns with manifold activities. Correspondingly facilities for young people's holidays are wide-ranging. To list them all is not possible in this book.

The Maison de la France (see Information) publishes a brochure containing all necessary details and information about travel (fare reductions, assembly points), accommodation (from youth hostels and camping sites to centres where young people from other countries can be met, and student houses), activity holidays (language courses, sport, cultural work, even jobs) and all technical matters.

## Hotels

Hotels in France are generally good and within their categories will satisfy every requirement. Apart from in the larger towns rooms are often furnished with the *grand lit*, the French double bed, and the charge for occupancy of such rooms by two people is only slightly more than for single occupancy.

Full board half board

In many hotels, particularly those on the coast and in winter sports areas, both full board (*pension complète*) and half board (*demi-pension*) are offered.

Classification

Most hotels are classified by the Ministère du Tourisme (17 rue de l'Ingénieur-Robert-Keller, F-75740 Paris Cedex) as *Hôtels de Tourisme* and are designated by one star (lowest category) to four stars (highest category) with the addition of the suffix L for luxury hotels. They are listed in the official hotel guide "Hôtels de France" published annually.

Price categories

Prices vary considerably within each category and according to season. The following list gives the price per night for two persons in a room with bath; single rooms are rarely available. In most hotels approximately 30% extra is charged for a third bed in a room.

| Category | Double room | in this guide |
|---|---|---|
| L**** | 600–2300 francs | L |
| **** | 400–2000 francs | A |
| *** | 300–700 francs | B |
| ** | 150–500 francs | C |
| * | 100–300 francs | D |

Logis de France

A considerable number of hotels of various categories, especially in areas in which tourism is encouraged, have been modernised with help from the Fédération Nationale des Logis de France (83 Avenue d'Italie, F-75013 Paris). They are mostly small and medium sized family run hotels, usually to be found outside the larger places in small towns and villages, with personal attention and comfort at reasonable prices. A guide is issued every year.

Relais

Many hotels, especially on the roadside outside built-up areas, are designated as "Relais" (the word actually means a posting house where horses were changed). They are mostly good independently run places and include the "Relais de Campagne et Château-Hôtels" and "Relais du Silence".
The inexpensive "Relais Routiers" are principally used by long-distance drivers and are, therefore, situated on main roads. They are generally more simple but nevertheless good. A "Guide des Relais Routiers", with over 3500 entries, is available.

Information

Current lists of the organisations mentioned can be obtained free from the Maison de la France and the Offices du Tourisme in the larger towns (see Information), and sometimes in bookshops. In addition each Office du Tourisme publishes a local hotel list. A further important source of information is the "Guide Michelin France", published annually and obtainable from booksellers.

Reservations

Advance booking is recommended. Reservations can be made in two ways: either by a simple payment (*acompte*) or by a deposit (*arrhes*) which can be retained by the hotel in the event of cancellation by the visitor or in a case where the hotel has defaulted on the booking can be recovered two-fold by the visitor.

Forty three Offices du Tourisme are associated with the Accueil de France organisation; in the area covered in this guide book these are in Avignon, Cannes, Nice, Nîmes and Toulon. Here hotel rooms can be reserved seven days in advance in the town concerned and in other places where the organisation is represented. Any reservation fee will be reimbursed by the hotel.

Valuables

In France the proprietor of a hotel is responsible if a car is broken into while in a secured hotel car park. If a hotel room is burgled the proprietor's liability is limited to 100 times the cost of the room. Nevertheless, valuables should be deposited in the hotel safe.

**Aigues-Mortes**

B: Hostellerie des Remparts, 6 Place A.-France, 19 r.; Saint-Louis, 10 rue Amiral Courbet, 23 r.

C: Quatre Vents, Route de Nîmes, 15 r.; Victoria, Place A.-France, 15 r;
D: Provence, Route de Nîmes, 28 r.

**Aix-en-Provence**
A: Mas d'Entremont, Montée d'Avignon, N7, 17 r.; Pigonnet, Avenue du Pigonnet, 50 r.; Roi René, 24 Boulevard du Roi René, 134 r.
B: Augustins, 3 rue de la Masse, 35 r.; Novotel Aix Beaumanoir, Autoroute A8, 102 r.; Novotel Aix Sud, Arc de Meyran 80 r.; Paul Cézanne, 40 Avenue Victor Hugo, 55 r.; Manoir, 8 rue d'Entrecasteaux, 43 r.; Grand Hôtel Nègre Coste, 33 Cours Mirabeau, 37 r.; Résidence Rotonde, 15 Avenue des Belges, 42 r.
C: Casino, 38 rue Leydet, 24 r.; Concorde, 68 Boulevard du Roi René, 39 r.; France, 63 rue Espariat, 38 r.; Globe, 74 Cours Sextius, 45 r.; Grill Campanile, Jas de Bouffan, Route de Valcros, 60 r.; Moulin, 1 Avenue Robert Schumann, 37 r.; Prieuré, Route des Alpes, N96, 30 r.; Saint-Christophe, 2 Avenue Victor Hugo, 56 r.; Terrasses, 21 Chemin du Belvédère, Val St-André, 23 r.
D: Paul, 10 Avenue Pasteur, 24 r.

**Antibes**
A: Thalazur, 770 Ch. des Moyennes Breguières, 75 r.
B: First Hotel, 21 Avenue des Chênes, 18 r.; Mas Djoliba, 29 Avenue de Provence, 13 r.; Josse, 8 Boulevard James Wyllie, 28 r.; Mercator, Chemin des Groules, 18 r.; Royal, Boulevard Meréchal-Leclerc, 40 r.
C: Brasero, Chemin des Ames-du-Purgatoire, 12 r.; Belle Epoque, 10 Avenue du 24-Août, 9 r.; Caméo, Place Nationale, 8 r.
D: Méditerranée, Avenue Maréchal Reille, 21 r.; Modern'Hotel, 1 rue Fourmillière, 24 r.; Nouvel Hotel, Place Guynemer, 18 r.; Ponteil, 11 Impasse J.-Mensier, 16 r.

Cap d'Antibes
L: Cap Eden Roc, Boulevard Kennedy, 134 r.
B: Résidence Beau Site, 141 Boulevard Kennedy, 26 r.; Gardiole, Chemin de la Garoupe, 21 r.; Garoupe, Boulevard du Cap, 24 r.; Miramar, Chemin de la Plage la Garoupe, 14 r.; Motel Axa, Boulevard de la Garoupe, 20 r.
C: Chateau Fleuri, 15 Boulevard du Cap, 19 r.
D: Jabotte, Avenue Max Maurey, 12 r.

Juan-les-Pins
L: Belles Rives, Boulevard du Littoral, 42 r.; Juana, Avenue Gallice, 50 r.
A: Beachotel, Avenue Alexandre-III, 43 r.; Beauséjour, Avenue Saramartel, 30 r.; Hélios, 3 Avenue Dautheville, 70 r.; Parc, Avenue Guy de Maupassant 28 r.
B: Astoria, 15 Av. Maréchal Joffre, 49 r.; Passy, 15 Avenue Gallet, 36 r.
C: Eden, 16 Avenue Gallet, 17 r.
D: Charmettes, 25 Vieux Chemin de la Colle, 17 r.

**Apt**
B: Auberge du Luberon, 17 Quai L. Sagy, 17 r.
C: Aptois, 6 Cours Lauze de Perret, 26 r.

**Arles**
A: Jules César, Boulevard des Lices, 55 r.; Nord-Pinus, 14 Place du Forum, 35 r.
B: D'Arlatan, 26 rue du Sauvage, 42 r.; Atrium, 1 rue E. Fasin, 94 r.; Auberge La Fenière, N453, Raphèle les Arles, 24 r.; Cabanettes, N572, Hameau de Saliers, 29 r.; Cantarelles, Quartier Villevieille, 35 r.; Forum, 10 Place du Forum, 45 r.; Mas de la Chapelle, north on the D35; Mercure, 45 Avenue Sadi Carnot, 67 r.; Mireille, 2 Place St-Pierre, 34 r.; Rodin, 20 Avenue Rodin, 30 r.; Select, 35 Boulevard Georges Clemenceau, 24 r.
C: Cloître, 18 rue du Cloître, 33 r.; Calendal, 22 Place Pomme, 27 r.; Montmajour, 84 Avenue de Stalingrad, 20 r.; Saint-Trophime, 16 rue de la Calade, 22 r.
D: Lamartine, 1 rue M.-Jouveau, 32 r.; Poste, 2 rue Molière, 15 r.

**Avignon**
A: Europe, 12 Place Crillon, 53 r.; Mirande, 4 Place de l'Amirande, 19 r.
B: Mercure Avignon Sud, Route de Marseille, 105 r.; Bristol Terminus, 44 Cours Jean Jaurès, 91 r.; Novotel Avignon Sud, Route de Marseille, 79 r.; Cité des Papes, 1 rue J. Vilar, 63 r.; Midi, 53 rue de la République, 57 r.
C: Angleterre, 20 Boulevard Raspail, 40 r.; Central Hotel, 31 rue de la République, 29 r.; Constantin, 46 rue Carnot, 40 r.; Ferme, Chemin des Bois,

Ile de la Barthelasse, 20 r.; Magnan, 63 Portail Magnanen, 31 r.; Médiéval, 15 rue de la Petite Saumerie, 20 r.; Palais des Papes, 1 rue Gérard Philipe, 23 r.; Régina, 6 rue de la République, 30 r.
D: Bourse, 6 rue Portail Boquier, 10 r.; Hostellerie de l'Île, La Barthelasse, 15 r.; Parc, 18 rue A. Perdiguier, 12 r.

**Bandol**

A: Pullman Ile Rousse, Boulevard L.-Lumière, 55 r.
B: Baie, 62 rue Marçon, 14 r.; Ker Mocotte, rue Raimu, 19 r.; Provençal, rue des Ecoles, 22 r.; Réserve, Avenue de la Libération, 16 r.; Résidence Beau-Rivage, Boulevard L.-Lumière, 23 r.
C: Bel Ombra, 31 rue la Fontaine, 18 r.; Brunière, Avenue Lumière, 16 r.; Ermitage, Résidence du Château, 29 r.; Galets, Route de Toulon, 27 r.; Golf, Plage Renécros, 22 r.; Splendid, 83 Plage Renécros 28 r.

**Les Baux**

L: Oustau de Baumanière, 24 r.
A: Cabro d'Or, 20 r.
B: Bautezar, Grande Rue F. Mistral, 10 r.; Benvengudo, Les Arcoules, 20 r.; Mas d'Aigret, D27 A, 17 r.
C: Reine Jeanne, rue Porte Mage, 12 r.; Hostellerie de Servanes, in Mouriès (D17, 11km).

**Beaulieu-sur-Mer**

L: Métropole, 15 Boulevard du Général Leclerc, 53 r.; Réserve de Beaulieu, 5 Boulevard du Général Leclerc, 42 r.
A: Carlton, Avenue E. Cavell, 33 r.
B: Comte de Nice, 25 Boulevard Marinoni, 33 r.; Don Gregorio, 3 Avenue Maréchal Joffre, 69 r.; Frisia Hotel, 2 Boulevard Général Leclerc, 36 r.; Résidence, Boulevard Albert-1er, 29 r.
C: Havre Bleu, 29 Boulevard Maréchal Joffre, 22 r.; Victoria, 47 Boulevard Marinoni, 79 r.
D: Marcellin, Avenue Albert-1er, 21 r.

**Bonnieux**

Aiguebrun, 9 r.; César, 15 r.; Prieuré, 10 r.

**Cagnes-sur-Mer**

B: Brasilia, Chemin Grands Plans, 18 r.; Cagnard, Rue Pontis Long, 24 r.; Paddock, 26 Boulevard de la Plage, 22 r.
C: Chantilly, Rue de la Minoterie, 20 r.; Savournin, 17 Avenue Auguste Renoir, 32 r.; Tierce Hotel, 22 Boulevard Kennedy, 23 r.
D: Golf, Avenue de la Gare, 24 r.

**Cannes**

L: Pullman Beach, 13 rue du Canada, 94 r.
A: Cannes Palace Hotel, 14 Avenue de Madrid, 100 r.; Carlton, 58 Boulevard de la Croisette, 335 r.; Gray d'Albion, 38 rue des Serbes, 186 r.; Grand Hôtel 45 Boulevard de la Croisette, 76 r.; Majestic, Boulevard de la Croisette, 262 r.; Martinez, 73 Boulevard de la Croisette, 420 r.; Montfleury, 25 Avenue Beauséjour, 235 r.; Savoy, 5 rue Einesy, 106 r.; Sofitel-Méditerranée, 2 Boulevard Jean-Hibert, 150 r.
B: Abrial, 24–26 Boulevard de Lorraine, 47 r.; Acapulco, 16 Boulevard d'Alsace, 60 r.; Belle Plage, 6 rue Dolfus, 40 r.; Canberra, 120/122 rue d'Antibes, 62 r.; Century, 133 rue d'Antibes, 35 r.; Château de la Tour, 10 Avenue Font de Veyre, 42 r.; Embassy, 6 rue de Bone, 60 r.; Licorn'Hotel, 23 Avenue Francis Tonner, 45 r.; Ligure, Place de la Gare, 36 r.; Mondial, 77 rue d'Antibes, 65 r.; Orangers, 1 rue des Orangers, 43 r.; Palma, 77 Boulevard de la Croisette, 52 r.; Paris, 34 Boulevard d'Alsace, 48 r.; Provence, 9 rue Molière, 30 r.; Ruc Hôtel Cannes, 13–15 Boulevard de Strasbourg, 30 r.; Solhotel Cannes, 65 Avenue du Docteur-Picaud, 100 r.; Splendid, 4/6 rue Félix Faure, 64 r.; Univers Hotel, 2 rue du Maréchal Foch, 68 r.
C: Amirauté, 17 rue du Maréchal Foch, 41 r.; Atlantis, 4 rue du 24-Août, 37 r.; Atlas, 5 Place de la Gare, 52 r.; Campanile, Aéroport La Bocca, 49 r.; Etrangers, 6 Place Sémard, 45 r.; France, 85 rue d'Antibes, 34 r.; Moliére, 5–7 rue Moliére, 45 r.; P.L.M., 3 rue Hoche, 25 r.; Select, 16 rue Hélène Vagliano, 30 r.; Touring, 11 rue Hoche, 28 r.; Wagram, Route d'Antibes, 23 r.
D: Bourgogne, 13 rue du 24-Août, 11 r.; Nord, rue Jean Jaurès, 21 r.

## Hotels

| | |
|---|---|
| **Carpentras** | A: Moulin de la Roque, Althen-des-Paluds (D89), 25 r.<br>B: Univers, Place Aristide Briand, 25 r.; Safari, Avenue Fabre, 42 r.<br>C: Fiacre, 153 rue Vigne, 19 r.; Théâtre, 7 Boulevard Durand, 17 r. |
| **Castellane** | B: Nouvel Hôtel Commerce, Place de l'Eglise, 44 r.<br>C: Levant, Place Sauvaire, 31 r.; Verdon, 14 Blvd. de la République, 22 r.<br>D: Auberge du Teillon, La Garde, N85, 9 r. |
| **Château-Arnoux** | A: La Bonne Etape, Chemin du Lac, 18 r. |
| **Châteauneuf-du-Pape** | A: Château des Fines Roches, D17, 7 r.<br>B: Logis d'Arnavel, Route de Roquemaure, 15 r. |
| **Digne** | B: Hermitage Napoléon, Route de Nice, 59 r.; Grand Paris, 5 Boulevard Thiers, 27 r.; Mistre, 65 Boulevard Gassendi 37 r.<br>C: Hostellerie de l'Aiglon, 1 rue de Provence, 27 r.; Bourgogne, 3 Avenue de Verdun, 20 r.; Central Hôtel, 26 Boulevard Gassendi, 22 r.; Coin Fleuri, 9 Boulevard Victor Hugo, 15 r.; Saint Michel, Les Sieyes, Route des Alpilles, 21 r.<br>D: Julia, 1 Place Pied de Ville, 23 r. |
| **Draguignan** | B: Bertin, 13 Blvd. Foch, 40 r.; Col de l'Ange, Route de Lorgues, 29 r.<br>C: Dracenois, 14 rue du Cros, 14 r.; Moulin de la Foux, Chemin de la Foux, 29 r.; Parc, 21 Boulevard de la Liberté, 20 r.; Postillon, 27 rue Gisson, 35 r.; Semeria, 12 Avenue Carnot, 23 r. |
| **Eze** | A: Cap Estel, Bord de Mer, 44 r.; Château de la Chèvre d'Or, Rue du Barri, 14 r.; Château Eze, Rue de la Pise, 9 r.; Eze Country Club, Route de la Turbie, 75 r.<br>C: Soleil, Avenue de la Liberté, 11 r. |
| **Fountaine-de-Vaucluse** | C: Ermitage Vallis Clausa, Plan de Saumane, 11 r.; Grand Hôtel des Sources, 12 r.; Parc, 12 r. |
| **Fontvieille** | A: Regalido, Rue F. Mistral, 14 r.<br>B: Grâce de Dieu, 90 Avenue de Tarascon, 10 r. |
| **Fréjus** | B: Catalogne, St-Aygulf, Avenue Corniche d'Azur, 32 r.; Résidences du Colombier, Route de Bagnols, 60 r.; Ligure, 1074 Avenue de Lattre de Tassaigny, 64 r.<br>C: Azur, St-Aygulf, Avenue Corniche d'Azur, 60 r.; Il était une fois, Rue Frédéric Mistral, 20 r.; Oasis, Impasse J.B. Charcot, 27 r.; Palmiers, Boulevard de la Libération, 52 r.<br>D: Bellevue, Place P. Vernet, 13 r.; Horizon, Blvd. de la Libération, 15 r. |
| **Gap** | B: Grille, 1 Place F. Euzières, 30 r.<br>C: Carina, Chabanas, Route de Veynes, 30 r.; Clos, 20 Avenue du Commandant Dumont, 42 r.; Ferme Blanche, Rue de Villarobert, 30 r.; Fons Regina, Rue de Fontreyne, 24 r.; Mokotel, Route de Marseille, 28 r.; Paix, 1 Place F. Euzières, 24 r.<br>D: Méridional, 1 bis, Avenue Jean Jaurès, 26 r.; Pavillon, Chabanas, Route de Veynes, 30 r.; Verdun, 20 Boulevard de la Libération, 28 r. |
| **Gordes** | A: Bastide de Gordes, 18 r.; Domaine de Moulin Blanc, Chemin du Moulin, 18 r.; Domaine de l'Enclos, Route Sénanque 10 r.<br>B: Ferme de la Huppe, Les Pourquiers, D156, 12 r.; Gordos, Route de Cavaillon, 18 r.; Gacholle, Route de Murs, D15, 10 r.; Mayanelle, 6 rue de la Combe, 10 r.<br>C: Auberge de Carcarille, Les Gervais, D2, 9 r. |
| **La Grande-Motte** | B: Altea, 140 rue du Port, 135 r.; Azur, Presqu'île du Port, 20 r.; Europe, Square Navigarde, 34 r.; Méditerranée, 277 Allée du Vaccarès, 52 r.; Quetzal, Allée des Jardins, 52 r. |

C: Acropolis Hotel, La Motte du Couchant, 22 r.; Saint-Clair, Avenue de l'Europe, 27 r.
D: Copacabana, Route des Plages, 21 r.

**Grasse**

A: Regent, Route de Nice, 40 r.
B: Aromes, N85, 7 r.; Bellevue, 14 Avenue Riou-Blanquet, 30 r.; Parfums, Rue E. Charabot, 71 r.
C: Oasis, Place de la Buanderie, 11 r.; Panorama, 2 Place du Cours, 36 r.

**Gréolières**

C: Domaine du Foulon, 14 r.

**Grignan**

A: Roserale, Route Valréas, 12 r.
C: Sévigné, Place de Castellane, 20 r.

**Hyères**

B: Bona, Plage de l'Hippodrome, 32 r.; Manoir, Port-Cros, 25 r.; Pins d'Argent, Plage, 16 r.; Vieille Auberge St-Nicolas, Les Salins (N98), 11 r.
C: Méditerranée, Plage, 13 r.; Parc, 7 Boulevard Pasteur, 40 r.; Mozart, 26 Avenue A. Denis, 13 r.; Suisse, 1 Avenue Aristide Briand, 22 r.; Thalassa, 6 rue J. d'Agrève, 22 r.

**Le Lavandou**

L: Club de Cavalière, Plage de Cavalière, 32 r.
A: Le 83 Hôtel, La Fossette, 28 r.; Roches Fleuries, 1 Avenue des Trois Dauphins, 40 r.
B: Auberge de la Calanque, 26 Avenue du Général de Gaulle, 38 r.; Belle Vue, St-Clair, 19 r.; Cap Nègre Hôtel, 45 Avenue du Cap Nègre, 30 r.; Espadon, 2 Place Reyer, 20 r.; Lune, 10 Avenue du Général de Gaulle, 24 r.; Orangeraie, Plage de St-Clair, 20 r.; Roc, St-Clair, 26 r.
C: Beau Rivage, Boulevard Front de Mer, 23 r.; Flots Bleus, St-Clair, 26 r.; Ilot Fleuri, Avenue Charles Cazin, 26 r.; Neptune, 26 Avenue du Général de Gaulle, 35 r.
D: California, Route de St-Tropez, 27 r.; Terminus, Place Vieille, 25 r.

**Marseilles**

L: Petit Nice, Rue des Braves, 17 r.
A: Concorde Palm Beach, 2 Promenade de la Plage, 161 r.; Concorde Prado, 11 Avenue Mazargues, 100 r.
B: Altea Marseille, Rue Neuve St-Martin, 200 r.; Bompard, 2 rue des Flots Bleus, 46 r.; Bristol, 18 Canebière, 35 r.; Castellane, 31 rue du Rouet, 55 r.; Grand Hôtel de Genèvre, 3 bis, rue Reine Elisabeth, 48 r.; Grand Modern-'Hotel, 5 Canebière, 48 r.; Manhattan, 3 Place de Rome, 41 r.; Novotel Marseille Est, St-Menet, 131 r.; Paris-Nice, 23/25 Boulevard d'Athènes, 33 r.; Petit Louvre, 19 Canebière, 35 r.; Pullman Beauvau, 4 rue Beauvau, 72 r.; Résidence du Vieux-Port, 18–24 Quai du Port, 52 r.; Rome et Saint-Pierre, 7 Cours St-Louis, 65 r.; Saint-Georges, 10 rue du Capitaine Dessemond, 27 r.; Sofitel Vieux-Port, 36 Boulevard Charles Divon, 130 r.
C: Breton, 52 rue de Mazenod, 49 r.; Continental, 6 rue Beauvau, 46 r.; Corbusier, Unité d'Habitation, 280 Blvd. Michelet, 24 r.; Deux Mondes, 46 Cours Belsunce, 50 r.; Européen, 115–117 rue Paradis, 43 r.; Ibis Prado, 6 rue de Cassis, 118 r.; Grand Hotel Californie, 60 Cours Belsunce, 67 r.; Lafayette, 9 Allées Gambetta, 50 r.; Méditerranée, 13–15 Quai des Belges, 45 r.; Normandie, 29 Boulevard d'Athènes, 58 r.; Paris, 11–15 rue Colbert, 90 r.; Porte de l'Orient, 6 rue Bonneterie, 50 r.; Préfecture, 9 Boulevard Louis-Salvator, 41 r.

**Martigues**

B: Saint-Roch, Le Moulin de Paradis, 38 r.
C: Eden, Boulevard Emile Zola, 38 r.; Gril Campanile, Boulevard de Thonon, 42 r.; Lido, Cours du 4-Septembre, 19 r.
D: Clare Hotel, Boulevard Marcel Cachin, 39 r.

**Menton**

B: Beau Rivage, 1 Avenue Blasco Ibanez, 40 r.; Chambord, 6 Avenue Boyer, 40 r.; Europ, 36 Boulevard de Verdun, 33 r.; Méditerranée, 5 rue de la République, 90 r.; Napoléon, 29 Porte de France, 40 r.; Parc, 11 Avenue de Verdun, 72 r.; Prince de Galles, 4 Avenue du Général de Gaulle, 68 r.;

Princess et Richmond, 617 Promenade du Soleil, 45 r.; Saint-Georges, 24 bis, Avenue Cochrane, 35 r.; Viking, 2 Avenue du Général de Gaulle, 34 r.
C: Arcades, 41 Avenue Félix Faure, 40 r.; Bristol, 24 Avenue Carnot, 40 r.; Carlton, 6 Avenue du Général de Gaulle, 42 r.; Celine Rose, 57 Avenue de Sospel, 35 r.; Floréal, 276 Cours du Centenaire, 60 r.; Magall, 10 rue Villarey, 43 r.; Paris Rome, 79 Porte de France 15 r.
D: Mondial, 12 rue Partouneaux, 41 r.; Villa Louise, 10 Avenue K. Mansfield, 22 r.

**Monaco** (Principality of Monaco)

L: Hermitage, Square Beaumarchais, 236 r.; Hôtel de Paris, Place du Casino, 271 r.; Loews Monte Carlo, Avenue des Spélugues, 636 r.; Métropole Palace, 4 Avenue de la Madone, 170 r.
A: Beach Plaza, 22 Avenue Princesse Grace, 316 r.; Mirabeau, 1–3 Avenue Princesse Grace, 100 r.; Monte-Carlo Beach, Route du Beach, 46 r.
B: Abela, 23 Avenue des Papalins, 192 r.; Alexandra, 35 Boulevard Princess Charlotte, 55 r.; Balmoral, 12 Avenue de la Costa, 68 r.; Louvre, 16 Boulevard des Moulins, 34 r.; Miramar, 1 Avenue Prés. J. F. Kennedy, 14 r.; Versailles, 4 Avenue Prince Pierre 15 r.
C: Siècle, 10 Avenue Prince Pierre, 35 r.; Terminus, 9 Avenue Prince Pierre, 54 r.; Résidence des Moulins, 27 Boulevard des Moulins, 12 r.
D: Cosmopolite, 4 rue de la Turbie, 24 r.; France, 6 rue de la Turbie, 24 r.; Helvetia, 1 bis, rue Grimaldi, 28 r.

**Montélimar**

A: Parc Chabaud, 16 Avenue d'Aygu, 22 r.
B: Motel Vallée du Rhône, 148 Route de Marseille, 50 r.; Relais de l'Empereur, Place Marx-Dormoy, 40 r.
C: Dauphiné Provence, 41 Avenue de Gaulle, 26 r.; Printemps, 8 Chemin de la Manche, 16 r.; Sphinx, 19 Boulevard Desmarais, 20 r.

**Montpellier**

L: Alliance Metropole, 3 rue Clos-René, 92 r.
B: Altea Antigone, 218 rue du Bastion Ventadour, 116 r.; George V, 42 Avenue St-Lazare, 39 r.; Grand Hôtel Midi, 22 Boulevard Victor Hugo, 48 r.; Mercure Montpellier Est. 662, Avenue de la Pompignane, 122 r.; Noailles, 2 rue des Ecoles-Centrales, 30 r.; Novotel, 125 bis, Avenue de Palavas, 97 r.; Royal Hotel, 8 rue Maguelone, 46 r.; Sofitel, Le Triangle, 98 r.
C: Climat de France, Rue du Caducée, 42 r.; Edouard-VII, 120 rue Oliver, 47 r.; France et Lutétia, 3–4 rue de la République, 40 r.; Ibis, 164 Route de Palavas, 102 r.; Inter Hotel L'Hotel, 6–8 rue Jules Ferry, 55 r.
D: Imperator, 20 rue Boussairolles, 48 r.

**Nice**

A: Aston, 12 Avenue Félix Faure, 157 r.; Beach Regency, 223 Promenade des Anglais, 335 r.; Méridien, 1 Promenade des Anglais, 315 r.; Negresco, 37 Promenade des Anglais, 150 r.; Pérouse, 11 Quai Rauba-Capeu, 65 r.; Plaza, 12 Avenue de Verdun, 200 r.; Sofitel Splendid, 50 Boulevard Victor Hugo, 128 r.; West-End, 31 Promenade des Anglais, 96 r.; Westminster Concorde, 27 Promenade des Anglais, 110 r.
B: Acropolis, 25 Boulevard Dubouchage, 113 r.; Albert-1er, 4 Avenue des Phocéens, 74 r.; Bedford, 45 rue du Maréchal Joffre, 50 r.; Brice, 44 rue du Maréchal Joffre, 60 r.; Busby, 36–38 rue du Maréchal Joffre, 76 r.; Chatham, 9 rue Karr, 50 r.; Florence, 3 rue Paul Déroulède, 57 r.; Gounod, 3 rue Gounod, 52 r.; Grand Hôtel de Noailles, 35 Boulevard Raimbaldi, 76 r.; Napoléon, 6 rue Grimaldi, 84 r.; New-York, 44 Avenue Maréchal Foch, 52 r.; Vendome, 26 rue Pastorelli, 60 r.; Windsor, 12 rue Dalpozzo, 65 r.
C: Berne, 1 Avenue Thiers, 58 r.; Bruxelles, 17 rue de Belgique, 54 r.; Frank-Zurich, 31 rue Paganini, 76 r.; Harvey, 18 Avenue de Suède, 62 r.; Midland, 41 rue Lamartine, 50 r.; Mulhouse, 9 rue Chauvain, 54 r.; National, 64 Avenue Jean Médecin, 61 r.; Nations, 25 Avenue Durante, 57 r.; Nouvel Hotel, 10 bis, Boulevard Victor Hugo, 54 r.; Rivoli, 47 rue Pastorelli, 70 r.; Roosevelt, 16 rue du Maréchal Joffre, 66 r.; Saint-Gothard, 20 rue Paganini, 63 r.; Sibill's, 25 rue Assalit, 56 r.; Univers, 9 Avenue Jean Médecin, 75 r.
D: Calais, 2 rue Chauvain, 50 r.; France, 24 Boulevard Raimbaldi, 45 r.; Gemeaux, 149 Boulevard de l'Observatoire (Grande Corniche), 12 r.

**Nîmes**

A: Imperator, Quai de la Fontaine, 62 r.
B: Cheval Blanc et des Arènes, 1 Place des Arènes, 49 r.; Grand Hôtel du Midi, Square de la Couronne, 105 r.; Mercure, Rue Tony Garnier, 100 r.; Novotel Nîmes Centre, 5 Boulevard de Prague, 119 r.; Tuileries, 22 rue Roussy, 10 r.
C: Amphithéatre, 4 rue des Arènes, 20 r.; Auberge de l'Eau Bouillie, Route d'Alès, 17 r.; Carrière, 6 rue Grizot, 55 r.; Lisita, 2 bis, rue des Arènes, 27 r.; Milan, 17 Avenue Feuchères, 32 r.; Provence, 5–7 Square de la Couronne, 33 r.; Royal Hotel, 3 Boulevard Alphonse Daudet, 32 r.; Terminus, 23 Avenue Feuchères, 34 r.
D: France, 4 Boulevard des Arènes, 16 r.; Couronne, 4 Square de la Couronne, 18 r.

**Orange**

A: Château de Rochegude, Rochegude (D976/11/117, 14km)
B: Altea Orange, Route de Caderousse, 99 r.; Arène, Place de Langes, 30 r.; Louvre et Terminus, 89 Avenue Frédéric Mistral, 34 r.
C: Boscotel, 764 Av. Ch. de Gaulle, 57 r.; Princes, 7 Av. de l'Arc de Triomphe, 52 r.; Arts, 1 Cours Pourtoules, 19 r.; Cigaloun, 4 rue Caristie, 29 r.

**Orgnac-l'Aven**

D: L'Aven, Vallon Pont-d'Arc, 27 r.

**Plan-de-la-Tour**

C: Parasolis, Hameau de Courruero, D44 (near Ste-Maxime), 15 r.

**Port-Grimaud**

A: Giraglia, Grande Rue, 48 r.
B: Port, Place du Marché, 20 r.

**Roquebrune-Cap-Martin**

A: Monte-Carlo Beach Hotel, Av. Princesse, 46 r.; Vista Palace, Grande Corniche, 76 r.
B: Alexandra, 93 Avenue Winston Churchill, 40 r.; Victoria, Promenade du Cap Roquebrune, 32 r.
D: Europe-Village, Avenue Hériot, 26 r.; Westminster, 14 Avenue Louis Laurens, 31 r.

**St-Gilles**

C: Cours, 10 Avenue François Brifeuille, 34 r.
D: Globe, Place Gambetta, 23 r.

**St-Maximin-la-Sainte-Baume**

C: France, 1–3 Avenue Albert 1er, 23 r.; Relais de Saint-Maximin, Route d'Aix, 12 r.

**St-Paul-de-Vence**

A: Mas d'Artigny, Rte. de la Colle, 82 r.; Saint-Paul, 86 rue Grande, 15 r.
B: Augergo dou Souleu, 1334 Route de la Colle, 7 r.; Colombe d'Or, Place des Ormeaux, 24 r.; Hameau, 528 Route de la Colle, 17 r.
C: Remparts, 72 rue Grande, 15 r.

**St-Raphaël**

B: Beausejour, Promenade du Président Coty, 40 r.; Golf de Valesure, Valesure, 40 r.; San Pedro, Avenue Colonel Brooke, 28 r.
C: Arènes, 31 Avenue du Général Leclerc, 27 r.; Excelsior, Boulevard Félix Martin, 40 r.; Europe Gare, 9 rue Amiral Baux, 32 r.; France, Place Galliéni, 28 r.; Moderne, 331 Avenue Leclerc, 25 r.; Provençal, 197 rue de la Garonne, 28 r.; Touring, 1 Quai Albert-1er, 23 r.

**St-Rémy-de-Provence**

A: Hostellerie du Vallon de Valrugues, Chemin de Canto Cigalo, 34 r.; Château des Alpilles, D31, 18 r.; Domaine de Valmouriane, D27, 12 r.
B: Antiques, 15 Avenue Pasteur, 27 r.; Castelet des Alpilles, 6 Place Mireille, 19 r.; Château de Roussan, Route de Tarascon, 20 r.
C: Canto Cigalo, Chemin de Canto Cigalo, 20 r.; Cheval Blanc, Avenue Fauconnet, 22 r.; Van Gogh, 1 Avenue Jean Moulin, 18 r.
D: Provence, 36 Boulevard Victor Hugo, 27 r.

**St-Tropez**

L: Byblos, Avenue Paul Signac, 107 r.; Residence de la Pinède, Plage de la Bouillabaisse, 40 r.
A: Bastide de St-Tropez, Route de Carles, 27 r.; Mandarine, Route Tahiti-Plage, 41 r.

B: Bastide des Salins, Route des Salins, 12 r.; Capucines, Domaine du Treizain, 24 r.; Ermitage, Avenue Paul Signac, 29 r.; Levant, Route des Salins, 28 r.; Lou Troupelen, Chemin des Vendanges, 44 r.; Mas de Chastelas, Domaine Bertaud, D19, 31 r.; Paris, Place Croix-de-Fer, 65 r.; Ponche, Place du Revelin, 23 r.; Provençal, Chemin Ste-Bonaventure, 18 r.; Résidence des Lices, Avenue A. Grangeon, 40 r.; Tartane, Route des Salins, 12 r.
C: Palmiers, 26 Boulevard Vasserot, 22 r.; Sube, at the harbour, 26 r.; Yaca, Boulevard d'Aumale, 23 r.

**Stes-Maries-de-la-Mer**

A: Auberge Cavalière, Route d'Arles, 48 r.; Mas de la Fouques, Route d'Aigues-Mortes, 14 r.; Pont des Bannes, Route d'Arles, 25 r.
B: Cabane du Boumian, 28 r.; Clamador, Route d'Aigues-Mortes, 22 r.; Etrier Camarguais, Chemin Bas des Launes, 25 r.; Galoubet, Route de Cacharel, 20 r.; Mas de Calabrun, D85 A, 27 r.; Mas de Rièges, Route de Cacharel, 16 r.
C: Camille, Av. de la Plage, 32 r.; Mirage, 27 r.
D: Mas des Lys, Route d'Arles, 26 r.

**Salon-de-Provence**

A: Abbaye de Sainte-Croix, Val de Cuech, D17, 24 r.
B: Devem de Mirapier, Cornillon, N113/D19, 16 r.
C: Grand Hôtel d'Angletere, 98 Cours Carnot, 26 r.; Ibis, Les Roquessiers, Route de Pélissanne, 60 r.; Midi, 518 Allées de Craponne, 27 r.; Roi René, 561 Allées de Craponne, 30 r.; Vendôme, 34 rue du Maréchal Joffre, 24 r.

**Sisteron**

B: Grand Hôtel du Cours, Place de l'Eglise, 50 r.
C: Chênes, Route de Gap, 21 r.; Citadelle, Rue Saumerie, 24 r.; Tivoli, Place du Tivoli, 19 r.; Touring Napoléon, 85 Avenue de la Libération, 28 r.

**Sospel**

C: Auberge Provençale, Route de Menton, 10 r.; Etrangers, 7 Boulevard de Verdun, 35 r.

**Tarascon**

B: Provence, 7 Boulevard Victor Hugo, 11 r.
C: Terminus, Place Berrurier, 25 r.; Provençal, 12 Cours A. Briand, 22 r.
D: Moderne, Boulevard Itam, 28 r.

**Toulon**

B: Altea Tour Blanche, Boulevard Amiral Vence, 92 r.; Corniche, 1 Littoral Frédéric Mistral, 22 r.; Grand Hôtel, 4 Place de la Liberté, 45 r.; Résidence du Cap Brun, Chemin de l'Aviateur Gayraud, 20 r.
C: Amirauté, 4 rue Guiol, 64 r.; Continental Métropole, 1 rue Racine, 48 r.; Dauphine, 10 rue Berthelot, 57 r.; Maritima, 9 rue Gimelli, 43 r.; Moderne, 21 Avenue Colbert, 39 r.; Napoléon, 49 rue Jean-Jaurès, 43 r.; Terminus, 7 Boulevard de Tessé, 40 r.
D: Allées, 18 Allée Amiral Courbet, 14 r.; Lutétia, 69 rue Jean-Jaurès, 30 r.; Rex Hotel, 51 rue Jean-Jaurès, 31 r.

**Uzès**

B: Entraygues, 8 rue de la Calade, 19 r.
C: Champ de Mars, 1087 Route de Nîmes, 7 r.; Saint-Géniès, Route de Saint Ambroix, 18 r.; Taverne, 4 rue Sigalon, 10 r.
D: Hostellerie Provençale, 3 rue Grande–Bourgade, 10 r.

**Vaison-la-Romaine**

B: Domaine de la Cabasse, in Séguret, 10 r.; Hostellerie l'Oustau, 11 r.; Table du Comtat, in Séguret, 8 r.
C: Bellerive, in Rasteau (D69), 20 r.; Logis du Château, Haute Ville, 40 r.; Beffroi, Haute Ville, 20 r.; Burrhus, Place Montfort, 14 r.; Escargot d'Or, Route d'Orange, 20 r.

**Vence**

L: Château du Domaine St-Martin, Route de Coursegoules, 15 r.
A: Relais Cantemerle, 258 Chemin Cantemerle, 20 r.
B: Diana, Avenue des Poilus, 25 r.; Floréal, 440 Avenue Rhin et Danube, 43 r.; Mas de Vence, 539 Av. E. Hugues, 41 r.; Miramar, Plateau St-Michel, 17 r.
C: Provence, 9 Avenue Marcellin Maurel, 20 r.; Regina, Avenue des Alliés, 26 r.; Roseraie, Av. Henri Giraud, 12 r.
D: Closerie des Genêts, 4 Impasse M. Maurel, 10 r.

D: Moulin de Provence, 12 r. — **Vauvenargues**

**Villeneuve-lèz-Avignon**

A: Prieuré, Place du Chapitre, 36 r.
B: Atelier, 5 rue de la Foire, 19 r.; Magnaneraie, 37 rue du Camp-de-Bataille, 29 r.; Vieux Moulin, Rue du Vieux Moulin, 27 r.
C: Li Cigaloun, 40 rue du Général Leclerc, 10 r.; Résidence les Cedres, 39 Avenue Pasteur-Bellevue, 23 r.
B: Beauséjour, 61 Avenue Gabriel Péri, 15 r.; Hostellerie de l'Ile, Barthelasse, 15 r.

## Information

Maison de la France

Under the name "Maison de la France" the French tourist organisations have created for themselves a new image. References to "Maison de la France" in this book have the same meaning as "Tourist Office". Most local tourist offices are designated "Office de Tourisme".

Headquarters

Maison de la France
8 Avenue de l'Opéra
F-75001 Paris; tel. (1) 42 96 10 23

### Information outside France

Great Britain

Maison de la France
178 Piccadilly
London W1V 0AL; tel. (071) 499 6911

United States

Maison de la France
610 Fifth Avenue
New York NY 10020; tel. (212) 757 1125

645 N. Michigan Avenue
Chicago IL. 60611; tel. (312) 751 7800, 337 6301

World Trade Centre No. 103
2050 Stemmons Freeway
Dallas TX 75258; tel. (214) 742 7011

9401 Wilshire Boulevard, Room 840
Beverly Hills CA 90212; tel. (213) 272 2661, 271 6665

1 Hallidie Place, Suite 250
San Francisco CA 94102-2818; tel. (415) 986 4161

Canada

1981 McGill College Avenue, Suite 490
Montreal, Quebec, H3A 2W9; tel. (514) 288 4264

30 St Patrick Street, Suite 700
Toronto, Ontario, ONT. M5T 3A3; tel. (416) 593 6427

### Information in France

Regional committees

Comité Régional du Tourisme de Provence-Alpes-Côte d'Azur
2 rue Henri Barbusse, F-13241 Marseille Cedex 01; tel. 91 39 38 00

Comité Régional du Tourisme de Riviera-Côte d'Azur
53 Promenade des Anglais, F-06000 Nice; tel. 93 44 50 59

## Information

Comité Régional du Tourisme du Languedoc-Roussillon
20 rue de la République, F-34000 Montpellier; tel. 67 92 67 92

Departmental Committees

Alpes-de-Haute-Provence
Comité Départmental du Tourisme
42 Boulevard Victor Hugo, B.P. 170, F-04005 Digne Cedex; tel. 92 31 57 29

Ardèche
Comité Départmental du Tourisme
8 Cours Palais, F-707000 Privas; tel. 75 64 04 66

Bouches-du-Rhône
Comité Départmental du Tourisme
6 rue Anacharsis, F-13001 Marseille; tel. 91 54 92 66

Drôme
Comité Départmental du Tourisme
1 Avenue de Romans F-26000 Valence; tel. 75 43 27 12

Gard
Comité Départmental du Tourisme
3 Place des Arènes, B.P. 122, F-3001 Nîmes Cedex; tel. 66 21 02 51

Hautes-Alpes
Comité Départmental du Tourisme
5 ter rue Capitaine de Bresson, F-05002 Gap; tel. 92 53 62 00

Var
Comité Départmental du Tourisme
1 Boulevard Foch, B.P. 99, F-83000 Draguignan Cedex; tel. 94 68 58 33

Vaucluse
Comité Départmental du Tourisme
La Balance, Place Campana, B.P. 147, F-84008 Avignon Cedex; tel. 90 86 43 42

**Aigues-Mortes** Porte de la Gardette, F-30220 Aigues-Mortes; tel. 66 53 73 00

**Aix-en-Provence** Place du Général de Gaulle, F-13100 Aix-en-Provence; tel. 42 26 02 93

**Antibes** 11 Place du Général de Gaulle, F-06600 Antibes; tel. 93 33 95 64

**Arles** Esplanade Charles de Gaulle / Place de la République, F-13200 Arles; tel. 90 96 29 35

**Avignon** 41 Cours Jean-Jaurès, F-84000 Avignon; tel. 90 82 65 11

**Bandol** Allées Alfred-Vivien, F-83150; tel. 94 29 41 35

**Les Baux** Hôtel de Manville, F-13520 Les Baux de Provence; tel. 90 54 34 39

**Beaulieu-sur-Mer** Place G-Clemenceau, F-06310 Beaulieu-sur-Mer; tel. 93 01 02 21

**Cagnes-sur-Mer** 6 Boulevard Maréchal-Juin, F-06801 Cagnes-sur-Mer; tel. 93 20 61 64

**Cannes** Palais des Festivals, 1 La Croisette, F-06400 Cannes; tel. 93 39 24 53
Information bureau at the station (Gare SNCF); tel. 93 99 19 77

**Carpentras** 170 Avenue Jean-Jaurès, F-84200 Carpentras; tel. 90 63 00 78

**Castellane** Rue Nationale, F-04120 Castellane; tel. 92 83 61 14

| | |
|---|---|
| Place Portail, F-84230 Châteauneuf-du-Pape; tel. 90 39 71 08 | **Châteauneuf-du Pape** |
| Rond-Point, F-04000 Digne; tel. 92 31 42 73 | **Digne** |
| 9 Boulevard Clemenceau, F-83300 Draguignan; tel. 94 68 63 30 | **Draguignan** |
| Place de l'Eglise, F-84800 Fontaine-de-Vaucluse; tel. 90 20 32 22 | **Fontaine-de-Vaucluse** |
| Place Calvini, F-83600 Fréjus; tel. 94 51 53 87 | **Fréjus** |
| 12 rue Faure du Serre, F-05000 Gap; tel. 92 51 57 03 | **Gap** |
| Place du Château, F-84220 Gordes; tel. 90 72 02 75 | **Gordes** |
| Place du 1er Octobre, F-34280 La Grande-Motte; tel. 67 56 62 62 | **La Grande-Motte** |
| Place de la Foux, F-06130 Grasse; tel. 93 36 03 56 | **Grasse** |
| Grande Rue, F-26230 Grignan; tel. 75 46 56 75 | **Grignan** |
| Avenue de Belgique, F-83400 Hyères; tel. 94 65 18 55 | **Hyères** |
| 1 Boulevard Guillaumont, F-06160 Juan-les-Pins; tel. 93 61 04 98 | **Juin-les-Pins** |
| Quai Gabriel-Péri, F-83980 Le Lavandou; tel. 94 71 00 61 | **Le Lavandou** |
| Place du Docteur-Joubert, F-04100 Manosque; tel. 92 72 16 00 | **Manosque** |
| 4 La Canebière, F-13001 Marseille; tel. 91 54 91 11 | **Marseilles** |
| Quai Paul-Doumer, F-13500 Martigues; tel. 42 80 30 72 | **Martigues** |
| Palais de l'Europe, Avenue Boyer, F-06503 Menton; tel. 93 57 57 00 | **Menton** |
| Allées Champ de Mars, F-26200 Montélimar; tel. 75 01 00 20 | **Montélimar** |
| 78 Avenue Pirée, F-34000 Montpellier; tel. 67 22 06 16 | **Montpellier** |
| Acropolis, 1 Esplanade Kennedy, F-06058 Nice; tel. 93 62 82 82<br>Information bureau at the station; tel. 93 87 07 07 | **Nice** |
| 6 rue Auguste, F-30000 Nîmes; tel. 66 67 29 11 | **Nîmes** |
| Cours Aristide Briand, F-84100 Orange; tel. 90 34 70 88 | **Orange** |
| 20 Av. P.-Doumer, F-06190 Roquebrune-Cap-Martin; tel. 93 35 62 87 | **Roquebrune-Cap-Martin** |
| Place F.-Mistral, F-30800 St-Gilles; tel. 66 87 33 75 | **St-Gilles** |
| Rue W.-Rousseau, F-83700 St-Raphaël; tel. 94 95 16 87 | **St-Raphaël** |
| Place Jean-Jaurès, F-13210 St-Rémy-de-Provence; tel. 90 92 05 22 | **St-Rémy-de-Provence** |
| Quai Jean Jaurès, F-83990 St-Tropez; tel. 94 97 41 21 | **St-Tropez** |
| Avenue Van Gogh, F-13460 Saintes-Maries-de-la-Mer; tel. 90 47 82 55 | **Stes-Maries-de-la-Mer** |
| 56 Cours Gimon, F-13300 Salon-de-Provence; tel. 90 56 27 60 | **Salon-de-Provence** |

| | |
|---|---|
| **Sisteron** | Avenue Paul-Arène, F-04200 Sisteron; tel. 92 61 12 03 |
| **Tarascon** | 59 rue des Halles, F-13150 Tarascon; tel. 90 91 03 52 |
| **Toulon** | 8 Avenue Colbert, F-83000 Toulon; tel. 94 22 08 22 |
| **Uzès** | Avenue de la Libération, F-30700 Uzès; tel. 66 22 68 88 |
| **Vaison-la-Romaine** | Place du Chanoine Sautel, F-84110 Vaison-la-Romaine; tel. 90 36 02 11 |
| **Vence** | Place du Grand-jardin, F-06140 Vence; tel. 93 58 06 38 |
| **Villeneuve-lèz Avignon** | Place Charles David, F-30400 Villeneuve-lèz-Avignon; tel. 90 25 61 55 |

### Principality of Monaco

| | |
|---|---|
| Monaco | Direction du Tourisme et des Congrès<br>2a Boulevard des Moulins, MC-98030 Monaco Cedex<br>tel. 93 30 87 01 and 93 50 60 88 |

## Insurance

General

Visitors are strongly advised to ensure that they have adequate holiday insurance, including loss or damage to luggage, loss of currency and jewellery.

Health

Nationals of other European Community countries are entitled to obtain medical care when on holiday in France. Treatment can be obtained free of charge, but medicines must be paid for.
It is essential for visitors from non-EC countries, and advisable for EC nationals, to take out some form of short-term health insurance providing complete cover and possibly avoiding delays. Nationals of non-EC countries should certainly have insurance cover.

Vehicles

Visitors travelling by car should ensure that their insurance is comprehensive and covers use of the vehicle in France.

See also Travel Documents.

## Language

French is of course the official language of Provence, although visitors will often hear the Provençal dialect (see Fact and Figures, Provençal Language) especially in the more rural areas. Visitors who have at least some knowledge of French, therefore, should have no difficulty in making themselves understood.

Pronunciation

Characteristic features are the placing of the stress towards the end of the word and the frequent nasalisation of vowels.
Vowels (always pronounced without the diphthongisation found in English): *ai* like English *ay; ais* an open *e* as in "bed"; *é* like *ay; è* and *ê* an open *e; an, en, em* at the end of a syllable like a nasalised *on* (not quite *ong); un, im, in, ein* at the end of a syllable like a nasalised *un* (not quite *ung); eu* a little like the *u* in "fur"; *oi, oy* like *wa; ou* like *oo; u* a sound obtained by pronouncing *ee* with rounded lips.

Consonants: *c* before *e, i* or *y* and *ç* before other vowels, like *s; c* before *a, o* or *u* like *k;* j, and *g* before *e, i* or *y*, like *zh; g* before *a, o* or *u* like a hard English *g; ch* like *sh; gn* usually like *ny* in "canyon"; *h* always silent; *ll* between vowels often palatalised to a consonantal *y* sound, but sometimes a light *l* (e.g. in *elle); q, qu* like *k.*
The following letters are usually silent at the end of a word (and often also at the end of a syllable): *d, e, r* (only after *e), s, t, x, z.*

### Numbers

| | | | |
|---|---|---|---|
| 0 | zéro | 22 | vingt-deux |
| 1 | un, une | 30 | trente |
| 2 | deux | 40 | quarante |
| 3 | trois | 50 | cinquante |
| 4 | quatre | 60 | soixante |
| 5 | cinq | 70 | soixante-dix |
| 6 | six | 71 | soixante et onze |
| 7 | sept | 80 | quatre-vingt(s) |
| 8 | huit | 81 | quatre-vingt-un |
| 9 | neuf | 90 | quatre-vingt-dix |
| 10 | dix | 91 | quatre-vingt-onze |
| 11 | onze | 100 | cent |
| 12 | douze | 101 | cent un |
| 13 | treize | 153 | cent cinquante trois |
| 14 | quatorze | 200 | deux cent(s) |
| 15 | quinze | 300 | trois cent(s) |
| 16 | seize | 400 | quatre cent(s) |
| 17 | dix-sept | 500 | cinq cent(s) |
| 18 | dix-huit | 1000 | mille |
| 19 | dix-neuf | 1001 | mille un |
| 20 | vingt | 2000 | deux mille |
| 21 | vingt et un | 1,000,000 | un million |

### Ordinals

| | | | |
|---|---|---|---|
| 1st | premier, première | 7th | septième |
| 2nd | deuxième | 8th | huitième |
| | second(e) | 9th | neuvième |
| 3rd | troisième | 10th | dixième |
| 4th | quatrième | 11th | onzième |
| 5th | cinquième | 12th | douzième |
| 6th | sixième | 100th | centième |

### Fractions

| | | | |
|---|---|---|---|
| Half | demi(e) | Quarter | quart |
| Third | tiers | Three-quarters | trois quarts |

### Useful Expressions

When addressing anyone it is usual to add the polite *Monsieur, Madame* or *Mademoiselle,* and any request or enquiry should be accompanied by *s'il vous plaît* ("please").

| | |
|---|---|
| Good morning, good day! | Bonjour! |
| Good evening! | Bonsoir! |
| Good night! | Bonne nuit! |
| Goodbye | Au revoir |
| Do you speak English? | Parlez-vous anglais? |
| I do not understand | Je ne comprends pas |
| Yes | Oui |
| No | Non |
| Please | S'il vous plaît |
| Thank you | Merci |
| Yesterday | Hier |
| Today | Aujourd'hui |
| Tomorrow | Demain |
| Help! | Au secours! |
| Have you a single room? | Avez-vous une chambre à un lit? |

| | | |
|---|---|---|
| | Have you a double room? | Avez-vous une chambre à deux lits? |
| | Have you a room with private bath? | Avez-vous une chambre avec bain? |
| | How much does it cost? | Combien (est-ce que) ça coûte? Quel est le prix de . . .? |
| | Please wake me at 6 | Veuillez me réveiller à six heures |
| | Where is the lavatory? | Où sont les toilettes? |
| | Where is the chemist's? | Où est la pharmacie? |
| | Where is the post office? | Où est la poste? |
| | Where is there a doctor? | Où y a-t-il un médecin? |
| | Where is there a dentist? | Où y a-t-il un dentiste? |
| | Is this the way to the station? | Est-ce le chemin de la gare? |
| Months | January | Janvier |
| | February | Février |
| | March | Mars |
| | April | Avril |
| | May | Mai |
| | June | Juin |
| | July | Juillet |
| | August | Août |
| | September | Septembre |
| | October | Octobre |
| | November | Novembre |
| | December | Décembre |
| Days of the week | Sunday | Dimanche |
| | Monday | Lundi |
| | Tuesday | Mardi |
| | Wednesday | Mercredi |
| | Thursday | Jeudi |
| | Friday | Vendredi |
| | Saturday | Samedi |
| | Day | Jour, journée |
| | Public holiday | Jour de fête |
| Festivals | New Year | Nouvel An |
| | Easter | Pâques |
| | Ascension | Ascension |
| | Whitsun | Pentecôte |
| | Corpus Christi | Fête-Dieu |
| | Assumption | Assomption |
| | All Saints | Toussaint |
| | Christmas | Noël |
| | New Year's Eve | La Saint-Sylvestre |
| Food and drink | See entry | |
| Rail and air travel | Airport | Aéroport |
| | All aboard! | En voiture! |
| | Arrival | Arrivée |
| | Baggage | Bagages |
| | Baggage check | Bulletin de bagages |
| | Bus station | Gare routière |
| | Couchette | Couchette |
| | Departure | Départ |
| | Flight | Vol |
| | Halt | Arrêt |
| | Information | Information, renseignements |
| | Lavatory | Toilette(s) |
| | Left luggage office | Consigne |

| | |
|---|---|
| Line (railway) | Voie |
| Luggage | Bagages |
| Non-smoking | Non-fumeurs |
| Platform | Quai |
| Porter | Porteur |
| Restaurant-car | Wagon-restaurant |
| Sleeping-car | Wagon-lit |
| Smoking | Fumeurs |
| Station | Gare |
| Stewardess | Hôtesse (de l'air) |
| Stop | Arrêt |
| Ticket | Billet, ticket |
| Ticket collector | Contrôleur |
| Ticket window | Guichet |
| Timetable | Horaire |
| Train | Train |
| Waiting room | Salle d'attente |
| Window seat | Coin fenêtre |

At the post office

| | |
|---|---|
| Address | Adresse |
| Express | Exprès |
| Letter | Lettre |
| Letter-box | Boîte à lettres |
| Parcel | Paquet, colis |
| Postcard | Carte postale |
| Poste restante | Poste restante |
| Postman | Facteur |
| Registered | Recommandé |
| Small packet | Petit paquet |
| Stamp | Timbre(-poste) |
| Telegram | Télégramme |
| Telephone | Téléphone |
| Telex | Télex |

## Topographical terms

| | |
|---|---|
| Abbaye | Abbey |
| Aiguille | Pinnacle, crag |
| Anse | Bay |
| Archipel | Archipelago |
| Arène | Amphitheatre |
| Autoroute | Motorway |
| Avenue | Avenue |
| Bac | Ferry |
| Baie | Bay |
| Bain | Bath(s) |
| Barrage | Dam; reservoir, artificial lake |
| Bassin | Dock; ornamental lake, pond |
| Belvédère | Viewpoint |
| Bibliothèque | Library |
| Bois | Wood |
| Boulevard | Boulevard, avenue |
| Bourse | (Stock) exchange |
| Butte | Low hill, bluff |
| Cabane | Hut |
| Cabinets | Lavatory, toilet |
| Campagne | Countryside |
| Camping | Camping site |
| Capitainerie | Harbourmaster's office |
| Carrefour | Road intersection |
| Carrière | Quarry |

| | |
|---|---|
| Cascade | Waterfall |
| Cathédrale | Cathedral |
| Cave | Cellar |
| Caverne | Cave |
| Chaîne | Chain, range (of hills) |
| Chalet | Chalet; mountain hut |
| Champ | Field |
| Chapelle | Chapel |
| Château | Castle, country house, manor-house |
| Chemin | Road, track |
| Chemin de fer | Railway |
| Cime | Peak, summit |
| Cimetière | Cemetery |
| Citadelle | Citadel |
| Cloître | Cloister |
| Clos | Enclosure, field, vineyard |
| Col | Pass |
| Collégiale | Collegiate church |
| Colline | Hill |
| Colonne | Column |
| Corniche | Corniche road (along side of hill) |
| Côte | Coast; slope (of hill) |
| Coté | Side |
| Cour | Courtyard |
| Cours | Avenue |
| Cours d'eau | River, watercourse |
| Couvent | Convent, religious house |
| Crête | Crest, ridge (of hill) |
| Défilé | Defile, gorge |
| Dent | Crag, pinnacle (of mountain) |
| Dôme | Dome; rounded hill |
| Donjon | Keep |
| Ecluse | Lock (on canal) |
| Ecole | School |
| Escalier | Staircase |
| Est | East |
| Estuaire | Estuary |
| Établissement thermal | Spa establishment |
| Etang | Pond, lake |
| Fleuve | River (flowing into sea) |
| Fontaine | Fountain |
| Forêt | Forest |
| Fort | Fort |
| Forteresse | Fortress |
| Fosse | Pit; grave |
| Fossé | Ditch; moat |
| Gare | Railway station |
| Gare routière | Bus station |
| Golf | Golf-course |
| Golfe | Gulf, bay |
| Gorge | Gorge |
| Grotte | Cave |
| Hauteur | Height, hill |
| Hôpital | Hospital |
| Hôtel | Hotel; aristocratic mansion |
| Hôtel de Ville | Town hall |
| Île | Island |
| Ilot | Islet |
| Impasse | Cul-de-sac |
| Jardin | Garden |
| Jardin des plantes | Botanic garden |

| | |
|---|---|
| Lac | Lake |
| Lagune | Lagoon |
| Maison | House |
| Maquis | Scrub(land) |
| Marais | Marsh, bog |
| Marché | Market |
| Marécage | Marsh, bog |
| Mer | Sea |
| Mont | Mount(ain) |
| Montagne | Mountain |
| Municipalité | Local authority, municipality; town hall |
| Mur, muraille | Wall |
| Musée | Museum |
| Nez | Nose, cape |
| Nord | North |
| Ouest | West |
| Palais de justice | Law courts |
| Parc | Park |
| Pays | Country |
| Phare | Lighthouse |
| Pic | Peak |
| Piscine | Swimming pool |
| Place | Square |
| Plage | Beach |
| Plaine | Plain |
| Plâteau | Plateau |
| Pointe | Cape, point; peak (of hill) |
| Pont | Bridge |
| Porche | Porch |
| Port | Port, harbour |
| Portail | Doorway |
| Porte | Door |
| Poste | Post office |
| Presqu'île | Peninsula |
| Promontoire | Promontory |
| PTT | Post office |
| Puits | Well |
| Quai | Quay; embankment |
| Quartier | Quarter, district (of a town) |
| Rade | Anchorage, roadsteads |
| Refuge | Traffic island; mountain hut |
| Remparts | Ramparts |
| Rivière | River (not flowing into sea) |
| Roc, roche, rocher | Rock |
| Route | Road |
| Rue | Street |
| Sable | Sand |
| Saline | Salt-pan |
| Salle | Hall, room |
| Saut | Waterfall |
| Source | Spring; source of river |
| Square | Public square with gardens |
| Stade | Stadium |
| Station | Resort; station |
| Station thermale | Spa, health resort |
| Sud | South |
| Téléférique | Cableway |
| Thermes | Baths |
| Tombe, tombeau | Tomb |
| Torrent | Mountain stream |
| Tour | Tower |

| | |
|---|---|
| Trésor | Treasure, treasury |
| Trottoir | Pavement |
| Trou | Hole |
| Tunnel | Tunnel |
| Université | University |
| Val, vallée, vallon | Valley |
| Village | Village |
| Ville | Town |

## Maps and Plans

Visitors who are travelling away from the major holiday routes should take a map or maps in addition to the general map provided with this guide. Below is a selection:

1:1,500,000 Shell Motoring Map of France

1:1,000,000 Michelin France, sheet 989

1:750,000 Shell Large Motoring Map of France

1:200,000 Michelin detailed maps of France; for the area covered in this guide sheets 80, 81, 83 and 84

1:100,000 IGN maps 60, 61, 66, 67 and 68

## Medical Assistance

French medical services are excellent and the country is well supplied with doctors, many of whom speak English.
British visitors will find it helpful to obtain a free booklet prepared by the Department of Health "The Traveller's Guide to Health" which gives advice about health precautions and how to get urgent medical treatment when abroad.

Insurance See entry

## Motoring

See Car Rental, Emergencies, Getting to Provence, Roads, Traffic Regulations, Travel Documents.

## Opening Times

Banks

Not all banks have the same closing day; some are closed on Saturdays, others on Mondays. Hours of business also vary; as a general rule banks are open for business between 9am and noon and from 2 until 4pm. They close at noon on the eve of a public holiday.

Post Offices

Hours of business of post offices also vary; in the larger towns they are open on Monday to Friday from 8am until 7pm, in smaller places from 9am until noon and from 2 until 5.30pm. On Saturdays offices are generally open from 8am until noon.

Shops

There are no official early-closing days in France and no regulations as to when a shop may be open. Individual shops are normally open from

9.30am until 6.30pm. Shops selling foodstuffs frequently open very early, but most close from 12.30pm until 3 or 4pm and remain open in the evening until quite a late hour. Normally shops are closed on Sundays, but bakers, butchers, wine-dealers and florists are often open until 12.30 or 1pm. Shops which open on Sundays generally remain closed on Mondays and sometimes also on Wednesdays.

Department stores

Department stores and large shops are open on weekdays from 9.30am until 6.30pm.

Shopping Centres

Even quite small places usually have a large and well-stocked supermarket, often situated on the edge of the built-up area.

These shopping centres (*centre commerciale, supermarché*) are generally open from Monday to Saturday from 9am until 7pm (and some stay open until 9pm). Frequently establishments which stay open late are closed on Monday morning.

Places of interest/ Museums

Many places of interest (châteaux, excavation sites, and some churches) are closed from noon until 2pm. However, there are exceptions during the main holiday season. Visitors will, of course, refrain from looking round a church while a service is in progress.

Most National museums (Musée National . . .) are closed on Tuesdays and public holidays; municipal museums on Mondays. Entry is normally permitted up to half an hour before closing time.

## Post

Opening Times

See entry

Stamps

Stamps can be obtained in post offices and at tobacconists and sometimes also at newsagents and souvenir shops. A letter to Great Britain costs 2.20 francs, to Canada (air-mail up to 5 grams) 2.80 francs and to the United States (air-mail up to 5 grams) 4.20 francs. Postcards to Great Britain and Canada cost 2 francs and to the United States 2.80 francs.

## Private Rooms

Chambre d'hôte

The *Chambres d'hôte*, especially in country districts, are an excellent and comparatively inexpensive alternative to rooms in hotels of modest or average standard. In addition they often have a very pleasant atmosphere. Visitors should look out for the green shield on houses which are generally situated away from main roads.

Meublés

Furnished rooms and apartments can be rented from private landlords in both small and large towns. They are officially classified in three categories – normal, comfortable and luxury – and are usually rented for at least a week. ("Normal" private rooms which are taken for only one night come into the category of Chambre d'hôte.)

Information

Current lists of private rooms and holiday homes can be obtained from any Comité Départmental du Tourisme or Office du Tourisme and also from Gîtes de France (see Rural Holidays).

## Public Holidays

Fixed holidays

January 1st: *Jour de l'An*, New Year's Day
May 1st: *Fête du Travail*, Labour Day
May 8th: *Armistice* (1945)
July 14th: National holiday (storming of the Bastille 1789)
August 15th: *Assomption*, Assumption of the Virgin Mary
November 1st: *Toussaint*, All Saints Day
December 25th: *Noël*, Christmas Day

Movable feasts

*Lundi de Pâques*, Easter Monday
*Ascension*, Ascension Day
Whit Monday

Monaco additional holidays

Corpus Christi
November 19th: National holiday
December 6th: Immaculate Conception

## Radio and Television

Radio

British radio programmes can be received in the south of France on the short wave band (BBC World Service).
During the holiday season some French stations (including Radio Provence, from Marseilles, Avignon, Digne, Gap and Toulon) transmit daily programmes in English for the benefit of visitors.

Television

French television uses a different system and British portable sets can not receive French programmes.

## Railways

The most important railway route to Provence is the line from Paris and the channel ports via Lyon to Avignon, Arles, Marseilles, Toulon, Nice and Monaco into Italy. This route is served by many express (*rapide*) trains many of which have evocative names such as "Mistral", "Ligure", "Phocéen", "Rhodanien", etc., and the historic "Train Bleu".
Since 1981 the historic "Train à Grande Vitesse" (TGV) has run between Paris and Lyon, with a continuation to Avignon and Marseilles, and to Montpellier and Nice; this is the fastest train in the world in a regular timetable, reaching speeds of up to 260km/162 miles per hour.
In the area of the French Riviera rail services are good. In addition to the route mentioned above there are lines from Avignon via Salon, Fos-sur-Mer to Marseilles and from Nice to Turin via Breil and Tende. A branch line goes from Marseilles to Hyères. The mountainous hinterland of Haute Provence is served by the line from Marseilles to Aix-en-Provence, Sisteron and Gap, with a branch to Digne. The "Pine-cone Train" runs from Nice to Digne. This rail-bus is an excellent shuttle service for walking excursions in the area of the lower Var and a trip on the antiquated narrow-gauge line gives the passenger a special feeling of actually being in Provence. On the stretch between Puget-Theniers and Annot trains are hauled by steam locomotives on certain days (see Entrevaux).

Special fares

Reduced fares are available according to the period in which a journey is undertaken – these are designated in the *Calendrier Voyageurs* (calendar for passengers) as red, white and blue periods. There are special fares for children, for young people aged 12 to 26 (carte jeune, Inter-rail), for senior citizens over 60 (carte vermeil), for couples and families (carte couple/carte famille) and season tickets (billet de séjour, France Vacances).

France Vacances

This card is valid on the entire French rail network for 15 days or a month (passengers may travel without paying a supplement on trains on which one is normally payable, but seat reservations, couchettes and sleeping car places must be paid for). Within the period of validity of the card journeys may be undertaken on four or nine days respectively at the choice of the holder. In addition, reductions are granted on motorail (*train + auto*) journeys, on entrance fees to museums and other places of interest, and on accommodation in the hotels of the Pullman/Altea and Ibis/Urbis chains. The France Vacances card can be obtained at any French railway station and also at French Railways offices in Great Britain and many other countries.

Motorail

See Getting to Provence

Car rental

In association with various firms French Railways (SNCF) operate the service Train + Auto (car at the station). Within the area covered in the guide this sevice is available at Aix-en-Provence, Les Arcs/Draguignan, Antibes, Arles, Avignon, Beaulieu-sur-Mer, Cagnes-sur-Mer, Cannes, Gap, Hyères, Marseille, Menton, Monaco, Montélimar, Montpellier, Nice, Nîmes, Orange, St-Raphaël, Toulon. For addresses see Car Rental.

Bicycle Rental

See entry

Excursions

Partly in association with local undertakings French Railways organise sightseeing and excursions by rail, boat and bus under the title "Excursions, Services de Tourisme SNCF". Starting points include Aix-en-Provence, Arles, Aubenas, Avignon, Cannes, Cap d'Agde, Gap, La Grande-Motte, Grasse, Hyères, Marseilles, Menton, Montpellier, Nice, Nîmes, St-Raphaël, St-Tropez, Toulon.
Further information can be obtained at any local Office de Tourisme and at railway stations.

Travel for the Disabled

See Help for the Disabled

Information

Detailed information and particulars of fares can be obtained from French Railways:
179 Piccadilly, London, W1V 0AB; tel. (071) 409 9731
610 Fifth Avenue, New York, N.Y. 10020; tel. (212) 582 2110
1500 Stanley Street, Montreal, H3A 1R3; tel. (514) 288 8255

## Restaurants

Most hotels have a restaurant. In the list below these restaurants are only given in exceptional cases; otherwise they can be found under "Hotels".

Food and Drink

See entry

**Aigues-Mortes**

Arcades, 23 Boulevard Gambetta; Camargue, Rue de la République; Goulue, 2 ter, rue Denfert-Rochereau

**Aix-en-Provence**

Abbaye des Cordeliers, 21 rue Lieutaud; Bistro Latin; Caves Henri IV, 32 rue Espariat; Clos de la Violette, 10 Avenue Violette; Deux Garçons, 53 Cours Mirabeau; Poivre et Sel, 9 rue Constantin; Semailles, 15 rue Brueys; Salon de Thé Arbaud, Cours Mirabeau; Vendôme, 2 bis, Avenue Napoléon; Vieille Auberge, 62 rue Espariat

**Antibes**

Auberge Provençale, 61 Place Nationale; Bacon, Bd. Bacon, Cap d'Antibes; Bonne Auberge, on the N7; Calèche, 25 rue Vauban; Caméo, Place Nationale, Ecurie Royale, 33 rue Vauban; Marguerite, 11 rue Carnot; Vieux Murs, Avenue Amiral de Grasse

**Arles**

Guele du Loup, 39 rue des Arènes; Lou Marquès, Boulevard des Lices; Olivier, 1 bis, rue Réattu; Paillotte, 28 rue du Dr Fanton; Provence, Place St-Pierre; Vaccarès, Place du Forum

## Restaurants

**Avignon** Bonne Croute, Rue des Teinturiers; Brunel, 46 rue de la Balance, Café des Artistes, Place Crillon; Christian Etienne, 10 rue de Mons; Grangousier, 17 rue Galante; Hiély-Lucullus, 5 rue de la République; Mirande, 4 Place de l'Amirande; Petit Bedon, 70 rue Joseph Vernet; Pied de Boeuf, 49 Av. Pierre Semard; Tache d'Encre, 22 rue des Teinturiers; Trois Clefs, 26 rue des Trois Faucons; Venaissin, 16 Place de l'Horloge; Vielle Fontaine, 12 Place Crillon

**Bandol** Auberge du Port, 9 Allées J.-Moulin; Fleurs, Av. du 11 Novembre; Réserve, Route de Sanary

**Les Baux** Berengère; Prince Noir; Porte d'Eyguières; Riboto de Taven

**Cagnes-sur-Mer** Josy-Jo, 4 rue Planastel; Peintres, 71 Montée Bourgades, Haut-de-Cagnes; Bourride, Port, Cros-de-Cagnes

**Cannes** Caveau "30", 45 rue Félix Faure; Corvette, 48 rue des Serbes; Félix, 63 Boulevard de la Croisette; Festival, 52 Boulevard de la Croisette; Mère Besson, 13 rue des Frères Pradignac; Mirabelle, 24 rue St-Antoine; Orangeraie, 73 Boulevard de la Croisette; Oriental, 286 Avenue Jourdan; Poêle d'Or, 23 rue des Etats-Unis; Quatre Saisons, 38 rue des Serbes; Royal Gray, 38 rue des Serbes; Santons de Provence, 4 rue du Maréchal Joffre; Toque Blanche, 3 rue de la Fontaine

**Carpentras** Orangerie, 26 rue Duplessis; Rapière du Comtat, 47 Bd. du Nord; Saule Pleureur, Route d'Avignon; Vert Galant, Rue Clapies

**Digne** Origan, 6 rue Pied de Ville; Petit St-Jean, 14 Cours Arès

**Eze** Richard Borfiga, Place de Gaulle; Troubadour

**Fontaine-de-Vaucluse** Hostellerie du Château; Parc; Philip

**Fréjus** Colombe d'Or, Route de Bagnois (D4); Lou Calen, 9 rue Desaugiers; Potiers, 135 rue des Potiers; Toque Blanche, 394 Av. V. Hugo (Fréjus-Plage); Vieux Four, 57 rue Grisolle

**Gap** Café du Lycée, 41 Bd. de la Libération; Patalain, 7 Avenue des Alpes; Petite Marmite, 79 rue Carnot; Roseraie, Rue de Villarobert (N85)

**Gordes** Bories, on the road to Sénanque; Mas Tourteron, Les Imberts

**Grasse** Amphitryon, 16 Boulevard Victor-Hugo; Aromes, Route de Cannes (N115); Brasserie du Patti, Place du Patti; Ormeaux, Plan de Grasse; Palais des Congres, Cours H. Cresp; Richelieu, Traverse Sidi-Brahim

**Hyères** Delfin's, 7 rue du Dr Roux-Seigneuret; Roy Gourmet, 11 rue Ribier; Taverne Royale, 23 rue de Limans; Toison d'Or, 1 rue Galiéni

**Le Lavandou** Bouée, Avenue Ch. Cazin; Grill, 22 rue Patron-Ravello; Roches, in Aiguebelle; Vieux Port, Quai Gabriel Péri

**Marseilles** Bellecour, 26 Cours Julien; Calypso, 3 rue des Catalans; Caruso, 158 Quai du Port; Cousin-Cousine, 102 Cours Julien; Dent Creuse, 14 rue Sénac; Epuisette, Vallon des Auffres; Jambon de Parme, 67 rue de la Palud; Michel, 6 rue des Catalans; Miramar, 12 Quai du Port; New York, 7 Quai des Belges; Oursinade, Rue Neuve St-Martin (Centre de la Bourse); Panzani, 17 rue Montgrand; Pavillon d'Or, 45 Route de la Treille, Camoins-les-Bains; Pavillon du Lac, Parc Borély; Pescadou, 19 Place de Castellane.

**Martigues** Auberge Mirabeau, Place Mirabeau; Gousse d'Ail, 42 Quai du Général Leclerc

**Menton** Au Pistou, 2 rue Fossan; Auberge Provençale, 11 rue Trenca; Calanque, 13 Square Victoria; Chez Mireille – L'Ermitage, Promenade du Soleil

**Monaco** Aurore, 8 rue M. de Lorraine; Bacchus, 13 rue de La Turbie; Bec Rouge, 11 Avenue Grande-Bretagne; Café de la Mer, 12 Av. des Spelugues; Castelroc, Place du Palais; Chaumière, Pl. du Jardin Exotique; Chez Gianni, 39 Avenue Princesse Grace; Coupole, 1 Avenue Princesse Grace; Louis XV, Place Casino; Rampoldi, 3 Avenue des Spélugues; Saint Nicolas, 6 rue de L'Eglise

**Mondragon** Beaugravière, on the N7

**Montélimar** Auberge Provençale, Boulevard Marre-Desmarais; Grillon, 40 rue Cuiraterie; Vendôme, Place d'Armes

**Montpellier** Chanderlier, 3 rue Leenhardt; Jardin des Sens, 11 Avenue St-Lazare; Louvre, 2 rue Vielle; Mas, Route Vauguières (D24/172E); Menestrol, 8 Impasse Perrier; Olivier, 12 rue Aristide Olivier; Réserve Rimbaud, 820 Avenue St-Maur

**Mougins** Amadier de Mougins; Bistro de Mougins; Feu Follet; Manoir de l'Etang, 66 Allée du Manoir; Mas Caudille; Moulin de Mougins, Chemin du Moulin; Estaminet de Remparts

**Nice** Ane Rouge, 7 Quai des Deux Emmanuel; Barale, 39 rue Beaumont; Bistrot de Nice, 2 rue S. Guitry; Boccaccio, 7 rue Masséna; Café de Turin, 5 Place Garibaldi; Caracolès, 5 rue St-François-de-Paule; Chalutier, 13 Quai des Deux Emmanuel; Chantecler, 37 Promenade des Anglais; Chapon Fin, 1 rue du Moulin; Chez les Pêcheurs, 18 Quai des Docks; Dents de la Mer, 2 rue St-François-de-Paule; Don Camillo, 5 rue des Ponchettes; Florian, 22 rue A. Karr; Gourmets, 12 rue Dante; Jacques Maximin, 4 rue S. Guitry; Massoury, Villefranche-sur-Mer, Av. Léopold II; Merenda, 4 rue de la Terrasse; Nissa-Socca, 5 rue Ste-Réparate; Pizza Coco, 38 B. Risso; Safari, 1 Cours Saleya

**Nîmes** Alexandre, Garons/Route d'Aéroport; Chapon Fin, 3 rue Château Fadaise; Grillade, 44 rue Nationale; Magister, 5 rue Nationale; Mas d'Abeilles, Route de St-Gilles

**Orange** Aigo-Boulido, 20 Place Sylvain; Forum, 3 rue du Mazeau; Parvis, 3 Cours Pourtoules

**Peillon** Auberge de la Madone

**Port-Grimaud** Amphitrite; Marine; Tartane

**Roquebrune** Grand Inquisiteur, Rue du Château; Hippocampe, Avenue Winston Churchill; Lucioles, 12 Place de la République

**St-Gilles** Rascasse, 16 Avenue Griffeuille

**St-Jean-Cap-Ferrat** Provençal, 2 Avenue Séméria

**St-Martin-du-Var** Belle Route (Issautier) on the N202

**St-Raphäel** Pastorel, 54 rue de la Liberté; Scirocco, 35 Quai Albert-1er; Voile d'Or, 1 Bd. Général de Gaulle

**St-Rémy** Belle Emilie, 18 Boulevard Victor Hugo; France, 2 Avenue Fauconnet; Jardin de Frédéric, 8 Boulevard Gambetta; Marceau, 13 Bd. Marceau; Mirabeau, 26 Boulevard Mirabeau

**St-Tropez** A casa mia, 38 bis, rue G. Clemenceau; Auberge des Vieux Moulins, Ramatuelle, Route de Pampelonne; Canastel, 12 rue de la Citadelle; Chabichou, Avenue Foch; Chez Madeleine, Route de Tahiti; Citadelle, 22 bis, rue de la

Citadelle; Girelier, at the harbour; Leï Mouscardins, at the harbour; Mas de Chastelas, Route Gassin; Ramade, Rue du Temple

**Stes-Maries-de-la-Mer** Brûleur de Loups, Avenue G. Leroy; Chalut, 39 Avenue Frédéric Mistral; Impérial, 1 Place des Impériaux

**Salon-de-Provence** Café des Arts, 20 Place Crousillat; Craponne, 146 Allées Craponne; Francis Robin, 1 Boulevard Georges Clemenceau; Poêlon, 71 Allées Craponne

**Tarascon** Midi, 1 Boulevard Victor Hugo; Trident, Place Colonel Berrurier

**Toulon** Au Sourd, 10 rue Molière; Bartavelles, 28 rue Gimelli; Corniche, 1 Littoral F. Mistral; Dauphin, 21 bis, rue Jean Jaurès; Ferme, 6 Place Louis Blanc; Madeleine, 7 rue Tombades; Poivre et Sel, 20 Allées Courbet

**Uzès** Abbaye, 24 Bd. Charles Gide; Coté Jardin, 10 Pl. Dampmartin; Césarine, 1 Bd. Victor Hugo; Fontaines, 11 rue Péllisserie; Jardins de Castille

**Vaison-la-Romaine** Bateleur, 1 Place Aubanel

**Valréas** Etrier, 2 Cours Tivoli; Remparts, Place Gutenberg

**Vauvenargues** Mas de Bonfillon, Route de Rians

**Venasque** Fontaine, Pl. de la Fontaine; Luminaire, Pl. de la Fontaine; Four à Chaux, in Caromb

**Vence** Augerbe des Seigneurs, Place Frêne; Auberge des Templiers, 39 Avenue du Maréchal Joffre; Closerie des Genets, 4 Impasse Maurel; Portiques, Rue St-Veran

**Villeneuve-lèz-Avignon** Cèdres, 39 Bd. Pasteur; Saint-André, 4 bis, Montée du Fort

## Roads

The French road network is close-meshed; even minor roads are generally in good condition.
Since the network of roads is so dense and the population density generally quite low, traffic is not particularly heavy; hold-ups occur principally at holiday times and particularly at the beginning and end of the school holidays (beginning of July/end of September) on the major trunk routes.

Lead-free patrol is widely available, but not every filling station can be relied on to supply it, especially those in villages and on country roads. It should be pointed out that many filling stations are closed on Sundays. Automatic pumps accept only 10 franc coins.

Motorways

French motorways have a total length of 7000 kilometres/4350 miles. Apart from short stretches near large towns they are subject to tolls (*péage*; Eurocard, Mastercard and Visa International can be used). Toll booths at frontiers accept foreign currency.
As far as the area covered in this guide is concerned the motorways (especially the A7 "Autoroute du Soleil" and the A8 "Autoroute Provençale") function only as access routes; the tolls, and the fact that points at which they can be joined and left are situated considerable distances apart make it advisable for visitors to use the national roads for exploring the area.

National Roads

Long-distance traffic still makes great use of the excellently engineered national roads (*routes nationales*) which correspond approximately to A roads in Great Britain. They are designated by red and white kilometre posts which bear the road number (e.g. N555) and frequently have three lanes, the centre lane being used for overtaking.

Provincial Roads

Provincial roads (*routes départementales*) are marked by yellow and white kilometre posts (e.g. D666); important stretches are of similar quality to the national roads.

## Shopping and Souvenirs

A speciality of Provence is perfume (especially in Grasse) and toilet water (lavender water, etc.). Also popular are the *herbes de Provence*, aromatic herbs which are on sale everywhere, nougat from Montélimar of various kinds, soft or hard, perfumed or plain, and *callissons*, a tangy marzipan confection, from Aix-en-Provence.

The well-known resorts of the Côte d'Azur all have similar luxury shops stocking everything which is both of good quality and also expensive; the range extends from haute couture through jewellery and perfumes to luxury cars. The markets, where all kinds of culinary products can be found, and the narrow lanes of the old parts of these towns are particularly attractive.

The typical pleasantly rural-looking cotton material of Provence, which is used for women's clothes, has small floral patterns printed on a plain coloured background.

Articles of daily use and handcrafted objects made from olive wood can be found in great variety and catering for every taste; the same is true of pottery (especially from the world-famous potteries of Vallauris). Unusual souvenirs are the so-called "santons" – Provençal crib figures.

*Everything for the tourist . . .*

It must be remembered that all these things are produced specially for tourists.
Music lovers will also be attracted by records, cassettes and CDs of Provençal songs.

## Son et Lumière

In places of touristic interest the spectacle Son et Lumière (sound and light) takes place after sunset during the summer. Accompanied by lighting effects often of theatrical quality, historical or legendary episodes are presented to the audience as a kind of radio play; sometimes scenic effects are also introduced.

## Sport

Water sports

The varied nature of the coast is favourable for many kinds of water sports. As well as stretches of sand and pebbles which are especially suitable for families and wind-surfers, there are in the more rocky parts (for example along the Corniche des Maures) many charming bays and good places for diving. Unfortunately the amount and variety of marine life have declined considerably in recent years through overfishing, underwater hunting and pollution.

Diving Information

Féderation Française d'Etudes et de Sports sous-marins
24 Quai de Rive-Neuve
F-13007 Marseille
Tel. 91 33 99 31
The "Annuaire officiel" published by the above association contains a list of diving clubs and courses available.

Beach warning system

Since conditions of wind and current can change very quickly, most of the larger beaches have a warning system which should be strictly observed; coloured pennants indicate the prevailing conditions.

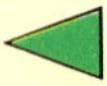
Bathing without restriction

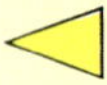
Bathing dangerous

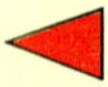
Bathing prohibited

Golf

Golf clubs which are affiliated to the "France Golf International" organisation always welcome visiting golfers. The relevant golf courses are at Digne, Mandelieu, St-Raphaël, Roquebrune St-Argens, Nans-les-Pins, Mouries, Les Baux, Morière-les-Avignons, Avignon/Vedene, Montelimar/Montboucher-sur-Jabron. Other courses can be used under certain conditions; information from France Golf International, 2 rue Linois, F-75740 Paris Cedex, and the Fédération Française de Golf, 69 Avenue Victor Hugo, F-75783 Paris Cedex.

Winter Sports

In the area covered by this guide are the Alpes Maritimes, where the winter sports resorts lie between 50 and 100km/31 and 62 miles from the Mediterranean. The great advantage of this region is the combination of exceptionally good snow conditions and warm sunshine. Among the leading resorts are Barcellonette with Pra-Loup and La Foux-d'Allos as well as Auron, Vallberg and Isola 2000. Most of these places have been built to provide accommodation for skiers and they are not particularly attractive.

Cycling

See entry

Walking

See entry

## Telephone

In France area codes are included in the telephone number. Only for calls to Paris (Île de France) is it necessary to dial 1 before the number and from the provinces to Paris an additional 16 must first be dialled.
Most telephone boxes accept only télécartes which can be obtained from post offices, tobacco kiosks (*tabac*), the offices of France Telecom, railway ticket offices, and other outlets (showing "Télécate en vente ici"). A card is valid for 50 or 100 units.
A local call from a coin-box costs 1 franc per unit.

International telephone codes

From the United Kingdom to France 010 33
From the United States or Canada to France 011 33
From France to the United Kingdom 19 44
From France to the United States or Canada 19 1
After dialling 19 wait for the dialling tone before continuing.

When dialling from France the zero prefixed to the local dialling code must be omitted.

## Time

France observes Central European Time, one hour ahead of Greenwich Mean Time. Summer Time (two hours ahead of Greenwich Mean Time) is in force from the last Sunday in March until the last Sunday in September.

## Tipping

Tips (*pourboire*) are normally given in similar circumstances and in similar amounts to those in the United Kingdom. In restaurants a tip of 5–10% is a recognition of good service (a service charge of 15% is normally included in the bill – *service compris*)

In addition a tip is usual in the following situations:

Hotel

Porter 5–10 francs per case. Room-maid up to 10 francs per day.

Museums
Châteaux

For the guide 5 francs per person

Cinema, Theatre

2 francs per person for the usherette

Taxi

10–15% of the fare

Hairdresser

10% of the bill

Toilets

For the attendant 2 francs; in restaurants and theatres up to 5 francs

## Traffic Regulations

General

As in other continental countries vehicles in France travel on the right. Drivers and passengers must wear seat-belts (including those on rear seats). Motorcyclists must wear a helmet. Children under 10 may not travel in front seats.

In general a vehicle approaching from the right has priority (*priorité à droite* signs are often displayed); at a roundabout, however, vehicles actually negotiating the roundabout have priority. Roads on which traffic has the right of way are marked *priorité à droite* at the approach of a junction. Roads without priority generally are signed *vous n'avez pas la priorité* or *Cédez le passage.*
The horn may only be used to warn other drivers. Between sunset and sunrise flashing of the headlights must be used instead. In built-up areas the use of the horn is permitted only when danger is imminent.
In rain and snow dipped headlights must be used. Motorcyclists must use headlights at all times. Foreign motorists are not compelled to convert headlights to the yellow beam normal in France. Spare bulbs for all lights must be carried.

Speed limits

Maximum speeds for vehicles:
on motorways 130kph/80mph; when wet 110kmph/68mph
on main roads with two lanes in each direction 110kph/68mph; when wet 100kph/62mph
on national and country roads 90kph/56mph; when wet 80kph/50mph
in built-up areas 50kph/31mph
Mopeds are normally restricted to 45kph/28mph
Drivers who have held their licence for less that 12 months may not exceed 90kph/56mph

Drinking and Driving

The alcohol limit is 0.8 pro mille – corresponding to two glasses of wine. Penalties for exceeding the limit are severe; a positive test can result in confiscation of the driving licence, and if an accident has occurred, even if no injury has been caused, a prison sentence of two months to two years and fines of 2000 to 30,000 francs can be expected. If anyone is injured the penalty can be up to four years imprisonment and confiscation of the driver's licence.

Procedure in the event of an accident

In the event of an accident the drivers concerned must each make a statement (*constat amiable d'accident automobile*) and sign it. Automobile clubs will provide the necessary formulae. Where damage has occurred it is advisable to have the circumstances of the accident and details of damage confirmed by a *huissier* (a kind of lawyer's clerk), He is paid by the person or persons who summon him according to the time taken. The police need only be called if there are personal injuries or if a driver has driven off after an accident; the police are not concerned with accident damage. In the case of severe damage the offices of an expert should be obtained so that assessment can be simplified and expedited.

Parking Regulations

See Car Parks

## Travel Documents

Personal documents

For citizens of the United Kingdom, the United States and Canada a passport only is required for entry into France. Children can be entered in their parent's passport if they do not have one of their own.

Vehicle Documents

A national driving licence and vehicle licence are recognised and must be taken. A "green card" (international insurance certificate) is advisable. Vehicles must bear the oval nationality plate.

Health Insurance

See Medical Assistance

Advice

In case papers are lost photocopies are very helpful (for example so that the Police can disseminate details and the consulate can issue provisional documents). These copies should be kept separately from the originals.

## Walking

The hinterland is an interesting and a rewarding area for walkers, but the Provençal coast is also becoming more and more popular. A paradise for nature-lovers and mountain walkers is the Mercantour National Park. It is important to remember that even outside the narrow areas of the Alps there are stretches of an Alpine character and so equipment must always be in good order and weather and conditions taken into account when embarking on a walking holiday.

Long-distance footpaths

A few long-distance footpaths (*sentiers de grande randonnée* – GR for short, plus the number of the footpath) in the area of Provence are dealt with in some greater detail below:

GR 9

GR 9, coming from Grenoble, reaches the area covered in this guide near Dieulefit. It runs first via Nyons through the baronies to Brantes, follows the northern slope of Mont Ventoux and descends to the Gorges of the Nesque. Beyond Apt and Buoux it climbs the Montagne du Luberon (Mourre Nègre), crosses the Durance at Pont-de-Mirabeau and comes to Vauvenargues at the Montagne Ste-Victoire. After ascending the Croix de Provence it continues east along the crest, turns south and via Trets reaches the Massif de la Ste-Baume (St-Pilon). Still going east it leads via the Barre de Cuers and Rochbaron into the Massif des Maures; it then skirts La Garde-Freinet before reaching the sea near Port-Grimaud.

GR 4

GR 4 first leads through the area of the Gorges de l'Ardèche (with several alternative paths), crosses the Rhône at Pont-St-Esprit and reaches Mont Ventoux via Vaison-la-Romaine and Malaucène. It continues along the northern foot of the mountain to Brantes; part of the path coincides with the GR 9, then it leads via Sault, Simiane-la-Rotonde and the Canyon d'Oppedette to the eastern part of the Luberon and to Manosque. Near Grenoux-les-Bains it reaches the Verdon, follows the Colostre as far as Moutiers and descends to the Gorges du Verdon, following the river as far as Castellane. In a great curve the path skirts Entrevaux on the upper Var, turns south-west into the area of the Alpes Maritimes, crosses the Montagne du Choiron to Gréolières and arrives at Grasse across the Plaine des Rochers.

GR 5

GR 5 leads from Nice over Mont Chauve near Aspremont to the Gorges of the Vésubie. From here it climbs to Utelle, crosses Mont Tounairet and via St-Sauveur-sur-Tinée comes to the area of Mont Mounier. It then continues north into the Parc Régional du Queras and to Briançon.

GR 98/90/51

This series of long-distance paths covers the immediate hinterland of the Mediterranean coast from Marseilles to Menton.

Information

Comité National des Sentiers de Grande Randonnée
9 Avenue Georges V, F-75008 Paris; tel. (1) 47 23 62 32

C.N.S. Centre d'Information
64 rue de Gergovie, F-75014 Paris; tel. (1) 45 45 31 02

Club Alpin Français
14 Avenue Mirabeau, F-06000 Nice; tel. 93 62 59 99

"Transhumance"

By prior arrangement it is possible to accompany shepherds as they move with their flocks among the mountain pasture. The walk lasts between three and ten days.
Information and arrangements through:
Centre de Découverte de l'Espace Pastoral
Les Deux Moulins, Gontard, Dauphin
F-04300 Forcalquier; tel. 92 79 58 33

Maps and guidebooks

The walkers' guide in the Topo series "Topo-Guide des sentiers de Grande Randonnée" (short form "Topo Guide") includes maps to a scale of 1:50,000 and, with information about routes, accommodation, time-planning, geography, nature and culture, is an excellent reference book for a successful walking tour. It can be obtained in bookshops in France or it can be ordered from the C.N.S. Centre d'Information (see above) or through Editions Chiron, 40 rue de Seine, F-75006 Paris.

## When to Go

General

Spring/early summer and autumn (September/October) are the best times to visit Provence or the Côte d'Azur. During these seasons the weather is fine (or at least not liable to unexpected changes) and the French school holidays are avoided. A visit in winter can also be a pleasant experience.

Spring

Because of the relatively mild climate blossom appears early (mimosa blossom from the end of January). This and the pleasant water temperature early in the year make spring an ideal time for a visit to the Côte d'Azur. It must be added, however, that at this time of year there is quite a lot of welcome rain (many fossils washed out of the rocks on the hillsides can be found). For places at a higher altitude late spring and early summer are more suitable for a visit.

Summer

In the very dry summer season, the heat of which is often interrupted by the cold currents of the Mistral, the real character of Provence comes into its own, especially when the lavender is in flower. At this season the gorges of Haute Provence, which at other times are accessible only with difficulty, can be explored, or the calanques to the east of Marseilles can be visited without undue risk. On the other hand a visit to the coast in July and August – that is in the high season – can suffer from the effects of overcrowding (school holidays in France last from the beginning of July until the beginning of September). Thanks to the warm sea water bathing is sometimes

Autumn

possible until well into the somewhat rainy season in autumn.

Winter

Mild winters made the coast of Provence attractive from the earliest days of tourism. Well-known and well-equipped winter sports resorts are to be found chiefly in the alpine parts of Haute Provence and in the Alpes Maritimes.

## Wine

General

Among the wines of Provence the full-bodied dark-red Châteauneuf-du-Pape enjoys an excellent reputation. On the other hand rosé wine – the actual typical Provençal wine – is still, even in southern France, referred to as "uncomplicated table-wine", a description which is very misleading. In its freshness it is in no way light or undistiguished; acidity, bouquet and alcoholic content are ideally balanced and give the wine the character of the region far better than any other.

Viniculture in Provence goes back to the Greek colonisation in the 7th and 6th c. B.C. – it has therefore the longest tradition in France – and is carried on essentially in two areas, the "Lower Rhône" in a triangle between Montelimar, Avignon and Apt, and the "Provence" in its narrower sense, that is the country between Aix/Marseilles and Nice. There is also a third area, the adjoining territory of Languedoc-Roussillon between Nîmes and Stes-Maries-de-la-Mer.

Lower Rhône

Wine is classified according to the so-called "Appelation-Contrôlée" regions (AC), and in descending order: the Grands Crus of the Côtes du

Rhône with individual names such as Châteauneuf-du-Pape, Gigondas, Tavel, Lirac, Rasteau, Muscat de Beaumes-de-Venise, Côteau de Tricastin, Côtes du Ventoux, Clairette de Bellegarde and Muscat de Lunel; the AC wines of the Rhône villages (e.g. from Cairanne, Séguret, Vacqueyras), AC Côtes du Rhône with the département added and finally AC without the departmental name. There is also wine labelled VDQS (*vin délimité de qualité supérieure*): Côtes du Luberon, Côteaux de Pierrevert, Costières du Gard; and finally table wine (*vin de table*).

Châteauneuf-du-Pape, almost exclusively red wine, is produced from thirteen varieties of grape – every estate has its own "recipe" – and the vines are grown on the gravelly plains of the Rhône in widely separated rows. It was here that the idea of "Appellation Controlée" was born; in 1923 Baron Le Roy decided to introduce designations of quality and to define them in terms of variety of grape, time of harvesting (*vendange*), maximal yield and alcohol content. Châteauneuf-du-Pape is a full-bodied dark-red wine (minimum alcohol content 12.5%) which requires four to five years to reach maturity; recently attempts have been made to make the wine less heavy and thinner, so that it can be drunk after only two years. The same is true of the Gigondas which obtained its own AC in 1971.

Tavel is a well-known rosé as is the wine from Lirac where red wine is being produced in increasing quantities. From Rasteau, Beaumes-de-Venise and Lunel come very aromatic white wines (Muscat), the residual sweetness of which is achieved by the addition of spirit. The other areas of viniculture produce both red and rosé wines.

A peculiarity is Listel, a "sand wine" (*vin de sables*) which is made from grapes grown on the wet sandy plains to the east of Aigues-Mortes.

Provence

Some 60% of the wine produced in Provence is the fruity aromatic rosé; red wine accounts for 35% and white for 5%. There were once only four AC areas: Palette (near Aix, producing all three types but only from one estate); Cassis (east of Marseilles, with very dry full-bodied white wine); Bandol (mainly red wine) and Bellet (in the hilly hinterland of Nice). The AC Côtes de Provence appeared in 1977 and includes extensive areas around Bandol, between Toulon and St-Tropez and between Toulon and St-Raphaël (approximately along the N 97 and N 7). The wines made here are predominently rich fresh rosé and a lighter white.

The former VDQS Côteaux d'Aix-en-Provence and Côteaux des Baux have been raised to the status of AC, the description VDQS Côteaux Varois was a new designation; all these names indicate that the wine of Provence is gaining in appreciation, and that it is produced with increased attention to quality.

## Youth Hostels

The French youth-hostel organisations FUAJ and LFAJ together operate some 330 youth hostels which can be used by young people holding a card issued by their national youth-hostel association.

In July and August (school holidays) advance booking is necessary; generally in the main holiday period a stay in any one hostel is limited to three nights.

In the area covered by this guide there are hostels in Aix-en-Provence, Arles, Avignon, Cassis, Fontaine-de-Vaucluse, Fréjus, La Foux-d'Allos, Jausiers, Manosque, Marseilles, Menton, Montpellier, Nice, Nîmes, La Palud-sur-Verdon, Saignon (near Apt), Savines-le-Lac, St-Dalmas-de-Tende, St-Etienne-de-Tinée, Stes-Maries-de-la-Mer, Tarascon, Tende, Le Trayas (near Théoule-sur-Mer), Séguret (near Vaison-la-Romaine) and Var.

## Youth Hostels

Information

Fédération Unie des Auberges de Jeunesse
27 rue Pajol, F-75019 Paris
Tel. (1) 46 07 00 01

Ligue Française des Auberges de la Jeunesse
38 Boulevard Raspail, F-75007 Paris
Tel. (1) 45 48 69 84

## Index

## The Principal Sights at a Glance

*(Continued from page 6)*